PIMLICO

488

GOODBYE, TWENTIETH CENTURY

Dannie Abse is a doctor and poet and both vocations have inspired his work; as has his Welsh and Jewish ancestry. A poet, reviewer and playwright, he has written some 15 books of poetry, including his collected poems, *White Coat, Purple Coat*, as well as fiction and books about medicine.

GOODBYE, TWENTIETH CENTURY

CENTURY

An Autobiography

———

DANNIE ABSE

PIMLICO

Published by Pimlico 2001

2 4 6 8 10 9 7 5 3 1

Copyright © Dannie Abse 2001

First published in Great Britain by Pimlico 2001

A Poet in the Family
first published by Hutchinson, 1973

Pimlico
Random House, 20 Vauxhall Bridge Road,
London SW1V 2SA

Random House Australia (Pty) Limited
20 Alfred Street, Milsons Point, Sydney,
New South Wales 2061, Australia

Random House New Zealand Limited
18 Poland Road, Glenfield,
Auckland 10, New Zealand

Random House (Pty) Limited
Endulini, 5A Jubilee Road, Parktown 2193, South Africa

The Random House Group Limited Reg. No. 954009
www.randomhouse.co.uk

A CIP catalogue record for this book
is available from the British Library

ISBN 0-7126-6829-2

Papers used by Random House are natural,
recyclable products made from wood grown in sustainable forests;
the manufacturing processes conform to the environmental
regulations of the country of origin

Typeset by Deltatype, Birkenhead, Merseyside
Printed and bound in Great Britain by
Mackays of Chatham PLC

Author's Note

To the early version of *A Poet in the Family*, published in 1973, I have added footnotes and brought the book up to date by writing about my life from the late 1960s to the year 2000. Should you wonder why I bothered to tell such a silly story I can best answer by quoting Pushkin: 'What's it to you? I wanted to.'

Acknowledgements are owed to Emanuel Litvinoff for allowing me to quote his poem 'To T.S. Eliot'; to Vision Press Ltd, for the poem from *The Book of Hours* by Rainer Maria Rilke; to New Directions for quotations from William Carlos Williams' *The Autobiography*; to Faber and Faber for the lines of Ezra Pound; to Eyre and Spottiswoode for C. Day Lewis's 'Where are the War Poets?'; and to Glenys Ormond for permission to reprint 'Cathedral Builders' from John Ormond's *Selected Poems* (Seren).
D. A.

Contents

PART ONE

A Poet in the Family

Nine-tenths of our lives is well forgotten in the living. Of the part that is remembered, the most had better not be told: it would interest no one, or at least would not contribute to the story of what we ourselves have been. A thin thread of narrative remains – a few hundred pages – about which clusters, like a rock candy, the interests upon which the general reader will spend a few hours, as might a sweet-toothed child, preferring something richer and not so hard on the teeth. To us, however, such hours have been sweet. They constitute our particular treasure. That is all, justly, that we should offer.

WILLIAM CARLOS WILLIAMS (*The Autobiography*)

This before all: ask yourself in the quietest hour of your night: must I write? Dig down into yourself for a deep answer. And if this should be in the affirmative, if you may meet this solemn question with a strong and simple 'I must', then build your life according to this necessity; your life must, right to its most unimportant and insignificant hour, become a token and a witness of this impulse.

RAINER MARIA RILKE (*Letters to a Young Poet*)

1. A Poet in the Family

There were few poetry books in the house. Palgrave's *Golden Treasury*, the *Oxford Book of English Verse*, and two slim Faber volumes in Leo's bookcase. These books had nothing to do with me. I was too young. Like the row of Charles Dickens and the set of Joseph Conrad, stoutly bound in navy blue with great gold lettering, they were there to be read later when I was an old teenager. My father, in his palmy days, had bought these sets along with some grey-bound, luxurious encyclopedias from a glib travelling salesman, years before I was born.

I was a shy ten-year-old. I was interested in the fortunes of Cardiff City Football Club, and the Glamorgan cricket eleven. Poetry was something to do with short-long-short, or long-short-long. But Leo, seven years older than I, used to read out loud Browning's 'The Lost Leader' or 'Porphyria's Lover'. Wilfred, then nineteen, occasionally recited,

> 'Tears, idle tears, I know not what they mean,
> Tears from the depth of some divine despair.'

And the eldest of us, my sister Huldah, all skin-cream and perfume, could be heard upstairs healthily singing in the echoing bathroom: 'Some day he'll come along, the man I love.'

'Tears, idle tears', or 'Some day he'll come along', were all the same to me. They were manifestations of what grown-ups called 'soul'. I never heard my father recite a line from a poem. When he was gay he told jokes; when moodily sad he would take down his violin and, with eyes closed like a lover, play Kreisler's *Humoresque* until he became, for all the grey and green world of Wales, a model for Chagall. My mother exuded 'soul' any time – any time at all. She knew off by heart long stanzas and even longer stanzas of 'Hiawatha'. At the drop of an eyelid she'd be off moaning, 'O the famine and the fever! O the wasting of the famine! O the blasting of the fever! O the wailing of the children! O the anguish of the women!' And so on, until one of my older brothers would cry: 'Put a sock in it, moth.'

Certainly I had no ambition to become a writer. I was not even particularly pleased when I won a school prize for the set essay on 'The Evils of Drink'. I didn't want to become anything. I wanted to keep on sucking mintoes for ever. 'What do you want to be when you grow up?' was a question one had to endure from adults, like having cheeks pinched or being told to 'Wee wee, wash, and comb your hair.' My eldest brother, Wilfred, decided that I should be a doctor. He was going to be one. Moreover, I had two uncles who were doctors, and five cousins who were destined to wear the honourable white coat. In my family it seemed there were only two choices – either you became a doctor or went on the dole to play a marvellous game of snooker. I was neutral about the matter.

One afternoon, though, a few years later, I saw Edward G. Robinson in a film about the German bacteriologist, Paul Ehrlich, called *The Magic Bullet*. I came out of the Olympia Cinema at half past five with my eyes shining. Before I had crossed St Mary's Street, a metaphorical stethoscope in my pocket, I had saved an old lady from asphyxiating, administered first aid to a policeman shot by Tiger Bay gangsters, and operated on Adolf Hitler without success. Back home, still uplifted by Hollywood heroics, I expressed some vague interest in medicine, and before I could change my illusions Wilfred responsibly put my name down to go to Westminster Hospital, London. 'It's the best hospital in the country,' Wilfred said. He paused. 'It's the best hospital in Europe,' he said. I nodded uncertainly. 'I wouldn't mind being a vet,' I said. 'It's the best hospital in the world,' he said.

I was then attending St Illtyd's College, a high school in Splott, Cardiff. Poetry was still something rather dreary like the school song: 'Green and gold, green and gold, Strong be your heart and bold, To remain unsullied our great name, Adding to ancient glory, modern fame . . .'

But I was fortunate during those early Cardiff years for, at home, I was exposed to the adult dialogue of the thirties – to the dialogue between Sigmund Freud and Karl Marx, as it was interpreted and argued by my two elder brothers, by Wilfred who would become a psychiatrist and by Leo the future MP for Pontypool. Leo, already, was quite a persuasive orator, and used to stand on a soapbox in Llandaff Fields. I heard him quote: 'It is given to man to live but once and he should live not to be seared by the shame of a cowardly and trivial past, but so live that dying he might say, "All my life and all my strength have been given to the finest cause in the world, the enlightenment and liberation of mankind."' I was moved perhaps for the first time by words, by the order of words – not by poetry, though, but by rhetoric.

Outside, in the streets of Cardiff, there were yellow, bouncing tramcars, and occasionally a hearse would pass by pulled by six coal-black horses. The newspaper headlines were about Mussolini and Abyssinia, later about Hitler and 'Last Territorial Claims'. Always J. C. Clay was taking wickets for Glamorgan and Cardiff City lost at home. BLUEBIRDS FLATTER TO DECEIVE headlined the back page, and somewhere in the middle pages of the *South Wales Echo*, Beverley Baxter irrevocably wrote about 'The Red Sea of Bolshevism'. It was colour, colour all the way, and one of my non-doctor uncles had more than a drop to drink. 'Leo will be Prime Minister one day,' he said to my father. 'Wilfred's got an 'ead on 'im.' He looked at me then. 'Never mind, you've got a diabolical right foot. *Diabolical.*' And he shouted, 'Up the City.'

Stimulated by my brothers' conversations and arguments I began to write essays in a little blue exercise book. I wrote these essays in order to clarify my own attitudes. They were 'On Fascism', 'On Socialism', 'On Jazz', and so on. I showed them to Wilfred who seriously encouraged me to write more. Wilfred was infallibly kind. But there was still no poetry in the little, blue exercise book. Just one line of Keats: 'No hungry generations tread thee down'. For that I thought was the greatest line ever written – not that I had read many lines. In this reference to a nightingale, and its inference about his brother's and his own pulmonary tuberculosis, the poet had captured my youthful social conscience. After all, I knew of the miners who coughed, the TB that was rife in the valleys, the processions of the unemployed. That line was the embodiment of the sad, bitter soul. 'No hungry generations tread thee down.' It contained my father playing *Humoresque*, my mother wailing Longfellow, quotations of Lenin, and even the lyric my sister sang in the bathroom: 'Ten cents a dance, that's what they pay me, Lord how they weigh me down' – and the old pipes in the house knocked and shook because of an air bubble.

But it was my youthful engagement with the tragedy of Spain that oddly led me to 'modern poetry'. That war seemed to me, as it did to many others much older, to be a straightforward case of white *v.* black. The *News Chronicle* used to come into the house with its bitter accounts of the fighting in Spain and its attacks on the Government non-intervention policy. Besides, I lived in the same house as Leo and was moved by his declamatory and righteous protestations. Also, I went to a Catholic school where I was taught by Christian brothers. I was the only boy in the school who was against Franco. There is nothing like being in a minority of one, especially at fourteen years of age, to be wholly and fiercely committed to a cause – especially if that cause is a losing one. 'Do you know what the Reds would do if they came here?' said one of the brothers in his black grieving gown. 'Why, boy, they'd burn me down and the school wid me,' and when my fist clenched I think he mistakenly assumed I was giving a surreptitious communist salute. 'Green and gold, green and gold, Strong be your heart and bold.'

So I find it strange to read a poem by Donald Davie, a poet and critic of my own generation, who, remembering the thirties, writes:

> The Anschluss, Guernica – all the names
> At which those poets thrilled, or were afraid,
> For me mean schools and schoolmasters and games;
> And in the process someone is betrayed.

For me Guernica meant Cornford dead, Lorca dead, Caudwell dead, Fox dead, heroes dead, dead, dead. It meant a long fight in the back lane with the school's hooker because he saw Franco as a knight on a white horse, a protector of nuns. It meant particularly a book of poems that came out two years later.

Yes, it was 1940, when I was still a schoolboy, that I came across a book of verse in a yellow jacket, edited by Stephen Spender and John Lehmann, called *Poems for Spain*. Some of the work in that volume was of the public platform variety where what was said was more important than how it was said. The poems of Miguel Hernandez, particularly, seemed urgent. They were articulate and terrible cries for help. Hernandez was a young Spanish peasant poet who fought against Franco, who in his poems begged the democratic nations to intercede against Franco, who later was imprisoned by Franco and who, in 1942, died in one of Franco's dark jails.

I read Hernandez with rapt assent and growing anger. Here was a voice that could arouse a reader's indignation and, perhaps, *move him to action*. Here was a persuasive, pleading, prophetic and admonitory voice and one which, in some unspecified future, I hoped to emulate:

Singing I defend myself
and I defend my people when the barbarians of crime
imprint on my people their hooves
of powder and desolation.

The lament pouring through valleys and balconies
deluges the stones and works in the stones,
and there is no room for so much death
and there is no word for so many coffins . . .

Blood, blood through the trees and the soil
blood in the waters and on the walls,
and a fear that Spain will collapse
from the weight of the blood which soaks through her meshes
right to the bread which is eaten . . .

Hernandez wrote such poems during the worst of the Spanish civil war – when Spain was being turned into 'a vast cemetery, red and bombarded'. One of Leo's friends, Sid Hamm, had been killed out there fighting for the International Brigade. I knew Sid Hamm. He used to come to our house and he was old enough for me to call him Mr Hamm, and I was young enough to be teased by him and to be given a shilling – and now Sid Hamm was dead. I remember the memorial meeting for Sid Hamm at a dolorous little hall in Cardiff, misnamed Sunshine Hall. A platform, one hundred wooden chairs, some women in black, the chairman reciting with a Welsh fervour, 'They shall not grow old, as we that are left grow old,' and then sipping water as a few people coughed. A man near me, a grown man crying, crying for Sid Hamm and the Spanish Republic. A pamphlet, orange, white, and black, poorly printed, with Sid Hamm's face over a caption: THERE CAN BE NO VICTORY WITHOUT SACRIFICE.

Leo regularly brought home a magazine into the house called *Left Review*. It would contain a short story by Ralph Fox – in a later issue there would be Fox's obituary. It would contain an article by Christopher Caudwell – in a later issue there would be Caudwell's obituary. One week, a poem by John Cornford, and then, later, inevitably, in another edition of *Left Review*, Cornford's obituary. I had never seen photographs of Fox or Caudwell or Cornford. But I imagined them to look very much like Sid Hamm. Sid Hamm, killed at Brunete, and apparently very few people caring.

I found a most beautiful love poem in the yellow-jacketed *Poems for Spain*. It was called 'Huesca' and it was by John Cornford. Not yet twenty-one, Cornford had been killed at the battle of Huesca while

7

fighting for the International Brigade. How poignant his melancholy premonition of his own death; how terrible those lines of his, the last lines he ever wrote:

> Heart of the heartless world,
> Dear heart, the thought of you,
> Is the pain at my side,
> The shadow that chills my view.
>
> The wind rises in the evening,
> Reminds that autumn is near.
> I am afraid to lose you,
> I am afraid of my fear.
>
> On the last mile to Huesca,
> The last fence for our pride,
> Think so kindly, dear, that I
> Sense you at my side.
>
> And if bad luck should lay my strength
> Into the shallow grave,
> Remember all the good you can;
> Don't forget my love.

'Huesca' was the first poem that I ever voluntarily memorised. I can recite it still, and it moves me still, its piquant directness, its sad music, its silence between the quatrains, the time and the place and the young man who wrote it, and the woman he wrote to, whom I can imagine reading that love poem addressed to her, reading it after he was dead, reading it in privacy, in a room, in a house, somewhere in England.

To be sure, my schoolboy political awareness of 1940 derived from Leo's altogether more informed and enduring engagement. Ever since I can remember, he had spoken persuasively about class injustice, about unemployment in the Welsh valleys, about the Fascists in Italy, the Nazis in Germany and so on. Even before I was ten years old Leo had told me, as I listened, big-eyed, the truth about imperialistic Cowboys and oppressed Red Indians. So while my friends were firing Tom Mix guns, bang bang bang you're dead, from bosky paths in the local park, Waterloo Gardens, I crouched behind the summer house ready to ambush them with my Ugh and my imaginary bows and arrows. When I was a small boy, Leo not only taught me an alphabet that began:

A stands for Armaments the Capitalists' pride
B stands for Bolshie the thorn in their side

but also took me along to hear orators like Arthur Horner, the miners' leader. True, I could not understand what Arthur Horner was saying exactly but I sat privileged in the front row and stared, fascinated, at his false teeth that were much too loose for him and which perpetually threatened to slip out of his mouth as he pointed one index finger up to heaven and the other towards Barry Island. It had all the excitement of watching a trapeze artist who threatened Death and Destruction to all Fascist Hyenas and Cowboys.

No wonder poems with a political colouration made such an impression on me in 1940. For at school the poems we were nudged to read were too often about nightingales, celandines, daffodils, larks, mermaids – hardly matters relevant to my young life. Since St Illtyd's College happened to be a Catholic school the only twentieth-century poems the Christian brothers directed us to were by those rather tiresome Catholic poets, Chesterton and Belloc. Worse, we had to learn many verses off by heart. There were, of course, moments of illumination, even pleasure. I recall the time when one member of our class, Tubby Davies, who could not pronounce his Rs was asked by a new teacher to turn to page 496 of Palgrave's *Golden Treasury* and read out loud Chesterton's 'Before the Romans came to Rye'. With delight we watched the new master's face change into a paranoid maniac's as innocently Tubby continued with:

Before the Womans came to Wye or out to Severn stwode
The wolling English dwunkard made the wolling English woad,
A weeling woad, a wolling woad, that wambles wound the shire
And after him the parson wan, the sexton and the squire.
A mewwy woad, a mazy woad, and such as we did twead
The night we went to Birmingham by way of Beachy Head.

Apart from *Poems for Spain*, I soon discovered the fashionable 'pink' poets of the day: W. H. Auden, Stephen Spender, Louis MacNeice, and Cecil Day Lewis. They were OK. They were on our side – and We were the People. Auden and the others had reacted unequivocally, like litmus paper to acid, to European conflict and the civil war in Spain. They were hostile in their writings and in their ancillary activities to the rise of Nazism in Germany and Fascism in Italy. But I could not help noting that they also wrote poems that had nothing to do with the world of politics, that they were concerned about

9

political events without being overwhelmingly and singularly committed to any thorough system of political thought, to any dogma which held that poetry was important primarily as a missionary weapon. They never had the public urgency, say, of Wilfred Owen who, under the exceptional pressures of the First World War trenches, had written that the poetry was in the pity and that the poetry did not matter. Auden and the other 'pink' poets were content to compose poems that were ordered carnivals of the interior life. They were content to give readers pleasure. They were not trying to save our souls.

George Herbert, the seventeenth-century 'divine' poet, on his deathbed, asked his friend, Farrer, to let his book of poems, *The Temple*, be published only if it would do good, only if it would help 'any dejected poor soul'. Otherwise, Farrer should burn it. Herbert was not concerned whether his poetry would give pleasure or not. His poems, he felt, were valuable if they were effective as God's propaganda. His aspiration was to bring despairing men nearer to God. His intention, in short, was missionary. George Herbert, then, was a typically committed poet.

The first poems I wrote also had a missionary intention. My arrogance was only matched by my ignorance. True, I owned no religious commitment – but I wanted my poems to change the world. For at seventeen years of age I was an evangelical socialist. I had not yet learned that 'convictions can be prisons'; more to the point I had not learned how to write unflawed poems. I had not George Herbert's knack and skill. Still I knew the story of the provincial in Shaftesbury Avenue who asked a street musician how to get to the Albert Hall. 'Practise,' the musician directed him solemnly, 'practise.'

With practice, surely, my empty rhetoric would magically change into irresistible eloquence? It might take me years to become a proficient poet. Eventually, though, one day I would raise high the banner of Revolution and Poetry: I would legislatively searchlight the scandal of easy, adult accommodation; I would reveal – hey presto – how Violence himself merely slumbered, unbuttoned after his Sunday dinner, in the armchairs of Britain; I would cry out against the paradox of slums and cripples in a world of colours.

Yet these aspirations, if the truth be told, were peripheral and, occasionally, faltering. The writing of poetry was not a central need and activity for me as it is now, as it has been for so many years. More often, frankly, I daydreamed that I was the blue-shirted boy wonder who scored the winning goal for Cardiff City while my girl friend watched me from the Canton Stand; or I was hitting a six to make a century for Glamorgan (with a broken arm); or at the Prince of Wales Theatre, the audience, comprised of beautiful, busty young women, rose in unison shouting, 'Author! Author!' as I modestly bowed on stage. Indeed, apart from being such an extraordinary athlete, etc., I played, in my spare time, a variety of musical instruments at a night club. I played a clarinet like Benny Goodman, a saxophone like Tommy Dorsey, trumpet like Louis Armstrong, piano like Fats Waller. I sang a bit too – like Bing Crosby. Owning all these varied accomplishments I hardly had time to dream that one day I would be a great poet who might write lines like Walt Whitman's:

> Not a grave of the murder'd for freedom but grows seed
> for freedom, in its turn to bear seed,
> Which the winds carry afar and re-sow, and the rains and
> the snows nourish.
>
> Not a disembodied spirit can the weapons of tyrants let loose,
> But it stalks invisibly over the earth, whispering, counselling,
>   cautioning,
> Liberty, let others despair of you – I never despair of you.
>
> Is the house shut? is the master away?
> Nevertheless, be ready, be not weary of watching.
> He will soon return, his messengers come anon.

Though I could not write lines like these, my voice, when I began writing in 1940, was raised, my sixth-form school face red with indignation. Soon, secretly, I began to send out these 'committed' poems to magazines like *Penguin New Writing* and *The Welsh Review*. Moreover, the rejection slips I received with little notes decorating them, 'I like many things in this,' signed J.L., didn't discourage me. But now that it was war-time my two brothers, called up, left home. And so I was deprived of my immediate and reluctant audience.

In 1942, during my first year of medical studies at Cardiff, I resolved to show my notebook of poems to S.L. Bethell who was not only a Shakespearean scholar at the university but had also had poems published. Shy, I kept putting off my plan to ambush him. One afternoon, though, in the foyer of the university, I saw him come through the swing doors and since I was clutching my red-hot notebook of poems in my hand, I involuntarily sidestepped towards him.

'Please, sir,' I mumbled, 'would you be kind enough to er, to er, to er . . .' He looked down at me, puzzled, not knowing me from Adam. 'What?' he said. 'My poems, sir. Would you read them perhaps? I know you're busy, but –' He took the notebook from me. I wanted him, of course, to take the poems away and read them later. He opened up the notebook there and then. I stood awkwardly by, fidgeting, as students rushed in and out of the swing doors. I don't know what I expected him to say. But whatever he said would be of desperate importance to me. Suddenly, as he read down the page, his mouth opened slightly and he made a quiet noise. 'Pardon, sir?' I asked. The noise became louder, and his body seemed to shake. I stood there blushing and heard him distinctly: 'Ha ha ha. Ha ha ha. Ha ha ha HA HAHAHAHA. Oh ha ha, well, boy, well, well, there you are, boy.' He thrust the notebook back into my hands, and smiling cheerfully disappeared down the corridor.★

I don't think Professor Bethell intended to be unkind. The poems probably merited that kind of treatment. He just had not agreed with Johnson who once said, 'The price of reading other people's poetry is praise.' But he discouraged me for a whole year in one sense. I ceased to send my poems out to the literary magazines. The following year I continued my medical studies in war-time London. Still I wrote poems. Still there was the inevitable notebook. This time the front pages consisted of notes taken during lectures on anatomy and physiology. But the back pages, as usual, were noisy with poems.

One day in 1944, after a session in the dissecting room, I saw on the notice board that the poet, Edmund Blunden, was to give a lecture to the literary society. So, instead of returning to my digs, I hung around till six o'clock, and then went to Blunden's lecture. I don't remember what he talked about now. I don't recall what questions I asked him afterwards. He evidently discerned that I was interested in poetry for he invited me to have a drink with him. So, clutching my notebook, I, with the president and secretary and vice-president and vice-vice-secretary and vice-acting treasurer of the literary society, followed him down the Strand to The Coal Hole. He took the book away with him. I have the letter he wrote me still. It's

---

★ I had my moment of empty triumph in 1960 when four of my poems were included in an anthology, *Dragons and Daffodils*. I noted with mathematical and malicious glee that S.L. Bethell had only two poems selected.

on yolk-yellow paper and he used red ink. He was exceedingly generous, especially as I now realise that those early poems I showed him, though interiorly composed and directed, though no longer missionary in intent, were still extreme failures.

When I went home to Cardiff next I proudly read out Edmund Blunden's letter to my parents. They were baffled by his kind remarks. My father said, 'He can't be much of a critic. Besides you should be studying medicine hard, not wasting time composing poems.' But they listened intently when I read them my latest windy verse in my best front-room voice. There was a puzzled silence from my parents afterwards until my mother moaned, 'O the famine and the fever, O the wasting of the famine, O the blasting of the fever!' and Dad shouted above her wailing, 'I don't care if he's Homer. He's got to earn a living.'

2. A Jew in the Mirror

I had but the vaguest conception of the difference between Christian and Jew. As a child, I knew there was something different in the way Christian and Jew worshipped. They prayed on their knees. We stood up. They took their hats off. We kept them on. It was all rather baffling. 'Who's Jesus Price, mama?' I asked. 'Not Price, son,' my mother said. Once again she explained to me that, as far as Jews were concerned, Jesus was not the son of God. 'A good man,' my mother insisted, as if she knew him personally, 'but not divine, not the son of God. Do you understand?' My mother knew many things. She could speak Welsh as well as English, Yiddish as well as Welsh. Some of the 'wise' sayings from Welsh and Yiddish she loosely translated into English. I know them still – but I am not quite sure, even now, which proverbs are Welsh, which Yiddish:

> *If a man stares in the mirror too long he will see the devil.*
> *Love lasts as long as there are two people.*
> *If the rich could hire the poor to die for them what a*
> *   wonderful living the poor could make.*
> *When you visit a restaurant take a seat next to the waiter.*

My guess is that the first two 'philosophical' sayings are Welsh and the latter two, wry practical remarks, are from the Yiddish.

At the school I attended before St Illtyd's, Marlborough Road Elementary School to be precise, a building that later, during the war, was to be destroyed by bombs, I became aware of a vague, minimal otherness. The class register, each morning, proved something. Thirty boys shared the names of Evans, Davies, Jones, Morgan, Thomas, and Williams. Abse seemed a fancy name in that incestuous context. Besides, with another Jewish boy called Sidney Isaacs, during scripture classes, I was banished next door. While Evans-Davies-Jones-Morgan-Thomas-Williams bowed their heads over the New Testament, we, in our exile, discussed religiously the merits of the touring Australian cricket eleven: St Don Bradman and the Rev Ponsford. The googlies of Pope O'Reilly and that holy man, Grimmett. Anti-semitism hardly exhibited itself in the ambience of that elementary school in Roath so no pressures existed to make us feel basically different from our non-Jewish friends.

It just seemed quirky that we did not attend scripture classes with the other boys. It was of no great moment that on Saturday mornings we were bundled off, tidy to a 't', Lifebuoy soap under our armpits, to Windsor Place synagogue instead of to church the following morning. I did not like the synagogue. I could not understand the Hebrew address to the one God which the elders there uttered so devoutly. Their chanting seemed so ineffably sad and, like God, inexplicable. The sermon, it is true, was delivered in English and sometimes the rabbi would refer to the outrages in Nazi Germany. 'We should be sad this November. For it is the anniversary of the Kristallnacht when Hitler's insane violence towards the Jews of Germany became official. On the ninth and tenth of November, ruthlessly, all the synagogues in Germany, in Austria, in Sudetenland, went up in flames. With Teutonic efficiency the Nazis burnt down shops owned by Jews and flats occupied by Jews. Imagine what it's like to wake up in your house and to find the house on fire while maniacal mobs of uniformed men stand outside in the street shouting, with flaring torches in their hands. Oi, that black night, some 30,000 Jews were rounded up – a crowd that could fill the Arms Park when Cardiff play the Barbarians – and those Jews, those same Jews were dispatched to the concentration camps. Shouldn't this day be a day of mourning?'

The rabbi folded his arms and nodded his head up and down, up and down repetitively, silently, until he resumed, 'Some of you may have in your hearts vengeance, may have in your hearts wrath. Understandable . . . I say understandable. An eye for an eye, some of you may think. Yet . . . you should know that a primitive demand for retaliation is alien to our Jewish ethic. Our laws demand justice not blind retaliation. For the old law of an eye for an eye was not a law of retribution but of compensation. Apart from the commentary of the Talmud there is evidence for this in the holy scripture. The law of Moses meant that the equivalent value of an eye – not an eye itself – had to be paid for an eye. The equivalent value of a hand – not a hand itself – had to be paid for the loss of a hand. Do you follow? If a man lost an eye he should not have compensation worth two eyes or indeed something worth less than one eye. But he should have an eye for an eye, no more, no less. The primacy of justice not revenge is the notion Jews should be committed to. That is what our Mosaic law teaches us . . .'

I could not understand such academic argument. It was not too relevant to a young boy who, fortunately, was not exposed to anti-semitism. True, it was possible to hear, very occasionally, snide remarks about some Jewish villain who had made the headlines in the *South Wales Echo*. But men named Evans or Williams similarly figured in scandals, and of course, because of their numbers, more often. Besides, any doubts derived from having heard remarks about vagrant Jews so crooked that they had to be screwed into their graves were counteracted by my mother's insistence that I should be proud to be Jewish. 'Why?' I demanded, in a voice perpetually stranded on top doh. My mother would simplify for me our ancient traditions, pronounce on our heritage of high moral codes, and finally, defeated, resort to name-dropping. 'Spinoza and Disraeli were born Jews. And Yehudi Menuhin and Kid Berg are Jewish,' she said, proving something. I also learned from my parents about the more melancholy legacy of European anti-semitism, of pogroms and dispersion, of 'enemies on stilts'. I used to sing to the Smetana melody of the Hatikvah (the present Israeli national anthem):

> Austria, Rumania,
> And Russia too,
> All com-bined
> To persecute the Jew.

On the whole, though, if you were a schoolboy in South Wales, being Jewish had advantages. There were the usual holidays, Christmas and Easter and Whitsun, and there were the Jewish fasts and feasts also to keep or celebrate – which meant more days off from school. Again, one of the masters at elementary school, George Thomas – who was to become an MP and Secretary of State for Wales★ – unashamedly favoured the Jewish boys in his class. Possibly his pleasant bias had a complex aetiology. Or it may be that he showed us particular kindnesses merely in the hope that he alone, singlehanded, could compensate for certain disadvantages that we were sure to experience as we grew older, some time, somewhere else. Other gains derived as much from the idiosyncrasies of my parents as from the fact that we were Jewish. Thus, when I was about ten, I returned home one day from school with a form for my parents to sign. The form turned out to be a notice of intent that I, along with the other boys in the class, would be given a scientific lecture by some visiting educational sex expert. My parents sighed, and signed. So, in due course, I listened to a ghastly pale, flogged-out looking gentleman from the wrong side of Chepstow, humourlessly pontificating on the facts of life. One fact that I learned that afternoon worried me. 'In a year or two,' said the sex expert, 'you will experience nocturnal emissions. That is to say you will have wet dreams. Now let me explain . . .' I did not like the idea of having nocturnal emissions. I liked my dreams dry. And now, because soon I would break through some biological age barrier, they were going to become wet. It wasn't fair. For days I thought it over, and my mother sensing that I was anxious about something eventually asked me what I was worrying about. 'Wet dreams,' I confided, whispering. She looked at me, distressed.

'Oh, you are not to worry about that,' she said, hesitating.

'But it does worry me.'

'It won't happen,' said my mother suddenly, and I felt a sense of growing relief at her confidence. 'It just won't happen to you.'

'Why not?'

'Because you are a *Jewish* boy,' she said blandly.

And I believed her, so ceased worrying. Yes, I was fortunate to be a Jew.

True, it was irksome that certain evenings, instead of playing

★ Later Speaker of the House of Commons and, later still, Lord Tonypandy. But his 'Order! Order!' was first rehearsed in the classrooms of my primary school.

cricket or football in the back lane, I had to go to *Cheder,* that is to Hebrew classes. Here, in the basement of the Windsor Place Synagogue, I learned the aleph-beth, the Hebrew alphabet. Soon I could articulate the correct Hebrew noises without, however, understanding what those noises meant. It seems to me now that such a discipline was quite absurd; yet the fact that one could utter prayers to God in a language that had no meaning did not seem to me, then, to be peculiar. Prayer, after all, was a ceremony, and required a ceremonial language that should have no ordinary significance. If God was a mystery that could not be understood by man then the language in which man addressed Him directly should perhaps be equally mysterious. Or so I reasoned. Yet learning the correct noises was a bore and all the youngsters in that shabby basement room with its maps of ancient Palestine on the wall yawned repeatedly. It was a relief when we were taught Old Testament stories in English. For the first time, in that small room, I heard Goliath's large forehead cruelly splintering as the small stone pierced it; I saw the ten-mile-long horizontal shadow cast across the desert of Shinar by the tower of Babel; I smelt the hot acrid breath of the lions panting in Daniel's face.

It wasn't until I was about eleven that I questioned whether I believed in God. Reading of the disasters abroad, aware of unemployment and the dole queues in the Welsh valleys, without having heard of Nietzsche, I wondered whether God was dead, or whether God had just simply forgotten that he had created the world. I soon discovered that a Jew who doubts the existence of God, or who goes further to dismiss frankly the relevance of the idea of God and all the mumbo-jumbo prayers, all the antediluvian rituals that are bound up with that idea, does not, as a result, cease to be a Jew. The Cohen who becomes Conway, the Levy who becomes Lee, it makes no odds – once a Jew always a Jew. It seemed being a Jew was not a matter of religion only or even race. It was a destiny. And judging from the newspaper reports and from the seemingly paranoid fears of Jewish adults it was a destiny that would become increasingly awesome and deplorable. 'Chosen People,' I heard my mother say bitterly. 'Chosen to be persecuted.' Hitler, those days, was too much alive in the world, and one had to remain a Jew with dignity and with pride. All else was a pretence, a false name, a betrayal.

When I left Marlborough Road Elementary School to study at St Illtyd's, my parents were anxious lest I should be indoctrinated by the

Christian brothers. Apparently, the school had a small number of Protestant pupils but they had never had a Jewish lad before. 'You must tell them at the first opportunity that you are a Jew, son,' my mother insisted. So, the first morning at St Illtyd's I sat at a desk in Class 2B staring at the crucifix high above the blackboard and wondered when I could obey my mother's injunction. The muscular gym master, a Mr Welch, one of the few lay teachers, had breezed into the classroom. He appeared to be a fearsome man. Only later did I discover him to be all bark and no bite. That morning, though, he roared dragon fire. 'You mean to say that none of you have brought your gym shoes and gym shorts,' he bellowed. We all sat there, our eyes widening. 'If any boy comes in tomorrow without them I'LL FLAY THAT BOY ALIVE,' he shouted, louder than any Hell preacher. Then, 'ANY QUESTIONS?' The class sat there dumb. At last I stood up. 'YES, BOY?' he roared, thumping the desk with a huge fist. 'Please, sir,' I stammered, 'please, sir . . . I am a Jewish boy.' Edgar Welch looked at me, baffled. After an interval of silence he said, foxed, 'What's that got to do with gym?'

Though I was the only Jewish boy in St Illtyd's I did not feel any great sense of alienation. I enjoyed playing cricket and rugby so my very normal interests allowed me to be fully integrated into that schoolboy world. Soon, too, I became used to observing the rest of the class crossing themselves before and after each lesson, and to hearing pathological stories related by one crazy brother about demoniacal agents. Indeed this particular Brother R. repetitively told us an admonitory tale about a student who could not cross himself because of being possessed by the devil. One day Brother R. disappeared from the school. I think he must have had a nervous breakdown.

Nor had my parents any need to fear my being converted. By the time I was fifteen I had read Llewellyn Powys's *The Pathetic Fallacy* and I had come to dislike Christianity as a theological proposition if only because it seemed to me to be death-rooted: the dead Jesus on the cross, the way the church itself was surrounded with littered graves. And then there was the church's deep anti-sexuality. I would like to think that I would feel the same antagonism even if I wasn't born a Jew. Though I liked a number of the Christian brothers who taught me, I felt that there was something unhealthy about celibate disciplinarians in long black skirts bringing down their canes far too often on to this or that boy's raw, shuddering hand. Frankly, I was repelled by the conjunction of the dry murmur of devout prayers and the buzzing cane that caused a boy's involuntary yelp, in the name of the Father, the Son and the Holy Ghost.

Not that I dared discuss Christianity, then, with any of my non-Jewish friends. Gentiles, such as Llewellyn Powys, could attack Christianity philosophically, but a Jew, I was led to believe, should not comment. Jews are powerless; Jews should be quiet; Jews should be inconspicuous; Jews should do nothing to offend. Was not that the code of the ghetto and the lesson of centuries of pogroms? It is a code and lesson that takes a long time to unlearn.★

But at fifteen, absurdly juvenile, I merely wanted Judaism to be a better religion than Christianity – rather as I wanted Cardiff City to be a better football team than Swansea Town. Not that I ever went, by then, to synagogue or said Hebrew prayers. I really believed in religious anarchy where everybody could have their own God and where worship was expressed only in terms of action, in terms of *doing*. Leo had said, 'Well, Judaism is essentially a practical religion, it does believe in action; it is a religion which, after all, defined the Ten Commandments. Perhaps the main ethic of Christianity is "Love thy neighbour as you would yourself," an impossibly idealistic aspiration, whereas the main ethic of Judaism is probably, "Do unto others as you would have done unto yourself."' I liked Leo's analysis. I wanted it to be true. I wanted Christianity to be an inferior theology. I was not glowingly proud of the history of the Jews in the Diaspora through the ages. I felt the harassment of a relatively threadbare cultural heritage – the absence of beautiful cathedrals, the absence of magnificent paintings, the absence of great sculpture; little music and only a limited secular literary tradition. Two thousand and more years ago seemed too long a time to go back to our cultural glory. Still, guilt-ridden Christianity with its doctrinal sense of sin, the gloomed history of the Church that had waxed on suffering, had its own spite and lack of charm.

By 1941 abstract theology had become an irrelevance in my young life. I had become interested in writing poetry and any religious

★ Many years later when I first visited Israel and over lunch discussed theological concerns with the Hebrew novelist Moshe Shamir, he suddenly asked me, 'Why do you lower your voice every time the waitress comes close to our table?' I answered, 'Well, we were talking about the parthenogenesis of Jesus and I didn't wish to offend the waitress.' Shamir stared at me with penetrating pity. 'She's Jewish,' he reminded me. 'All the people serving us here are Jewish. Everybody here is Jewish.' It seemed odd to me to be in the majority.

formulations I had defined for myself had pertinence for me only insofar as they could help concretely in the making of poems. The language I spoke was English and it was the only language I knew. Here was my commitment. Solomon Molko and St Joan ceased to be Jew and Christian. Deluded, schizoid, they had more in common with each other than with their saner co-religionists. I was a Jew but that hardly seemed to matter very much. I did not wake up in the morning screaming, 'I am a 5 feet $8\frac{1}{2}$ inches Welsh Jew.' Simply I had resolved to start with the visible and to be startled by the visible. I was in the sixth form in school. I was going to study medicine. I needed to write poems. I was interested in girls, and in football, and in talking politics, and in the green ordinary world where God only existed because He was absent.

3. Girls

We lived in a rented, semidetached house in Windermere Avenue, a few doors away from the allotments. Over a period of sixteen years my family had moved from 'the smoky house' in Whitchurch Road where I was born to 298 Albany Road near the White Wall, to 237 Albany Road, to 66 Albany Road, to 66 Sandringham Road near Waterloo Gardens, to the house in Windermere Avenue. Every two or three years when we moved, I would ask with anomic anxiety, 'Mama, why are we moving?' I was always reluctant to shift even half a mile away from the pitch I had made my own. 'The new house will be more convenient,' my mother would always explain to me. Later, years later, I learned the truth. It seemed we moved whenever the house we rented needed redecorating.

Soon I began to like Windermere Avenue. It was a short road – not an avenue – of relatively new houses. It had a smell of fresh tar and lilac as it wound up a small incline from the side of Roath Park Lake to loop above Lake Road West and stop abruptly at the allotments. But I liked Windermere Avenue less for its topography than for some of its occupants. Three girls lived within one hundred yards of me: dark, smouldering Valerie Thomas; smiling, juicy Joyce

Bullivant; and pert, saucy Natalie Lewis who, however, at fifteen I considered to be rather young for I was now almost seventeen. Even before I had spoken to any of these three I had claimed them for my own. Condescendingly, I had allowed them to join my private, delightful, imaginary harem, my dream of fair women.

Valerie Thomas was the first to be expelled from the diaphanous brothel in my head. For one September evening, at the twilight hour, when the necks and heads of swans grew into particularly white question marks on the darkening lake, when men in bicycle clips doused the fires in the allotments before blackout time, I took a short cut home through the quiet, murky back-lane. There, in the shallow recess of a garage door, Valerie Thomas stood face to face with that tall, incredibly humourless fellow, Charley May. 'Good evening, Charley,' I said, ignoring Valerie Thomas whom, in any case, I had never actually spoken to − though I had seen her in my imagination nude and willing many a time − the slut.

Back home, no one was in. Not even the dog. 'Mother,' I shouted. Where the hell was everybody? '*Moth-er.*' No reply. Charley May, of all people. He was so hoy tee toi, so Cyncoed, with his front-room, madeira cake and sherry, up-the-hill, English accent. He was the only chap of my age that I knew who walked around with an umbrella − like Chamberlain, for God's sake. In a year or two, no doubt, he would be wearing a bowler and Harley Street trousers to match. Thinking of Chamberlain brought to mind Churchill. In the sideboard drawer there was, I knew, a box of cigars that recently my father had received as a gift. I had never smoked a cigar. If Charley punily identified himself with Chamberlain then why should I not become Churchillian?

Outside it was now almost dark. I did not light up until I entered the shuttered lane. I pulled at the fat cigar and blew out smoke like billyho, as I passed the garage where Charley and Valerie were necking. Their oval faces, one higher than the other, pale in the shadow, turned towards me. I pulled at the cigar and said nothing. I hoped Valerie was impressed. She was so vital, like her statistics, and he so effete. I proceeded past the dustbins outside the back doors of houses until I reached the bottom of the lane. But now there was no place to go particularly. I could barely see the water on the lake below. It was a depth of water, secret, ageless, turned into itself, alienated from the rest of the world. There was nothing better to do than to walk back up the lane again.

So I climbed towards the garage once more, dragging at the cigar. When I reached them they were standing apart, not even holding hands. Obviously I had dazzled Valerie Thomas. Surely, by now, she could see the difference between a Charley like Charley and a man like me? Suppressing a cough, I took the cigar from my mouth, flicked ash with my hand extended delicately to the right, and said, 'Goodnight, Charles.' I did not give him a V sign. I heard him mumble something indistinctly but already I had begun to feel nauseous.

At home, I felt terrible and threw the cigar dibby into the lavatory where it hardly sizzled. I lay down on the couch feeling dizzy and noticed how the keyholes in the doors stared at me. I closed my eyes but I felt the earth turning round in its circles. Soon I had to stagger on a tilting carpet and linoleum back to the lavatory where I was properly sick. Afterwards, exhausted, I thought, 'Fucking cigars. That Valerie Thomas isn't worth a light.'

I had better luck with Joyce Bullivant and Natalie Lewis. That late summer, with one or the other, I swam in the dubious waters of Roath Park Lake, risking the dangers of a duck-shit rash. And afterwards, with towels under our arms and our bathing costumes wrapped up in the towels, we walked beside the sunset mirror glittering in the hoofed lake and past the long boathouse under tall trees drawn in charcoal. What did we talk about, I wonder, as we dodged the midges that, hanging on invisible elastic, drew their oblique lines back and fore tirelessly? When we leaned over the railings of the west side of the 'promenade' of Roath Park Lake and stared down at the lathering water, at the far drop of the philosophical waterfalls, what profundities did we utter? Was it about the war and heroes whose faults could console us – or about those insane specks of energy, the midges, that presumably began their Sisyphus work before man appeared on this earth and will, I feel sure, continue to inhabit the sunset hour when man on this earth is no more?

I can't remember. Most likely we talked, Joyce and Natalie and I, about the latest film in the Capitol or the Empire or the Park Hall. Or about the previous night's radio programme – *ITMA* perhaps, or of Gracie Fields throatily singing 'Sally' to the troops who, afterwards, clapped and stamped their feet as if a great victory had been won. Perhaps I told Natalie Lewis my Max Miller joke: 'My wife is so stupendously ugly it is easier to take her with me than to kiss her goodbye.' And did Natalie obligingly laugh, I wonder? Did I read out to Joyce Bullivant the John Pudney poem that had been printed in that morning's *News Chronicle*? I don't remember. I do not recall any of our small conversations. They have gone, like so much else, into the backward distance where the fire glows still though all is ashes – gone beyond hearing.

In fact, I saw more of Joyce Bullivant than of Natalie. Occasionally I would take out a boat and row her with creaking oars to the more isolated, more secretive, north end of the lake where the deserted islands were. But our meetings were more innocent than randy and, gradually, became desultory, eventually to peter out altogether – much to the relief of my mother who irrationally thought I spent too much time in Joyce's company, too many evenings in her house. My mother, deluded of course, always tended to believe that her sons were being hunted and ogled by scheming women. How often have I heard her say, 'She needs a bucket of water over her, my lad. That'll cool her ardour.' Generally, though, sex was a subject my parents did not talk about – not in front of the children anyway. My father never said one word about sexual matters to me all his life except once when I was a student in London, at King's College. He, having heard that I had been seeing one girl called Nancy rather frequently over a period of months, drew me to one side secretively. Then, after an initial, trenchant silence, he said to my astonishment, 'Listen, son – I don't mind how many women you have. But don't keep on having the same one!'

At St Illtyd's, now in the sixth form, I studied not only physics and chemistry but, for the first time, biology too. Biology was not a subject taught to the younger boys. Perhaps the Christian brothers felt that a discussion about the mating habits of frogs, say, might act as an undesirable aphrodisiac – and cause their pupils to lust after girls. As a matter of fact, one boy in the school (his surname, I remember, was Hopkins) had been seen accompanying in a very affectionate manner, and in a public place, one of the girls from Highfield House School. Worse, Hopkins had been wearing, at the time, the school blazer and the green and gold school cap. As a result he had been made to wear the brown blazer and skirt of the girls' school and to parade on the stage of our school assembly hall so that we all could savagely hoot at this juvenile transvestite.

The new headmaster, Brother Michael, had arrived after the disgrace of Hopkins. He had always been pleasant to me personally. But one day I was summoned to his office and I felt a certain foreboding even though I should have been 'in his good books'. After all, I had done reasonably well scholastically and I played rugby and cricket and even chess for the school. But that September Monday afternoon of yellow sunshine on parquet floors I stood inside the headmaster's office like a (guilty) miscreant. His face was as solemn as an executioner's – I had been summoned obviously to be strongly reprimanded. 'Sit down, Abse,' he said, gathering about him his long black gown. He seemed to be a worried man. Of course it was wartime and he had especial administrative problems. Recently, not only had most of the lay staff been called up but Brother Bonaventure, our excellent history teacher, had left the school having volunteered to become a bomber pilot.

'Last Friday evening,' Brother Michael said in his Irish brogue, 'you gave a talk to the Sixth Form Society, did you not now?'

'Yes, sir,' I said, puzzled. 'It was a debate actually.'

'The subject of your talk was "The Bankruptcy of Marriage" am I entirely right?'

'Well, Brother . . .' I began.

Abruptly he lost control and shouted, 'I don't want you talking about that sort of t'ing to the boys at all. Not in this school. It's a good Cat'olic school and I won't have you undermining the morale of the others. One of the boys, offended, reported to me your desperate opinions and . . .'

'But Brother Michael, I . . .'

'*Quiet*,' he yelled.

I was amazed. There had been a debate the previous Friday evening and I had advocated that Marriage was an unnecessary institution. True, only one boy had voted for me – and he had been a Protestant – but surely nobody would have been offended enough to complain to the headmaster? I could hardly credit Brother Michael's own apparent disgust and anger. However, he now once more controlled himself. He sighed, pushed his rimless spectacles higher up the bridge of his nose and continued more reasonably, 'Now, Abse, sure, I know you would say nothing pornographic at all. I mean you do not have a dirty mind – unlike some of the other boys I could mention – but I will not have you –' and at this point his face suddenly suffused with blood and his voice grew dominantly loud, '– present a PERVERTED CREDO ABOUT MARRIAGE – do you understand?'

'I assure you, Brother Michael . . .' I began, almost shaking with anger.

'Quite so,' he interrupted me. 'I don't want to hear any more of this TRASHY VIEW OF YOURS ABOUT MARRIAGE.'

I almost wanted to cry. If I spoke I might well cry. It was best to be silent. For a moment I heard the faint sound of traffic outside the window. He rose and came round his desk and placed his hand briefly on my shoulder in a reassuring way. Perhaps he sensed how upset I was. Maybe he felt he had gone too far. Now he said quietly, manufacturing a smile, 'That will be all.'

But at the door he spoke again, as if driven. 'By the way, what are your attitudes about sex?' I turned around. He seemed to be looking at me with an extraordinary, almost violent alertness. He was waiting for me to talk about sex. In no circumstance would I talk to this celibate priest about such matters.

'Excuse me, sir,' I said.

I stood there miserably waiting for him to give me permission once more to quit that office of his – that stuffy office with its black Bible on the large desk and its crucifix on the wall.

'Do you go ballroom dancing, Abse?' he asked sternly, as if dancing were a mortal sin.

I was astonished by his question, and he, I think, realised it sounded absurd. For he now opened the door for me, indicating that I need not answer. 'I don't dance, sir,' I said, and he nodded and I quit and I heard his door close softly behind me. For all I know, afterwards he sat down in the armchair and brought both his hands to his face.

For my part, cycling home that evening I wondered why Brother Michael wished me to discuss sex with him. Did he want to correct my wayward, demonic views; to save me with missionary zeal from a Don Juan life of promiscuity and guilt and retribution? When I arrived home I told my sister, Huldah, who happened to be visiting us that evening, about my interview with Brother Michael. But all she said was, 'You should know how to dance,' and then irrelevantly, flatteringly, 'You're the good-looking one of the family.' My sister has always tried to bolster my self-esteem by telling me, in latter years, how gifted I am, and earlier, when a youth, how much more handsome I was than my elder brothers. I looked at the mantelpiece photographs of Wilfred and Leo in uniform. They did not exactly resemble Robert Taylor and Cary Grant. To be told I was better-looking than they were hardly assuaged my adolescent doubts about my physical appearance.

'I'll get by,' I muttered without confidence.

'But you should learn how to dance,' my sister said vaguely. 'Your headmaster is right.'

There was no point in telling her again about my interview. Evidently she had not listened to my story attentively. Later, in my own room, I observed myself in the mirror. I was almost ugly, I decided. If only I did not have any signs of acne and if only my nose was a little bit shorter. I pushed the distal end of my nose upwards with my index finger. If I could only sleep in that posture it might stop the damn thing from growing. Why couldn't they invent a brace for noses? And yet . . . and yet . . .? From some angles I was almost good-looking. If I turned my head *so* – showing a fraction only of my left profile and if I raised my right eyebrow *so*, at the same time, just a little, I looked quite laconic, debonair. I descended the stairs, a youthful Clark Gable, with one of my eyebrows slightly raised and my head fixed at an angle on my neck and waited for applause in the living room. Neither mother nor Huldah noticed.

Afterwards, when I put one of my records on the radiogram – perhaps Dinah Shore singing 'Memphis Blues' or 'Sophisticated Lady', my sister said again, 'You ought to learn how to dance. Next year at University you will just have to dance.'

'Leave the boy alone,' my mother said. 'He spends too much time already with Joyce Bullivant.'

'I hardly ever see her these days,' I protested.

'Very nice people, mind you, the Bullivants,' my mother said. 'He's a civil servant, you know.'

But Huldah was rolling back the carpet. She was going to show me how to dance. 'Your father was an excellent dancer in his day,' my mother said. 'Show Dannie how to do the polka, Huldah.'

'The polka – for heaven's sake, mother,' Huldah laughed.

She showed me the first easy steps of a fox trot. 'Keep your legs together. Don't splay them apart,' she commanded. 'For heaven's sake, you look as if you've wet your trousers.'

Huldah arranged that I should take dancing lessons with one of the Miss Williams sisters who lived off Penylan Hill. It was an ironic sequel to Brother Michael's threatening interview. That autumn of 1940, the Battle of Britain had been fought and won and it was a great victory. But none of us really knew how great – though

Churchill had said in his characteristic way, 'Never in the field of human conflict was so much owed by so many to so few.' And Brother Michael was worried about the sexual attitudes of the sixth form and there I was, worried about blackheads, listening to Miss Williams saying, '*One* two three and *one* two three and *one* two three. Hold me closer, c'mon don't be shy, hold me *closer*,' while the record player sounded 'Toodleoodle ooma, toodleoodle ooma, don't mind the rain.'

That winter I joined the ranks of Saturday night dancers. We shaved, we sprinkled tap-water on our hair, combed it and went out slamming the door behind us as one of our parents shouted, 'And don't be late.' We whistled all the way to the bus stop. We travelled from Roath, or Llandaff, or Penylan, or Ely, or Cyncoed, or Splott, or some other district of Cardiff, towards the consolation of noise. In town, we barely noticed people fumbling through the blackout. We ignored the unlit shop windows and the River Taff flowing noiselessly under the bridge near the Castle. The Taff did not exist. We were going into Saturday night where the others were. Wherever a crowd gathered, singing at a pub, at a students' dance at the City Hall, wherever they joked, quarrelled, laughed, it was Saturday night. Elsewhere it was no time at all – though some were in uniform and some were casualties already, or like my cousin, Sidney, missing at Dunkirk, presumed dead with my Uncle Boonie and Aunt Cissie in mourning for him and cursing the bloody Huns. *One* two three, *one* two three and *one* two three, hold her closer and *one* two three, do you come here often and *one* two three:

South of the Border
Down Mexico Way

I was going to become a doctor. It had been planned. It had all been planned for me. When I was thirteen my name had been put down for Westminster Hospital. Now I was studying 'sciences' in the sixth form. Next year I would be doing my first MB at Cardiff University. Then I would continue my studies in London, at King's College in the Strand and finally at Westminster Hospital. 'The best hospital in the world,' Wilfred had said. There was no decision to be taken. All I had to do was to travel down the metalled ways towards next year and the year after. Meanwhile it was the last dance and it was time to go home, back to where my parents listened to the radio with its news about the defeat of the Italians at Sidi Barrani, and stroked the dog and spoke about their children and the war, about what was and what might be.

After one Saturday dance, some weeks before Christmas, I accompanied a WAAF, Peggy, who wore her raven hair tight around her skull with a parting dead centre, back to her parents' home somewhere beyond Victoria Park. She told me with the sing-song voice of the valleys, that it was her last night on leave and that she was stationed in an RAF camp with the comical name of Middle Wallop. She did not ask me my age. I sensed that she was more experienced than Joyce Bullivant or Natalie Lewis or any other girl I had known. The blue-lit tram rocked through the town towards more desolate outskirts and gradually unloaded its passengers before we reached the terminus. There we alighted on to a still wet pavement and walked past blacked-out, hermetic houses while searchlights dragged their diagonal white cones through the sky until they pooled and smoked in clouds.

Outside her house she drew me close to her. After a while I did not hear the remnants of rain dripping from the surrounding eaves and drainpipes. Peggy complained it was too cold and too damp. 'Come in,' she said, 'and I will make you a cup of tea.' I hesitated. I had a long, long walk home and already it was late. But she gave me her hand and her eyes promised me so much that my doubts became soluble. We climbed the few steps to her front door. Her mother, it seemed, had gone out to play cards with some neighbours.

'When she do play whist, see, she never gets back before midnight,' Peggy said. 'Yes, when it comes to cards mam is an absolute demon.'

Inside the house, Peggy seemed to forget about that cup of tea. In the front room, in the dark, near a silent piano, I swooned while elsewhere, in a different district of Cardiff, no doubt Brother Michael, also with his eyes closed, prayed on his knees. His prayers must have been mightily powerful for, suddenly, we heard the noise of a front door banging and footsteps in the hall. Quickly Peggy turned on the light and arranged herself. Her mother had come home and it was she who made us tea. I remember making polite, punctuated conversation about how I was hardly familiar with the Victoria Park district – though I knew of the seal that used to swim in its pond.*

---

* Every Cardiff youngster was taken to the pond at Victoria Park sooner or later to

'Billy the seal swam down Queen Street during the floods,' Peggy's mother said. 'But you wouldn't remember that.'

'Of course I do,' I replied.

'Mind you, we used to live in Ferndale in those days,' she said.

Afterwards, I went back to Windermere Avenue, still a virgin . . . just – which is more, I think, than could have been said for Peggy.

My parents were waiting up for me. It was late, very late.

4. Abse of the Sixth Form

As I was ushered into the cramped, messy, editorial offices of the *Western Mail and South Wales Echo* I screwed up the green and yellow cap of St Illtyd's College and thrust it into the pocket of my blazer. 'This boy wants to write articles for us, Jim,' said the man in shirt sleeves. I had told Sidney Isaacs and Eric Philips that I could write better articles than Beverley Baxter. 'Last week you boasted you could write a better play than *Young Woodley*,' sneered Sidney, adding provocatively, 'go on, tell the editor, you're a wizard journalist.' His remark propelled me through the newspaper's doors in St Mary's Street. I left the two of them startled on the pavement. Once inside the building I felt impelled to run out again into the sunlit street of shadows. It was too late; someone in shirt sleeves asked me what I wanted and stupidly I said in a gush of embarrassed words, 'I could write better articles than that idiot Beverley Baxter. He's worse than Negley Farson.'

'Sit down,' said Jim. 'Sit down, son. How old are you?'

'Sixteen.'

'Have you written articles before?'

I could hardly refer to those reports in the most recent issue of the St Illtyd's magazine about the school cricket matches. They were signed by a certain D.A. who described, dispassionately of course, how a boy called D. Abse had scored with leg glides and straight

---

observe Billy the seal. He was a great favourite with the kids but, after the war, when Billy died, a post mortem revealed 'he' had ovaries!

drives reminiscent of Hammond, eight not out against Cathays High School and five l.b.w. against Monkton House School.

Nor could I boast, 'Mr Graber, our English master, always gives me eight for my essays, sir.' The only time he had not given me eight was for that essay Leo had written for me. Earlier my brother had said, 'I'll do your composition for you. Then you will get nine or ten.' I believed him. Had not Leo won, a few months earlier, the first prize, offered by *Reynolds News*, for an article on a socialist theme? I was grateful for Leo's assistance. After he wrote an essay specially for me I copied it out neatly into my homework exercise book and handed it in to Mr Graber. Alas Mr Graber gave me seven and had written in red ink: 'Do not use words like "aberration" unless you know exactly what they mean.'

'Whose articles do you admire?' asked Jim.

'I quite like William Forrest of the *News Chronicle*,' I said. 'I used to admire A. J. Cummings too.'

'You've outgrown him, I suppose,' said Jim, with heavy sarcasm.

I felt my cheeks become hot and the silence elongated until the phone on the editor's desk rang. Then he said above its clamour, 'Look, son, come back in a couple of years' time when you've left school.' I rose and made my way down the undistinguished corridor into the yellowing street of a late summer afternoon where two boys waited for me. I felt free, uncaged, marvellously free. 'They've got Beverley Baxter on a contract,' I explained.

'Besides you're much too busy thinking about writing a play better than *Young Woodley*,' said Sidney Isaacs sarcastically, 'to write a regular column for the *Echo*.'

'You could call your play *Abse of the Sixth Form*,' said Eric Philips. Then he added more seriously, 'If you do ever write a play I hope you bring into it the real issues of the day. State the case for Revolution as against Evolution.'

'Yes,' I said without confidence.

Afterwards, when I was on my own with Sidney Isaacs I told him what really happened inside the editorial offices of the *South Wales Echo*. 'He thought I was too young,' I told Sidney bitterly. 'Too young for Christ's sake. We're *sixteen*. People don't realise these days that sixteen is quite old. Some people can be very mature at sixteen.'

'I feel hellishly old sometimes,' said Sidney earnestly. He consoled himself by adding, 'Ripeness is all, as the master says.'

'The master?' I queried.

'Shakespeare, Shakespeare,' said Sidney scornfully.

That autumn of 1940 I went several times with Sidney Isaacs to the Prince of Wales Theatre. We sat in row N near the outside aisle. It was better than listening to the radio, to Gracie Fields singing 'Sally' to the troops, or to Henry Hall playing 'Here's to the next time'. We felt very grown up in the Prince of Wales watching Donald Wolfit in *King Lear* or Eugene O'Neill's *Desire Under the Elms*. In the interval we would chance the bar to smoke cigarettes and drink one wicked gin. 'It's just hooch these days,' I told Sidney languidly.

I enjoyed these evenings out at the theatre. It was so different from going with my parents as I had done occasionally in the years before the war. Not that my parents had ever taken me to see a play. They preferred Variety shows. 'A very good turn,' my father would say, wondering whether he could employ some unheard-of juggler or impersonator to amuse the audiences in the Aberdare cinema he managed before the two main films. 'It would make a change from the organ,' he argued. As a Saturday night treat my father about once every two months had taken us to one or another variety theatre in Cardiff or even in Newport. The safety curtain would be down before the show began and we would stare at projected slides of local advertisements while an unseen orchestra in the pit would play sweet, old-fashioned music. My mother would hum.

Afterwards as we munched the Black Magic chocolates that Dad invariably presented to my mother on such occasions, the curtains would rise and eventually we would listen to that star turn, the Cheeky Chappie, Max Miller in his gaudy jacket and plus fours, as he cracked the dirtiest jokes in the world. 'That's a good one,' my father would say while my mother stared at the distance, her eyes somehow unfocused as if she had not understood. Once we went to hear Issy Bonn singing 'My Yiddisher Momma' and my mother, from time to time, raised to her eyes a handkerchief that always smelt of eau de cologne.

'I hate Variety,' I said to Sidney Isaacs during the first interval of *Desire Under the Elms*.

'Yes,' said Sidney, 'muck compared to this sort of thing. It's all right when you're very young. But when I see a Variety show these days I feel older than the old man of the sea.'

'Who's he?' I asked.

It was in the bar of the Prince of Wales during an interval (I can't remember which play) that we saw and heard – to be accurate heard and saw – Mr Inky Williams holding forth on the social function of drama. Both Sidney and I had once been in his class at Marlborough Road Elementary School. We both recalled how Mr Williams had handed on 'the torch of history from age to age'. He used to stand in the classroom speaking with tears in his eyes of Owain Glyndwr whom he declared was a great hero 'though the English of course denounced him as a traitor'. Often Mr Williams read out to us in ringing tones a text from a book written by an equally fervent Welshman: 'Owain Glyndwr's grave is well known. It is beside no church, neither under the shadow of any ancient yew. It is in a spot safer and more sacred still. Time shall not touch it; decay shall not dishonour it; for that grave is in the heart of every true Cymro. There, forever, from generation unto generation, grey Owain's heart lies dreaming on, dreaming on safe, forever and forever.' Rousing stuff.

Mr Williams had always appeared to us to be pronouncedly correct, dignified and respectable. He spoke a proper biblical English. Yet once I had observed him go berserk at Ninian Park. At that particular football match he had screamed at the opposing hulk of a centre-forward from Luton or Gillingham, 'Go back to Hong Kong, you bleeder,' and 'Get your bloody hair cut, you filthy Mona Lisa,' – or some such words. Inky Williams, I had discovered, was a secret swearer.*

Now he was calm, sober, otiose. And what we noted with some surprise as we glanced across the bar was how *young* he appeared. When we had attended Marlborough Road Elementary School five years earlier he had seemed so old. Once again, with a shock, we realised it was we who were getting older. We were catching him up. It was another age already since we had sung in his classroom with

---

* In 1979, while I was giving a reading in the Town Hall of a Northern provincial town, a Christian brother who once taught me at St Illtyd's sat in the front row. He was not sober. After each poem the priest in his long black gown addressed me too audibly, 'Thassa wonderful poem, sure it is, Dannie,' or, sherry-happy, exclaimed, 'Tip-top, tip-top. Entirely tip-top.' Finally he turned to the audience. 'I taught Dannie when he was a boy. No doubt about it at all, he's become a desperately wonderful poet. But I have to rebuke him. In one of his poems which I'm glad he hasn't disturbed you wid tonight, he used the word Fuck.' Suddenly, as he swayed, his scolding voice rose higher and higher. 'It's a poem that *uses the word fuck*. I repeat . . . *fuck*.' The audience sat there somewhat rigidly, I thought.

piping voices, 'Land of My Fathers', 'Men of Harlech', and 'Cwm Rhondda' in Cardiff English. That picture of ourselves as ten year olds had begun so soon to fade. The songs themselves had already become ghostly like an echo of an echo of an echo.

Suddenly in that theatre bar I felt for a moment the sad impermanence of things and then the bell rang indicating that the interval was over, that the play was the thing and about to restart. As Mr Williams left the bar he stared at us without recognition. Vacantly, Sidney and I returned to our seats in row N.

5. Sticks and Stones

Our sports field extended beyond the grounds of Cardiff Castle. Between the rugby pitch and the Castle grounds proper, green acres fumed an indistinct morning mist. In the distance a line of very tall trees, negrescent, devoid of foliage, poised themselves for vertical flight into the faded blue of a February sky, and nearer, the sparse spectators urged us to 'heel', to 'sling it out', and to 'get stuck in'. Throughout the game I was aware of a girl in a yellow skirt sitting some three hundred yards behind the goal posts all on her own. She sat on some sort of groundsheet reading a book, totally uninterested in the rugby. Her presence seemed quite incongruous because it was too cold really, the air too brisk, just to sit there as if at a picnic. In any event, immediately after half time we were leading Canton High School by 9–3. The whistle shrilled for a scrum. Sixteen boys in coloured jerseys, their breath smoking in the air, bent down, locked themselves together, and the ball came out cleanly, 'sweet as a bird'. We broke away, and I remember calling 'Kevin'. He gave it to me, and I was away on the blind side, accelerating, hugging that oval to my chest with my right hand. But I was too slow. Tackled high, my arms pinned, I fell hard to the frosty ground on to my right shoulder. I heard the light snap of a bone being broken and I lay still on the earth, astonished that I felt no pain.

The referee was a Mr Kennedy, our cheerful chemistry master. He attempted to pull me up to my feet as the rest of the team, in their green–and–gold–hooped shirts, gathered round. 'What's the matter, boy?' Mr Kennedy asked.

'I've broken my collar bone, sir.'

'Don't be ridiculous,' he said, irritated.

But he pulled my jersey back, then said, puzzled, 'Oh . . . it does look a bit bent.' And so it was: there had been the noise of a bone fracturing and the red-faced chemistry master stared at me, non-plussed, while in the middle distance, sitting in her yellow skirt, oblivious of the game, not belonging to anybody, sat a girl reading. (I wonder what brought her there that cold Saturday morning to settle on the frostbound grass, as the sun broke through the milky traces still loading the early air?) I think the other boys and the chemistry master believed me to be rather brave but actually I experienced no pain whatsoever. I walked towards the touchline, supporting my right elbow with my left hand, and the school's fullback, as I passed him, murmured sympathetically, 'We'll do Nigger Rees for you.' He was referring to the swarthy Canton lad who had tackled me, but it had all been an accident. Still a false hero I passed the few sympathetic spectators who gave me a little clap, and now, accompanied by a boy called Bill Williams, I proceeded to the dressing room. I didn't think of the consequences of a broken bone. All that troubled me was that that very afternoon I would not now be able to play soccer as had been planned. For, although I liked rugby, I loved soccer; and those days I was fit enough to play them both, as I frequently did, on a Saturday. Our two shadows were flung forward on the bottle-green turf, and behind us I heard the game recommencing – the distant sound of a cry frozen in the air, and the familiar thud of a leather ball being kicked, perhaps, for touch.

To enter the dressing room in the wooden pavilion, though, one had to bend down slightly through the small cut-out door. This trivial exercise resulted in my feeling the pain for the first time. Bill, solicitous, sixteen years of age, pulled out a packet of Woodbines and said, 'Have a drag.' I sat down, wincing, and waited for the taxi somebody had called and which would take me to Cardiff Infirmary where only a few years earlier Wilfred had been a medical student. I wished he were there still. He would have looked after me; but he was away in the Army. I leaned forward and it hurt again, quite an acute pain. 'Swear if you want to, mun,' said Bill. I didn't feel like swearing. The dressing room stored darkness and smelt of dried, sour sweat. Instinctively, in the gloom, one looked towards the oblong of light in the far entrance.

It seemed hours before I sat on the wooden bench in the Casualty Department of Cardiff Infirmary. Most of the people waiting looked old and tired: people bandaged, people with crutches, people who didn't seem to have anything wrong with them at all. The conspicuous thing, though, was that everybody seemed to be defeated – maybe it was because everybody spoke in humble whispers and nobody dared to laugh out loud. One day I would be familiar with this world; not as a patient but as a medical student and a doctor. However I had not seen then those who had fallen out of 'the splendid procession of life'. I had not then assented to Boycott's remark: 'I do not wonder that people die; that is easy enough. What I marvel at is that they go on living with bodies so maimed, disordered, and worn out.'

The X-ray room, also, with its floor of polished linoleum and intricate machinery, seemed utterly cheerless and impersonal. The metal of the cassette pressed cold against my bare chest as I obeyed the order to, 'Breathe in. Hold it.' There was the whirr and click of the X-ray machine and, later, a man in a white coat held up an X-ray plate to the screen. There I was – the picture of a flat man without flesh, and my own, alien, cream ribs curved on a grey background.

A nurse commanded me to sit on an upright chair, behind which the doctor stood.

'I'm going to be a medical student,' I told him. I mentioned this, I think, in the vague hope of receiving some preferential treatment but he pulled my shoulders towards him forcibly and at the same time placed his knee in my back. 'I'm sorry,' said the doctor as I stared momentarily at the light reflected on a chromium surface. It was over quite soon. 'You see,' the doctor smiled, 'nothing to it.'

When I returned home to Windermere Avenue, bound up, my arm in a sling, very far from comfortable and visibly pale, my father unaccountably shouted at me. 'You're no damned good. If you get injured like this it means you're no good at the game. You shouldn't play if you can't take care of yourself. What a damn fool you are!'

'What are you shouting for?' my mother asked, puzzled.

I, too, was startled by my father's vehemence. I expected sympathy but he merely scolded me. Indeed, he looked as if he could thump me. Generally, my father was a quiet man, not over-demonstrative, and certainly not given to hitting his children. I do not recall him even once slapping me. (True, he had, years before, thrashed Leo for smoking or rather for telling lies about smoking but that had been a most uncharacteristic event.) Now, though, he scowled malevolently. He was like a half-doused bonfire, smoking, almost out – likely though to flare dangerously with any new casual wind.

'These days you so easily go off the handle,' my mother complained.

It was enough. 'You drive me up the wall,' he yelled, and he began to exit from the room. 'BOTH OF YOU.' And he slammed the door so emphatically behind him that our dog, tail between legs, hid himself under the sideboard. Dismayed, I changed my position in the armchair for I was experiencing twinges of pain. 'He's not really angry,' my mother said thoughtfully, 'he's just upset that you're hurt, son.'

Four years earlier I had to have thirteen stitches in my leg. After a muddy afternoon game of soccer in the Rec., I had arranged to meet a friend. I was late and instead of taking a shower, I bathed my feet in the washbasin in the bathroom. I stood on a chair and gingerly placed my right foot into the basin. I leaned over to grab some soap when I fell and the basin gave way. Jaggedly the sharp china ripped open the red and white flesh down the back of my leg and thigh. Fortunately, Wilfred had been at home to attend to me with iodine and bandages and he took me to Casualty at Glossop Terrace. And all Dad said was, ''At's a dirty habit, washing your feet in the basin.'

'But he yelled when Wilfred had concussion that time,' my mother reminded me. I had heard the story many times before – how, on one occasion, Wilfred had been playing cricket for his 'House' at Cardiff High School. Wilf fancied himself as a wicket keeper. 'Yes,' Mother continued, 'when Wilfred very cleverly stumped this lad out this same boy turned around and *coldly* hit Wilfred over the head with the cricket bat. Was that fair?'

'Not cricket,' I said.

'That boy was expelled,' my mother said.

'Well,' I said.

'And when they brought Wilfred home still dazed, poor boy, your father was tamping mad with *Wilfred*. Isn't your father ridiculous? He should stick to fishing,' my mother added irrelevantly.

By way of apology, my father gave me money to buy some books. Partly immobilised because of my collar bone, and off from school for a few weeks, I had plenty of time to read. Of course, there were books in the house I still hadn't opened. The blue-bound sets of Dickens and Conrad had only been dipped into. These, I felt, could be read any time. They had been on display so long in the front-room bookcase, a status symbol for neighbourly visitors, that I grew assured they would be there in the future, just waiting faithfully for genuine attention. Meanwhile they were loved, honoured and neglected. For other books offered greater excitements. With my good arm, I brought back, from W. H. Smith's, *The Betrayal of the Left* edited by John Strachey and Nietzsche's *Thus Spake Zarathustra* in the Everyman edition. I also picked up the newest edition of *Penguin New Writing* which contained some poems I immediately responded to: W. H. Auden's 'Lay Your Sleeping Head'; David Gascoyne's 'Snow in Europe'; and C. Day Lewis's 'Where are the War Poets?'

> They who in panic or mere greed
> Enslaved religion, markets, laws
> Borrow our language now and bid
> Us to speak up in freedom's cause.
>
> It is the logic of our times
> No subject for immortal verse
> That we who live by honest dreams
> Defend the bad against the worse.

But the 'worse' couldn't be worse: that ranting, homicidal Hitler, and all those murdering, fanged Nazis roaring, 'Sieg Heil' in unison and singing 'Germany Over All'. What could be worse than the mindless, rough, blond beast, its hour come round at last, goose-stepping over pavements of blood towards Valhalla to be born? And the local result on the civilians in Cardiff?

I don't fancy time-bombs. Don't know when the buggers will explode.

Gimme one of those under-the-counter cigarettes.

Duw, that's no nun – Look at her long *steps*. It's a man. A spy, I'm positive.

And the News At Six, and, afterwards, the mournful siren and the droning bombers and the ack-ack fire and *Be British, Don't Panic* on the cinema screens of the Olympia, the Empire, and the Park Hall. I had not forgotten that recent January air raid. As I approached Roath Park Lake the intensity of noise increased alarmingly. I began to run up the moonlit lane to Windermere Avenue. And less than thirty yards behind me I heard bits of shrapnel clanging against the dustbins.

One of the prose writers contributing to the February *Penguin New Writing* used the pseudonym of Fanfarlo. He remarked: 'Suppose during an air-raid I held Botticelli's *Venus* under one arm and an old woman unknown to me under the other, with the chance of saving one but not both, which should I choose? Immortal painting or crumbling flesh and blood. The first! As an artist, I claim that right.' I pondered that existential choice and knew that without doubt, I, Dannie Abse of the sixth form, would save crumbling flesh and blood. I had no doubts. Did that mean that I did not own, like Fanfarlo apparently, the sensibility of an artist? Or was Fanfarlo talking through his hat anyway? Or was it simply that, already, I had the bourgeois humanist mind of a doctor?

On the radio, we had listened to Churchill's stirring biblical rhetoric addressed only indirectly to Roosevelt. 'We shall not fail or falter. We shall not weaken or starve. Neither the sudden shock of battle nor the long-drawn trial of vigilance and exertion will wear us down. Give us the tools and we will finish the job.' That language, then, did not seem particularly inflated. It was 1941 and the diction of war will always be purple. Astonishingly enough, nobody I knew ever imagined we could lose the war. It was just a question of how long it would take us to beat the bastards. And if things did get desperate, as Dad said – as everybody said – the Yanks would come in sooner or later. They would not let us down. They were our rich cousins. We had 'a special relationship' didn't we? They were just Australians or Canadians with a different accent, weren't they . . . surely? They would be helping us sooner or later by coming into the war. It would be more than lend-lease and giving us fifty clapped-out destroyers. But, Jesus, why didn't they hurry up?

The 'sudden shock of battle' came to our house in Windermere Avenue in earnest only a week or two after I had broken my collar bone. That night my father was out and it was a particularly bad raid. One could hardly distinguish the noise of gunfire from that of bomb explosions. We tried to ignore it all, my mother and I, as we sat before the coal fire, not talking much. When my father did come in he seemed excited. 'It's as light as day outside,' he said. 'You could pick up a pin.' He persuaded me to leave the blacked-out house for a minute and witness how the surrounding district was bathed in a luminous, eerie green. And indeed it was so. I have never seen anything like that sick light. It was the colour of gangrene. Flares were floating down like chandeliers – a number of small lights clustered around a big central green flare, and the pattern was repeated over and over.

'Incendiaries,' an ARP warden said and, indicating my arm which was in a sling, he urged my father and me to go to a shelter or at least to return inside.

'All right, Mr Davies,' my father said, 'don't fuss now.'

When the explosions rooted themselves nearer to our house, my father ushered us into the little cloakroom below the stairs, and he hung up a thick coat against the window lest glass should fly dangerously. Just in time, too, for there was the distinct whine of a bomb falling. The sound advanced, changed its note into a high-pitched whistle. They used to say, in the war, that if you could hear that whistle you would be all right – that some other poor bugger had his name written on it. No one is alive to contradict that fable. The poor bugger in this case who was literally blown to bits was the ARP warden who had only spoken to us a few minutes earlier. So our neighbour, Mr Davies, had been killed, and I remember hearing the thin scream of some woman outside in the street, now very close to us, for a hole had appeared in our wall and the ceilings were down. I lay on the floor in the smell of dust and plaster, and my shoulder was hurting again, and the green light crept indoors.

'Are you all right? Are you all right?' my father and mother were saying.

Soon after I was admitted to a small cottage hospital just outside Cardiff.

6. Reg

In the next bed, his right leg swathed in bandages, in a Hodgen splint, that same leg slung up by a pulley affair at an angle of almost forty-five degrees, reclined Reg. He'd lain for months in that ridiculous posture, staring at ceilings from sunken pillows through nameless days of routine similarity and, no doubt, long restless hospital nights. It was enough to turn any man, any ordinary man, never mind Reg, into a sex maniac. The bed itself was tilted, the furthest end raised up a foot, and surrounded by a Balkan frame. What with the uprights, pulleys and weights, the bed was a contraption that looked as if it could zoom up to the ceiling at any moment, with Reg in it, waving to the nurses.

But I wasn't feeling very comfortable myself. Ridiculously, they had placed a small sandbag under my back, between my shoulder blades, and I lay near a window to stare outside at the far roof-top of a house. Often, having nothing better to do, I watched the smoke from its miniature chimneys drift away till it became invisible – the sky pinned up blue behind it, or more often grey on white. Or closer, a pattern of rain on the window pane caused me to think blankly of particulars, a snail on a wall, the same colour as the wall, rain falling on to a gravel pathway, framed reflections of the sky in a rainpool, oh I don't know what I thought of as I had to lie like that, quite still, with my arms folded on my chest. The doctor explained that my collar bone would heal very cleanly. Apparently, film stars in Hollywood with broken collar bones were given this fastidious and radical kind of treatment. Ronald Colman, Don Ameche, Brian Aherne, Robert Taylor, Melvyn Douglas, according to that doctor who forever winked when he spoke to me, had endured this sandbag therapy. In any event, it was the only time in my life that I had been treated like a film star. So I lay back there, like Reg, in my own way also immobilised, and feeling as vacant as a mirror in an empty room.

It was a small ward. Three beds against one wall, three beds against another, and in between the two sets of beds a long polished table carrying vases of flowers. On our side of the room, myself, Reg, and Old Billy, an ex-collier with a silicosis cough. 'Duw, my breath is bad today!' Old Billy used to say, 'An' I'm a bit deaf, too.' A bit deaf, Christ! His deafness was almost total and perpetual, not a fluctuating ailment as Billy would pretend. Every morning Reg used to yell at him, 'How are you today, Dad?' and Old Billy, after prompting Reg, at the top of his voice, to repeat his inquiry, would reply suspiciously, 'Enough of that, you cheeky devil.' Because his deafness prevented communication Old Billy never said much. But we were under the illusion that we knew him because of what he was and where he came from. At least we knew miners exactly like him. We knew the mining communities in the valleys – the terraced houses, the sheep in the cobbled streets, the skyline of the mountains, the Socialist orators he had listened to, and grief kneeling in the sow-coloured chapel. I don't remember very well the other three who occupied the beds on the far side of the room beyond the polished table; one of them, I recall, suffered, perplexed, from of all things a complication of measles.

Soon Reg became friendly. Apparently he had smashed his femur in several places as a result of a motor-bike accident. But he didn't tell me much about that. He was more concerned in letting me know about his girl friends. The fact that I was still a schoolboy didn't deter him from speaking to me, man to man. 'If this leg don't mend soon, see, some other swine will be shaggin' them.' I was the right age, I suppose, to be impressed by Reg's amorous entanglements, and, to confirm his bragging, erotic tales, letters arrived for Reg almost daily.

Sometimes he would read out, shamelessly, a few paragraphs to the whole ward. They were from Betty, or Sian, or Rosemary, or Gwen, or Sandra. Most of them worked with Reg in the munitions factory at Bridgend. They all had yellow fingers and hands, Reg told us, from working with chemicals, but their bodies he insisted were beautiful, mun, white as cream. 'Not that I'd mind screwing a Chink,' he informed us, unprejudiced and progressive. And, one day, feeling generous, he pulled out from his wallet a sheaf of snapshots of girls, girls, girls, and passed them over for my watering eyes. Girls sedate in ATS uniform, girls in bathing costumes, land girls, girls in close-up, girls reclining on grass, looking at Reg's camera rather expectantly, I thought. I gave the snapshots back to Reg who studied them anew. On his face then, one could discern the shifting blanks of sadness that can be seen on violinists' faces as they play yearning melodies.

One late, dragging afternoon, the ward was suddenly disturbed from its slow conversational vacancies by Old Billy.

'Do you notice it?' he cried out, dramatically.

'What, Dad?' roared Reg.

'Ye-es, it's there all right.'

I remember how the whole ward paid attention for Billy, being deaf, rarely began a conversation.

'To be candid,' Old Billy shouted, 'I have an acute sense of smell.'

He was sitting bolt upright, and seemed alarmed. 'Concha smell it?' he said. 'Bloody terrible it is, letting that happen, by here, in a ward which is in a hospital.'

He sniffed once or twice, then grumbling inaudibly, lay back resigned. Whatever odour Billy perceived, it wasn't of this world. And the ward hesitated, oddly quiet, not even Reg being moved to utter some ribald remark. It was as if Billy's mysterious protest had changed something, as if his worried interruption of the afternoon, that until then had progressed forward mindlessly, had left behind significant absences. But soon the nurses broke the delicate fabric of clock-ticking air by pushing in tea trolleys – and then Old Billy's olfactory hallucination was forgotten. Reg, as usual, began to twit noisily, 'Charming,' at the nurses. Or to be exact, for he cut his 'a's short, 'Chamin, chamin!'

Certainly, all the nurses appeared happy to do things for Reg. Even the rather plump one that Reg called 'Jumbo'. They engaged in naughty flirtations and semi-amorous scuffles with him. They even co-operated in writing his love letters to Betty or Sian or Rosemary or Gwen or Sandra. It was awkward physically for Reg, sunk back, his head lower than his good foot, to write himself. So, shamelessly, he dictated his wicked love to his yellow-fingered women via the poker-faced nurses, and what I overheard sounded like fragments from erotic masterpieces. But Love on the antiseptic page was obviously not enough for Reg. One night I woke up to hear whisperings and shufflings from the next bed. Reg in his grotesque posture, and the good-natured night nurse who bent over him shadowily, seemed to be engaged in do-it-yourself sex. But all he said to me next morning was, 'I'm browned off of lying here. I'm so damned well browned off.'

And I was browned off, too, already tired of my sandbag – so how much worse it must have been for Reg. It would be marvellous to turn, if only for a moment, on one's right or left side. It would be a joy to have the elastic bandaging removed from my chest. For that adhesive stuff made my skin itch. Indeed, years after I left that cottage hospital I slept on my back with my arms folded across my chest, like a dead man tidily arranged. When I think of it now it was rather drastic treatment the doctor prescribed for me. And while I lay there Swansea was bombed three nights in succession and ruined; Bulgaria joined the Axis; Kid Berg beat Mizler; and there was talk of the USA giving us Lease-Lend. But all this seemed unreal. The small events in our ward – Old Billy saying, 'Enough of that, you cheeky devil,' and Reg dictating his love letters to his girls in Bridgend – appeared more important, real – though much of the trivia that occurred during those hours and hours and hours is now blurred or utterly unremembered. I recall eventually having the elastic bandage removed, I remember having my first bath and fainting in it – the first time I had fainted in my life – and I remember talking to Reg about poetry.★

When I spoke feelingly about the war in Spain, and the urgent poetry that had come out of it, Reg was hardly impressed. He had no interest in politics – as for poetry the only things he liked were limericks:

> There was a young lady from Chislehurst,
> Who had to whistle before she could wee wee first.
> One day in June,
> She forgot the tune,
> Wooooooooooooooo
> Bladder burst!

Jumbo, the spreading nurse, who had overheard Reg's recitation suddenly exploded into uncontrollable laughter. She laughed like a small child, quite without inhibition, so that we all laughed at her laughter. The hilarious noise in the ward became infectious, confluent, gained in volume. Even Old Billy, I remember, noticing that people rolled in their beds with laughter, began to cackle in the peculiar way that deaf people do. Jumbo could not stop laughing, and we, too, continued hysterically, so that soon Sister entered the ward to restore order. The ward became gradually quiet until it was altogether too silent. Each person lay back in his bed defeated, each on his own.

★ More than twenty years later I visited Cardiff jail while making a programme for the BBC. The governor asked me if I would read some poems of one of the prisoners. I could hardly say 'No'. Two minutes later, accompanied by the governor and the prison doctor, Gus Barry, I entered a cell where a man stood at soldierly attention. 'Show him your poems,' commanded Dr Barry. I felt embarrassed. I was expected to comment on the poems there and then. I looked at the prisoner standing in that stiff, artificial posture. I felt I had seen him before somewhere. I read the poems in the exercise book he handed me. His verses were peppered with dead words: with 'twixt' and 'tis' and 'amaranthine' and 'myriad'. I murmured some encouraging noises. What else could I do? Gladly I left the cell. Later, when I discovered his first name was Reginald, I realised where I had seen him before. He was Reg, an older Reg, surely?

7. A Porthcawl Sojourn

I never did discover why we stayed the wrong side of the bay in more formal Porthcawl rather than Ogmore. After all, the Abse family belonged to Ogmore-by-sea, Ogmore of turf and sweet extra air, Ogmore of ferns interrupted by sheep-runs and spectacular chemical sunsets. Ogmore of cliffs and rocks and pebbles and sand and a snail-bright track across the river's mouth where, on the shore, my father hunched over a fishing rod while the long grey tides of the Bristol Channel crept in. Indeed, though born in Cardiff, I may well have been conceived at Ogmore-by-sea. My father and mother, in the old-time sepia-tinted days of fewer people moving more slowly, must have spent many honeymoons there.

Before the war, like a seasonal ritual, each long summer holiday, we stayed in borrowed bungalow or wooden villa, tipping out sand from our daps, arguing the toss, shouting 'Mine, mine,' and singing bars of 'Stormy Weather'. Or else, we shared lyrical accommodation with earwigs and beetles as big as Welsh dragons in a tent or caravan pitched behind a rusted grey wall on tilted Hardy's field while the sheep marked H munched away at the turf all afternoon, all evening, till gradually the stars became more visible one by one, one thousand by one thousand, one million by one million, until the night sky over Ogmore was as beautiful and terrible as the music of Bach.

But that April of 1941, convalescent, I joined my parents in a furnished terraced house in Porthcawl. 'We'll stay here for a few months,' my mother explained. 'After that, we'll move back to Cardiff. Your father is already looking for another house to rent. As for school, it's your last term anyway. You can go in daily by train when you feel up to it.'

The rooms of the Porthcawl house were too poky; the wallpaper too conspicuous; the furniture too oppressive. One had the sense of stuffed birds slowly leaking sawdust behind glass cases; a clock with a tic, hiccuping solemn chimes on the hour; china dogs cheaply won at the local fair on the mantelpiece; the sweet smell of decaying mice under the floorboards and a too beautifully printed 'Old Chinese Saying' framed on the wall: *If you have two pennies to spend, spend one penny on bread that you may live; spend the other penny on a flower that you may have a reason for living.*

'My Swansea is destroyed, my Swansea is destroyed,' my mother said dramatically. That very day she had visited her long-lost schoolfriend, short Mrs Beasley, at Sketty. 'Gone Swansea market, gone Ben Evans's store, gone – '

'Listen,' my father interrupted her, 'does he 'ave to take *all* the crusts off *every* loaf?'

'I was hungry,' I muttered.

'Yes, but do you 'ave to peel off the crusts as if the bread was a square banana?' complained my father.

'He's a growing boy,' my mother defended me. 'And he likes crusts. Listen, Swansea's finished, Rudy. You wouldn't recognise – '

'I like crusts,' my father breathed heavily, 'but do I go tearing them off every loaf, do I?'

'There's a war on,' my mother said, as if that explained everything.

'I'm not a savage,' my father grumbled. 'I don't scalp the bread.'

While I was in hospital, Cardiff also had further raids – none as severe as those on Swansea but there had been casualties and the spire of Llandaff Cathedral had been blown off. One of my friends who had visited me at hospital – Sidney Isaacs or Alan Greedy was it? – had told me about the sadness of Charley May. Apparently, raw glass had fallen out of a building over Charley and severed a main artery in his leg. He had been rushed to hospital but, because of complications later, his leg had to be amputated. I did not know that Charley, also, happened to be convalescing nearby at Rest Bay, Porthcawl.

Several weeks later though, ahead of me on the prom, I saw a dark-haired girl pushing a fellow in a wheelchair. Soon I recognised Valerie Thomas and Charley May. I did not know whether to stop or to continue walking until they smiled at me as if I were a close and valued friend. We hesitated opposite the Esplanade Hotel and I said, 'I'm sorry, Charley,' and he stopped smiling and he gazed out to the horizon over the unceasing sea.

'Do you like my ring?' Valerie Thomas said too quickly.

Startled, I expressed my admiration. I heard my own unchained voice: more enthusiastic than it should have been, fit for a florid eulogy.

'Thank you,' Valerie said.

So they were engaged. Neither was yet eighteen but they were to be married in the autumn. 'I wish you happiness,' I said tidily. Charley nodded and I thought of them together in a bedroom. Somewhere else a rifle-butt smashed the stained-glass window of a church.

'Mam says I'm a bit young to get married,' Valerie Thomas said. 'But what's the point of waiting if you're in love, if you are right for each other?'

'That's so,' said Charley, with his surprisingly measured English voice. 'That's absolutely so.'

And then, as if he had read my thoughts, he added with some aggression, 'We'll make out.'

The sea thudded against the wall of the promenade sending spray on to the pavement some twenty yards away from us. 'The subject of your talk was,' said Brother Michael, 'the Bankruptcy of Marriage, am I entirely right?' I heard the background noise, the disordered rhythms of the sea, and I said, 'Well, I'd better push on.' But I did not move.

'They're making a film down at the Slip,' Valerie said.

'I expect it's because of the jetty and the lighthouse,' Charley May remarked. 'Natural décor and all that.'

'With Jack Doyle and Movita,' said Valerie enthusiastically.

For a moment I was tempted to confess to Charley that I was sick that time – that time in the lane when I had smoked the cigar. Afterwards I had been sick as a dog. But I noticed Charley and Valerie smiling at each other as if they shared a secret, one I should never know, and I suddenly felt like a stranger to them which indeed I was.

'Well, I'll see you,' I said. 'Must press on.'

And while she pushed Charley May in his wheelchair towards Rest Bay I walked on towards Porthcawl Slip as close to the promenade railings as I could so that the sea spray flying could splash right over me, over and over again.

At the jetty a small, listless crowd had gathered. A few men clustered around a camera. I could not see anyone who resembled the singing Irish, curly-headed ex-boxer. But the lady in dark sun glasses talking to a brick-faced man in a camel-coloured overcoat was no doubt Movita. Somehow she looked a little seedy for a film star. I did not expect that. Perhaps it was the excessive make-up that paradoxically made her look shagged, scandalously shagged in a sudden throw of sunshine. I waited for some action. I waited for a quarter of an hour. Nothing happened. A few seagulls were carried like paper in a swirl of wind and the sun went behind a cloud. Ogmore is so much nicer than Porthcawl, I thought. Yes, Ogmore-by-sea is a really nice place. I could see it right across there, across the bay. The shadows were racing across the sea.

8. Absent Brothers

After our Porthcawl sojourn, we moved to a small house in Vaughan Avenue, near Llandaff, and I left school for university. It was important for me, I realise now, that Wilfred and Leo were no longer at home to influence me. Already I owed them too much, had taken in, as if by osmosis, not only their more enlightened opinions but their prejudices also.

'What's best, Labour or Liberal?' Wilfred appealed to me when I was five years of age.

'Labour,' prompted Leo.

'Liberal,' said Wilfred.

'Labour.'

'Liberal.'

'LABOUR.'

'LIBERAL.'

'Well, what do you say?' Leo said to me, as if I were the judge.

I liked Wilfred best in the whole wide world but I could not pronounce the word 'Liberal'. I said *cimena* and they laughed. I said *emeny* and they laughed. So I certainly was not going ever to attempt the word 'Liberal'.

'Labour,' I said.

'There you are,' said Leo triumphantly. 'Even a child *knows*.' Wilfred looked at me as if I had betrayed him. After all, had he not brought me, the day I was born, *Comic Cuts*? Did he not protect me when Leo teased or thumped me? Did he not give me pennies to cheer me up when I was crying? And here I was, ungrateful beast, five years old already and not even a Liberal.

Later, Wilfred bequeathed me his Ten Commandments which began: *Do not wash your hair in the bath while taking a bath*; continued with, *Do not jump off a tram without paying the fare even if the conductor happens to be busy upstairs*; and concluded, *Try not to walk in dog's excrement.* If Wilfred, because of his fastidiousness and moral scrupulosity, sometimes made me feel like a common sinner, Leo made me feel like an uncommon ignoramus. 'You mean to stand there,' he would thunder, his mouth suddenly consisting of thirty-two ivory teeth, all canines, 'you mean to stand there and tell me you have never *heard* of Rosa Luxemburg. Ieusu Grist!'

It was hard going sometimes. 'Wilfred and Leo were always in the first three in school,' my father would say, 'and you come home, pleased with yourself, because the report says you're fourth. Dummkopf.'

On a boat on Roath Park Lake Wilfred would instruct me, 'Watch me carefully now. You feather like this' – and he let the oars skim gracefully over the surface of the water. 'Whatcher think of that, hey? Not bad, eh? Not half bad, what? Now you do the same.' And I would try to copy his action but would fail miserably and Wilfred would lose his composure. 'You fool, you idiot – you'll tip the boat over in a minute. Watch it, watch it, you . . . nitwit.' Or taking down a magazine from the shelf, Leo would read out loud some lines written by a member of the International Brigade in Spain. 'Now you read it,' he would say to me.

> A handsome young airman lay dying
> And as on the aerodrome he lay
> To the mechanics who round him came sighing
> These last dying words he did say:
>
> Take the cylinders out of my kidneys,
> The connecting-rod out of my brain,
> Take the cam-shaft from out of my backbone
> And assemble the engine again.

Reading these lines I felt the bravery of the dying young airman. I read the verses with emotion and thought I had read them well. But Leo said, 'My God, your Cardiff accent is terrible. You could do with some elocution lessons.'

To this day, out of habit, my brothers unfailingly criticise me. Recently Leo attended a concert at the Queen Elizabeth Hall where I happened to be one of several poets reading their own poems.

Afterwards he commented: 'You read your stuff all right – but for heaven's sake, the way you *stand*. Do you realise that you look like a cripple? Really, I'm not joking.' And Wilfred: 'You mean to say you find the idea of God an irrelevance. My dear chap, all the great philosophers since the beginning of time are prepared to come to grips with the concept of God. But *you* – *you* say, as far as *you're* concerned, God is an irrelevance. Ha ha ha.'

Wilfred was born to be a psychiatrist. He was always willing to listen to, and be interested in, other people's problems. Yet, as a small boy, judging from all the stories I have heard from my parents, he had been particularly abstracted. Once, apparently, late for school, he rushed out of the lavatory and put his overcoat on, leaving his trousers off. Arriving at school and shedding his overcoat in the lobby, he was assaulted by corrosive laughter. Embarrassed, he ran all the way home only, finally, to collide with the lamp-post near our house, knocking himself silly. No wonder Wilfred became a psychiatrist.

After qualifying at the Welsh National School of Medicine and doing the usual house jobs at Cardiff Infirmary, he took a job at Abergavenny Mental Hospital where he began his psychiatric career and took his Diploma of Psychological Medicine. Nowadays he is very eminent in his field and writes learned papers and books with such snappy titles as *Hysteria and Related Mental Disorders*. 'I don't know how he can bear to work with all those queer people,' my mother iterates and reiterates. Perhaps she remembers that day we first visited him at Abergavenny Hospital just before he was called up into the Army. My mother and I (neither of us had visited such an establishment hitherto) walked across the tranquil lawns of the mental hospital towards the main building where Wilfred was located. On the way we heard someone obsessively swearing. My mother, who has never uttered any oath stronger than 'damn' all her life, pretended to be deaf. But as we proceeded the swearing became louder, the man's voice more strident. He had his back to us and, disturbingly, addressed a blank wall: 'Fuck, shit, cunt, fuck, shit, cunt, bugger, bloody, bastard, bugger, bloody, bastard, fuck, shit, cunt, fuck, shit . . .' My mother did not turn her head. She marched on, as if only the Monmouthshire blackbirds and thrushes whistled in the wounded air. 'How can he stand it?' she asked me afterwards. Never have I heard a question so genuinely asked.

Leo was born to be a politician. He has always been conspicuous by his presence. His organisational ability, like his oratory, has always been formidable. Yet he did not articulate one coherent word until he was almost four years of age. One day, though, one of my mother's brothers, my uncle Joe – Joe Shepherd, a doctor – took him from Cardiff to Swansea. It seems that during the journey Leo became fractious and when my uncle attempted to assert his authority Leo started his revolt with aphasic grimaces. This earned a reprimand which stimulated Leo to kick Joe Shepherd's shin. Ultimately, enraged, my uncle held Leo out of the window while the train was still in motion. Leo, then, uttered a most surprising adult sentence or two. He has hardly ceased speaking ever since. Shortly after Leo had begun to compose such imposing sentences my father pushed him on to the spotlit stage of the Aberdare cinema that he then managed. 'Ladies and Gentlemen,' Leo, three feet high, would announce, 'next week we have a treat for you. Not only can you see Cecil B. De Mille's *Male and Female* but also Charlie Chaplin in *The Kid*. I'm sure you all look forward to that as much as I do.'

It has not been to announce forthcoming attractions that Leo has since exercised his rhetorical gifts – unless a programme of modified socialism and a concern for the quality of individual life can be counted as such. In his own way, Leo was – is – as much 'a sensual puritan' as ever Aneurin Bevan had been. When I was a small boy how righteously Leo would address those solemn people sitting attentively in rows and rows of wooden chairs as he reminded them of the debasement of spirit resulting from widespread unemployment in the valleys, of the cheerless slums that sprawled across bleak mountain sides near colliery wheels no longer turning. I have heard him recite, like one inspired, from a soapbox in Llandaff Fields the amazing phrases of a poet: 'Freedom is more than a word, more than the base coinage of statesmen.' How thrilling I would find his speeches when I was a schoolboy, even though, critical, the previous night, I had caught him practising impromptu gestures in front of a mirror.

But the year I began my medical studies at Cardiff University both my elder brothers were away. My sister was married and in London. My parents' house seemed unnaturally quiet. Their absence allowed me to make my own decisions, form my own opinions, blunder in my own way. Moreover, at university, I had more freedom than at school. I attended lectures when I felt like it, studied in my own green time. I lit up a fag, no longer surreptitiously; swaggered into a pub as if I owned it; perched my father's trilby hat on my head at an Emlyn Williams angle; played poker and listened to the older medical students' bawdy stories.

'A bloke came into Casualty today with a bottle on his penis,' said Cyril Evans.

'You're kidding.'

'No, honest. Know what he said when we asked him how it happened?'

'What?'

'He said – I swear to you – he said . . . it fell off a shelf!'

'C'mon Cyril . . . deal.'

The year that I was a freshman there were so many firsts! First time I slept with a woman, 'Take it off, take it off, I haven't got VD.' First time I drove a car – nobody told me how to brake and I took my feet off everything so that eventually, at 10 m.p.h., I crashed into a wall on which was written OPEN UP THE SECOND FRONT NOW. First time I even read *The Times*!

I had bought *The Times* because a girl called Bernice Rubens had mocked me. 'Fancy, you've never read *The Times* – and you're eighteen years of age. Tough shit.' Bernice, at that time, impressively planted oaths in her sentences like a docker. Though not interested in her sexually I did find her rather different from other girls. She had a mass of black hair. One had the impression, wrongly of course, that her hair went straight down all the way to the pavement. She also had very bright eyes, a triangular jaw, a smile 'not quite in the middle of her face', and sometimes, a laugh near to lunacy. Nowadays she is well known as a novelist; but when I first encountered her she was as much interested in Zionism as in literature. She did not easily dispense sympathy. If she had heard, say, that Cyril Evans had shot himself in a field in Llandaff one dark night (as he in fact did) with a Home Guard rifle because he thought he had put a certain usherette at the Queen's Cinema in the family way, then Bernice's reaction might well have been nothing more than 'Tough shit'.

Perhaps one needed to react in an apparently callous way. There was so much to mourn. Recently, I have been looking at the front page of *The Times* dated April 1st 1942, in order to remind myself of this and that. There were so many deaths on active service then, so many missing. MISSING: *Brancher* – officially missing at Singapore;

Brown – reported missing after fall of Singapore; *Dean* – reported missing in Malaya, Feb. 1942. Etc., etc., missing, missing, name after name, a long roll call, and always the small advertisement concluded with the plea, 'Any information gratefully received by his parents.'

April 1st 1942 happened to be the first day of Passover. That night, if my brothers had been at home, there would have been a *Seder* – that is to say a festive meal to celebrate the ancient exodus of the Jews from Egypt. Though neither I nor my brothers and sister were generally interested in Jewish ritual, in the synagogue and its schedules, in the dull prayers of dull religious maniacs, I think we all welcomed, as a warm family occasion, the *Seder* ceremony. We enjoyed the dinner with wine, the arguments about, and explications of, symbols and prayers some two thousand years old, the songs and the jokes and the momentary opening of the door for the angel Elijah who might be standing outside, mantled, tall, in a stranger's guise.

But April 1st 1942, only my father, my mother and I sat down to the rationed evening meal. And instead of a *Seder* ceremony my mother lit two candles, put her hands over her face and mouthed a prayer silently. Then she said out loud, 'Next year may there be Peace in the world and may all the family be together again.' That night no door was opened for the invisible angel and the flames on the two candles did not tremble but continued to stand up straight like two small, yellow, clown hats.

9. Ezra Pound and My Father

There is no doubt that Ezra Pound's speeches were his own. No Italian propagandist would have been capable of writing them. I never heard of anyone who heard these broadcasts over the radio, although they were received and monitored in the United States. As a radio figure, Pound did not command the interest of Lord Haw Haw, Axis Sally, or Tokio Rose.

JULIAN CORNELL, *The Trial of Ezra Pound*, Faber, 1966

I was surprised when I read that statement by Ezra Pound's lawyer,

Julian Cornell. For though I never listened to Tokio Rose or Axis Sally, I had heard Pound on the radio loud, if not clear. Not long before hearing him broadcast from Italy I had come across his *Selected Poems* in Cardiff's Central Library. In that centrally-heated building which often smelt of wet mackintoshes, I had taken down a green volume from the Poetry shelf and as I arbitrarily flicked the pages over I came across:

> Upon learning that the mother wrote verses,
> And that the father wrote verses,
> And that the youngest son was in a publisher's office,
> And that the friend of the second daughter was undergoing a novel,
> The young American pilgrim
> Exclaimed:
>   'This is a darn'd clever bunch!'

I took the book home and became an Ezra Pound fan. I did not know of his bizarre economic theories, or his *Cantos*, or his anti-semitism. But when I told my new enthusiasm for the poems of Ezra Pound to one of my more literate acquaintances – perhaps it was Bernice Rubens or John Stuart Williams – I was informed that Pound 'broadcasts regularly from Italy. He's working for Mussolini.'

So, in July 1942, I fiddled with the knobs of our ancient radio set. The black-out curtains were drawn. The photograph of my brothers, in uniform, stared from the mantelpiece; my father stared at me from the armchair near the empty firegrate; our black mongrel dog stared at me from his favourite place under the sideboard, and then, for the first time, I heard the twanging accents of Ezra Pound. His voice kept on coming and going; it became a strain to try to identify what he was saying. I had heard earlier, 'Europe calling, Ezra Pound speaking,' but now the radio set effervesced with atmospherics, crackled with the noise of burning sticks, and finally a high-pitched jamming note dominated everything so that the dog's ears suddenly lifted in alarm. I said apologetically to my parents, 'Well, it makes a change from the BBC or Lord Haw Haw.'

'Even hearing you read us *your* poetry would be better than this,' my father said, teasing me. And he laughed as if he had recounted the greatest joke in the world.

But then the râles and rhonchi in the radio cleared, the adventitious noises miraculously vanished, and Ezra Pound's voice became stridently distinct.

'Listen to this,' I said to my reluctant parents. 'Listen to the second greatest poet in the world!'

My father and mother said nothing for a while. Despite Fascist Italy, my own left-wing views, and the fact that my two elder brothers were in the Forces fighting the bastards, winning the war on their own as a matter of fact, our living room in Vaughan Avenue, Llandaff, grew reverently hushed.

'It's a saw,' my mother said at last, 'he's got a voice like a human saw.'

The voice heckled: 'I ask Archie to say openly why he handed out four billion dollars . . . to a dirty gang of kikes and hyper-kikes.'

'Who's Archie?' asked my father, baffled.

I shrugged my shoulders and the ranting voice continued, 'Had you had the sense to eliminate Roosevelt and his Jews or the Jews and their Roosevelt . . .'

'He's a lousy anti-semite,' said my father.

'I'll switch it off,' I said, disappointed.

Strangely, my father became addicted to the voice of Ezra Pound. Twice a week he would try and listen to him, unable to understand, any more than I could, what was being broadcast by E.P. Every now and again, two continuous sentences, plain and unadorned, came through, syntax and all – all quite comprehensible to both of us. Then followed intricate divagations, private references, then a line perhaps from some poem in a state of nascence or a botched aphorism. It all seemed like some recondite insult. To some, perhaps, it was meaningful – but to us, in Vaughan Avenue, his broadcasts appeared to be merely the ravings of an eccentric poet, the paradox of a sensitive Fascist.

I got fed up of that nasal harangue. My mother became fiercely irritated. 'I would rather hear Gloomy Sunday than that anti-semite,' she kept saying. But my father, week after week, month after month, would just hiss at us imperatively, 'Shut up, for Gawd's sake. Shut up and listen.'

And he would sit there, his armchair pulled close to the radio, his ear close to the loudspeaker, his forehead puckered with concentration and his mouth falling open. Sometimes I would dare to ask my father to switch over to the Bob Hope show. 'After all,' I said logically, 'you don't understand what Pound is talking about.'

'No, but he's interestin',' my father would reply, turning the volume on full blast. 'Idle darkness. You are in black darkness and confusion . . . you have been hugger-muggered . . . Hitler taught the Germans manners . . . Health is more interesting than disease . . . We have, most of us, been buffaloed . . . Beardsley was no slouch. He was a courageous invalid. He was a heroic invalid. He said, "Beauty is so difficult." I repeat that. Beauty is so difficult . . .'

'Turn it down,' my mother cried. 'For heaven's sake, Rudy, it's too loud. His voice will break the valves.'

'Sssh,' my father said.

And so we had to listen to: 'You can put me in with Dante but I've got a pretty low opinion of Shakespeare . . . I see Roosevelt and his Jews and his monopolists setting out on a scheme that implies very expensive trade routes . . . Ezra Pound speaking. I know I haven't got very far in this talk so wait for the next one. Health dammit. Think about Health in the interim. Pound speaking.'

It took me a long time to understand why my father listened with such persistence. Like us all, Dad longed for the war to end and for my two elder brothers to be demobilised. After all, he himself had had his basinful during the 1914–18 war. But he knew that the 'authorities' couldn't give true and vital news about battles and events. What filtered through was radically censored, milk and water stuff, just enough for home consumption. Dad was hungry for truth, absolute. Lord Haw Haw obviously told lies. You couldn't believe 'Jarmany calling, Jarmany calling.' Pound, on the other hand – well, who knew?

Deep in that gibberish and rhetoric and near obscenity, why, my father instinctively felt, there might be a grain, a small, hidden, precious, grain of truth about the war, about the events of the war. Nobody told lies like that, reasoned my father.

It was an alien, crazy language that Ezra Pound spoke to my own father those early war years. If only he could find the key, translate it, interpret it, then he half believed he would have heard the one true word, the beautiful gospel, the annunciation of divine verity. He would have perceived the unperceivable, known the unknowable. ABOVE ALL, HE WOULD HAVE BECOME ACQUAINTED WITH THE EXACT DATE THE WAR WOULD END.

When I said as much to my father, of course he denied it. He just gave me a foxy look and once again turned the knob that made the radio louder.

'Don't be damned soft, boy,' he said above the din. 'It's interesting, just interesting, that's all. He's a man which is interesting, that's why I listen. The Italians just wouldn't put a madman on the radio. There's something in it, if I could understand – and it's interesting.'

'He's a saw,' my mother moaned. 'A saw.'

I didn't speak again of Ezra Pound to my father until about twelve years ago. I was staying for a week-end in Cardiff with my parents. We sat in the small living room of the flat that they had moved to. The same ancient radio rested on the same ancient stand but now my father and mother, twenty years older, ignored it. Instead, they faced a dominating television set. Night after night, the soiled images flickered across its screen with its advertisements of *Daz* and *Kattomeat*. All through the evening, my father sat in the armchair and stared, unemployed, at programme after programme, indiscriminately. Bored, at last I fingered through the *Radio Times* to discover Ezra Pound, that very evening, was to read some of his poems – to broadcast not through the microphones of murderers, but to intone over the civilised octaves of the Third Programme.

'Dad,' I asked, 'could we have the radio on?'

'What?'

'Could we knock off the TV? Your favourite poet is on the radio.'

He thought that I was referring to myself, that it was my immodest and teasing way of saying that I had recorded a broadcast. Reflexly, he said out of long years of habit, 'Poetry will get you nowhere, son. Now why don't you write a play for television? Look at this rubbish – even you could do better than that. And they would pay you too, better than any old Third Programme.'

I told him that Ezra Pound was broadcasting – not me; but he stared blankly back at the television set, at 'the rubbish' which fascinated him.

'You remember Ezra Pound?' I said. 'Surely you do. Why you listened to him every night for God knows how long, during the war.'

He remembered Ezra Pound. He smiled the smile of nostalgia, and then he stopped smiling. 'You made me listen to him,' my father said seriously. 'You made our lives a misery making us listen to 'im.'

'It was the other way round,' my mother protested. 'That's how he's gone lately, your father – turning things around.'

'You can't talk to her,' my father replied, showing the ceiling the palms of his hands. 'Anyway, those days it was war. In wartime, *everybody* is mad. It's a mass madness is war. Those days they put mad things in the papers and on the wireless. And mad people lapped it up.'

'He who knows little, often repeats it,' my mother said, bristling for an argument.

'*Poetry*,' my father shouted, as if it were a swear word, and then, victorious, he turned back to the television set, staring at its grey, violent, and perverted images.

10. To London Then I Came

I did not want to leave. I liked Cardiff. Best place in the universe, I thought, never having travelled further than Aberystwyth. Oh yes, I was fond of my home patch but my borrowed zipped bags were packed and my little green ticket lay secure in my lost-property-found wallet. 'When you get to London, look up my friends, the Bowens,' my Uncle Sol Shepherd said. 'Nice family, the Bowens. Among the élite, you could say, of Ystalyfera. Aye, even Dai Bowen had his points. Talk about agitators. Why, your Leo has nothing on Dai. Moscow Bowen they called him. Very good personal friend of mine he was. He watched me that time I made a break of 120 . . . ah then, you didn't know I was once billiard champion of the Swansea valley, did you?'

'Never trust men who play billiards too well and women who dance too well,' interrupted my father acidly. 'Signs of a misspent youth.'

Armed with such sad, secret wisdom I entered the GWR third-class carriage filled with men in uniform, men with kitbags going back to war. The doors slammed their blank gunshots, the guard waved his little flag that was as red as Moscow Bowen, and blew out his cheeks to a piercing whistle. Then the train unsheathed the platform to puff its way onward from what I was, and to travel fifty tamping miles an hour towards what I would be. Through Newport, over the bridge above the Usk (in the mud of which river, according to winking adults when I was a child, there used to be crocodiles); through the Severn Tunnel (nice place for a murder), into England (where the rain and the sheep stopped), on and on towards the smoke where the distance was. 'Rejoice,' Moses said, 'Zebulun in thy going out; and Issachar in thy tents.'

When I read accounts by older writers of how they came to London many, quite naturally, appear to have journeyed there with one, dry, open eye on a future literary career. Sooner or later they called at the offices of *The London Mercury* to see J. C. Squire and departed with an armful of books to review. Or they talked to Harold Monro in the Poetry Bookshop or sported themselves at the Café Royal. At a later date, young writers presented themselves at the *Tribune* offices in the Strand where George Orwell, so I am told, hid himself in a cupboard so that he did not have to offend them by saying, 'No'. Of course, many young writers had come straight from Oxford or Cambridge and their student days were over whereas mine had hardly begun. Moreover, on arriving in London I thought of poetry-writing (I still do) as a vocation rather than a career and I had no intention of actively contacting any editor or any literary man of influence. To have met one such, say T. S. Eliot, or Herbert Read, or Stephen Spender, would have only caused me acute embarrassment. (Edmund Blunden, whom I was soon to meet, was a different matter – I had not, at that time, read his poetry!)

Besides, I had come to London to study medicine, to work for two years at King's College in the Strand on anatomy and physiology before 'walking the wards' at Westminster Hospital. I was allotted a part of a human body to dissect which I had to share with another student, Russell Barton, who I was happy to discover wrote poetry also and who even knew bits of Ezra Pound off by heart:

> For a moment she rested against me
> Like a swallow half blown to the wall,
> And they talk of Swinburne's women,
> And the shepherdess meeting with Guido,
> And the harlots of Baudelaire,

intoned Russell Barton, before whooping with delight. So, sometimes Russell and I, in the large Anatomy Room where, grotesquely, bodies and bits of bodies in different stages of dissection were laid out on the slabs, would recite lines of poems at each other. Other times we would talk about girls or the war or politics or about fellow students – about our friend, Titch, for instance, who had once been so fastidious. Recently, we had observed him accidentally drop his lit cigarette into the open cavity of a dead man's abdomen. Immediately, unthinkingly, he picked it up, put it back in his mouth and blew out the smoke of hell.

Most of the time we, too, investigated that forlorn thing, the cadaver, and pried into its bloodless meat that had pickling formaldehyde in its arteries. The sour formaldehyde fumes would stay with us, soak into our very clothes. Still we dug into the material of dead flesh with scalpel – scraped it, stripped it, cut deep into it, learned its thoroughways, yet had no spiritual shock of revelation. Our first disgust weakened to distaste, and our distaste was usurped by numbness, by an apathetic neutrality.

This progression of feelings arriving at non-feeling was true, I think, for even the most sensitive student. For the neck, say, exposed with all its muscles and its vessels mimicking a coloured plate in the anatomy book, seemed, soon enough, never to have belonged to a live person. The wonder of a hand, say, provoked no abstract questions, even in our youthful minds, about God or Death or the Meaning of Life – no metaphysical speculation whatsoever. That was to come later when we 'walked the wards' in hospital and attended post-mortems of people we had spoken to a day earlier. But now this hand, or rather this resemblance of a hand, had never held it seemed another hand in greeting or in tenderness, had never clenched a fist in anger, had never held a pen to sign an authentic name. For this thing, this – as the weeks, the months, passed by – decreasing thing, visibly losing its 'divine proportions', this residue, this so-called trunk of a body, this legless, armless, headless thing had never had a name surely?

Apart from the dissecting room, we attended lectures and had to submit to 'vivas'. I used to find Professor MacDowell's physiology lectures the most entertaining. 'We are governed by three instincts,' he asseverated, 'by the three Fs: Fear, Food, and Reproduction.' His talks often seemed irrelevant, full of witty, ornamental comments, anecdotes. In short, they were leisurely – suitable for peacetime. Other tutorials, lectures, were succinct, puritanically factual without decorative blurring. They were utility designed. We were there, nineteen years of age, to be trained urgently, to qualify as doctors who would then be drafted into the Forces. And, at night, meanwhile, while we studied in our digs or fire-watched on the roof of King's College, there was still occasionally the howl of the air-raid warning, the long chalk lines of the searchlights, the important, stuttering guns, the magnesium flares of fire, the bombers' intermittent drone, and the noise death makes when escaping from an exploding bomb.

My first digs in London were in anonymous Wandsworth, in the scrubbed house of a Scots clergyman. When his dominant wife gave me the front-door key she said, 'This doesn't mean you can come rolling in at ten o'clock at night.' She meant it too, for the door was bolted at 10 p.m. sharp. There were all sorts of other dust-free regulations also. One even had to hide in the spotless lavatory for a dirty smoke.

After a month in London, I had discovered only some streets in Wandsworth, the area around King's College in the Strand, the dejected, echoing railway station that was Paddington. Later, I was to understand that the more famous landmarks like St Paul's, Nelson's Column, the Tower, Buckingham Palace, were, in any case, but sly edifices to bamboozle the provincial, the tourist, the soldier on leave, from knowing the real London. Such landmarks were distractions, even decoys, to keep the casual visitor from the more characteristic features of the city. For London's centre lies, oddly, on its periphery: district after district, suburb after suburb, stretching on and on and on in a dour conspiracy of sameness in order to remain disguised and hardly knowable. It is no accident that London owns so many streets; it proliferates streets deliberately in order to remain arcane.

It takes a long time to like London's secret ways, its modesty. London doesn't, like Paris, whisper, 'Here I am. Take me!' You have to say, 'There you are,' and even as you say it, London disappears down smoky evenings, resenting your familiarity. The fogs only come when the leaves have fallen from the trees and the streets are bare. Yes, when London at last is naked, vulnerable, exposed to any casual voyeur, it pulls down the fog to hide itself, like any modest woman. But those first months in the autumn of 1942 I loathed the fogs, London's apparent offhandedness. I longed for the provincial friendliness of Welsh people. I wanted to hear a bit of Welsh spoken, or, at least, the accented sing-song voices that I knew so well with all their comic portentousness. At King's College I joined the Welsh Society and even gave a talk on Welsh poetry. I chanted William Barnes's translation of an anonymous ninth-century Welsh lament until tears of home-sickness came into my eyes:

Cynddylan's hall is all in gloom tonight;
No fire, no lighted room:
Amid the stillness of the tomb.

Cynddylan's hall is left alone tonight:
A hall with none to own.
O Death, take me where he is flown.

Cynddylan's hall is now unblest – tonight;
On Hydwyrth's rocky crest
No lord is there, no meal, no guest.

Cynddylan's hall! It makes me wan
To see cold hearths, and roofing gone.
My lord is dead, and I live on!

Cynddylan's hall is sad within – tonight;
For sons of Cyndrwyn,
Cynon, Gwion, and Gwyn.

No man says 'Goodbye' to the place he loves until he loves another place better. It took me many years of coming and going from London to Cardiff, Cardiff to London, before I could say 'Goodbye' to South Wales. And, even now, when I return there, as I still do, I am not absolutely sure that I have really travelled the 150-plus miles that can turn the hair grey.

After one term in digs at Wandsworth I decided to move. The London University lodgings bureau for students recommended a place in Aberdare Gardens, Swiss Cottage. The name, Aberdare, appealed to me. After all, I knew Aberdare in South Wales, for when I was seven years of age my father, before his fortunes slumped badly, part-owned a small cinema there and had driven me every Saturday afternoon to see Buck Jones, Wheeler and Wolsey, or Rin Tin Tin, or Jean Harlow, or Harold Lloyd. I associated Aberdare with my father winking and usherettes being nice to me because I was the boss's son, and a lit cinema organ rising from the dark pit, playing 'Goodnight Vienna' as it changed colours from purple to orange, to crimson and pure blood, to Cardiff City blue, to 1st March daffodil yellow, whilst all the time I resolutely chewed mintoes. So, in some curious and irrational way, I hoped for the best when I emerged at Swiss Cottage tube station into January 1943 and asked the newsvendor the directions to Aberdare Gardens.

Across the road from the station I saw the old-fashioned, ye olde cottage-like café, and further down, the tall, modern Odeon. I walked northwards, and on the opposite side of the road, though it was only afternoon, the lights were on inside the shops. Soon the black-out curtains would be drawn. I noted the names of the restaurants – The Cosmo next to the Victoria Wine Co. Ltd and The Glass House near the Silver Stores. But on the side of the thoroughfare where I walked, to my left, stood for the most part only abandoned houses. They hadn't been surgically exposed, like most bombed houses, to reveal a cross-section of a staircase here, or a segment of a room with peeling wallpaper there. The chipped porticoes with the fluted pillars merely jutted out above worn stone steps that had long been calcified by pigeon droppings. On each side of these protruding porticoes the oblong windows gaped unnaturally black. The eye did not take in immediately that these window frames had no glass in them. The leafless front gardens, of course, were tangled with the wild return of the countryside that lies everywhere under the concrete of London, even in winter lies in wait for its hour, and its hour had come, here, perhaps some twelve months before. It was hard to know why these once elegant houses had been deserted and allowed to rot. Perhaps fire bombs had rained down upon them on their averted side, or their foundations had been rocked by blast. But it seemed rather as if some disease had driven out the tenants, the insidious plague of another century, and these monuments containing the spirit of nothing had been left behind as elegies of another time.

In fact, in one of the houses at least, two rooms were still occupied; certainly, window frames retained their glass and net curtains could be seen behind them. Another house, too, was evidently occupied in some way; it owned a discreet sign, THE BLUE DANUBE CLUB, and as I passed it a man came out of the front door and slowly descended the steps. I did not know then, that some nine years later, after a morning registry office wedding I would lunch in that building with my wife. Now that tall house, with all the others too, has been pulled down and replaced by modern shops. Now shop faces shop in the Finchley Road at Swiss Cottage – and it looks like any place, like any High Street, any town in England. It was different then – more distinctive; but fortunately, now, no men and women in uniform constantly walk on the pavements, and columns of tanks and jeeps do not pass by.

I carried on, turned left, and strolled down an incline past tall, red-bricked houses whose basements were barred, down the wrong side of Hampstead as it has been called, towards the smudge of Kilburn, until I came to a quiet, curving, tree-lined road, Aberdare Gardens. Soon, near a pillar box, I reached No. 38. I pushed open a tidy wrought-iron gate, paced the short path to a black-painted front door and rang the bell.

I was to stay in this house for years – until the day I qualified as a doctor and had written almost two books of poems. In a pleasant room on the first floor, overlooking the long, narrow back garden, I was to unpack, light the gas fire (on a meter), test the bed, hang up my one and only suit in a huge wardrobe, put my shaving tackle on the shelf near the wash basin, place my few books in the small bookcase, tintack my Picasso and Miró reproductions on the wallpaper, and sit down and wait. I didn't know quite what for. Soon, after nightfall, there was a moaning wail from an air-raid warning. Before its sound quite died, it spawned another one, further off, small wail answering small wail, echo answering echo of an echo all over London, further and further, more admonitory, more mournful than any ghost-foghorn siren, this shaman wail of some mythical half-god, half-beast, this saddest sound in and out of this extraordinary world. Outside it was blackout dark. The same darkness from the upper slopes of hell. That very night, rooted explosions surrounded 38 Aberdare Gardens, blowing out yet again all the windows of John Barnes.★ In a road nearby a house ceased to exist. 'Fire converts to fire the thing it burns,' wrote Sir John Davies.

11. Survivors

38 Aberdare Gardens, London NW6, I now wrote on top of the letters to my mother who, in return, would send me home-made Welsh cakes. It was a large three-storied, red-brick house owned by a Mr Austin who had taught history, but now completely deaf let out rooms. He would attend to the garden (I would see him sometimes from my window leaning on a spade, bicycle clips round the bottom of his trousers as he watched, perhaps, a bonfire of leaves smouldering

★ Now this building is occupied by Waitrose.

away into smoke nearby). He would go back to his room to read one of the history books he was forever buying secondhand. He would be sent on bicycle errands by his wife. He would watch sometimes his son, John, playing Bach on the piano. Insulated from all sound he stared at the mouth of his wife who whispered to him with grotesquely emphasised lip movements. And the silence he had to endure irrevocably, seemed to inhabit the whole house.

When John Austin played Bach downstairs, when a door would suddenly bang or the geyser rumble to a blank explosion in the bathroom, or the telephone clamour in the hall, the silence was barely exiled from the house. It remained there all the time and, afterwards, resumed its domination like some dumb, temporarily insulted, emperor.

Amongst those lodging in this Victorian silent house were two ancient German Jewish ladies. Refugees. In the next room to myself lived Mrs Schiff, grey-haired, with no make-up, small and kyphotic, invariably dressed in black down to her ankles as if she were in mourning. And, in fact, she was in mourning – for relations in Germany who had disappeared, I came later to understand, into the death camps. No wonder her dresses were black, the colour of grief, the colour of wet earth newly turned over. Mrs Schiff looked like somebody's grandmother. Sometimes, when there was a telephone call for me she hovered on the shadowy landing, peeping down at the hall and after I had replaced the receiver I would hear her door close softly. She always tried to make herself as inconspicuous as possible, despite her inveterate curiosity. Her insecurity had an aetiology founded in some terrible experience she would not relate – one so evil that at the vaguest hint of a threat one felt the response would be not a dogmatic, 'Go away,' but a pleading supplication, 'Please, leave me alone. Please, I do not exist. Please, I am nobody.' So Mrs Schiff would disappear at the sound of a footstep, lower her voice, play her gramophone records with the volume turned down, hoping that in this way nobody would ever come for her again as they had for her relatives. Occasionally, when I went to collect my letters from the hall stand, I would find one of them in her hand as she peered at it curiously, shortsightedly. Abject, she always passed it over to me, mumbling apologies, before confusedly melting away back up the stairs. I liked Mrs Schiff.

In a room above mine, on the second floor, lived Mrs Blumenfeld. She did not look like a grandmother. Her grey hair was tinted gold and her wrinkled face was thick with white powder, an unreal clown's white, accentuated by garish lipstick. Though she had equal cause for mourning her dresses were not black but invariably floral and gay. They were shorter than they should have been considering her age. When I coughed she raised her hand to her head as if she were suffering from a headache. If I coughed again she would produce from her handbag a handkerchief drenched with eau de cologne. I did not care so much for Mrs Blumenfeld.

Mrs Blumenfeld liked Strauss. Mrs Schiff liked Beethoven. I do not think they liked each other. Often I heard them whispering in German on the dark landing, arguing in whispers, but as soon as I approached Mrs Schiff spoke in English and only resumed her German after she thought that I was out of earshot.

Mrs Schiff and Mrs Blumenfeld were the only Jewish people I had contact with when I first came to London, and we hardly ever spoke together. They were 'victims of Nazism'. But frankly I did not give them much thought at all. The women I was interested in were much younger.

One Sunday autumn afternoon in 1943 I happened to turn towards my window and look down at the back garden below. On the lawn stood Mrs Schiff in her long black gown. She appeared shorter than the high sunflowers near the fence. Suddenly Mrs Schiff began to wave both her arms rhythmically. The old lady, not knowing she was being observed – perhaps listening to some symphony in her head – had begun to conduct an invisible orchestra. Waving her arms like that it seemed she wanted to take off from the lawn and fly. There were the sunflowers just moving perceptibly in the wind, the apple tree full with its apples gently swaying, the grass, the one rosebush, the plants, the leaves, all obeying in slow movement the old grey-haired lady who was waving her arms about. I could see her distinctly smiling. She seemed so *happy*.

I turned away, thinking of her, thinking of what she had escaped from, to conjure up blurred images from my ignorance. I remembered how, when I had first arrived in the house some ten months earlier, there had been a particularly noisy air-raid and we had all filed down the stairs. Just after an explosion outside she had whispered a question: 'Mr Abse, please, are you a Jew?' I had nodded, and then she nodded and smiled and nodded again and took my hand momentarily as if I were a relative. Perhaps her own kith and kin in Germany were all dead. Perhaps she had no relatives in London. My name was Abse and I was born in Wales and her name was Schiff and she had been born in Germany. I was a very young man and she was an old old lady I did not know from Adam and so what, so what the hell, except that she had taken my hand like a relative. And I felt she was justified. I returned to the window remembering how I had thought she was justified. On the lawn, Mrs Schiff had stopped conducting. She had her back to me, her round shoulders still. Then it occurred to me that Mrs Schiff had not been conducting inaudible music at all. She had been dancing to it. Dancing, in spirit, with her arms, dancing without moving her eighty-year-old feet. Dancing, God knows when, in what year, what place, what world, and with whom I knew not, nor to which music.

There is one other small incident I should like to relate here regarding Mrs Schiff. It occurred about two years later. I recall one night when the house was particularly silent, silent as an empty well. Someone, in the house, an hour earlier, had been using a typewriter. It had emitted dropping little noises as it pecked away on paper reassuringly. Faintly, too, I had heard Mrs Schiff playing her Beethoven records next door. I was sorry when she put on 135. As soon as I heard the three ominous notes of the viola and cello asking, *Muss es sein?* I knew that the house would soon resume its customary night-silence. For the terrible inevitability of the answer, *Es muss sein!* – that jaunty and poignant resignation was always too much for Mrs Schiff. Why else did she invariably conclude her private recital with that record?

So when the typewriter ceased its strategy, and the record its turning, the silence, the audible silence, came back to occupy the house. By that time the war was over and the air raids had long ceased. Instead, occasionally, from the distance, the outgoing cry of a train could be heard. The cry, tiny, sharp, complaining. The mourning cry as it arrived somewhere, the mourning cry as it departed. In that, like us.

Downstairs, the telephone rang and I left my room to answer it. I can't remember now who phoned or what the conversation was about. After, I know I climbed the stairs blankly. The light was on in the hall which doubtless was full with the exact desolation of small, inanimate objects. But the landing was dark. Suddenly, Mrs Schiff's door opened just two feet, no more. She solemnly peered out, half concealed by the door, the light from the room behind her spreading on her white hair – a halo almost – and I said softly, '*Muss es sein?*'

Mrs Schiff did not reply. Mrs Schiff did not smile. Her old face, in the shadows, did not appear to change its expression. She merely closed the door quietly.

I suppose Mrs Schiff and Mrs Blumenfeld reminded me in a mild way, in their own way, that I was a Jew. There were other circumstances that occasionally made me identify myself as such. Not only mean, articulated expressions of anti-semitism, usually unthinkingly displayed in my presence and not directed at me, called forth the 'I-happen-to-be-a-Jew' response, but more commonly other people's curiosity about my surname. Thus, from time to time, I was asked, 'Abse? That's an odd name. Where are you from?' Initially I used to answer, 'Wales'. Generally, however, the questioner would probe further. 'Is Abse a common Welsh name?' So, finally, I would have to say simply, 'I am a Welsh Jew.' Eventually, bored by probings about my surname, I would say without prevarication, as soon as asked, 'I am a Welsh Jew.' Such a plain, unadorned statement though, however softly spoken, frequently seemed to the questioner a naked, aggressive response. At least many appeared to be embarrassed judging from their subsequent stuttering. They made me feel that they had made some indefinable faux pas.

I think it was Ehrenberg, the Russian writer, who declared that he was a Jew as long as there was one anti-semite alive. To this sentiment I assented, and still assent, but there is more to it than that. After the war years, I, like so many others, in Britain and elsewhere, learnt more and more about the death camps of Europe. I came to realise that what had happened to the relatives of Blumenfeld and Schiff was something that could not be irrevocably suppressed from consciousness, that in one sense I, too, was a survivor, that I could never encounter a German of a certain age-group without seeing him as a one-time inquisitor, that ordinary smoke towering over autumn gardens could trigger off a vision of concentration camps, false teeth, lampshades, soap. There was, not long ago in London, and probably all over Britain, a huge advertisement on the hoardings for Guinness which read 6,000,000 ENJOYED EVERY DAY. Only Jews, I imagine, found those ads obscene. They would hardly be acceptable in Israel.

Yes, Auschwitz has made me more of a Jew than Moses did. Indeed, as the years have passed, as I take in more fully the unbearable reality of what happened in Europe, as I read the biographies of Hitler, Himmler, Goebbels, Goering, as I read the testimony of actual survivors, as I see films, as I come to know the documents of history, then gradually I feel myself to be more of a Jew than ever. It takes a long time to become aware that here, in England, one is a survivor also. The realisation of the destruction of the Jews, of one single event only – that two million Jews have been exterminated in Auschwitz alone, that thousands of children there were thrown on the pyre alive and not even gassed – changes, poisons subtly, one's attitude to other people. I am aware that ordinary, decent people one has met, with ordinary passive prejudices, could be, under other circumstances, the murderers of one's own children, or the executioners of adults whom one loves and reveres. This is not a paranoiac delusion, alas. As a doctor, I know that listening to, say, Mr Robinson sitting opposite me, complaining of this or that minor symptom and ventilating strange anxieties, that I am hearing the muted voice of some potential Gestapo official. I have heard in the course of one week the heartbeat of Eichmann, palpated the liver of Goering, seen the X-rays of Himmler, read the electroencephalogram of Hitler. Almost every Jewish father and mother, however much they disaffiliate themselves from Judaism or Jewry, have, perhaps once a year, because of a remark uttered inadvertently, or because of a headline, looked across the table at their young children and wondered for half a second whether one day their beloved offspring might be forced to enter the gas chambers of another decade. Even the most optimistic Jew must admit the possibility to be there. This is something that many non-Jews can hardly credit.

Of course, it is difficult to sustain suspicious attitudes towards other people, now, here, in tolerant, liberal, mild, decent, democratic England. No doubt it would be sick to do so. As a Jew I was brought up to believe that man was essentially good. Didn't I, as a boy, say in my morning prayer 'My God, the soul which thou hast given me is pure' . . .? Karl Marx explained the evil in society in environmental terms. He wasn't a Jew, and an optimist, for nothing. But Sigmund Freud, another Jew, has given us back Original Sin not as a genetic or theological proposition, but clandestinely and more realistically in terms of our early and inevitable Oedipus complex. How can we be anything but (neurotically?) afraid of anti-semitism seeing what happened in Europe? Why is it that every Jew over-reacts, however much he feels himself to be delivered from a ghetto mentality, when a Jewish figure like Peter Rachman features villainously in some contemporary scandal? The fact is, I don't believe any Jew in the Diaspora, however much he proclaims the contrary, is other than a

Ghetto Jew in the deepest sense – and this is above all because of the wartime destruction of the Jew in Europe.

I do not know why so many German-Jewish refugees were attracted to Swiss Cottage. One could hear their guttural cries all down the Finchley Road between the Odeon and John Barnes – on the pavements, in the shops. Like Mrs Schiff and Mrs Blumenfeld they lived in one room with a sputtering gas fire, heavy furniture, frayed carpets, patterned faded wallpaper, and a photograph on the mantelpiece of someone forever smiling who had years before vanished. Many were old and sat out half the black-out hours in one of the Swiss Cottage cafés: The Cosmo, The Dorice, The Glass House or The Swiss, where they would argue about politics and literature in English and abuse each other in German.

One night, not long after I had moved to 38 Aberdare Gardens, coming home fairly late from town, as the bus jerked to a halt and an insensate conductress shouted out good-humouredly, 'Tel Aviv', I resolved to visit one of those cafés instead of going straight back to my digs. I sat in the Swiss Cottage corner café over my cup of coffee alone, hearing the thick accents all about me. It must have been almost midnight when a burly man entered, shouting, 'Germans, Germans, Germans.' Uneasily the café became conspicuous with silence. Towering over a middle-aged couple, the burly man swayed and shouted, 'Where do you come from?' They did not reply. Eventually, from the other side of the cafe a pleasant voice asked, 'Why don't you ask me where I come from?' Pappy, the Cypriot owner of the cafe, pretended nothing was happening and the waitresses looked away. The burly man ponderously turned round, puzzled. Hesitatingly, he asked, his voice a threat, 'Well . . . where *do* you come from?'

'Ireland,' came the surprising reply.

I was the only one who laughed and unfortunately, as a result, I attracted the burly man's attention. He deliberately thrust his face, magnified, into mine. He breathed out beer and I breathed beer in. 'And where do you come from? Germany, I suppose?' he yelled as if I were the other side of the room, not a mere six boozy inches away. I had to keep my voice level, not to betray the anxiety that I felt. 'I come from South Wales,' I said politely. To my surprise, everybody in the café laughed and the burly man benignly smiled at them all as if he had made a great joke.

'I thought you were all bleeding German Jews,' he said, nodding apologetically. And quite soon he quit the café.

Afterwards a bespectacled man with a narrow face – his name I learnt was Peter Berg – began talking to me.

'So you're Velsh,' he said.

I felt constrained to say that I was a Welsh Jew. He did not seem to know, until that moment, Welsh Jews existed. This information, of course, did not embarrass him. On the contrary, I became suddenly an exotic. I was introduced all round: 'He's a Velsh Jew.' I joined Peter Berg at his table and smiled at a fair-haired girl called Anna. From that evening my social life changed. I, too, became a habitué of the Swiss Cottage cafés. So, while during the day I dissected a part of a body at King's, at night I argued with Peter or Bondy or Hans or Kurt in the cafés – and usually late I went home alone but sometimes with Anna. And from time to time I wrote to Cardiff letters which began, 'Dear Parents, All is well here. Thank you for the Welsh cakes . . .'

12. First Doubts

Recently, in Cardiff, I opened a jammed desk drawer and happened on a few old letters I had written to my parents during the war years. I seem to have reassured them continually that I had good 'digs', that I had only lost weight because I was playing too much football, that I visited my sister, Huldah, from time to time in her apartment in Brownlow Court, Hampstead Garden Suburb, that though we had air raids still, they remained mild compared to the Blitz days and that, as a result, my fire-watching duties on the roof of King's College were hardly onerous.

I also wrote home in 1943 that I was reading (at different times) Ignazio Silone's *Fontamara*, E. M. Forster's *A Passage to India*, T. S. Eliot's *The Dry Salvages* (printed then in a thin blue pamphlet) and, of course, Gray's *Anatomy*. I had seen, moreover, walking down the Strand *within the short space of two days*, ARTHUR ASKEY, PROFESSOR JOAD (who was talking to himself) and WEE GEORGIE WOOD. Gosh. As for the war, well, we were going to win it. Definitely. With a little help of course from the Russians and the Yanks etc.

I told my parents all this with unblinking authority, with unerring pomposity. I told them other things that they most wanted to hear: that I was studying hard, that I had met Wilfred one Thursday teatime at Lyons Corner House in the Strand (on his way back from Banstead Military Hospital in Surrey), and that we had both enjoyed, that same evening, Michael Redgrave in Turgenev's *A Month in the Country*. I did not tell them that Wilfred had given me money some of which I had put on Persian Gulf in the Derby. (It lost.) I did not tell them about Anna either.

One night in her bedsitting room in Belsize Park I had woken up. It must have been four in the morning and Anna was shuffling around. 'What's wrong?' I asked. Anna, at first, did not reply. I turned the light on. 'What's the matter?' I insisted. Despondently she said, 'I'm looking for some tablets.' I thought perhaps she had a headache. But she said, 'I have to take these pills. You see, I should have told you before – I'm an epileptic.' I tried not to show how disturbed I was by that piece of information. On the contrary, I turned off the light and consoled her. Later, in the dark, I stared at the ceiling and I knew that Anna next to me was also not asleep. Poor Anna, I thought. And then – *supposing now she had a sudden devastating convulsion of body muscles and cried out terribly?* I was going to be a doctor, but the thought of it happening to Anna, with both of us in bed together, unnerved me.

'It won't make any difference, will it?' Anna asked me over breakfast.

'No, of course not,' I lied.

Gradually, I saw less of Anna. And I felt guilty about the whole thing. Guilty in a defined way. Often during my life I have felt a vague sense of guilt – though I may have done nothing precisely wrong. I have been just guilty of waiting, of not working, guilty of being almost dead for days, of postponements on rainy nights, of things not done and words not said. Guilty of inertia. Maybe writing poems, then, has been a restorative act, a pleading for pardon, a ritual to rid one of that sense of foreboding. But with Anna I knew why I felt guilty. Nothing could disguise it . . .

In Lyons Corner House with Wilfred, while the corny orchestra played Palm Court music, I steered the conversation towards epilepsy. 'You can tell the epileptics in a mental hospital,' Wilf told me, 'by noticing which patients go to church on Sunday. All the epileptics go. Perhaps epileptics themselves fear demoniac possession – it is an antique fear in us all maybe, and persists as an unconscious prejudice in our modern irreligious minds.' Perhaps Wilfred sensed I was concerned about a girl, for he suddenly gave me advice I was always to remember. 'When you decide to sleep with a girl,' he advised me, 'it's best to remember three things. Firstly, contraception. Secondly, the dangers of VD. And thirdly, and most important, the relationship, the emotional tie that occurs which may not be easily undone.' Wilfred looked thoughtful and I did not know quite what to say. The old-fashioned trio on the little elevated stage near the tea-tables played old-fashioned music decorously. Soon we quit, my brother and I, and went to the theatre.

A few days later, I visited a different kind of theatre – at Westminster Hospital where, in a year's time, I was to 'walk the wards'. Russell Barton had arranged for a few of us to see an operation. 'Why not?' I had breezily replied. After all, sooner or later I would have to witness such a spectacle, a surgeon bending with strange intimacy over a patient – for that was how I imagined it somehow – a white-gowned figure, white-masked, cutting with a silver scalpel while the patient breathed in, breathed out, in tidal and unremembering regularity. I would have to learn about surgery; yet truth to tell, I was not keen to hurry to the operating theatre.

'Titch is coming and Noel Rhys-Davies,' said Russell Barton. 'We'll be able to sneak you in as well.'

'Thank you,' I said.

Cutting with a scalpel through a dead body, that I had become used to, that was one thing – but dissection of live flesh that would be something else, surely? No matter, in order to qualify as a doctor and practise as a doctor, I would have to become used to many disagreeable things varying from epilepsy to the worst of surgery and even to the death struggle. I had never seen a human being die.

The operation that Russell Barton's friend arranged for us to attend was on a patient who suffered from a parathyroid tumour. The surgeon, in order to excise this tumour, would first have to remove a portion of the sternum, the breast bone. So in the charged, yet calm, hieratic surroundings of an operating theatre I donned for the first time a surgical gown and wore a surgical mask.

'Struth, that gown is spotless,' joked Russell Barton.

We needed to joke, to distance ourselves in some way from the significance of the instruments laid out ready for the surgeon. I peered at the prostrate patient or rather at a small exposed part of a human being, part of a nameless human being, part of a case of parathyroid disease, part of a white male, and then my eyes watched a bright scalpel in the gloved right hand of the surgeon. Noiselessly, the sharp blade drew a line across the skin and little rivulets of scarlet blood surfaced, summoned as it were by a cruel magician. It was enough. The operation had hardly begun but I had to back away. 'Excuse me,' I muttered. I felt faint. Somebody, possibly Titch, whispered to me, 'Go outside.' And quickly I quit the theatre and sat down on the parquet floor the wrong side of the doors feeling sick. I was worried too. Would I ever become used to the little knife cutting into the live flesh with no noise? Within a short space of time I had backed away not only from a girl who suffered from epilepsy but now also from a surgical operation.

'Am I fit to become a doctor?' I wondered silently. Russell's friend gamely tried to reassure me when the operation was over and the others joined me. 'Even those who go on to become brilliant surgeons,' he said, 'sometimes faint at their first operation.'

Hardly reassured, I mumbled that I wanted to become a physician not an extroverted surgical technician. Russell found my protestation funny. Much to my annoyance he laughed and laughed.

'You're like bloody little Audrey,' I said. And he laughed even more, while Noel Rhys-Davies and Titch smiled superiorly, as if they already had their brass plates in Harley Street.

13. Football, Nancy, and Swiss Cottage

I find it rather absurd now to admit how much I enjoyed playing football. I gained pleasure from playing rugby or cricket or tennis or squash – but soccer was something else. That season, 1943–4, when I played for King's first eleven along with three other medical students I enjoyed my soccer more than ever before. I can remember the details of some games with disturbing clarity. I am sure it sounds kinky, and I have never thought of myself as kinky, but I enjoyed my soccer then, at least on some days, as much as I have sexual intercourse on some nights with the right person.

One teatime, in the Refectory, John Oliver, the Captain of the first eleven, who like myself happened to be a third-year medical student, sat with MacLaren, the secretary, and one or two others over cups of coffee as they chose the three teams that were to play the following Saturday. At the next table, on her own, presumably waiting for somebody, I observed Nancy Tyler. She wore her straw-coloured hair short and, for a moment, she turned her extraordinary large, blue eyes that slanted in a peculiar way, towards me. That very morning in the physiology lab., as we took tracings of a frog's heart in systole and diastole, Titch had said thoughtfully that Nan Tyler resembled the actress, Joan Fontaine, a bit, didn't I think so? Neither of us had spoken to Nancy Tyler.

As I joined the 'football table' and listened to the conversation I was most keenly aware of Nancy Tyler's unnerving profile a mere three yards away.

'Don Sleep can't play this week,' Oliver was saying. 'He has to go home to Devon. A relative of his has died or got born or something. Anyway we'll have to play somebody else on the wing.'

'Alan Cohen has been playing regularly on the right wing for the second eleven,' MacLaren said. 'Quite well, I understand. So he can take over from Don.'

'No,' said Oliver firmly.

We all looked at him surprised because he was so emphatic: his 'no' had come through in italics. John Oliver usually was a most retiring captain of a football team. Like most goalkeepers he was a quiet fellow, good natured, apparently reasonable.

'No,' he said again, this time more quietly.

'Why not?' someone asked.

Blithely John Oliver proffered his incredibly ignorant, even innocent reason. 'Cohen can't play football. You see he's a Jew. Jews can't play football.'

There appeared to be no malice in his comment. His statement was as assured as any text from orthodox dogma. We were all stunned by the monumental absurdity of his remark. Then MacLaren laughed. 'What are you laughing at?' queried John Oliver.

'Dannie's a Jew,' MacLaren choked out.

John Oliver had known me for a year. We had attended the same lectures together on Anatomy and Physiology, Embryology, and

Histology, had dissected bodies in the same Anatomy Room, had played football and cricket together regularly, fire-watched on King's roof together.

'You . . . a Jew?' John Oliver said surprised, blushing.

'If you prick me I will bleed,' I said.

I should have been angry but John Oliver was so discomfited. I have never seen a face so suffused suddenly with blood as John Oliver's was. Everybody was laughing. There was nothing else to do. Alan Cohen's name went down on the team list, unfortunately. I say unfortunately because during the Saturday game the ball struck him forcibly in the face and as a result he suffered a detached retina. But, of course, none of us knew that would happen. We laughed and I still think John Oliver's prejudice benign. When the laughter dribbled away I turned towards the next table. Nancy Tyler had gone.

That year while I continued my medical studies at King's College my interest in poetry, if anything, quickened. During the last twenty years, if I have completed to my own satisfaction six poems a year, I have been content. In a good year, I may have finished seven publishable poems; in a bad one only five. It takes me roughly five years to collect enough related poems to have a book ready. In 1944, however, I was writing poems every week, if not every day. They were hardly genuine poems, though I did not know that at the time. I also read a great deal of poetry. Indeed any poem I happened on which I particularly liked would cause me to utter, subvocally, the common confession of the amateur writer, 'I wish I had written that.' Now I realise that no professional poet would own up to such feelings. For he desires to be only his own man, to speak with his own authentic voice, however dreary that voice may be, however faulty. Every genuine poet would rather be the first unknown Bloggs than the second T.S. Eliot. At twenty, I was even less sure of my identity than I had the right to be. All too easily I caught the accents of other people – whether in answering an American soldier on the top of a bus or through the communication of an individuated poem on the page.

Soon I was reading my poems (and other people's) to Nancy Tyler. After a College dance, I had taken her back to her home in Wembley. I had talked about God knows what – about my brothers who had recently been posted overseas possibly; about myself and poetry, no doubt. I did not win the cup at Wembley that night but I won through to the second round.

Before the end of term I reached the Final and introduced her to Swiss Cottage café life. Before long we became inseparable. When I returned to London after the Christmas holiday she moved into a room in 38 Aberdare Gardens for a while. Though Nan, too, was only twenty, I think Mrs Austin romantically hoped we would get married. Meanwhile we read books together, went to the films together, travelled into the country together. Once, Nan even watched me play football.

The Saturday afternoon that Nan stood behind the goalposts with my old, striped, green and gold, St Illtyd's scarf around her neck, John Oliver had a masterly game. His daring was conspicuous, his catching of the ball spectacularly safe, his kicking of a dead ball effective and *graceful*. He knew he was being watched surely, and he became a hundred-per-cent-protestant goalkeeper. Nan said, 'He's super.' I nodded glumly and squeezing my hand she tactfully added, 'You're very good too.'

When I try now to picture the young man who bore my name, who rested his forehead gently against the forehead of a trusting blonde girl called Nan so that everybody else and everything else seemed old in the world, the image blurs a little. I almost feel estranged from my own past and innocence. I suppose every autobiography begins with 'I' and ends with 'me' but there can be a huge gulf between those two pronouns. In any case I find it difficult to talk about Nan and myself because any boy and any girl imagining themselves to be in love for the first time cease to be unique. Unoriginally they ask 'Do you love me?' and invent pet names for each other, and delight in their own silly private jokes. Surely all those young lovers – Paolo and Francesca, Romeo and gentle Juliet, Gaspara Stampa and Collaltino – would have bored us unendurably if their lyrical affairs had not been starcrossed, tragically impeded? Would we have cared a jot for them if they had lived happily ever after?

Nan and I thought we were in love – our relationship was to last two years. We did not feel it to be, then, an approximate thing like the colours in a reproduction of a masterpiece. It was an enchantment I feel grateful for; and if so many days I shared with Nan have become indistinct one at least persists in being utterly clear.

We had walked that day, between tea and dinner, to the edge of Hampstead Heath, near the large glittering ponds close to Keats'

Grove. From a window in one house that backed on to the water a premature light nakedly reached across the surface of the pond, its reflection trembling. Within an hour it would be black-out time. Under a tall tree we stopped and listened to the cries and tiny blank honks of the waterfowl. Moorhens and ducks pulled away towards the houses, dragging their widening V's behind them. It was pleasant standing there silently. Each house facing us above the pond had some fourteen windows and, one by one, they lit up sending out long, vibratory golden reflections across the water. Then something happened to me. I had not eaten the root that is called peyote but it was such an awakening.

It was as if I had fallen through the unstitched air and everything had accompanied me: Nancy in profile faintly smiling; the pond with branch-shadows at the edge; the houses with their unsteady lights; the great classic trees becoming silhouettes; the flung sky with its first stagey star. And I was at one with it all – I do not know for how long – with the grass at my rooted feet, with the soaring trunk of that tree which I rested against. I was purely happy in that inward armistice, in those moments seemingly numinous that I have never quite recaptured again but from which, ever since, I have drawn a kind of uninterpreted nourishment.

I assumed Nan had been touched by these same feelings. I did not question her. We never discussed that hour. I do not know why.

What we did share together, indisputably in the same way, was something altogether less transcendental. In June, not long after I had taken my Anatomy and Physiology exams, the doodlebugs were catapulted from their ramps in France and aimed at London.

Albert Speer has written, 'Hitler and all of us hoped that this new weapon, the V–1, would sow horror, confusion and paralysis in the enemy camp.' In fact, they were much less frightening than ordinary bombs. Simply, as we heard them approach with their characteristic chugging noise we held our breaths for a moment hoping that their engines would not cut out. Providing the things passed over our heads all of us in London continued whatever we were doing: we put that chip on the suspended fork into our mouth; turned the page over that momentarily had been held halfway; resumed writing, shouting, swearing, laughing, making love. If an engine did cut, we would hold our breaths until we heard the inevitable explosion before resuming the lives that we were living. 'In Brueghel's *Icarus*, for instance: how everything turns away, Quite leisurely from the disaster . . .'

In July, the doodlebugs continued to nudge us into breathless moments regularly and many of those who could leave London did so. No matter, D-Day had come and passed and progress on the Second Front continued apace. At last, the war in Europe seemed finite. Besides, I had passed my examinations and this meant my studies at King's had ended. At Westminster Hospital they were short-handed in the Casualty Department. Because of the invasion, many staff and students at the hospital had already taken up duties on hospital trains and at reception centres for battle casualties. Part of the hospital, when the flying bombs started, was also evacuated to Staines and some of the students had gone there. But the Casualty Department at Horseferry Road, Westminster, now had queues of flying glass and blast casualties from the doodlebugs. And so student volunteers were called for. Worse, there were rumours that the Germans would soon unleash a new and even more terrible secret weapon upon London.

With Noel Rhys-Davies I went immediately to Westminster Hospital. It was not simply for patriotic reasons that I forwent my long summer holiday that year. I wanted to test myself, as a minor attendant, in the drama of suffering. I recalled too powerfully how, in 1943, I had almost fainted at that operation. In any case, it was no great sacrifice. Despite the doodlebugs I enjoyed my life in London. There was Swiss Cottage and Nan.

14. A Taste of Real Medicine

Relatively few people visited the common room of the Medical School Student Union during the summer months of 1944. Noel Rhys-Davies and I, though, would retire there to read the journals or play darts and shove-halfpenny after our exertions in Casualty where we were taught how to bandage varicose ulcers or sprains, give injections, take blood, put in stitches, transilluminate and tap hydroceles, administer 'laughing gas' anaesthetics etc.* I liked Noel,

---

* The second gas anaesthetic I administered I shall long remember. The Casualty

a tall, wheezy, hollow-cheeked Welshman. A month earlier, at our final physiology practical examinations at King's, Noel had been working on the bench near me and Professor Samson Wright, of text-book fame, came around to give us all a short 'viva'.

Professor Wright proved to be a charming, gentle man. He had interrupted my 'experiment' with 'I do hope you can give me a few minutes while I ask you some questions?' And my responses were encouraged with numerous nods of his head and a 'Good' and a 'Very good' and a 'Quite so'. Afterwards, he had turned to Noel Rhys-Davies on my right and had said, 'Ah, can you spare me the time, I wonder, so that we may talk about the function of the pituitary gland?' His question, of course, had been rhetorical but quickly Noel replied breathtakingly, 'No, thank you, sir. I would rather not.' Professor Wright hesitated before saying, 'Well, then, let us consider the pancreas.' And, cheerfully, Noel prattled on a subject he knew much more about. Noel's polite impertinence and spontaneity had paid off. In Casualty, I witnessed the same direct coolness of mind at work whether he was applying Unna's paste or calming an outraged old lady.

In any case, soon Noel and I adapted ourselves to our strenuous new tasks. Soon we were saying like veterans, 'Not to worry' and 'Just a little prick' and 'B.I.D.' (Brought in Dead) and 'How's the waterworks?' I remember, of course, my first patient. The Casualty Officer had told us how to take a case history. 'Ask the patient what he is complaining of. Then what illnesses run in his family. Then what illnesses he may have suffered from in the past. Finally, write down the onset and development of the symptoms he is presently complaining of. I'll repeat that for you: *a*, what complaining of; *b*, family history; *c*, personal history; *d*, present history. Got it?'

'Yes,' we said.

'Right. Abse, go into that cubicle there and take down the patient's case history. I'll be with you in a tick.'

He, then, went to speak on the telephone. Noel disappeared and I pulled back the curtains of the cubicle to be confronted by my first patient. A man, about thirty years of age, lay supine on a black couch.

Officer was about to remove a painful verruca from the sole of a man's foot when he was called away urgently from the theatre. I had just placed the anaesthetic mask over the man's face but had not yet turned the gas on. So I removed the mask only to find that the patient appeared to be deeply asleep and, indeed, difficult to rouse! Such is the power of suggestion.

I smiled but he did not regard me at all but continued to stare at the electric bulb above his head with an unnerving intensity. I placed a chair near the couch, sat on it, leaned a pad on my knee, wrote down, COMPLAINING OF and asked softly, 'What are you complaining of?'

The man did not reply but kept his terrible blue eyes fixed on the electric bulb. Perhaps he was deaf?

'What symptoms are worrying you?' I called.

He still refused to acknowledge my presence. I sat there defeated. At last he said, 'See that bulb?'

'Yes,' I replied, delighted that we were suddenly on speaking terms.

'It's fate,' the patient said.

'What?'

'It's FATE,' the patient thundered.

Christ, I thought. I had to write down something opposite COMPLAINING OF. I could hardly put down, 'Fate'. I did not even know his name.

'May I have your name and age, please?' I asked, trying to be business-like.

'Ring Belsize Park 1961,' he replied.

'Your name . . .' I persisted gently.

'Ring it,' he commanded. 'Ring it AT ONCE.'

I wished the Casualty Officer would soon come into the cubicle and help out.

'ARE YOU RINGING BELSIZE PARK 1961?' he shouted threateningly.

'Yes,' I said.

'Good,' cried my blue-eyed staring patient. 'Now let me have the phone.'

'It's engaged,' I said, inspired.

I looked at him but he was still staring at the lamp. He evidently believed that there was a phone in the cubicle.

'Keep trying that number,' he said reasonably.

'Yes,' I said.

They say humour a madman. But what do psychiatrists do? What would my brother Wilfred have done? Sitting there, waiting for the Casualty Officer to arrive, pretending a non-existent phone was at hand, that a telephone number was engaged, that that electric bulb was Fate made me aware in a magnified way of my own incompetence. I would have liked to have done something masterful, or if not masterful, at least something helpful. But the *Collected Papers* of Freud, Volume IV, which I had pinched from Wilfred's bookcase and which I had read so assiduously was hardly of use to me now. So the blue-eyed man stared on and on at the electric bulb as if, inside it, small but real, were the nestling, bright oak leaves of Dodona. He could see a deity invisible to me, hear an oracle that I was deaf to. He himself lay so still he seemed like a sculptured image; more than an image – a metaphor.

Relating the story of that unbalanced patient I am reminded of another, more arresting. It is told by the American poet, and physician, William Carlos Williams, after he had visited Ezra Pound at St Elizabeth's Mental Hospital in Washington. He writes,

It is surprising how open and apparently unguarded the whole grounds of the institution present themselves to a visitor: you walk about, you go in and out apparently unobserved and certainly unobstructed, but as I looked up from the mud where I was somewhat carefully stepping, I saw this man, naked, full-on and immobile, his arms up as though climbing a wall, plastered against one of the high windows of the old building like a great sea slug against the inside of a glass aquarium, his belly as though stuck to the glass that looked dull or splattered from the bad weather. I didn't stop, but kept looking up from time to time. I glanced around to see if there were any women about. There was no one in the grounds at that point but myself. The man's genitals were hard against the cold (it must have been cold) glass, plastered there in that posture of despair. When would they come and take him down? After all it was glass, window glass, bars though there were beyond it. The white flesh like a slug's white belly separated from the outside world, without frenzy, stuck silent on the glass.

For all I know, the man on the couch with frightened, blue eyes had been possessed by the same madness as the naked man pressed against that window in St Elizabeth's Hospital. I never did find out what exactly was wrong with him. The Casualty Officer, eventually, entered the cubicle with a nurse in attendance. He tried unsuccessfully to communicate with my patient (who now would not speak at all). It seemed to me the Casualty Officer felt as impotent as I did. His mask slipped a little. 'All right,' he rasped to me, 'off you go.' Half disappointed, half relieved, I quit the cubicle and stood outside a dream. Soon I was telling a ginger-haired man that he needed stitches in a wound caused by flying glass from a doodlebug. The man nodded, 'If you say so – but mind you numb it first, sonny.' The nurse nearby giggled. 'I'll just clean it up first,' I said, dominant. 'Can I have the trolley, nurse?'

My early, intimate encounters with suffering and dependent human beings stirred me up. Of course they did. Yet, like others, gradually I became used to the recurring decimal of calamity. Occasionally though, I felt drained inside, hollow as a zero. For some incidents were too touching, too raw. For instance, a young woman had brought her young child in to be circumcised. She had walked into the Casualty Department, a sprightly young mother. The child seemed happy . . . noisy, lively. An anaesthetic was administered – fortunately not by Noel Rhys-Davies or by myself. The child never woke up. The mother waited on a bench outside the Casualty Operating theatre, reading a magazine. The child lay dead on the table inside, and nothing would revive it. It won't take a few minutes, the nurse had told the mother. Breathe in, breathe out, there's a feller, the doctor had said to the child. The child breathed in and breathed out, then stopped breathing forever. It was an act of God. They had to tell her the child was dead. No, doctor, you don't understand, my husband doesn't know I brought our son to be circumcised. I did it without his permission. My husband was against the boy being circumcised. They stood there in white coats trying to explain to her again that the boy was dead. She would have to go home without her child – tell her husband, who did not know she had brought the child to the hospital in the first place. The mother had signed a form giving her permission for her child to be anaesthetised. The child proved to be allergic to the anaesthetic. A rare occurrence. So sorry. We're so very sorry. So rare for a patient to react to an anaesthetic like that. The mother comes into Casualty smiling, the child alive. The mother leaves without the child. The mother is crying. Next patient, please.

When I was asked to play cricket for a team called – of all things – Public School Wanderers, at Windsor, I accepted with alacrity. I was glad of the break – a break not only from the disturbing drama of the Casualty Department but from the doodlebugs that now came over too regularly. For Windsor, I was told, had not seen or heard a doodlebug.

The inevitable happened. That very day Windsor experienced its first flying bomb. I was fielding in the slips. The air-raid warning had sounded and almost immediately afterwards, the familiar stuttering noise of a doodlebug became more focused. The bowler was about to make his run to the wicket when we all saw it above – the batsman waved his bat to the bowler to indicate that he wanted him to 'hang on' for a minute. After all, his concentration had been affected. We waited for the doodlebug with the naked, visible flames in its tail to pass over. Chug, chug, chug, chug, chug, it sounded in Von Braun German before the engine cut. Then all of us, like a flock of birds after a gun has been sounded, moved together. We all began to run towards the pavilion. All of us, in white shirts and white trousers, the batsmen and stumper in their awkward white pads, the umpires in their long white coats, all scampered over the green turf. The flying bomb sailed over some trees out of sight and we stopped running even before we heard the explosion. It was stupid anyway to have run for cover to the wooden pavilion where there was glass waiting to be blown to pieces. But we all had reacted instinctively. Now we all felt foolish standing there immobile, our shadows tied to our feet on the green.

In the distance we could hear the sound of a fire engine and far behind the trees, half a mile away, a plume of smoke ribboned upwards in the blue sky. The batsman returned to the crease and asked the umpire for 'middle and leg'. The bowler ran his long loping run towards the wicket and I crouched down, hopefully awaiting a catch in the slips.

At Westminster Hospital Medical School, once more I heard rumours of the likelihood of London's suffering from another secret weapon and, indeed, we were told that much of the hospital was to be evacuated to the Canadian Military Hospital at Taplow. Then these evacuation plans were cancelled. One evening in early September, Nan and I, as we came off a bus in the North Circular Road – we had been invited to somebody's party – heard a distant explosion, a tremendous dull thunder-roll. It seemed as if some faraway gas mains had vaporised. But another explosion followed. These strange, unexplained explosions occurred from time to time in the coming weeks and indeed increased in frequency. Some had seen, after the explosions, flashes of white dazzle in the sky and talked about 'flying gas mains'. They were caused, we knew, though the newspapers would not tell us so, by Hitler's new secret weapon. In the autumn, about five of these explosions could be heard in London during the course of a single day. They caused no real alarm. We only knew about the V-2s *after* we heard them explode. There was no anticipatory fear. We heard them thud and echo, a rumble of thunder and, unharmed, we continued our daily trespasses and business without a thanksgiving prayer and with barely an 'alas' for those less fortunate.

In the early autumn, the rest of the students returned from Staines or from their holidays. And I left Casualty for my first medical firm along with other students including Noel Rhys-Davies, Russell Barton, Titch, Eric Trimmer, Neville Stotesbury, Charles Morgan, and a brilliant fellow called John Hargraves. Now we were in the wards and fitting on mental armour to face the intolerable. We came to realise that symptoms were signals, often non-articulated cries for help, and we were educated by watching excellent physicians in their daily practice.

Of course there were occasions for humour and horseplay. Once we were waiting for Sir Adolph Abrahams to take a ward round and his registrar, to fill the hiatus, instructed us in some of the elementary principles of medicine. He asked us how we would discover whether or not there was sugar in a urine sample. No one replied. A nurse was requested to fetch a test tube of urine. The registrar dipped a finger into it before tasting that finger with the tip of his tongue. The sample of urine was passed round. Each one of us, Barton, Morgan, Titch, Stotesbury, Rhys-Davies, Hargraves, Trimmer, foolishly licked his finger. 'Now,' said Sir Adolph Abrahams' registrar, grinning, 'you have learnt the first principle of diagnosis. I mean the Power of Observation.' We were baffled. 'You see,' he continued, 'I dipped my *middle* finger into the urine but I licked my *index* finger – not like you chaps.'

Sir Adolph Abrahams arrived and we all trooped into the ward. A senior consultant like Sir Adolph was treated with reverence by all the staff. He was a kind of god. Sister curtsied, almost, as he came into her vision, and the house physicians stuttered, 'sir'. We had been told about his likes and dislikes, briefed on what we could say and do. Sir Adolph may have been a great physician but he was also a pedant. 'Never,' the registrar had said with awe, 'never say the word "slightly" or "slight" to Sir Adolph. He abhors the word "slight".' Russell Barton and I had looked at each other. That afternoon I was asked to listen with my stethoscope to the heart sounds of a West Indian patient.

'Well?' asked Sir Adolph. 'What do you hear, professor?'

I could not resist it. 'I hear a slight systolic murmur, sir,' I said and the rest of the firm ruffled and smirked. The registrar half closed his eyes. Sir Adolph spluttered in his nasal pitched twang, 'Slight? Slight? What do you mean by slight, boy? There is no meaning to *that* word in *that* context. Be more definite. A woman is pregnant or not pregnant. She cannot be slightly pregnant. He has got a systolic murmur or he has not got a systolic murmur. Somebody else listen to that patient's heart.'

Russell Barton immediately thrust forward, his stethoscope at the ready. The firm waited. The registrar opened his eyes, looked pensive. Sir Adolph waited. At last, Russell stepped back from the bedside to where we were all standing, just out of earshot of the patient.

'Well, do you hear a slight systolic murmur?' sneered Sir Adolph in his catarrhal high-pitch.

'No, sir,' said Russell Barton firmly.

'Good,' said Sir Adolph smiling.

The registrar smiled too. But the firm knew Russell Barton better than that. They waited.

'No, I hear a slight diastolic murmur,' Russell said, innocent and poker-faced. The whole ward wondered why the students suddenly convulsed with laughter.

The medical student is given to such frivolity. Perhaps it is necessary for him to joke and be trivial for, in his early twenties, he is seldom mature enough to cope with the sheer proximity of ineluctable human sadness and sickness. What can a young man of twenty-one do but laugh, and respond by some form of activism – by trying to comfort and help those in the disarrayed sick wards that he uncertainly and inadequately walks through. This each one of us on the firm attempted to do even as we submitted to the ritualised indoctrination of medical orthodoxies. Of course, sometimes, we were critical of the judgement of some of our teachers. They too, in their powerful postures, had to cope with their own problems, their own inner violence. And I had not forgotten that the guillotine had been developed by a physician – Dr Joseph Ignace Guillotin.

Early in 1945, I joined my first surgical firm and assisted at my first operation. Apart from the minor surgery in Casualty I had not attended an operation since that occasion when I had almost passed out. With some trepidation I watched Mr MacNab make his grid-iron incision as he began the operation to remove an appendix. I was too active in the operating theatre to even think of feeling faint. When blood spurted from an artery in the subcutaneous tissues it was promptly ligated and Mr MacNab issued commands in a most routine fashion. He cut deep into the abdomen and after suitable retraction of the severed muscles the peritoneum was opened. 'Retractor please.' 'Swab please.' 'Readjust the retractor.' These were the imperatives I heard. And 'Don't touch that instrument table,' or 'Get out of the way, you're impeding my view.' All this, while the patient breathed in and out, in and out, dreaming for all I know of a field of bluebells.

Eventually, Mr MacNab inserted a finger into the deep abdominal wound that he had made and miraculously delivered the appendix so that it could be easily seen. A tubular worm of a thing, swollen, red and elongated. 'Grasp the caecum,' Mr MacNab instructed his main assistant. Then he asked a nurse for a Lane's forceps which he applied around the appendix. This organ he then crushed near its junction with the caecum before applying ligatures. Used and discarded instruments were passed back to the instrument nurse and the appendix at last amputated. The operation was soon over. He asked me to complete the final stitching. The patient was finally wheeled out of the theatre.

Afterwards, Mr MacNab said good-humouredly, 'Never mind, Abse, some are good at one thing and some at others.' I did not mind his gentle reproof. I did not want to become a surgeon. I may not have been very deft in the operating theatre but at least I had not made a fool of myself. I felt I had come through some kind of test. I felt that for the present, anyway, I had come through. 'Look,' I wanted to say, 'I have come through. And outside there are three strange angels. Admit them, admit them.'

In April 1945, when the war seemed almost as good as over, our firm was called together. Would any of us volunteer to nurse and treat critically sick prisoners in a camp that the Germans had abandoned? We were not told the name of that camp. Of course I volunteered. But unlike Russell Barton, Titch, Eric Trimmer, Hargraves and others, inexplicably I was not accepted. 'They must think I'm a duffer,' I told Titch gloomily.

Soon after, Titch and the rest were flown from an RAF camp near Swindon. Their destination hell. Some called it Belsen. They flew from RAF Lyneham on April 28th, the day the Italian partisans hung Mussolini and his mistress head downwards from meat hooks in a Milan garage. Two days later Hitler committed suicide and my friends in Belsen heard his emaciated victims cry pleadingly, 'Herr

Doktor, Herr Doktor.' They were covered, these barely living skeletons, with sores and ulcers and infested with every kind of body parasite. Hargraves contracted typhus and became seriously ill.

None of this I knew until much later when I guessed that I was not allowed to join the Belsen team because I was a Jew. Meanwhile, on May 8th, it was Victory Day. With Nan I joined the effervescent singing crowds in Trafalgar Square who were wearing paper hats as at a party.

I often think about my not going to Belsen.

15. Marrowells

As the four of us left the station at Walton-on-Thames it began to snow. 'Marrowells,' we had been told, 'is only a ten-minute walk from the station.' Soon Noel Rhys-Davies, Charles Morgan, Neville Stotesbury and I proceeded past the Lodge down the driveway between laurel hedges and high rhododendrons stopping every now and then to give Stotesbury a rest for he carried more luggage than we did. Amongst other pieces of furniture he lugged around with him was a black case in which he transported his precious clarinet.

At first there was no sign of the house. We seemed to be in the middle of a wood – high soaring trees and snow coming through them. 'This is the place to see ghosts,' Noel Rhys-Davies said with satisfaction. 'Marrowells is the kind of house that could be haunted.' Noel spoke seriously. 'I bet you we'll see a ghost of one or another variety before we leave here.' In the train we had discovered much to our amazement that Noel Rhys-Davies not only believed in psychic phenomena but actually was an expert in such matters. For instance, he had told us how ghosts could be classified into God knows how many different species and that according to their classification they behaved in this or that fashion. 'What are their mating habits?' we had joked; but Noel Rhys-Davies found our sceptical irreverence absurd – founded as it was, he maintained, on ignorance.

Suddenly, as we turned around a bend in the driveway, Marrowells came into view with its great hipped roof. It was not a sinister house, not a House of Usher. On the contrary, it was a pleasant red-brick mansion with white shuttered windows.

'Not a bloody ghost in sight, mun,' said Charles Morgan drily.

By mistake we went in the back way, through a courtyard with lofty, beautiful, red-brick walls. It was January, 1946 and Marrowells had been transformed into a Midwifery Unit and we were to remain there until we had delivered, or assisted in the delivery of, one hundred babies.

We were to be supervised by a 'lady doctor' who, however, had recently contracted some strange dental ailment and had to disappear for long intervals from Marrowells and remained for us a shadowy figure – a sort of female Cincinnatus. We were to summon her only in the event of an emergency – a high forceps delivery, for example. Most of the next two months we were left to our own devices and chivvied by good-natured midwives. For the time being, we forgot about Noel Rhys-Davies's promise of phantoms, varieties *a*, *b*, and *c*, and took ante-natal clinics, gave anaesthetics, delivered babies, and put in stitches when a perineum was torn. A consultant, Mr Bell, from Westminster Hospital, visited us once a week, Monday, on his round, and meanwhile, theoretically, we were under the charge of the experienced head sister whom neither Noel Rhys-Davies nor I liked.*

After a week, Noel and I offered to go on perpetual night duty so that we did not have to deliver babies when she was about. Since most human beings seem determined to enter this one and only world in the early hours of the morning we had an arduous schedule. After ante-natal clinics and ward rounds in the day, we worked in the delivery room at night. Charles Morgan and Neville Stotesbury began to look more and more alert as Noel and I gradually wilted with dark shadows under our eyes. No matter, it was a rewarding job. After the struggle, after the muscles tensed, after the shouts and the palaver of blood, after the routine and ritual that precede every birth, it was gratifying and refreshing to witness the pure, delighted smile of the new mother when she heard her own baby cry for the first time.

On one hundred occasions I saw that most tender, most inward smile. I never once failed to see it unambiguously breaking through, after the granular pain, when the mother heard her child whimper

---

*In dealing with patients she was too class-conscious. As soon as I arrived at Marrowells she asked me if I was listed in *Who's Who* or *Debrett's*.

like a seagull. It did not matter whether the baby was born out of wedlock or not, whether the mother had earlier wanted that child or not. Such a metamorphosis! One minute the mother had been moaning or sobbing and we had been shouting, 'Stop pushing,' as the baby's head was almost crowned; then, the next, the infant was safe in gloved, Dettol hands and the cord had been cut, the sick, sweet smell of the gas over, and the mother would listen amazed to her own child cry. And after the smile that would then begin and endure, a most astonishing smile, the rest would seem superfluous – the afterbirth, a blue, jellied umbilical cord descending, a fat blue worm winding its way downward between the mother's splayed thighs. Even the stitches that were sometimes necessary after a birth seemed of little consequence though these had to be given under an anaesthetic.

Having administered a number of anaesthetics during those summer months in Casualty, at the time of the V-1 bombs, Noel and I thought we were rather dab hands at it. But, on one occasion, an apparently unconscious Irish lady suddenly startled us all in the delivery room when she shouted at me from beneath the anaesthetic mask, 'You moight have a good bedside manner, doctor, but you can't give a bleedin' anaesthetic.' I felt, then, rather like the anaesthetist who was once cursed by the famous surgeon, Wilfred Trotter. Trotter, it seemed, exasperated in the middle of an operation, growled, 'Mr Anaesthetist, if your patient can keep awake, surely you can?'

Noel and I mostly fared better than that. We noticed how amorous half-anaesthetised new mothers could become, how when intoxicated with laughing gas, their arms would grasp us around the neck in a half-nelson. Maybe they just felt grateful their babies had been born whole and healthy and, at that moment, felt full of love for us. Had they not dreamt months earlier, most of them, that they had given birth to strange, deformed creatures? Oh, the dreams of pregnant women! They dream they are delivered of puppies, or kittens, or tortoises – all sorts of unlikely litters.

Once Noel and I were surprised to hear one anaesthetised patient speak endearments to us in fluent French, though awake she assured us she only knew the words 'oui' and 'non', 'après', and 'merci'. 'I can't understand it,' she said. 'True, I did spend two years in Normandy when I was a child. That I should speak fluent French under an anaesthetic, though, astonishes me.'

I was the one who was astonished the next day. I received a letter from Nan. Our affair had petered out some two months earlier. I had not expected to hear from her – certainly I was taken aback by her news. It appeared that now she was deliciously happy; that she had left the Admiralty where she worked; that, as she wrote to me, she had a new engagement ring on her finger and, indeed, intended to be married in a matter of weeks – after which event she would go to live in Johannesburg with her husband who was a South African and who was soon to be demobbed from the Army.

I suppose I had assumed she would pine after me for years, unable to discover anybody so gifted, so intelligent, so masculine, so desirable as Dannie Abse.

'Bleeding hell,' I told Noel, 'it's only seven and a half weeks.'

'Women are enigmas,' Noel said.

'I'm glad for her,' I explained to Noel. 'I really am. It's all for the best. But I'm astonished. I mean . . . so *soon*.'

'Write a poem about it,' Noel said, with scientific disregard.

I didn't, though. Instead I wrote Nan a congratulatory epistle. I wrote that letter in the early hours of the morning and probably I was maudlin with tiredness. I cannot remember what I wrote. She was my first shy love so I'm sure I wished her well. I still do.

The weeks ticked by and everything grew towards or from perfection for a little moment. But I left Marrowells prematurely and in disgrace. One wet Friday evening, with less than a week to go before we were all to pack our bags and quit, Morgan and I sat chatting and bragging in the small common room. For a change, there was no work for us. Nobody moaned in the labour room. Nobody had even been admitted with those first signals, those first faint desultory contractions as awesome to the mother as any holy annunciation. Nobody bothered us at all.

'All quiet on the western front,' Noel Rhys-Davies had sighed, and clambered upstairs to fiddle once more with the anaesthetic machine in the labour room. For Noel had some bright invention in mind, a refinement of the anaesthetic machine he hoped one day to patent – and which he eventually did. Neville Stotesbury had taken his clarinet to London – or so we thought – for every other Friday evening he played with some small amateur chamber orchestra. That Friday, though, he missed the train, and when he returned, disconsolate, in his wet mackintosh, he took out his clarinet from its little coffin and blew a frustrated, a most sour, a most unearthly note.

'If Noel had heard that noise from the woods,' Charles Morgan said, 'he'd summon the bloody President of the Psychical Society to Marrowells.'

Less than half an hour later, Charles Morgan and I, along with a reluctant, even suspicious Noel Rhys-Davies, walked down the driveway to investigate some weird noises I swore I had heard a little earlier. Somewhere out there, as the thin rain descended with the least of sounds, in the trickling darkness between the high trees, Morgan and I knew that Stotesbury would be waiting for us, would be standing hushed in his white medical gown and white headpiece with his spooky clarinet at the ready. Noel imagined Stotesbury to be in London. And he said, 'Those weird noises you heard were probably only some night birds or owls or something.'

'Thought you believed in ghosts,' I said, castigating him for his faithlessness.

'This is a fool's errand,' Charles Morgan said. 'I don't know why we let Dannie drag us out into the rain.'

At a bifurcation of the driveway the three of us stopped glued to the ground. In a small clearing of the woods, some sixty yards away against the wide girth of a tree trunk, a fluttering of white could be seen through the darkness.

'There,' I said, triumphantly.

Morgan, with great clarity of mind, poker-faced and poker-voiced, pretended he could not see anything and evidently convinced Noel of this spiritual blindness.

'Your optic nerve has gone,' I told Charles Morgan, managing not to laugh.

And as we quietly argued, Noel interrupted with, 'Struth, only you and I are psychic, Dan.'

Noel became quite agitated and his accent grew more pronouncedly Welsh as, astonishingly, he now knelt on one knee (despite the rainpools) to say, swaying like a praying man, 'Duw, I can see right through it. It's transparent, mun.'

'Stop mucking about,' said Morgan who, it seemed, was a born actor. 'If you chaps want to pretend you can see anything, you're welcome. I'm going back in.'

'Hold on,' I said, near to hysteria.

Noel Rhys-Davies, after all, was the expert in ghosts, a specialist, I argued. He knew what to do. But Noel's scholastic know-how about psychic phenomena dissipated in face of the fluttering white gown in the distance. 'Hello, ghost,' he yelled abruptly, startling us.

We decided that since only Noel and I were psychic the two of us would tackle the ghost together while Morgan, apparently bored, just watched. 'Slowly, slowly does it,' Noel whispered to me as we took one step, two steps, three steps towards the white thing in the distance. After some ten paces, Stotesbury let fly a most terrific ragged shriek of a high note on his clarinet. If I had not known that it was merely Stotesbury sounding off I think I would have collapsed with fright. As it was, Noel receded some four yards behind me. He seemed to have gone into a slight asthmatic attack for he was now wheezing and his eyes were protuberant. The shriek on that clarinet would have frightened a ghost.

'Are you all right?' I asked Noel.

'What's the matter?' demanded Morgan.

'Didn't you hear it?' wheezed Noel.

'What?' asked Morgan.

Eventually with great courage, Noel Rhys-Davies – much to Stotesbury's alarm and our delight – tore down a branch from a tree and went forward to attack the 'ghost'. The clarinet shrieks which Stotesbury emitted with increasing hysterical frequency as he was approached merely held Noel up momentarily. Finally, Neville Stotesbury retreated into the dark woods with Noel following him. They disappeared from view. Charles Morgan and I heard in the distance, in the anonymous night, the clarinet screaming like an enraged poltergeist until eventually the noises ceased.

Later, one hour later, Noel Rhys-Davies forgave us and Stotesbury offered to stay on duty that night while Morgan and I took Noel off to the pub. Noel and I had not been out 'for hundreds of years'. We had not had a drink once since we had come to Marrowells. We had been on duty night after night. We went from pub to boozy pub until closing time. We staggered back, the three of us, up the tilting driveway, singing Welsh songs. We must have been too clamorous because in the foyer we saw the head sister coming down the stairs in her dressing gown. 'How dare you?' she addressed us. I knew what I was doing but I did not care. 'Get up the stairs,' I yelled, spectacular as an aurora borealis, 'get up, you bitch.' She, abashed and astounded, immediately climbed up to the landing and tightly said, 'I will report you to Mr Bell when he comes on his round on Monday.'

'Do what you like,' I shouted, 'but get to BED.'

My outburst sobered up the other two. It almost sobered me up. Next day I decided to leave Marrowells before, scrubbed and scrupulous, Mr Bell appeared. The patients had heard us singing melancholy Welsh songs and heard me yelling at Sister. I thought it best not to wait until Wednesday, our last day at Marrowells. I had, in any case, delivered much more than the required quota of babies. I said goodbye to some of the mothers I had delivered, had a last look at some of their infants – a few, all with the same colourlessly blue eyes, had been named Daniel – shook hands with the midwives and said 'See you' to Stotesbury, Morgan and Noel. I walked down the driveway. The morning woods were assertive with bird calls in the clear air. I observed a squirrel. There were percentages of green moss on the concrete of the lane, the same pretty green moss on the tree trunks. Beyond the bend in the driveway I could no longer see the great house. I passed the lodge and made for the station. It was almost spring, the springtime of the year, and happily I was going back to London, to Swiss Cottage.

16. Green Shoots

For five years after the war the Swiss Cottage cafés became even more interesting. Among those who now lingered over their synthetic cups of coffee, despite growling waitresses, were William Turnbull, the sculptor; Tony Turner, Hyde Park orator; Jack Ashman who owned a studio in St John's Wood where, with girls in their season, parties would suddenly start like inflammable phosphorus; Theo Bikel who would not stop singing until he took his guitar to Hollywood; Glyn Davies who could not stop stealing books from Foyles until he was taken to a melancholy English gaol. (Glyn, fastidiously, would only steal books with suitable titles – *Crime and Punishment, The Prisoner of Zenda*, or *Thieves in the Night* for instance.)

A number of writers, also, gradually began to frequent The Cosmo, and The Cordial and The Winter Garden. These writers included Peter Vansittart, Emanuel Litvinoff, Elias Canetti, Andrew Salkey, and Erich Fried who sometimes could be seen to crash his large head against the nearest wall bang bang bang for our delectation.

Occasionally we were amused, too, by arguments so intense that they became virtually physical. Godfrey Rubens (who later became a painter) had a stand-up fight with David Sylvester (who later became an art critic).

Swiss Cottage could also be an utterly boring, even a desolate place. There may have been good conversations, parties, jollity, but there were also those stale hours when one did nothing, smoked too many cigarettes, sipped coffee without enthusiasm. There were nights when I quit 38 Aberdare Gardens for say, the Cosmo, and waited uselessly for somebody interesting to show up. On such occasions I experienced the neurosis of too much leisure and did not feel mentally energetic enough even to read a newspaper. I would peer through the glass at the darkness down the Finchley Road where the neon glowed to display its banal, small advertisements and where, no doubt, on such nights a thin, monotonous rain descended on the tyre-hissing road to match the weather in my soul.

Infrequently, I quit my Swiss Cottage stamping-ground for the Soho pubs where writers and artists more renowned than those in Swiss Cottage could be seen leaning against the bars. I was once taken to the Mandrake Club in Meard Street simply to scrutinise Dylan Thomas and John Minton. (And did you once see Shelley plain?) That particular night, though, they must have had other assignations. My companion, instead, pointed out to me a short-skirted, thin-legged, tall hag with a scraggy, ancient, fox-fur around her equally scraggy neck.

'*That*,' he said whispering reverently, as if in a cathedral, 'is Nina Hamnett.'

'Who?'

'Nina Hamnett.'

My ignorance was infinite. I had not known until that very moment that Nina Hamnett was the author of *Laughing Torso* and had been, in days of yore, a model for Modigliani and Epstein. Recently, I happened on Nina Hamnett's portrait by Roger Fry in London's Courtauld Gallery. It was a young Nina Hamnett that Fry had painted, unrecognisably young, unthumbmarked, not the hatchet-faced lady of the Mandrake Club with old flesh ruined and with eyes that watered with fluid as clear as gin.

Oddly, the following week I had a drink with Nina Hamnett at the Swiss Cottage pub. I descended the stairs of a No. 13 bus intending to exit into the summer evening at Swiss Cottage. She swayed on the pavement, confidentially leaning towards each alighting passenger and whispered hoarsely, 'Buy me a drink, dearie, my fucking cat is dead.' The other passengers blinked and hurried on to their respectable appointments. I, trying not to be bourgeois, turned the single half crown over in my pocket and took her to the pub across the road.

Once inside the electric, crowded saloon she demanded, with sour alacrity, a gin and tonic which, along with my own half pint, I steered towards her some minutes later. All she said was 'Cheers', gasped down the drink in one go and, with a shocking suddenness, darted for the door before I could even ask her about her fucking cat. Probably she sensed that I had no more money and hence could not repeat my gallantry. I imagine that all evening she had been accosting passengers alighting from the No. 2, the No. 13, and No. 113 buses. Perhaps, at first, she had said pleadingly, tearfully, 'Please buy me a drink, my cat has died.' Doubtless, after an hour of silent rebuffs, her demands had become more gruff and peremptory, and her cat had begun to copulate.

My one and only meeting with Dylan Thomas occurred in the Swiss Cottage pub. I sat at a table, on my own, when Dylan Thomas came in with a companion. His friend edged towards the bar and Dylan himself, looking like his photograph, made for my table. At that time I was full of admiration for his poetry. Many of the poems that were soon to be collected in *Deaths and Entrances* had been given an airing in the literary magazines, *Horizon, Life and Letters*, etc. and I had been spellbound by them. As he settled himself in the chair next to me I grew hysterical in my silence. I wanted somehow to say that I liked his poetry; on the other hand I did not wish to presume and certainly I did not want my mouth to be full of soap. Finally, I ventured timidly, 'You're Dylan Thomas.' He turned his head, surprised. 'I think you know my cousin, Leo Solomon, from Swansea,' I added quickly.

'Who?'

'Leo Solomon.'

Dylan Thomas seemed puzzled. My cousin had told me that he knew Dylan well, that they were old buddies, that he had taken Dylan back many a time to my uncle's, his father's house. *Didn't Leo Solomon even know Dylan Thomas's dreams?*★

★ Dylan Thomas had related one of his dreams to my brother Leo. He described how, in his dream, he had floated into a cavern where a biblical scene was being enacted: he heard the roar of the lions and saw Daniel emerging from the lions' den. Then he

'Leo Solomon, the painter,' I said, desperately.

Dylan Thomas hardly reacted. He seemed shy and preoccupied. His friend at the bar was having difficulty in drawing the barmaid's attention. I began to wish that I had not spoken, that I had not blundered so familiarly. It was too late now. 'Leo Solomon . . . my cousin . . . the painter . . . from Swansea,' I insisted. I had spoken very slowly with great deliberation and I hoped Dylan Thomas did not think I was treating him as a moron, or as one deaf who needed to lip-read.

'Yes,' said Dylan Thomas at last, and he looked around furtively, obviously wanting to get away.

Embarrassed, I thought it best to quit. After a decent interval of one and a half minutes, I finished off the half pint of the beer I had been half-drinking and rose. 'Bye,' I said to Dylan Thomas. He half smiled. He also half rose with deep courtesy and said, 'Bye, Mr Solomon.'

Naturally I wanted to tell him my real name. My name is Dannie Abse, the ego-clamour in me wanted to cry, and I write poetry too! I said nothing, of course. The bar doors swung behind me and I was on the Swiss Cottage pavement walking nowhere, making up witty remarks that had I said them would have, I reassured myself, had Dylan Thomas, or rather good old Dylan, in laughing stitches.

(Years later, by the way, when I first met Dylan Thomas's close friend, the painter Fred Janes, whose portrait of Dylan Thomas is in the National Museum of Wales in Cardiff, I told him of my frustrating lack of communication with Dylan. Fred Janes said, 'Of course Dylan knew Leo Solomon. We all were very friendly indeed with Leo.')

In the winter of 1945 I became friendly with a young poet, Rudi Nassauer, who was even more influenced by Dylan Thomas than I. I found Rudi's poems often impenetrable but I was always impressed by his Dylanesque booming reading of them. 'Listen to this new poem,' Rudi would say to me imperatively, and suddenly more solemn than any Welsh undertaker, his eyes becoming fanatical,

---

entered another cavern where Job sat afflicted with boils along with his comforters. From one cavern to another, going back in time, Dylan was witness to earlier biblical scenes: the boy David confronting Goliath; the white-haired patriarch, Abraham, smashing the idols; Cain, covered in blood, slaying Abel. Finally, in the last cavern, two skeletons sat side by side, bony hand in bony hand.

Of course, it all sounds too organised to be a dream as Dylan claimed it to be. Perhaps he had been reading Blake's 'The Marriage of Heaven and Hell'.

warning me hush!, his voice tuned in, short wave, to the noble and
the grandiloquent, he would chant and doom his long-as-a-sermon
revelations while I tried not to fidget or cough:

> O orb o sceptre
> animal of gold
> King of the first pained metamorphosis
> flesh apple bitten by the serpent hand
> dolphined o into you the power cracked
> divine o you, no one denies
> rain to the heavened seed.

My concentration would fail and his voice would diminish to
background noise. Occasionally I managed to rouse myself to hear his
magnificent medieval chant rise majestically, climactically:

> All is a oneness ever ever
> above, above, above, above,
> (flesh in the tie of dire coronation,
> rope of the sea-king's peopled sea and urge
> bound to the stake of pain.)
> Oneness, oneness, oneness, oneness,
> orb, or sceptre
> animal of gold.

Then Rudi would raise his self-hypnotised eyes from the book and
say to me with the pure conviction of a 21-year-old, 'Isn't that
marvellous? absolutely perfect?' I could not judge Rudi's poetry. My
own work was terribly defective, though of course I did not know it.
In very different ways Rudi and I were equally deluded. Each of us
played about on the wooden nursery rocking horse and called it
Pegasus. But Rudi was so stunningly certain that his poems were an
expression of genius that when challenged to utter an opinion about
his work I tended to hum and haw.

'Mmm,' I would say, 'I do like that line about the plastic cry of – '
'THIS STATUE IN THE PLASTIC CRY OF HORROR,'
Rudi chanted immediately. 'Yes, a great line.'

Rudi owned a very real talent even though his poems then were
too derivative of Dylan Thomas. In 1946 Bernice Rubens came to
London and I introduced him to her. A year later they married. In
turn, Rudi introduced me to, and kindly gave me books by, writers I
had not previously encountered. Rilke, for instance. To be exact,
translations of Rainer Maria Rilke from which I learnt much. One of
Rilke's poems from *The Book of Hours*, a wisdom piece, continues to

have significance for me: it still is for me, in Babette Deutsch's translation, a corrective personal text, inciting me to listen properly, as one might to unknown footsteps in a quiet house:

> If only there were stillness, full, complete.
> If all the random and approximate
> were muted, with neighbours' laughter, for your sake,
> and if the clamour that my senses make
> did not confound the vigil I would keep –
>
> Then in a thousandfold thought I could think
> you out, even to your utmost brink,
> and (while a smile endures) possess you, giving
> you away, as though I were but giving thanks,
> to all the living.

With Rudi Nassauer, I not only discussed Rilke's poetry but also Rilke's poetic attitude towards such things as death. Rilke seemed to believe that we each carried our own death within us – children a little death, old people a large one, almost ripe – and that each man's death was an individual thing, unique. Probably because of my medical studies, because I was seeing death in the wards and in the post-mortem room, I had become morbidly obsessed by the subject.

I kept a skull in my room and I would contemplate it, from time to time, so that I would remember my own transience, so that this awareness would prompt me to see all things with convalescent eyes, to perceive everything as fresh and as rinsed and as clean with colour as Adam did in those nascent days of Paradise. Maybe, too, I could act more selflessly if the skull reminded me how the flesh would fall away and how I had heard clearly the day before, or the day before that, a man in the ward, called Mr Jones, crying out with a dying voice, with a voice that was not his own, 'Mother, mam!'

Rudi Nassauer was not only interested in writing poetry; sensibly he wanted to have it published also. Why not? If the act of writing poetry is central in one's life and yet no one reads it, then the writer is likely to feel he is engaged in a too private, even a neurotic activity. If the poetry is appreciated by others that is another matter; poems serve then a useful, public function. Years later I was to write in a poem:

> Love, read this though it has little meaning
> for by reading this you give me meaning.

Meanwhile, in 1946, Rudi told me about literary magazines that I did not know existed. American ones like *Poetry (Chicago)*, *The Hudson Review*, *The Sewanee Review*, *Kenyon Review*, and *Partisan Review*. So, taking the tip, I sent a batch of poems to *Poetry (Chicago)* and much to my delight they accepted one. Soon after, the English poetry magazines *Outposts* and *Poetry Quarterly* also accepted verses of mine.

But these were merely trivial triumphs for Rudi had returned from a mysterious trip to Exeter and had announced, 'I met L.A.G. Strong who liked my poems and he has recommended Methuen to publish them.

'I shall call the book *Poems*,' Rudi added.

'Just . . . er . . . *Poems*?'

'*Poems*. By Rudolf Nassauer.'

'Not by Rudi Nassauer?'

'No, Rudolf.'

I thought about it for a moment. I could imagine clearly a bookshelf, and on that bookshelf a book called *Poems* by Daniel Abse. No, no – that did not sound right. *Poems* by Rudolf Nassauer. That had a more authentic ring. I must have been envious, I suppose – though, frankly, I cannot recall feeling any envy. Rudi's success simply encouraged me to put a collection together and send them off to Hutchinson. I sent them to Hutchinson only because a patient in the surgical ward happened to mention to Titch that Hutchinson were looking for books of verse – and Titch had passed that information to me.

In June 1946, my first book of poems, *After Every Green Thing* (the title taken from the Book of Job, *naturally*) was accepted by Hutchinson and Co. Ltd. I was given a generous advance of £50 on account of royalties and, not long after the book was published, Walter Hutchinson, the Chairman of the company, took a fatal overdose of drugs.

When, in September, I signed the contract I expected the book to appear the following year. It was nice. For years acquaintances, relatives, had said, 'So you're a *budding* poet? Have you had anything published?' And I would grunt, 'Well . . . no . . . but . . .' and the conversation would dwindle and finally peter out awkwardly. 'Never mind. Poetry's a nice hobby.' But poetry for me, of course, was no hobby. It was a need, an imperative need. Now I was able to say, 'I have one or two poems coming out in magazines and er . . . I have a book coming out next year.' I could relax, smile and swank.

A year later, however, I had not even received the galleys for *After Every Green Thing*. When I contacted the publishers they talked about paper shortage. In due course, they said, my book would appear. I just had to be patient. It was a time of many shortages, clothing coupons, butter rationing, meat rationing, sweet rationing. Billy Cotton, Ernie Bevin, Stanley Matthews, Denis Compton, Phil Piratin, dried egg, synthetic cream – and paper shortage. 'Yes,' I said. Nonetheless, it was embarrassing when the few literary people at Westminster such as Russell Barton and Norman Kreitman, or those in Swiss Cottage who had had books published or were about to have books published, asked me, at raised-eyebrow intervals, when *After Every Green Thing* would appear.

One of my friends was Denise Levertov with whom, at that time, I felt I had much in common. Not only did she write poetry – her first book, *The Double Image*, had been published in 1946 – but she had also been a nurse. Moreover her mother was Welsh and her father a Jew. Or to be exact an ex-Jew. For Dr Paul Levertoff (Denise, when she left for the USA, changed the spelling of her name) had not only been converted to Christianity but surprisingly had become a prominent Church of England Divine. I found it odd to hear Denise's gentle father who had an accent like a stage Jew discuss Jesus. 'And vasn't Jesus, Dannie, tempted by zer devil? Didn't our Lord respond viz, "It is written thou shalt not live by bread alone?" Vye do you tink Jesus Christ should say such a ting? Tell me for vye?' he once questioned me in his house in Ilford, Essex, while Denise's mother from Carmarthenshire poked the fire and interrupted our theological dialogue with, 'Duw, I do feel sure that Dannie would like a nice cup of tea now, wouldn't you?'

I think it was Denise who suggested that I should bring *After Every Green Thing* up to date by including the poems I had written during 1947. I had seen how Rudi's book *Poems*, when it appeared, had been devastatingly reviewed by Roy Fuller, and I began to worry whether I would get the same treatment. Wishing to make my book a little less critically vulnerable I rang up the editor at Hutchinson's. 'Could I extract one or two poems from the collection?' I asked tentatively on the telephone, 'and substitute them with new ones?' The editor was not keen on that. The book was at the printers in Red Lion Square and any minute now they were going to set things humming. 'We don't want to delay the book further,' I was told.

So without permission, unknown to Hutchinson and Co. and its shareholders, I furtively visited the printers at Red Lion Square, knocked on several doors, and nervously explained to anybody who would listen that I wanted to make some very *minor* emendations to my manuscript, please.

'Did you say your name was Abbey?'

'Abse.'

'Attlee?'

'Abse.'

Eventually I was given a chair. 'Just wait there a minute, Mr Abse.' Miraculously my very own manuscript appeared. When no one was looking I quickly extracted the newly typed ten new poems from my satchel and took out ten old poems from the manuscript, put in a new contents page, took out the old one, and sat back blankly, thinking, ''Tis done. I've changed one-third of the book.' I thanked whoever it was.

'That's all right, Mr Attlee, can you find your own way out?' In February 1949, *After Every Green Thing* at last appeared. Though it was not the book they had accepted, nobody at Hutchinson noticed. A week or so later I saw a copy of my book in the window of the Swiss Cottage bookshop. I felt like a virgin deflowered. I moved swiftly away from the window in case anybody saw me looking at my own book. I was pleased, of course, that the bookseller had placed my volume in the window – only I wished that he had not added that printed card beneath it which read: LOCAL AUTHOR. I did not want to be a local author. I wanted to be an INTERNATIONAL AUTHOR. After all, weren't Hutchinson trying to export a proportion of the 500 copies they had published to places like Australia, New Zealand, India, Ceylon, Rhodesia, South Africa, Nigeria, the Gold Coast, Sierra Leone, Canada, USA, and the Shetland Islands? Hadn't Sir Stafford Cripps himself, our very own 'iron chancellor', recently said that the prime goal of Britain for 1949 should be 'higher productivity and *more exports for dollars*'?

After Every Green Thing did not set the Taff on fire. The papers continued to report on the trial of Cardinal Mindszenty, the Primate of Hungary. They even published pieces about how the Bolivian Cabinet had resigned following the discovery of a plot against General Hertzog, and about the anti-government plot in Siam which had led to a declaration of a state of emergency in that country. They naturally reported on how President Rolan of Paraguay had been overthrown in a BLOODLESS coup d'état. Yet nobody seemed to realise that my book had been published. No reporter was imaginative enough to see any correlation between the recent international disturbances and my *After Every Green Thing*.

I see now that that first book of mine contained for the most part linguistically florid and faulty poems. When I had begun to write, as a sixth-form schoolboy, feeling passionately about the Spanish war, I had hoped one day to make poems politically urgent and publicly telling. The poems in *After Every Green Thing* hardly touched at all on public themes. They were too private. Perhaps the full significance of the dropping of the A-bombs on Hiroshima and Nagasaki, the horrific revelations about the death camps in Europe, combined paradoxically to make the political, gesturing poem, the platform poem, in England anyway irrelevant. The recent documents of history proved to be too awful. How could a writer, even one much more mature and gifted than I was, hope to compete with such blood-soaked documents?

When people have to mourn their millions dead they can do it best by public ritual, by planting six million trees or by standing bare-headed before a stone cenotaph. The two minutes silence is the public poem. The planting of trees is the public elegy. No words can match the sunken silences of such rituals.

Besides I had learnt that one had to write what one could, and not according to some earlier worked-out programme. Poetry is written in the brain but the brain is bathed in blood. Or as Shelley said,

A man cannot say, I will compose poetry. The greatest poet, even, cannot say it; for the mind in creation is as a fading coal, which some invisible influence, like an inconstant wind, awakens to transitory brightness; their power arises from within, like the colour of a flower which fades and changes as it is developed, and the conscious portions of our nature are unprophetic whether of its approach or of its departure.

There's eloquence for you! But true, true.

17. Conflict

The general public tend to think of poets, when they think of them at all, as 'sensitive plants', as peculiar, vulnerable personages who have been born with one skin less than other mortals and who, therefore, congenitally deficient in ordinary armour, feel too much. It does not matter whether this poet was a pirate like Walter Raleigh, or that poet a thief like François Villon – no, as a class, they are considered to possess that almost feminine aptitude to enter into the minds and feelings of others and so suffer the situational predicament of others.

Their anthropomorphic imagination can be seen in their work and, more importantly, their biographies reveal how they can identify themselves, sometimes to a batty degree, with creatures and even with inanimate things. Thus Rainer Maria Rilke admitted he did not like leaving a bar of soap behind in an hotel bedroom in case it felt lonely! Most poets are not that dotty, but to be able to identify oneself closely with another human being, to become the music while the music lasts, on occasions may be an advantage. It is not an advantage, for the most part, in the practice of medicine. Doctors, possibly, may make good poets; but poets rarely make good doctors. The good doctor's ability to distance himself from his patient's suffering is helpful, finally, for the patient.

In a novel I wrote several years ago called *O. Jones, O. Jones* the main protagonist was a medical student, 'Ozy' Jones, who could not cope with the demands of hospital life. He did not write poetry as I did, he did not have the same dilemma as I did – I mean the conflict that arises naturally out of the contrary claims of medicine and poetry – and yet part of him was part of me. I made him more in italics than myself: more blundering, more incompetent, more Chaplinesque, more sad, more insane than myself. But, in order to demonstrate his temperamental incapacity in dealing with certain patients I did call sometimes on my own experience as a medical student at Westminster Hospital.

For instance, one scene in that novel focused on Ozy Jones

examining a hunchback lady called Mrs Manson. At that point I was not writing fiction but autobiography – as novelists sometimes do. Titch, Eric Trimmer, Noel Rhys-Davies, Norman Kreitman, and myself attended a tutorial given by one of the consultant surgeons, Mr Wynn-Williams. We were to enter, one by one, the small examination room, and in turn take the history and examine the patient (Mrs Manson) waiting there. Afterwards we would sit in a half-circle of chairs around Mr Wynn-Williams and discuss our clinical findings with him.

While Titch and then Eric Trimmer had their five-minute sessions behind closed doors with Mrs Manson, I discussed poetry with Norman Kreitman who had plans to edit an anthology of anti-war verse. (Norman, needless to say, was a pacifist and incidentally one of the most sensitive and intelligent students at Westminster.) Norman admired the poetry of Alex Comfort. 'Do you know his "Notes for my Son?"' Norman Kreitman asked. I recited the opening lines:

> Remember when you hear them beginning to say Freedom
> Look carefully – see who it is that they want you to butcher.

Inside the examination room confronted by Mrs Manson I soon forgot the noise Alex Comfort's poem made in my head. She was tiny, an elderly lady hunchback clad only in a blue dressing gown and this garment she now drew tighter around herself with a pathetic modesty as she swivelled her extraordinary large eyes towards me.

'Mrs Manson?' I said at last, and fool that I was, I blushed. If she had not been a hunchback I would not have faltered. Her body was so twisted, her head too heavy, it seemed, for her frail neck, her eyes too big and too full of pain for the head. I thought how this tiny lady had been familiarly examined by Titch and by Noel Rhys-Davies before me. It seemed wrong that she should be displayed like some freak specimen. I was supposed to ask her about her past history but how could I presume to probe? How dare I question the tuberculous cause of that hump?

She stared at me curiously and, worse, sensed my pity and outrage, so that rightly she became proud. She didn't want pity from me – not from a young man *in a white coat*. I was not behaving like a medical student so evidently she resolved not to behave like a patient.

In *O. Jones, O. Jones*, I wrote,

I could see that she was staring at me curiously. I had a feeling she could read my thoughts and I stood there in silence. Outside the sun must have inched from behind the slovenly edges of a cloud for suddenly one wall bloomed with light, the ceiling shook alive, the metallic surfaces in the cubicle reflected dazzle of peach and silver. Brief, that paradoxical cheerfulness. For soon that illusion snuffed out and the wall that was light faded into gloom. Bleakness of brunette clinical couch, bleakness of brown hospital linoleum, and the paint all round no longer disguised but itself, neutrally itself. The walls quiet in their vertical, dejected serenity of institutional cream. They held the ceiling up. If one stares at any functional inanimate object long enough – doorknob, keyhole, curtain rail, weighing machine, nausea advances to the point where, defeated, one must move one's head. I turned to her again. She was conspicuous with ugliness. I wanted to quit, to escape from abnormality, and I felt sorry, so very sorry for her.

But I should have distanced myself from her. Pity was no use and, worse, pity inferred superiority on my part. She would not answer my questions. She would not allow me to examine her. I assumed the other medical students had had the same trouble – that when I quit the examination room Norman Kreitman, in his turn, would encounter the same obstructive difficulty.

Not so. When, later, we sat around Mr Wynn-Williams, the other four students recounted glibly Mrs Manson's medical history and their clinical findings. She had spoken to them. She had allowed each of them to examine her. They replied to Mr Wynn-Williams's questions in detail while I sat embarrassed, defeated and dumb.

Afterwards, in the medical students' union, I felt depressed. Near me Neville Stotesbury was arguing politics with Norman Kreitman. In 1948, Britain was dependent economically on American aid and we, on our way to a Welfare State, were enduring all kinds of urgent shortages, shortages of food and even shortages of fuel. A year earlier, after a very cold winter, we had actually run out of coal. So no electric lights had been available and only limited cooking had been allowed. Two months before that, every coal mine in the country had displayed with pride the sign:

THIS COLLIERY IS NOW MANAGED
BY THE NATIONAL COAL BOARD
ON BEHALF OF THE PEOPLE.

'Yes,' thundered anti-socialist Neville Stotesbury, 'and what a balls they made of it. And soon your lot will want to nationalise Health.'
'And quite rightly too,' responded Norman.

'People like Aneurin Bevan, Cripps, Dalton, Morrison – they'll ruin the country,' Neville Stotesbury blimped.

> Put the blame on Mame, boys,
> Put the blame on Mame –

crooned Russell Barton ending the argument as he gave an imitation of Rita Hayworth.

Glum, I left the medical students' union and I thought about Mrs Manson for days and days. In just over a year's time I would be a doctor, if I passed the necessary examinations. As a doctor, how would I cope with the Mrs Mansons of this world? More than that, in the post-mortem room didn't I too often think 'poetic' thoughts (not very good ones either) instead of scientifically concentrating on the remarks of the pathologist in his salmon-coloured rubber apron and salmon-coloured rubber gloves as he wielded his little silver scalpel? How many times had I entered the PM room, noted the naked dead body on that white porcelain slab patterned with herringbone grooves, watched the pathologist at work, seen the grooves fill with the remarkable clarity of real, red blood, observed the colours inside the abdomen of the dead body (the same colours as those seen in oilpools in the forecourts of garages) and, instead of taking notes about morbid pathology as the other students did, started instead a bit of a poem in my head or thought fanciful ideas unrelated to the forensic prose of the occasion?

How many times had I *not* censored that recurring fantasy when the pathologist sliced the brain in search of a haemorrhage or tumour, that fantasy in which I heard imaginary snatches of conversation from the dead man's past, old nostalgic songs falling away from the knife – even recent ones?

> Put the blame on Mame, boys,
> Put the blame on Mame.

It seemed impossible that memory should be obliterated completely. And, come to that, when the silver scalpel cut into the dead white flesh for the first time, why didn't the corpse cry out in pain, cry out that tiny, tiny cry that, if we heard it, would transform us all forever? He merely lay back dead with the fine particles of sulphur spread over his face, he lay back dead and doleful on the white porcelain slab. *Oh, who had come to live in him?*

In the process of becoming a doctor [Alex Comfort has written] one is introduced to death by way of the preserved cadaver. Soldiers and policemen are among the few groups besides doctors for whom human death, including their own, becomes tangible in their early twenties. The awareness of death becomes most intense in the post-mortem room after the demonstration that people like us and of our age sicken and die becomes emotionally ineluctable. This experience may disturb some: others more mature (and few of us are mature at the relevant age) are more upset by an intimate demonstration of the reality and multiplicity of human suffering.

I certainly was not mature, and there were times when I wanted to run away from the desolation of suffering and death. I wrote poems; but poetry was not a refuge. Poetry was not an escape from reality but an immersion into reality even though most of the poems I wrote seem now to me to be defective. I escaped, though, by not turning up at lectures, tutorials, ward rounds, and I felt guilty as a result. It was no surprise to me, nor to anybody else at Westminster, when I failed my Pathology examination.

Two years earlier when my book of poems had been accepted by Hutchinson, I must have written a murky letter home to my parents. Perhaps I had felt trapped then. For having my book of poems accepted made me feel temporarily that I should be living the bohemian life on the Left Bank in Paris, swigging absinthe, surrounded by courtesans, not swotting the signs and symptoms of respectable clinical medicine. My mother's response to my posturing youthfulness had been generous and maternal. I have her letter still.

'My dear young son,' my mother wrote, 'I hate to read your letter written in such an unhappy strain. My heart has ached all day. You should be full of the joy of life – just at this time, your beloved poems accepted and all your bright (PG) future before you. Snap out all gloom and be your cheerful self. We are all happy for you and thrilled at your news. Of course you will qualify – and some day your desire to spend a year in Paris will surely come to pass! You are young – a mere boy and life will stretch like elastic and hold all your dreams. Bless you son. Mother.'

Now I had more reason to write gloomily. I felt exhausted.

'All you need is a holiday,' Titch said.

I took a holiday. I did not go away. I hardly attended medical school for the next two months. When I did return I found myself far behind my contemporaries. I began to study hard for the Pathology examination once more, but to no avail. I again failed the exam and now, I wondered, in a panic, whether I should seriously give up medicine.

How would they take it in Cardiff? I was now almost a year behind. Leo was studying law having been demobilised from the RAF. Wilfred was helping him, I believe, financially. But my father was now struggling to make ends meet and so taking money from him in order that I might stay in London made me feel even more guilty. I returned to Cardiff, and told them, 'I want to write. I wouldn't mind giving up medicine altogether.'

'Can't you do both?' my father said aghast.

'You can write poems to your heart's content when you qualify,' my mother said reasonably.

'It would be better for you, indeed I'd say essential for you, from a psychological point of view, to finish something you've started,' Wilfred advised.

'Your father has spent a lot of money to keep you in London,' Leo shouted. 'You should be more responsible and work harder. Qualify first, then you can choose.'

'From a practical point of view,' my sister said, 'if you give up medicine now you'd be called up for National Service as a nursing orderly. Wouldn't it be better to qualify and enter the service as a doctor?'

'With a batman,' my mother added. 'He can't take care of himself. He's still a baby. He needs a batman, I'm telling you.'

I argued. I was not certain that I really wanted to give up medicine but the more they urged me to stop messing around the more I explained to them how I owned certain characterological traits not ideal for a doctor.

'Nonsense.'

'Good God, you've nearly finished for heaven's sake.'

'You've discovered this rather late in the day.'

'Pull yourself together, man.'

'Poetry won't make you a living, son.'

'You have moral responsibilities.'

They were right of course. I had always wanted to be good at things – at football, cricket, chess or whatever. Now because I had failed at the final Pathology examination twice, I wanted like a coward to give up. For, in more confident moods, I wanted to qualify also. 'We are only undefeated because we go on trying,' T.S.

Eliot has said. All I had to do was to return to London and, as Leo put it, 'Take my finger out.'

Late at night, alone with my father, as he stared into the fire and coughed I broached the matter again. I told him how I was having poems accepted by the poetry magazines in Britain and the USA, by *Poetry Quarterly* and by *Outposts* and by *Poetry* (*Chicago*); and how I had written a verse play called *Fire in Heaven* that some actor friends of mine had produced in a primitive way – Theo Bikel, Michael Flanders, Miriam Karlin among them. 'So you see, Dad,' I said, 'I think other people think that I have some talent for writing. It's not just a dream. I really wouldn't mind giving up medicine and becoming a professional writer.'

Then I noticed tears in his eyes. He said nothing. He looked away. I had never seen my father cry. He had banked on my becoming a physician. It had become one of *his* ambitions. I loved my father (I use the past tense because he died in 1964), and I loved him for his good nature, his never-failing kindness and his amazing tact. I never mentioned my conflict about becoming a doctor to him again. I returned to London and once more worked for my Pathology examination.

18. Joan

If somebody asked me, when I was not yet twenty, what kind of a wife would suit me best I would have protested that I had no intention of seeking out a life-mate but hoped to live a Don Juan dissolute life of variety and change for many years to come. If forced, though, to enumerate the qualities I would like to see in my future wife I suppose my catalogue would have included the common ones: she would need to be very physically attractive, intelligent with a sense of humour, sensitive and wise, honest and generous, etc. etc. In addition, it would be useful if she were devoted to me, to literature, to Cardiff City Football Club, and could play a reasonable game of tennis, squash, and even chess. Oh, and cook chips to perfection.

When I returned to London I met, in one of those Swiss Cottage cafés, my future wife. Her name was Joan Mercer. She did not seem especially enthusiastic about Cardiff City FC. She played tennis with an awkwardness more boring than endearing. Only with coaching could she distinguish a pawn from a bishop. Nor was she immediately devoted to me. Otherwise, no doubt, I would have known *at once* that here she was, abracadabra, the mother of my future children, the washer of my socks, corrector of my punctuation, comforter and perpetual lover, sweet ally and partner.

She was born and grew up in St Helens, Lancashire. As a schoolgirl she had been secretary of the local ILP – admirer of James Maxton and Fenner Brockway. She had left home to study at the London School of Economics and was now working in the library of the *Financial Times*.

She was twenty-two. I was twenty-five. I spoke of Walter Hammond and Ted Drake. She spoke of Harold Laski and Gandhi. She had brown eyes. I had grey eyes. She was ♀ I was ♂. We were a perfect couple. At first we liked each other, then we admired each other, then we loved each other. And though, at that time, neither of us had any thought of marriage, we were never, neither of us ever, to be truly singular and alone again.

Two years later, in Hampstead Register Office, on August 4th 1951, I, Dr Dannie Abse of 50 Belsize Square, married Miss Joan Mercer of 50 Belsize Square. I did not marry Joan for her money though at the time she had £35 in her Post Office account.

When the fellow at the Register Office said to Joan, 'And do you take this man to be your lawful wedded husband?' behind me, from Joan's mother, came an urgent whisper of 'I do.' A few seconds later Joan, herself, said 'I do,' and we were properly married. In the sunlight outside, Emanuel Litvinoff and his wife, Irene, who had been witnesses, shook our hands solemnly and someone with a camera shouted, 'Hold it.' It was a really nice occasion and I wish our children had been there to see it.

19. Riding the Two Horses

The small cinema in the Newport slums which my father partly owned and managed had begun to fail financially. The young married couples were moving away to the new housing estates the other side of the town and the older people who remained hardly visited their local flea-pit with its smell of perfumed disinfectant. Soon the TV screen would claim them completely and it was already evident that in the near future my father would have to close down the cinema. Besides, he was far from well. He had chronic bronchitis and emphysema and had become increasingly short of breath.

After paroxysms of coughing attacks, he would gasp for breath, having squandered all his oxygen, and when I used to say, 'For God's sake, Dad, why don't you give up smoking?' he would retort panting, 'You give it up – otherwise one day you'll be like me.'

At Westminster, I had begun to work diligently for my final examinations but, alas, my father could no longer afford to send money to keep me in London. So I began my secondary career as a freelance writer. Over the next year I wrote occasional book reviews, infrequent articles for the smaller magazines, and I also did theatre criticism for a drama magazine edited by Roy Walker. Self-importantly, I turned up with Joan Mercer at such fringe theatres as the Lyric, Hammersmith, the Mercury Theatre, and the New Lindsey Theatre in Notting Hill Gate.

One commission I had was to write an article, some 3000 words in length, on contemporary Hebrew poetry. The previous year, the new state of Israel had come into existence. Suddenly there was such a thing as 'Israeli Art'. I had no Hebrew (I have no Hebrew) but I knew something of the younger Israeli poets because of Noa Eshkol whom I had known well for some fifteen months a year or two earlier. Noa, the daughter of a future Prime Minister of Israel, had been a dancer, training with the Ballet Jooss at Swiss Cottage. She was a truly unconventional individual. She would stay in bed for days if she felt there was no good reason to get up, and would happily do nothing except play her one scratched Fats Waller record, 'My very good friend the milkman says', over and over, ignoring everything and everybody else.

Noa was a *sabra*, that is to say 'a cactus', one who is born in Israel and one who consequently is supposed to be a prickly person, at least on the outside. Noa could definitely be prickly. She mocked me incessantly in her Marlene Dietrich accent, 'You ees so clever, Dannie.' Or, if I ever boasted or told a story in which I figured as hero, she would respond with the sardonic Arabic expression, 'Yah bah yay' which roughly translated, I gather, means a most deflating, 'You don't say? You are simply *amazing*.' It was somewhat offputting if one had laughingly, even modestly remarked, that is, not over-playing it, 'Ye-es. I'm not too bad at soccer actually. Last winter I had a game with Cardiff City Reserves, ha ha ha!' to hear the stony, unsmiling response of, 'Yah . . . bah . . . YAY.'★

Noa, though, had told me about such Israeli poets as Nathan Alterman, Shlonsky and Leah Goldberg. At that time, Noa thought Alterman to be the most interesting Israeli poet. Alas, when I referred to English texts by Nathan Alterman I discovered these translations were by scholars rather than poets. For Alterman, like Shlonsky, like Goldberg, read as boringly as the most flat, old-fashioned Georgians. They all seemed to have been influenced by John Drinkwater and Lascelles Abercrombie which, of course, they were not.

It was difficult to enthuse about such poetry. On the other hand if no true Israeli talent existed to celebrate, there was hardly any point in writing the article. And I needed the money. So (quite wrongly of course) I invented a poet and called him by the good Hebrew name of Dov Shamir. With unbounded enthusiasm I purpled the ink and said what a marvellous, lyrical, promising, young poet Dov Shamir was. (Naturally this hero fought in the Palmach and worked on a kibbutz.) I continued unscrupulously for three pages about this genius

---

★ I never did play for Cardiff City Reserves. In the spring of 1944, Cyril Spears, the Bluebirds' manager, welcomed guest players to train at Ninian Park. After one such session he invited me to play for the Reserves in the Welsh League home match against Oswestry. But the following Saturday afternoon I did not wear the blue shirt of Cardiff City. Cyril Spears took me aside in the dressing room and explained that only ten of the Oswestry team had turned up. 'Would you,' he continued politely, 'be good enough to play for them?'

I wanted to play for Cardiff, not Oswestry, but soon I was in the visitors' dressing room pulling over my head the red shirt of Oswestry Town. I have written in greater detail about all this in *Perfect Pitch*, No. 1(1997), edited by Simon Kuper (Headline Books).

poet when I realised that I would have to illustrate my claims in some way. That is to say, I would have to present some lines of his in translation, as it were. Unabashed, I wrote a short song for Dov Shamir:

> Working is another way of praying.
> You plant in Israel the soul of a tree.
> You plant in the desert the spirit of gardens.
>
> Praying is another way of singing.
> You plant in the tree the soul of lemons.
> You plant in the gardens the spirit of roses.
>
> Singing is another way of loving.
> You plant in the lemons the spirit of your son.
> You plant in the roses the soul of your daughter.
>
> Loving is another way of living.
> You plant in your daughter the spirit of Israel.
> You plant in your son the soul of the desert.

After the article was published I liked Dov Shamir's *Song* well enough to extract it from the body of the article. (I still think it makes a nice noise.) I called it, *Song – after the Hebrew of Dov Shamir*. When, later, I sent a batch of poems to T.S. Eliot he kindly replied to me saying that he liked the Dov Shamir lines, and that I should do more of these translations because they were better than my own work! I am happy to say that since then Dov Shamir's *Song* has been translated into several languages including Hebrew.

Six months or so after receiving Eliot's letter Joan and I met him briefly – at the inaugural poetry reading of the Institute of Contemporary Arts in Dover Street. A dozen poets or more were to be called up to the platform by Herbert Read, the chairman. Halfway through this exercise T.S. Eliot came in quietly. 'Tom,' I heard someone whisper in the row behind me and he joined whomsoever it was. I was acutely conscious that the great man had sat down directly in the seat behind me. After a few minutes much to our astonishment Joan and I heard Eliot mutter, 'Which is Dannie Abse?' and foolishly I half-turned and introduced myself with fumbling embarrassment. He seemed equally embarrassed and mumbled, 'Ah, we have been in correspondence.' Almost immediately I heard Herbert Read announce that my friend, Emanuel Litvinoff, would read a poem.

Now Mannie had told me beforehand that he intended to read his astringent poem, 'To T. S. Eliot', which I knew well and which I admired. I wondered whether Emanuel Litvinoff was aware that T. S. Eliot sat amongst the audience. Herbert Read had evidently seen Eliot enter, as had others in the chairs near me, including Stephen Spender.

'"To T. S. Eliot",' Emanuel began in his customary rasping accent.

Herbert Read nodded with pleasure expecting that Litvinoff's poem would be one of proper homage. But Emanuel Litvinoff continued:

> Eminence becomes you. Now when the rock is struck
> your young sardonic voice which broke on beauty
> floats amid incense and speaks oracles
> as though a god
> utters from Russell Square and condescends,
> high in the solemn cathedral of the air,
> his holy octaves to a million radios.
>
> I am not one accepted in your parish,
> Bleistein is my relative and I share
> the protozoic slime of Shylock, a page
> in Stürmer, and, underneath the cities,
> a billet somewhat lower than the rats.
> Blood in the sewers. Pieces of our flesh
> float with the ordure on the Vistula.
> You had a sermon but it was not this.
>
> It would seem, then, yours is a voice
> remote, singing another river
> and the gilded wreck of princes only
> for Time's ruin. It is hard to kneel
> when knees are stiff.
>
> But London Semite Russian Pale, you will say
> Heaven is not in our voices.
> The accent, I confess, is merely human,
> speaking of passion with a small letter
> and, crying widow, mourning not the Church
> but a woman staring the sexless sea
> for no ship's return,
> and no fruit singing in the orchards.

Yet walking with Cohen when the sun exploded
and darkness choked our nostrils,
and the smoke drifting over Treblinka
reeked of the smouldering ashes of children,
I thought what an angry poem
you would have made of it, given the pity.

But your eye is a telescope
scanning the circuit of stars
for Good-Good and Evil Absolute,
and, at luncheon, turns fastidiously from fleshy
noses to contemplation of the knife
twisting among the entrails of spaghetti.

So shall I say it is not eminence chills
but the snigger from behind the covers of history?
Let your words
tread lightly on this earth of Europe
lest my people's bones protest.

Most of the audience began to clap at the end of the poem but Stephen Spender rose angrily and shouted that Litvinoff had grossly insulted Tom Eliot who was the most gentle of men. He continued with great emotion and spoke with great rapidity. Perhaps I did not hear Spender properly but he seemed to say something like: 'As a poet I'm as much a Jew as Litvinoff, and Tom isn't anti-semitic in the least.' In the confusion of anger, Spender was not entirely coherent but there was no mistaking his gutsy aggression towards Emanuel Litvinoff's attitude as it was forcibly expressed in the poem addressed to Eliot. For his part, Eliot, in the chair behind me, his head down, muttered generously, 'It's a good poem, it's a very good poem.'

Mannie Litvinoff attempted to reply to Stephen Spender but Herbert Read, with his chairman's hammer, violently struck the table and called for silence. He firmly indicated that he wanted no further discussion on the matter and would call on the next poet to read. There were a few lonely, scattered cries of 'Let Litvinoff reply, let him reply.' Most people, though, especially those sitting in the vicinity of Eliot sat silent and awkward. Others plainly appeared to be antagonistic to Litvinoff and had shouted 'Hear hear' when Spender had protested.

Litvinoff tried once more to reply to Stephen Spender's attack but Read, anarchist and defender of free speech, now, presumably because of 'good taste' and genuine feelings of loyalty to Eliot, tyrannically censored all further dissension. There was something sad and ironic about the whole incident. In retrospect, something comical too.

As for Mannie Litvinoff, he felt hurt and rejected. He had been invited to read a poem and he had read a poem, a passionate poem, in his usual abrasive way and he had been treated as one who had come into a sacred place and had spat. Bitter as coloquintida, he quit the platform, his whole posture one of aggrievement and smouldering protest. He strode to the back of the hall and stood there, white and exhausted, while Herbert Read called on the next poet to read. During the polite applause that followed that next reading Mannie, with his wife Irene, moved through the door, and as unobtrusively as possible we joined them.

The role of freelance writer, superior hack, after some months began to pall, not only because I was mostly unsuccessful and mostly abominably paid, but because of the continual pressure of thinking up something *new*. I have, as a result of this experience, a moderate admiration for those hardy fellows persisting in their unchosen careers of freelance literary journalism. It is so much easier to work as a medical practitioner than to have to patch together those hebdomadal essays and book reviews. It is Sisyphus work. One must imagine Sisyphus happy, cried Camus, arguing that Sisyphus, struggling towards the heights of the mountain, had no time to feel depressed. But can we truly envy those freelance journalists when every Monday they begin again at the lowest slopes of the hills? There they go still, on foot, wishing they had the leisure – 'Time, just time, that's all I need,' – to compose with breathtaking elegance their second novels.

In the cafés of Swiss Cottage nevertheless, I showed off the review slips inside the books Charles Wrey Gardiner had kindly sent me to review for *Public Opinion* or I fluttered my complimentary tickets given to me to cover Tennessee Williams's *Summer and Smoke* or Yvonne Mitchell's *The Same Sky*. So what about that you Swiss Cottage denizens, I boasted – you, Fred Goldsmith, struggling with your as yet unpublished detective novel; or you, Glyn Davies, temporarily giving Foyles a rest while you worked in some attic or garage in Belsize Park making lampshades that, lit up, revealed pornographic pictures.

As my final examinations drew closer I had little time to write book reviews or articles or visit the theatre. I stayed in my room in Aberdare Gardens studying the textbooks and making notes. Each evening, at 7 p.m., Mrs Austin would shake the ritual handbell downstairs in the hall and soon, in the silence of afterwards, I would leave my room and sit at the kitchen table for the evening meal with Mrs Schiff, Mrs Blumenfeld, and the other fast-ageing moody occupants of the house . . .

Later, back in my room, my notes and books spread out on the carpet, I would return to Sir John Conybeare's *Textbook of Medicine* and to E. Noble Chamberlain's *Symptoms and Signs in Clinical Medicine* (edition 1938, because it had been handed on to me by Wilfred, complete with his motto, *Nil Desperandum*, on the flyleaf). I studied the shiny pages of these books and others, until I even, inadvertently, memorised irrelevant details. For instance, the conclusion of Dr Chamberlain's preface to his book read: *Once again I gladly thank the publishers Messrs. John Wright and Sons for the careful production of this book and Dr Hunter, the medical editor, for his many useful criticisms.* Hardly vital information, but as I went to bed it stayed in my head, and I even dreamed once that some faceless examiner cross-examined me with, 'Now, professor, answer this if you can. What was the name of Messrs. John Wright and Sons' medical editor?' In truth I can't remember the rest of the dream but I fancy I answered with delight, 'Dr Hunter, Dr Hunter, Dr Hunter,' and no doubt all the grey-haired examiners jumped up and down in ecstasy waving their papers as they yelled in unison, 'Excellent, excellent, Mr Abse.'

More importantly I needed cash to pay the examination fees demanded by the Royal College of Physicians and Surgeons for the final examinations. Thus, I agreed to rewrite some foreign plays which had been badly translated into English. Half the money for this was paid in advance but I didn't have to complete the chore immediately. I could wait until my finals were over.

Happily I passed the examinations. I have a scroll to prove it. It reads:

I, Walter Russell Brain, D.M., President of the Royal College of Physicians of London, with the consent of the Fellows of the same College, have under the authority given to us by Royal Charter and Act of Parliament, granted to [*here my own name is beautifully written in*] who has satisfied the College of his proficiency, our Licence under the said Charter to practise Physic, including therein the practice of Medicine, Surgery and Midwifery, so long as he shall continue to obey the Statutes, Bye-Laws and Regulations of the College. [etc., etc., etc.]

I do not recall very well the small ceremony that followed the announcement of the examination results. In my shiny (only) suit I stood holding a glass of sherry having previously shaken the anonymous hands of my august examiners. Perhaps during that hour I swore the Hippocratic Oath – though I do not actually remember declaring: 'I will use treatment to help my patient according to my ability and judgement, but never with a view to injury or wrongdoing . . .' In all languages, for 2400 years doctors have been committed to the oath: 'I will abstain from abusing the bodies of men and women either free or slave . . .' and I, too, on that ceremonious occasion, in a cheerful state, must have sworn such, as doctors everywhere have done, are doing, and will do.

I wanted to quit the formality of that room, the company of those well-groomed elders. I wanted to phone home to Cardiff and tell my parents the good news. I had the presence of mind *not* to try and borrow a few bob for that purpose from the President of the Royal College. Instead, eventually, outside, in a smelly telephone booth, I reversed the charges and hustled my voice into the receiver, 'I qualified, mother. Yes. This is *Doctor* Abse speaking.'

'Well done, son,' my mother said.

'About bloody time, too,' said my father.

20. A Locum Tenens

In late August 1950, I journeyed back to South Wales having accepted an offer of a three-week locum tenens in my home town. I was only too aware, as most doctors must be when they first practise, of my inadequacies. The doctor who had employed me showed me over his surgery while his wife packed the bags before they departed on their holiday. He kept telling me, 'Not to worry' – the favourite expression of all doctors and one I, there and then, privately swore not to use. The more he reassured me the more he exacerbated my doubts in my own proficiency.

I was even more alarmed when he informed me that he generally dispensed medicines himself. 'Here,' he announced, opening the door of what seemed to be a pantry, 'is my little dispensary.' A row of large bottles containing different quantities of coloured fluids stared at me. I had never dispensed medicines before; it had not been part of the hospital teaching syllabus. True, I had passed an examination in pharmacology but few medical students failed to clear that one-foot hurdle. The course had consisted of very few lectures and all that I had to do, all that the others had to do, was to learn a very small, thin textbook off by heart for examination purposes.

The whole emphasis of medical education was, and is, on diagnosis, not on treatment. After all, it is only in recent years that specific drugs have been discovered that can deal with specific diseases. Since the training of a medical student was scientifically orientated, the timeworn prescriptions whose use was pragmatic or simply magical were, by and large, excluded from the curriculum.

'Not to worry,' my employer said. 'You will find labels on the different bottles.'

Sure enough, the bottle of red medicine was marked, *For Nervous Complaints*; the bottle containing the white, flocculent mixture *For Stomachs*. Even the doses were written out in such simple terms as a teaspoonful or tablespoonful three times a day. In the 'pantry' no mystique of Latin obscurantism dominated. It was evident that this old, knowledgeable doctor had employed newly qualified men before and he knew their limitations.

'This is the white aspirin,' he pointed out for me, 'and this is the pink aspirin for more sophisticated patients. You'll have to write out prescriptions for the newer drugs but up there you'll find plenty of samples you may want to try out.'

Soon he and his wife disappeared, and after I had blankly weighed myself on the machine in the corner, I sat down at his desk idling through the shiny advertisements from pharmaceutical firms. Well before the time for my first evening surgery approached, the telephone on the desk rang clamorously, too loud. Before picking up the receiver I remembered again the motto Wilfred had written on the flyleaf of his medical textbooks: *Nil Desperandum*. But I knew my patients needed the solace of that motto more than I.

My experience, my feelings of inadequacy, were not, of course, idiosyncratic. My education, apart from being prolonged, had been typical, my lack of certainty natural. When, after a day or two, I saw innumerable patients whose symptoms were nebulous, though real – 'This funny feeling I get here, doctor, often moves from place to place' – when they complained of pains in the back, sleeplessness, depression, headaches, indigestion, etc., I prescribed placebos, sedatives, or the pink or white aspirin. I soon discovered that diseases hardly ever presented themselves according to the textbook description, and, in any case, for the most part the symptoms exhibited did not seem to derive from any known organic ailment. I began to feel I was earning my money (£15 a week, a huge sum) for nothing. My advice was not based on the education I had received from Westminster. 'Yes,' I was saying reassuringly, 'not to worry.' I felt a fraud.

Where were the subacute combined degeneration cases? Where the women suffering from thyrotoxicosis? Where the young men afflicted with Hodgkin's Disease? Common things occur most commonly, they had taught me in hospital, meaning that signs and symptoms, say, of an anaemia suggested an iron deficiency rather than the anaemia of lead poisoning which was altogether more rare. But if, now, I prescribed an iron tonic it was without any concrete rationale – for it was not for a definite anaemia but for a complex of functional symptoms which would include tiredness – 'I don't seem to have any energy any more, doctor.' Nor, on the whole, did my patients expect me to approach them too scientifically. When I requested an examiner to take off his shirt so that I could examine his chest with a stethoscope, his previous experience of doctors prompted him to say, surprised, 'You're from Arley Street, are you?'

Of course, eventually, I encountered patients with the definite illnesses that my medical education had prepared me for. I felt like a scientific doctor rather than an incompetent, bungling, pseudo-magician when I immunised children against diphtheria; treated people with asthmatic attacks or in heart failure; injected penicillin into the thigh of a sailor suffering from gonorrhoea; and gave morphia to an incurable cancer case. Too often, though, there were patients with non-organic symptoms whom I could do little for. And I continually worried whether I would find myself in a medical situation which I could not handle. One night I was sure to be called out in some emergency and I was anxious about that too.

Each evening, after the day's work was over, I turned to those badly translated plays I still had to finish. Or else I wrote to Joan. I asked her to collect the skull, the femur, and the other bones from my room in Aberdare Gardens and to take them to that dealer in skeletons, Adam Rouilly Ltd. Joan had already moved into the mice-loud Belsize Square flat and we needed all the money we could muster.

Before long I would be called up into the RAF to do my National Service. The USA intended to double their defence expenditure following the North Korean offensive and more troops were also needed in Europe because of the 'cold war'. Our own Parliament had reassembled for an emergency session so that Attlee's government could prolong compulsory service from eighteen months to two years 'to meet the growing danger to world peace'.

Meanwhile, my father insisted on being my temporary chauffeur on my afternoon medical rounds. He sat patiently in the parked car in some mean street of dockland or outside some dismal railway house in Splott while I attended to an ATS girl on leave who had developed a paroxysmal tachycardia, or while I worried needlessly whether an old lady who had not been to the lavatory for a week had an intestinal obstruction. When I returned to the car he avidly asked me questions about what was wrong and how I had tried to remedy the situation. He would recall all kinds of better stories in which Wilfred figured as a doctor hero – and these thrilling escapades apparently always took place at dramatic dawn. Yet, if we encountered anybody he happened to know he would introduce me with pride as if I were a young Dr Kildare.

I received only one night-call and that was at the end of my locum tenens. I was summoned to visit a Mr Saul Jones. At about three in the morning I left the surgery alone with my medical bag hoping I would not fail in this emergency. Soon I arrived at a tall house and opened the gate to walk through the front garden. I passed the panic of a tree, its leaves fluttering like carbon paper. One high window in the dark house was ominous with light. I climbed the steps to the front door.

The bell, startled out of its sleep, rang – but the door was open and the hall unlit. I pushed forward anxiously and heard upstairs the faint moan of 'Oh God, oh God.' I called out, 'Hello, hello there.' Soon a woman's voice on the landing replied, 'Is that you, David?'

'No,' I replied in a voice not my own, 'it's the doctor.'

'Come up,' I was commanded.

The kingly name 'David' made me recall how purely, with what sensitive grace, that vulnerable boy once must have sung in the mournful tent of Saul. But this was Cardiff 1950 and, outside, were the night sounds of Cardiff in the wind: the moonstruck clock of the

City Hall, distant ship horn and train hooter. Upstairs a man was weeping, a man older than myself was weeping, and I, alas no David, climbed the dark stairs to the suffering attic tent of Saul. The woman said, 'He's been drinking, doctor.'

Next morning my father wanted to know why I had been called out in the middle of the night. I told him about Saul Jones. 'I do not know what really was wrong,' I said. 'Only he told me he didn't want to live any more. He said he was sixty-five and that was long enough for any man to live.'

My father, who was soon to be sixty-four, lit a cigarette and looked at me anxiously. 'When you're through with National Service,' he said, 'you couldn't do better than put up your brass plate by 'ere. The name of Abse is respected in Cardiff. In venyer a year they'll be queueing up to see you. They don't know how daft you are.'

'Thanks,' I said, smiling, 'thanks very much.'

21. Not All Bull

I was called up into the RAF for my National Service on May 1st, 1951 and sent to Moreton-in-Marsh, Gloucestershire, for one month's modified square bashing. As an officer, as a doctor, I was privileged, I knew that: I would not have to endure the legendary humiliation of each 'erk's' induction to the Royal Air Force. Even so, I hardly looked forward to my posting to Moreton-in-Marsh, a spoof name surely invented years before for Tommy Handley's radio programme, *ITMA*? Odd, too, to join as a Flying Officer, to be with Them instead of Us.

Worse, instead of blue, springtime skies arching over Cotswold stone buildings, snow unseasonably glided down across the high trees into morose, silent fields. With great efficiency they had allowed the coal supplies to be exhausted at the Camp and so we had no fuel to feed the primitive stoves that should have warmed the wooden huts in which we slept and also those other prefabricated buildings used as lecture rooms. There we sat, twenty young doctors in the blue greatcoats issued to us, while we listened to a military voice explaining RAF medical forms and who to call 'sir'.

'Don't forget,' he barked, 'you must consider yourself as an RAF officer first and as a doctor second.'

I thought shrilly, 'Never.' Each day we were marched briskly, an ill-assorted platoon, with breath fleeing vividly from our mouths while a senior NCO screamed until our feet thudded almost in unison on powdered snow. 'You're a shagged lot,' the NCO shouted. 'You're all about as fit as King Farouk.'

The snow melted. It rained instead, a cold evening rain even in the mornings. After the strenuous routine of each day, I sat in my hut fatigued, No. 501885, in a harsh blue uniform rough to the skin as a cat's tongue, and thought of Joan and Swiss Cottage, and wished I was back in London, back in the flat where the mice fornicated noisily behind the skirtings.

After two weeks at Moreton-in-Marsh I was presented with a form to fill in. One of the questions was 'geographical posting preference'. For the next two years I did not want to sit it out in 'compulsory and irreproachable idleness' at some Sick Quarters in Korea, Aden, the Persian Gulf, Singapore, Cyprus, or even on some RAF station somewhere beyond the Home Counties. I wanted London. To be precise, Swiss Cottage. Yet I could hardly put down that my preference was for NW3 and that my second and third choices were for NW6 and NW8.

A casual three-minute conversation with a short-haired Flight Lieutenant in the Mess Bar determined not only my next posting but, oddly, my whole medical destiny. He happened to remark, 'The RAF Mass Radiography Headquarters and Chest Clinic is situated in central London.'

Even as he spoke I recalled another question on that all-important form which read: *What speciality of medicine, if any, have you an interest in?* By the next morning I had an uncontrollable yearning to work in a chest clinic. Immediately I wrote on the form that I had a keen interest in mass radiography. No other doctor, surely, would express such an off-beat enthusiasm? I was right. Ever since, in and out of the RAF, I have worked in chest and mass radiography units.

Alas, much to my disgust, after having been trained at the London RAF chest clinic (happily close to the BBC), I was posted to a recruit induction centre to work in the mass radiography unit at Cardington. One airless summer morning, in civilian clothes, in a proud new lovat-green, Simpson's suit, I reluctantly alighted from the train at Bedford and joined the queue of servicemen outside the railway station who were waiting for transport to the Camp.

'What kind of station is it?' I asked the airman perspiring next to me.

'Shit hole,' he said.

'What's the medical set-up like?'

'Fuckin' ridiculous,' said the airman who then turned to the rest of the queue as if to receive an outburst of applause for his eloquence.

A blueish-grey road and half a field separated the Mess from the Camp. Apart from a severe, tall red-brick building that served as HQ, an ugly gas-works affair, an expanse of concrete known as the parade ground, and huge empty hangars that had once accommodated airships, as far as the eye could see, in the surrounding flat country, thousands of huts sweltered in the sun – an unpleasant, prefabricated, cardboard dream.

Later, from the Mess verandah, in the direction away from the Camp, I saw, across the level fields, the distant chimney stacks smoking over Bedford town and a toy Hornby train (disappearing behind a green slope of woods) bound for London probably where Joan was, where all that I held dear was. Here, in Cardington, I felt myself to be an impostor as fellow officers pleasantly called me 'doc' and strangers saluted me.

The mass radiography work was repetitive and dull. Most of the X-rays were normal of course, and I felt ashamed when, pleased, I picked up some pathology – a congenital heart condition or TB. It was always a small ordeal to tell some young recruit who thought he was fit – 'Look – there's a shadow on your lung. It needs investigation. It could be TB. It could be active. Probably not, but we must make sure.'

'But I feel well, doctor.'

'Yes . . . but more tests are needed.'

'TB you say?'

'Not necessarily – but possibly. In medicine everything is guilty until proved innocent.'

'TB is serious, isn't it, doctor?'

'It's serious if it is ignored – but not if it's properly treated. Not these days. But I repeat – it may not be TB. It may turn out to be only an old insignificant scar.'

'I've been leading a clean life, doctor.'

Apart from reading these X-rays I had general medical duties once a week. Sometimes I had to walk down a line of naked new recruits, hundreds of them, while an attendant sergeant shone a torch on their genitals so that I could see if anybody had a gonorrheal discharge or a chancre or crabs or scabies. FFIs they were called. Free From Infection parades. Each time I did it I recalled how D. H. Lawrence had once written how he, in Cornwall during the First World War, had to undergo such an examination and how he felt humiliated as a result.

Nor did I enjoy the dining-in nights. One has to become middle-aged to tolerate affectation which, after all, is no more than a pathetic grope for style. In my middle twenties I had no patience with formality and empty ceremony. There we sat, aping the upper classes as flunkeys served us and our soaped faces were reflected in the shining cutlery. There was port in the wine glasses as we raised them to toast the King.

'Gentlemen, you may now smoke.'

Afterwards, in the Mess ante-room, the traditional service games commenced. Two teams lined up, in single file, each team member having been supplied with a snooker ball that was held high up between thighs and crutch and buttock. At the other end of the room two buckets had been placed and towards these, now, each player awkwardly progressed in a relay race. At the bucket, each in turn would stoop in the posture of defecation in order to drop the billiard ball with a zinc clang into the receptacle. Or two men, blindfolded, would lie prone on the carpet as they tried to hit each other with a rolled-up *Picture Post* or *Life* magazine. These two blind antagonists lay on their stomachs, horizontal on the floor, swinging their arms and crashing down their weapons mainly on the carpet while other officers gathered round frenetically shouting, 'Smash him, Jocelyn. Attaboy, Robin.'

I was too critical, too sour about service life, never having had to endure these public school pranks, disliking the muted, homosexual undertone of it all. I was prejudiced from the start because of my own feelings of deprivation and resentment – deprivation of the intellectual life and resentment against all forms of regimentation. My opinions and interests in that ambience, in that Officers' Mess, political and literary seemed eccentric. Besides, I missed my wife too much.

I left Cardington for a brief spell to join the RAF mobile unit on its tour in Northern Ireland. In Aldergrove, near Belfast, I won my one and only victory while in the RAF. Earlier that week, the mobile unit had visited Ballykelly and Castle Archdale. On both camps there were so few officers in the Mess I never needed to change out of civilian clothes. Only in the Mess in Aldergrove was I suddenly challenged about my apparel. A Wing Commander with fantastic, thick, George Woodcock eyebrows asked me if I was in the RAF.

'Yes, sir,' I said serenely.

'In that case wear uniform in the Mess,' he said sharply.

Fair enough. Next morning, I changed into uniform only to discover that I had left my beret in Ballykelly. An officer in the Service cannot walk out of doors in uniform bareheaded – if he does so he is thought to be improperly dressed. So I changed back into civilian clothes before strolling over to the Mess for my bacon and eggs and ready with a fawning apology should I chance to encounter that particular Wing Commander.

He ignored my apology and shouted something about National Service officers having no sense of tradition and other officers present jerked their heads around. Once again I explained politely, reasonably I thought, how I had inadvertently left behind in Ballykelly my beret, my one sole beret; how I intended forthwith to telephone Ballykelly and ask them to post on to me *express delivery*, my precious beret; in twenty-four hours I felt confident armed with this same beret, this same blue beret that I had left behind so stupidly in Ballykelly, I would be able to walk over from my billet to the Mess resplendent in uniform . . . sir.

'Mind you do,' he said with cold contempt.

That morning I read the X-rays and examined the occasional chest. At lunchtime, still of course in civilian clothes, I returned to the Mess. I did not expect a further altercation with the heavy-browed Wing Commander. I had candidly told him everything about my blasted beret which, thanks to my telephone call a few hours earlier, was indeed moving at 30 m.p.h. towards RAF Aldergrove. There was nowhere else to have lunch and I did not intend to fast. I nearly choked on the rice pudding when I heard him screaming, '*I'll see that you are court martialled if you come into the Mess again without uniform.*'

'But I've explained everything to you, sir,' I said, genuinely dismayed. 'Tomorrow, when my beret arrives from Ballykelly, I'll come into this Mess in uniform.'

I woke up late next morning. If I did not hurry to the Mess I would miss breakfast. There was not time to go over to the post office in civilian clothes, collect my beret, return to my billet, and change into uniform before taking breakfast. I hesitated. The chances were that he would not be in the Mess so late.

He was. He was louder than the Crimean War. His voice thundered and volleyed. His eyebrows became blacker as his face reddened. I had to take it all, of course, in smouldering silence though I felt inclined to throw my Kellogg's corn flakes and milk into his unenjoyable face. For I felt sure that he had waited hopefully for me to come into the Mess that morning in civilian clothes. He found pleasure in insulting me and in trying to humiliate me. He was a Wing Commander. I was a Flying Officer. I could only say, 'Yes sir' and 'No sir'.

That afternoon all the officers at Aldergrove were to come over to the mobile unit to be X-rayed and I waited for him. When, at last, I read his 35 mm X-ray film, though it was normal, I asked the Corporal to get him back for a large-sized X-ray and *to keep him waiting*. It was a small vengeance, unheroic. I could not think of anything better. I sat there, with his normal chest X-ray on the blazing screen while he loitered outside. I stared at the X-ray for five minutes, sticking imaginary needles into it. The door opened. He came in without even knocking. Christ!

'Well,' he rasped, 'is there anything wrong?'

'What?' I asked.

'MY X-RAY, YOU IDIOT. IS IT ALL RIGHT?'

Abjectly, I was about to say, 'Yes – everything is OK.' It did not even seem worthwhile objecting to him calling me an idiot. Then my eyes rested on his X-ray, on the shadow of his aortic knuckle. It was normal but I thought of aneurysms, aortic stenosis, and happily I said quietly, 'There's just one question I want to ask you, sir.'

'What's that?' he replied aggressively.

'Have you ever had syphilis, sir?'

His eyebrows did not exactly jump. He stood leaning towards me about to erupt. As a doctor I had every justification in asking him about any hypothetical past medical history.

'Have you ever suffered from syphilis?' I repeated solemnly. I did not smile. 'SYPHILIS?' I asked very loudly. He turned away, defeated. Fortunately for me, my beret had arrived earlier that day in RAF Aldergrove's post office. So at teatime, wearing battle dress, my beret in my hand, I swaggered nonchalantly into the Mess.

Soon after, I flew back in a small Anson aircraft to England. I enjoyed that very first flight of mine until the pilot suddenly began swooping the plane down over a house on the outskirts of Liverpool. I must have turned pale. 'Just letting my girl friend know I'm back,' said the pilot before he aimed the aircraft for nearby RAF Hawarden.

After that brief spell on the mobile X-ray unit, I was lucky enough to be posted to Central Medical Establishment in London. There, officers were requested *not* to wear uniform. I worked in the chest clinic first as an assistant before, after a year, becoming the officer in charge of it with the rank of acting Squadron Leader. I was responsible directly to Air Vice Marshal Sir Aubrey Rumball who was then, probably, the best physician in the RAF. I did not have to consult him often but he was invariably kind to me as he was to others. I no longer had feelings of deprivation or resentment. I lived as a civilian, seeing my own friends, living my own life – and there was no question of regimentation at CME. All the main medical specialists for the RAF, civilian as well as those actually in the service, had consulting rooms there. I discovered that the higher the rank of the officer the more intelligent and agreeable he tended to be.

Air Vice Marshal Rumball suggested I joined the RAF permanently. I did not want to do that. I agreed to take a temporary commission for a further year provided that I was not posted away from Central Medical Establishment. In fact, I worked in the RAF chest clinic until 1955 (when I was offered the job as a civilian). I was not only given an assistant but also five other National Service doctors worked beneath me in the sub-sections at Cardington, Padgate, Lytham, etc. They would ring me up from time to time for my clinical opinion and call me 'sir'. It was fucking ridiculous.

22. Poetry and Poverty

Permanently stationed at the RAF chest clinic in London my life suddenly seemed to become very legal and regular. Each clock-watching day I would work in the RAF chest clinic and in the evenings I would write – between poems – my autobiographical novel, *Ash on a Young Man's Sleeve.*★ Sometimes Joan and I would visit the Swiss Cottage cafés. These had become less interesting: the inmates were less wild, more attenuated. We were not so often surprised.

Nevertheless one evening while we sat at a table listening to Theo Bikel singing in different languages, a young man of my own age, whom I shall call here Henry, introduced himself. He was a rich South African. 'Come to the pub,' he commanded. 'I want to buy you a drink.' We discovered he was an ardent admirer of the roneoed magazine *Poetry and Poverty* which three years earlier I had been associated with.

In 1949, two friends of mine, Godfrey Rubens and Molly Owen, had declared that they would willingly produce a duplicated magazine if I would edit it. Soon we had agreed on a title, *Poetry and Poverty*. That title had seemed propitious because it pointed to our lack of money and it also summarised the editorial intention of publishing good poems (naturally) as well as focusing critically on the imaginative poverty of certain well-known contemporary writers.

Of course, almost all the contributors were discovered in the Swiss Cottage cafés or were acquaintances of ours. We were young and it was summer time when *Poetry and Poverty No.* 1 appeared, price 6d. We had sold the 1000 copies with relative ease; we had been delighted with the one review (Desmond MacCarthy in the *Sunday Times*); we had been apologetic for the profusion of typographical errors; we had been proud of the contents. We had been cheerful, full of enthusiasm for our new magazine. Of our friends, Michael Hamburger alone had groaned pessimistically, 'You'll get fed up with it soon.' We had not felt too depressed by Michael's remarks. After all, his gloomy prophecy had been in character. Hadn't we all not

---

★ It was first published by Hutchinson in 1954. When Penguin reissued it in 1982 they promoted it, much to my annoyance, as if it were my autobiography, not the fiction it is. The book went into eight further Penguin editions with the classification 'autobiography' persisting on the back cover. It became a text studied in schools. As a result, too many people continue to tell me erroneously that they have read my autobiography. In the introduction to my novel, *There Was a Young Man from Cardiff* (1991), and elsewhere, I have tried to draw attention, vainly it seems, to the fact that *Ash on a Young Man's Sleeve* is fiction fiction fiction.

True, a number of the characters I portrayed resembled, at least in silhouette, some of my relatives. For instance, one of my uncles tended to be physically combative. In *Ash* I related how he had a fight with a professional boxer. Years later, my mother said to me after my uncle died, 'Remember how he had that fight with Killer Williams?' 'I made that up, mother,' I said. 'Of course you didn't, son. Your father witnessed it. He told me all about it.'

long before sat round a café table when somebody remarked, pointing at his temples, 'I'm losing some hair here.' Emanuel Litvinoff had said, 'Yes, I'm getting a widow's peak too.' And Lewis Greifer had added, 'I'm going a bit bald there as well.' Michael Hamburger had given a deep sigh. We all looked at him. He sighed again. He shook his head sorrowfully. 'I haven't lost any hair,' he had said at last, before sighing again and adding with measured melancholy, 'What's wrong with me?'

But Michael's pessimism about the magazine proved to be just. Godfrey Rubens and Molly Owen had begun to find the physical effort of 'borrowing' paper and producing *Poetry and Poverty* too much. We had been unable to raise enough cash to have the magazine printed. It had seemed that the first issue would also be the last.

But now, amazingly, in the Swiss Cottage pub, a stranger was insisting we drank with him and was actually offering to pay for the printing of the magazine if I would revive it and edit it. Moreover, Henry did not write poetry himself and promised not to interfere in editorial policy. It seemed too good to be true.

It was. When *Poetry and Poverty No.* 2 appeared in 1952 with contributions by Herbert Read, Lawrence Durrell, Kathleen Raine, etc. Henry exploded. 'So much bourgeois formalism,' he cried, startling me. 'I can't support this any longer unless you take a more sensible Marxist line.' Henry, it seemed, was being analysed by a doctor who somehow contrived to be a Freudian Communist. Overnight, Henry had also become a Communist. Now we heard nothing from him but the tired vocabulary of 'the supreme crime of cosmopolitanism', 'industrial proletariat', 'reactionary trouble-makers', 'bourgeois elements', 'class enemy' – and evidently in editing *Poetry and Poverty* I had been 'guilty of a serious error of political judgement'. Henry had seen the red light and it wasn't outside a whore-house. Honourably, he paid for the printing of No. 2, but that was that. Meanwhile, however, money had come in from subscriptions, and unsolicited cheques, too, amazingly came through the letterbox. I remember with particular gratitude donations from the novelist, Joyce Cary, and the actress, Margaret Rawlings.

As a result, *Poetry and Poverty*, for the next few years, appeared approximately every six months, and gradually it began to change in character. (Our own routine changed somewhat too: Joan and I

leased a sunny, tree-high flat in Eton Avenue and in December 1953
our first daughter, Keren, was born.)

Cyril Connolly has remarked that 'little magazines are of two kinds,
dynamic and eclectic. Some flourish on what they put in, others by
whom they keep out. Dynamic magazines have a shorter life . . . If
they go on too long they will become eclectic although the reverse
process is very unusual.' True enough; but *Poetry and Poverty* was an
exception. For though it began as an eclectic magazine, by No. 4 it
had become 'dynamic' in tendency.

This was because by 1954 a very real change had taken place in the
literary scene. Poems appearing in the weekly journals were more
formal than they had been a few years earlier; the diction used was
cooler, more chaste; the subject-matter tamer, more confined,
domestic. But as editor of *Poetry and Poverty* I did not want to publish
civilised, neat poems that ignored the psychotic savagery of
twentieth-century life. Why, only the previous decade there had
been Auschwitz and Belsen, Hiroshima and Nagasaki – so shouldn't
poetry be more vital, angry, rough, urgent – in short, Dionysian?
Should not poets write out of an urgent, personal predicament rather
than compose neat little clever exercises?

At odds with the prevailing critical climate of opinion *Poetry and
Poverty* changed from an eclectic magazine into a crusading, dynamic
one that finally found expression in the controversial anthology,
Mavericks, which I edited with Howard Sergeant, and which was
intended to rival the fashionable *New Lines* anthology which featured
Kingsley Amis, Robert Conquest, Donald Davie, D. J. Enright,
Thom Gunn, John Holloway, Elizabeth Jennings, Philip Larkin, and
John Wain. Yet, editorially we failed. This was because the best poets
in the opposing camp had a genuine, even an exciting talent. More
important, there were too few poems written during the 1950s that
lived up to my editorial ideal of being written out of the heat of
personal predicament and therefore imbued with a strong current of
feeling. There were some of course – among them Litvinoff's *To
T. S. Eliot*, Jon Silkin's *Death of a Son* and David Wright's *Monologue
of a Deaf Man*. But Ted Hughes, Sylvia Plath, and Robert Lowell had
not yet produced the poems that I, as an editor, was looking for.

It was not until 1962 that A. Alvarez published *The New Poetry* and
echoed more directly, more succinctly, the sentiments I had been
vocal about some eight years earlier. 'We are gradually being made to

realise,' wrote Alvarez, 'that all our lives, even those of the most genteel and enislanded, are influenced profoundly by forces which have nothing to do with gentility, decency or politeness.' In *Poetry and Poverty* the editorials had raged against poetry that was merely a formal exercise, a social accomplishment. Years later, A. Alvarez called this same poetry by another name, 'Poetry that was part of the gentility principle.'

Yet *The New Poetry* also failed. Even in the 1960s, Alvarez could not find enough poems of quality 'beyond the gentility principle'. The anthology he put together was generally not in accord with his editorial. The revised edition of 1966 allowed him to include Sylvia Plath and Anne Sexton but the anthology remained a mish-mash.

If I seem to dwell on Alvarez's failure it is only to excuse my own – what I was after was even further away in the early 1950s, and so I feel I had the right to fail.

There were those few who kindly wanted the magazine to continue. After all, apart from established poets and the contributors to *Mavericks* many others with their reputations not then secure contributed to *Poetry and Poverty*. These included Thomas Blackburn, Alan Brownjohn, Patricia Beer, and Edwin Brock. But I had become bored with the magazine. I wanted to concentrate on my own work. Also I was tired of worrying about subscriptions, of pleading with publishers for advertisements, of being accused by some poets of carrying on a 'literary gang warfare', of hawking *Poetry and Poverty* around the bookshops. I swear that in some shops the manager, if he had his way, would set a bloody big dog on to those who try to sell little literary magazines.

I never enjoyed, for instance, visiting Zwemmer's in the Charing Cross Road while Mr Friedman managed the literary side of that important bookshop. Standing there impressively, over six feet tall, in an immaculate suit, a carnation in his buttonhole, he was apt to snatch a book out of some poor woman's hand and shout in a voice, loud as an aristocrat's, 'Madam, that's hardly for you. *That* is by James Joyce.' And he would look at the lady's hands as if she had blackcurrant jam on her fingers.

Once when I entered the shop with my eight copies of *Poetry and Poverty* he yelled cheerlessly, 'I suppose, Mr Abse, you want your pound of flesh?' I tried to divert his evident hostility with, 'Well, Mr Friedman, not quite a pound – only sixteen shillings unless you have any copies of *Poetry and Poverty* to return.' He regarded me imperiously, and suddenly barked, 'Call me sir when you speak to me. DO YOU HEAR ME? CALL ME SIR, CALL ... ME ... SIR.' I heard him. Everybody in the shop heard him. I imagine Mr Zwemmer heard him too. When Mr Friedman's behaviour became even more bizarre he was replaced by the mild assistant manager, Norman Hart, who was five feet six inches tall, called customers 'sir' politely and never snatched a book out of anybody's hands, not even those of Glyn Davies.

With Norman in charge I happily visited Zwemmer's, especially after the demise of *Poetry and Poverty* when I no longer had to consider such pedestrian matters as invoices. Many writers used to browse in Zwemmer's including temporary visitors from the USA – John Malcolm Brinnin, Peter Viereck, and Ted Roethke among them. I recall Roethke startling me with, 'Ah, yeah, you're on the Gravy Train too,' referring to Princess Caetani's *Botteghe Oscure*, a most handsome, fat journal published from Rome in several languages which paid its contributors generously. No longer having to rush off with copies of *Poetry and Poverty* to the next bookshop I could linger under Norman Hart's benevolent gaze, and listen to the conversations of the Fifties – about CND and Aldermaston; about Alger Hiss, guilty spy or victim; about the Royal Court Theatre; about the lightning rise and lightning fall of Colin Wilson; Suez and Mr Eden's gall bladder duct; Hungary and Hugh MacDiarmid; *The Catcher in the Rye*; and all that nonsense about Angry Young Men. In the cafés of Swiss Cottage, juke-boxes for the first time became evident and the music went around and around yo ho ho ho, ho ho and it came out there; and in Torino's, too, in Old Compton Street, and the French pub round the corner. In Zwemmer's Norman Hart said, 'You know it's a peculiar thing but we don't sell books of translations of Rilke and Lorca like we used to.'

Yet one could have forecast that. A discernible nationalism had informed post-war, I-like-it-here, English writing and readership. The writers who had gained particular success in England during those years – John Braine, John Osborne, John Betjeman among them – may have owned undoubted gifts; but they would have gained much less attention had they not preoccupied themselves with the 'British' theme of class. Yet our changing sociological drama was a topic almost meaningless outside England. (What could they make of 'Phone for the fishknives, Norman,' in Portland, Oregon, or in Delhi?) It was dependent so much on acute, local observation of manners and owed little to broad, intuitive psychological insight. It failed to achieve a lasting *universal* vitality. And if English literature deserved, in the past, circumspect attention from students in Stockholm or Amsterdam or in Delhi, it was because writers chanced themes that transcended barriers of custom and nationality. Now the whole critical climate in England seemed parochial and limited by a barely conscious chauvinism.

And this, of course, was part of the quarrel between *New Lines* and *Mavericks*. On the surface it seemed merely an argument about style, a rather barren, technical argument. But the preference for one style rather than another was a symptom of more general attitudes and loyalties.

In September 1957, another volume was added to Zwemmer's poetry shelves. It was published by Hutchinson and called *Tenants of the House*. It consisted of all the poems I had written since qualifying as a doctor – or rather all the poems I wanted to keep which could contribute towards making a homogeneous volume. Arrogantly, I felt it to be different from the typical flat British poetry of the time. I'm still half-proud of half of it – though, since then, my poetry has tended to become less hortatory, more conversational in tone. I have grown to like Edward Thomas as much as, if not more than, Dylan Thomas. I have become as attached to the peculiarly modest 'English' tradition as to the distinctive, aspiring 'European' one. There is no competition between the two.

23. The Passionate Transitory

My mother demonstrated to Joan how to nurse Keren in the Welsh fashion. 'In a shawl like this I nursed them all,' my mother told Joan triumphantly. The spring of 1954 my parents visited us at 8 Eton Avenue so that they could take a peek at their new grandchild. They were much taken with Keren. 'She smells of apricots,' my mother declared. My father, having also paid proper homage to the baby, turned his attention to our three-roomed apartment. He gave it nought out of ten.

'Swiss Cottage is a nice neighbourhood, I agree,' my father said, 'but this room – it's a barn, it's ridiculous.'

'I saw a very nice-looking Chinese gentleman go into the house next door,' my mother said, trying to be more positive.

'You ought to let this room out as a dance hall,' my father said.

'Huldah, Wilfred, Leo, and you, son,' said my mother, 'all of you I nursed this way.'

'You could 'ave a game of tennis in 'ere,' my father said, thoughtfully.

'Dannie, you were no trouble as a baby at all,' my mother continued. 'You were as good as gold.'

'Or badminton. Hindoor badminton. Make a mint if you let it off for that,' mused Father.

That chilly April evening my father sat in his overcoat in front of an ineffective gas fire that burned with a put put put noise.

'If you weren't useless you would have fixed this fire,' he said to me, and added, 'Joan, you think you've got one baby. I tell you you've got two.'

When I had lived in South Wales my parents had frequently aired their prejudices about mixed marriages. And, at first, they made it plainly evident that they were disappointed I had not married a Jewish girl. But lower-middle-class Welsh Jews, like Spanish Royalty, can alter their 'irrevocable' attitudes. Before Columbus made his discovery the Spanish Royal Family believed the Straits of Gibraltar to be the last outpost of the world. Their coat of arms depicted the Pillars of Hercules, the Straits of Gibraltar, with the motto *Nec Plus Ultra* (No More Beyond). After Columbus set sail the Royal Family, with great economy, did not change their coat of arms. They merely erased the negative so that their motto now read *Plus Ultra* (More Beyond). My parents also, as it were, erased the negative, and soon Joan was cherished, all prejudices dissolved. Later Leo, and Wilfred in the USA too, married out and my parents did not demur. Why should they? The ship had already sailed into the blue beyond and had not fallen off the horizon.

My mother was busy telling Joan how some months earlier she had called into Lear's bookshop in Cardiff to inquire how my book of poems was selling. 'I asked how is my son's book selling and the assistant asked, "Who is your son, madam?" So naturally I said Dannie Abse and do you know what he said?'

'No,' said Joan.

'He said Not as well as Dylan Thomas's *Collected Poems*, madam, which has also recently been published. So I told him – My son, I said, my son is the *Welsh* Dylan Thomas.'

The previous November Dylan Thomas had died in New York. Like many others I felt, unreasonably, as if I had suffered a personal bereavement. He seemed like a cousin, an older cousin. Not only lines from his poems immediately came to mind but a number of his sayings too: 'Art is an accident of craft'; 'When in doubt, fox 'em'; 'the printed page is the place to examine the works of a poem, and the platform is the place to give the poem the works'. Dylan Thomas had not only been a marvellous, if uneven, poet, but he also owned a genius for comedy, verbal and situational. Not many contemporary poets were gifted in that way.

Like many others I wrote an 'Elegy for Dylan Thomas'. A month after his death I had the opportunity to read that poem out loud at a poetry reading that took place in an echoing hall in Fleet Street. Three other poets shared the platform with me. Each of us was asked to read five poems. In the middle of my first poem I heard a disturbance at the back. I looked up from my book and saw Charles coming into the hall very late and pushing forward a blonde companion. I had met Charles a few nights before the reading, having been introduced to him by Emanuel Litvinoff. Charles, I was told, wrote a gossip column about 'cultural events' for a national newspaper. Evidently he was now on duty. Unfortunately he was also somewhat drunk. He clumped down the aisle between the rows of wooden chairs as I continued my poem. He hustled his disinclined blonde girl in front of him and people turned their heads, hissing, 'Shush.' I came to the end of my first poem that nobody, of course, had listened to.

Without too much chagrin I announced the title of my second poem. Charles, settled in the middle of the sixth row, smiled sweetly at me. I had read only the first few lines when Charles rose suddenly, swayed, and stage-whispered 'Excuse me' as he urgently shoved past bony knees on his way to the aisle and the exit door. I addressed my second poem to his disappearing back and to rows of profiles. Charles had left, I noticed, the posterior door open. All was quiet as I began the third poem, glaring at the blonde girlfriend who had stayed behind. I progressed through at least six lines unimpeded. The hush was positively reverent, the audience solemn. Alas, in the middle of my poem, the audience and I heard the distinct noise of a lavatory chain being pulled. And, worse, my fourth poem was also interrupted, this time by Charles returning down the long aisle. When, at long last, Charles's weighty feet were still, I began to read my 'Elegy to Dylan Thomas'. I began the poem uncertainly. Yet all the eyes above those rows of wooden chairs stared up at me with good will. Charles and his blonde friend were now amazingly quiet. Neither fidgeted. I continued with rising optimism:

> Now, one second from earth, not even for the sake
>   of love can his true energy come back.

> So cease your talking
> Too familiar, you blaspheme his name and collected legends:
> Some tears fall soundlessly and aren't the same
>   as those that drop with obituary explosions.
>   Suddenly, others who sing seem older and lame.

At this point, there was a dreadful howl from the sixth row. Charles, who apparently had been a good friend of Dylan's, suddenly began to cry uncontrollably. He sounded like a wailing wall. His blonde friend plucked crossly at his sleeve and I could do nothing but raise my voice to a megaphone boom in order to be heard above his weeping.

> But far from the blind country of prose,
>   wherever his burst voice goes about you, or through you,
>   look up in surprise, in a hurt public house
>   or in a rain-blown street, and see how
>   no fat ghost but a quotation cries.

'Shush,' somebody shouted out loudly at Charles. 'Why don't you leave the hall?' another kind member of the audience roared.

> Stranger he is laid to rest
>   not in the . . .

I gave up. I sat down. I could not compete with the howls of a man in drunken mourning and an audience metamorphosed into a potential lynch mob. Unpopular Charles and friend once more stood up to leave – this time for good. The next poet coughed, rose, coughed again and read his five poems to a great, tame silence. And that was it, the most disastrous reading I have ever been involved in – also the most comic. Next day I read in Charles' column that the previous evening he had attended a poetry reading in Fleet Street and that he had heard a most moving elegy for Dylan Thomas written and read by the young poet, Emanuel Litvinoff.

Perhaps youthful readers, today, may find it difficult to understand why Dylan Thomas's reputation soared so high during his life-time, why he was called 'the Rimbaud of Swansea'. With Dylan Thomas's death the vogue of his own day and the enthusiasm of his contemporaries did not diminish at once. On the contrary, his popularity flared, became brilliant. Those who had not heard his name before began to read his poems or, at least, came to know *Under Milk Wood* and his other radio pieces. More and more people claimed acquaintance with him: 'I remember old Dylan telling me, etc.' (Strangers called him by his first name as if he were a child.) His death seemed to start up, with a great hum, the mysterious machinery of myth-making.

It seems that each generation needs to create a young martyr–poet – and what better than one who could have been first cousin to the Marx brothers, always and forever outrageously deflating stiff-shirted pomposity? So, in the mid–fifties, it was Dylan Thomas. A generation earlier, Wilfred Owen. Now many would cast Sylvia Plath for that role. There are those who feel that somehow the poet soars to forbidden heights, steals the ambrosia of the gods, illicitly brings heavenly fire to earth, and must suffer, as a result, degradation in life and the consequences of an early death, by drink, by drugs or by suicide.

'Yes, that Dylan Thomas,' said my father, surprising me, 'was no good. That's what I think. Not a proper man I'm telling you.'

'There are some people in your family,' my mother retaliated indignantly, 'who are just as bad and *they* have no talent at all. There's your brother, Boonie, for a start. Don't I have to lock up the drawers when he comes into the house?'

'Listen, you should talk,' my father replied. 'The Shepherds are a terrible lot. Your Isaac is so mean, so bigoted.'

'Your brother Philip,' my mother interrupted him.

'And your David,' my father responded.

Joan had tactfully vanished into the kitchen to take care of the dinner and I, therefore, took my young daughter from my mother who had been nursing her. I did not listen again to the familiar dialogue between my parents – Mother abusing the Abse family, Father denigrating the Shepherds, as I rocked Keren in my arms. She opened her eyelids suddenly staring at me with smiling baby eyes. I could feel her warm skull against my arm. If I cared to I could have felt for the fontanelle in it. Instead I brought her head to my face and I breathed in the faint sweetness of apricots.

Life was changing fast. Joan and I were becoming a much married couple. We were intemperately anxious parents. Pram, nappies, baby-sitters, early mornings, bottles of milk to heat, interrupted nights. We were anchored. Something was slipping away from us but something was being added also.

24. Ticket to Golders Green

We moved because the five-year lease on our flat was drawing to a close. Besides, in February, Susanna had been born; we needed more room. 'It would be useful if we had a house of our own,' Joan said wistfully, 'where we could put the pram out in the garden.' Alas, the houses in our immediate neighbourhood, in Belsize Park and Hampstead, were beyond our means.

'Perhaps we'll try Golders Green,' I said without enthusiasm. Golders Green was bourgeoisieland: red roofs, green cautious hedges, cherry blossom, short-haired men polishing their Sunday cars. But it was on the Northern Line, the next station after Hampstead, and it would be convenient for travelling to Goodge Street where my job took me regularly. (Central Medical Establishment, where I worked, was situated in Cleveland Street directly across the road from the main Middlesex Hospital.)

We discovered a house we liked in Hodford Road not too far from Golders Green Station and also near to Golders Hill Park which Ezra Pound had once called the most beautiful small park in London. We looked at the house again, at its front garden ostentatious with rose-bushes, at its hall that smelled of biscuits, at the spacious rooms that badly needed redecorating. We ambled in Golders Hill Park, up the green sloping lawns to the little zoo with its ravenous peacock cries, and beyond, to the pretty round bandstand with its ghosts of military music. We sat in Golders Hill Park's walled garden under the too-ripe magnolia trees and pondered. An aeroplane passed overhead. Soon they were going to explode the first British hydrogen bomb on Christmas Island. Both Joan and I were sympathetic to CND. But now there were personal things to think about. The house we contemplated buying would cost us £4650 leasehold and we had to arrange a mortgage.

We joined the propertied classes. It was goodbye to the Swiss Cottage emigré café life that had anyway lost its earlier vitality. It seemed more than a dozen years since Peter Berg had cried excitedly, as if I were the Messiah, 'He's a Velsh Jew,' and Erich Fried had astonished us all by swinging his head back and fore like a pendulum against a gonged wall. It seemed more than a decade since, in the Swiss Cottage arcade's secondhand bookshop, I had been confronted by Itzik Manger, the Yiddish poet, who was clutching a half-emptied bottle of vodka. Manger was a fine poet whom the Quakers had brought over to England after the fall of France. He had lost, of course, his considerable audience in Eastern Europe. Those Yiddish-speaking Jews had been slaughtered in their millions and so he wrote now in a language that was dying. He himself was unwell, visibly unwell. He had lurched towards me, through a vodka-haze, a wiry man with a lined face, and eyes much too melancholy. We had hardly spoken to each other before.

'You're a good-looking boy.'

'Thank you, Mr Manger,' I had replied, surprised.

'And you're a good poet.'

'Thank you.'

And then he had brought his bunched fist to my jaw. That swift uppercut had startled more than hurt me. Venomous, his face oddly contracting and becoming bonier, he had yelled at me, '*You killed all the Jews in Europe.*'

It seemed years ago, too, since Elias Canetti, another considerable emigré writer, had told me one of his unpalatable truths in the Cosmo. 'The man suffering from paranoia is correct. Someone *is* standing behind each door pumping invisible gas through the keyhole. For we are dying right now, a little every minute.' We are dying, Swiss Cottage, dying, and not expecting pardon ... In Golders Green I felt no one was likely to announce the advent of a Welsh Jew or crack his head deliberately against a café wall or, vodka-soaked, punch me on the jaw, or for that matter whisper such revelatory and inspirational secrets as Canetti did.

I am not a superstitious man (touch wood) but the evening after we paid the deposit on the Golders Green house a curious yellow-green bird percussed the window of our living room with its beak. The highest part of that window consisted of a leaded pane and the bird pecked at the strips of lead that made a pattern on it.

'Is it a budgerigar?' Joan asked.

'It's too big for a budgerigar,' I said.

We observed its long tail, its curved grey beak and yellow-green feathers. It seemed too small for a parrot. It nibbled away irritably at the lead on the window. I raised my hand and tapped the window glass but the bird continued to peck away as if the lead were a part of a cage, as if the bird wanted to return to a cage, having escaped from one.

'You don't get wild birds like that in London,' I said inanely.

'Perhaps it's escaped from the zoo?' Joan said.

London Zoo with its aviaries lay less than a mile away, the other side of Primrose Hill. As Joan spoke the bird flew away from the window into the plane tree the other side of the road – its yellow-green body soon camouflaged in the green leaves. I believe we were glad that it had gone; yet I was thinking that probably the other birds would destroy it. It would perish on the claws of the less brightly coloured bird-crowd.

We turned away. Joan resumed reading her book. (Those final days in Swiss Cottage, Joan always seemed to be reading *The Journals of André Gide*.) Ten minutes later, eerily, the bird returned to the identical place. The window banged gently and then we saw its body and long tail flattened and glued on the glass. I do not know why I felt so uneasy, why this incident seemed so full of significance. The bird gnawed at the strip of lead, turning its head in jerky movements to stare deliberately into the room. When I moved to the curtains and pulled the red curtains a fraction, it flew off at once. It disappeared into the same tree. I stood at the window for a long time. Other birds, sparrows, blackbirds, thrushes, flew in and out of the branches but I could not discern the over-sized budgerigar – if it was a budgerigar – against the green, slightly trembling leaves. I did not see it again though I must have delayed at that window for half an hour or more.

In November, as arranged, we moved to Hodford Road. Golders Green was, with the wind behind you, only a ten-minute walk from Hampstead. Our neighbours were always quick to point that out; yet

I have never heard anybody in Hampstead saying, 'We are quite close to Golders Green.' That is because Hampstead is an altogether more desirable and charming place to live in. It owns a respectable literary tradition. Golders Green, in comparison, is positively non-U where people say 'toilet' instead of 'lav', 'serviette' for 'napkin', 'sweet' for 'pudding', 'mirror' for 'looking glass' and, as John Betjeman has put it, 'switch on the logs in the grate'. *The Tatler*, finely aware of such social distinctions, photographed my neighbour, Dan Jacobson, the novelist, and the caption read *The Author in his Hampstead home.* Doubtless readers of *The Tatler* were sensitively aware of T. S. Eliot's lines:

> The red-eyed scavengers are creeping
> From Kentish Town and Golder's Green.

No wonder I soon began to reply to friendly inquiries of 'Where do you live?' defensively. Golders Green, even to those who live in it, is not only a place but a state of mind – a mind suburban, respectable, conformist. I came to discover that Golders Green did not consist only of quiet roads of semi-detached houses with wine-coloured rooftops, visible between spreading green leaves fussed by a gentle wind. A place is compounded of the people who live in it and it was a mere coincidence that the cherry blossom trees of Golders Green happened to be the same colour as the *Financial Times*.

After living in Golders Green for six months I knew that thousands of its inhabitants were, fortunately, raving mad. I began to feel at home there. In Hodford Road there lived one brilliant eccentric who, at midnight, crawled on all fours in his garden looking for slugs with a torch. Another neighbour with cotton wool in his ears I swear shouted 'Shush' at the woodworm, as sensitive to noise as Mrs Blumenfeld had been. Most of my neighbours I soon decided had gone mad with too much prose, too many shoeshops, too much central heating, too much TV, too much salt beef.

When I first moved from NW3 to NW11 I did not realise I was moving from relative sanity to relative insanity. I knew many Jews chose to live in Golders Green and that was fine; but I hardly expected a fifteen-minute walk (the wind against you) to make all that difference. After all there were striking bearded men in both places, though beards in 1957 were out of fashion. Artistic young men in corduroys wore them in Hampstead; black-coated schnorrers and orthodox rabbis in Golders Green. There were pretty girl students to ogle in Hampstead; pretty 'au pairs' in Golders Green. In Hampstead a bookshop, in Golders Green W. H. Smith's. In Hampstead the fair, in Golders Green the crematorium.

I discovered that my next-door neighbour was no other than the famous comedian, Bob Monkhouse. This was splendid. For I learnt that people in Hodford Road, Golders Green, did not need numbers on their houses. They lived 'five doors away from Bob Monkhouse' or 'three doors away from him'. The nearer to Bob Monkhouse, the higher one's social status. Strangers would occasionally stop me as I left the house, saying, 'Did you watch Bob on the TV last night?' or 'Did you read in the paper that Bob judged a beauty competition?' When Bob moved to St John's Wood I feared the price of our house would plunge. I need not have worried. People said instead, 'Don't you live next door to where Bob Monkhouse used to live?'

Despite my sudden fame as Bob Monkhouse's next-door neighbour my routine hardly changed. I wrote at home as before and continued with the diagnostic chest work at the clinic. I still played the fool with my children, assuming that gluey voice adults use when addressing the youthful dwarfs of our species: 'This little piggy went to market, this little piggy', etc. and tickled them to make *me* laugh. I played tennis regularly with Peter Vansittart and hardly ever shouted 'Out' when it was 'In'. I played chess with my philosopher friend from LSE, John Watkins, and swallowed hard, wearing that blank loser's smile, whenever he gloated, 'Checkmate.' On occasions, too, I would travel by train the 150 miles that took me to the rain the other side of the Severn Tunnel so that I could see my parents and relatives in Cardiff. One aunt of mine told me all the disasters. 'It's been a really bad year,' she said gloomily. 'So many deaths.' I looked puzzled. 'Kay Kendall,' she continued, 'Victor Maclaglen, Paul Douglas, Gerard Philippe, Margaret Sullavan, Errol Flynn.'

'Joan says I look a bit like Gerard Philippe used to look,' I said gamely.

'No resemblance whatsoever,' my aunt said. 'You should be so lucky. Ye-es it's been a bad year. Mind you, the year before was bad too. Ronald Colman dropped dead.'

'I knew Ronald Colman when I was a young girl in Ystalyfera,' my mother interrupted.

'Ronald Colman,' repeated my aunt relentlessly, announcing the register of the dead. 'Oliver Hardy, Michael Todd.'

'A Jewish boy,' my mother once again interjected.

My mother would show me airmail letters from Wilfred and Huldah who now lived in the USA. Afterwards, after feeding me with her *knaidlach* soup she would ask me my news. I told her about Joan and her grandchildren. Also I mentioned that I had passed my driving test. I was proud of that. I had learnt to drive in only three weeks. That was something to boast about. (True, I had driven a jeep around years before in Northern Ireland when I had been in the RAF).

'What's that?' my mother said, trying to give me more *knaidlach* soup.

'I said I passed my driving test, mother.'

'How long did it take you to learn?'

'Three weeks,' I said, pushing out my chest for a medal.

'Never mind, son, lots of people take a long time,' my mother said, consoling me.

Then she told me about Leo who had been adopted as a prospective candidate for a safe Welsh Labour seat. My driving capabilities could hardly compete with that.

A month or so later, in early December, after visiting Joan in Westminster Hospital where our son, David, had recently been born I walked over to the House of Commons to greet the new MP for Pontypool. He was dressed informally in a polo-necked jersey and a suede jacket. He looked very youthful and did not resemble a respectable Member of Parliament.

'How's my brother, the MP?' I said.

'At forty every man should start life anew,' he grinned.

He led me to the deserted medieval Westminster Hall, telling me the pertinent guide-book facts about it. We looked up at the large-scale hammerbeam roof. The timbers were massive. Then, in that cool ancient building of stone and wood and echoes beyond hearing, phantoms unseen, we heard a most tangible, solemn noise. Big Ben struck nine times.

'Hearing Big Ben like that,' Leo commented afterwards, 'you know that was an ambition of mine, ever since I've been a little boy, to stand here as an MP in the Palace of Westminster and hear Big Ben strike the hour.'

He spoke so quietly, so gravely, that I felt moved. I hesitated. 'No further ambitions?' I asked eventually. 'No interest in becoming a Minister one day?'

'No,' he said, sincerely. 'As a backbencher one may be able to do a little, change the laws of the land a little. Not much, one cannot do much. But one can try. Being an MP, that's enough. I've achieved my ambition.'

I could not help but wonder, as our footsteps followed us out of that stony hall, how Leo would make out as a Member of Parliament. He could be a charismatic orator, he had an alert, tenacious mind, a smoking energy and a deeply logical organising ability – but with too much ease he gathered to himself enemies. For he would clown and be irreverent; worse he had an obsessive habit of analysing people and events, at the drop of an eyelid, with a Freudian yardstick. In being loudly vocal about this Cabinet Minister's anal sadistic tendencies or that backbencher's helluva Oedipus complex, he would be sure to offend.

Outside the House of Commons I mumbled, 'Well, I had better get back to Golders Green,' and this immediately prompted him, reflexly almost, to say gruffly, 'Haven't you any sense of architecture at all? Why do you choose such an uninteresting place to settle in? It's a suburban wilderness.' He relented. 'Mother and Father, at least, are glad you're living in an area where you can so easily buy *The Jewish Chronicle*.' He laughed.

He was right about Golders Green having a large Jewish population. It was not, though, as he extravagantly made out, a ghetto with all mod. cons. On the other hand, years later, Keren, at the local school, because of the preponderance of Jewish classmates, did momentarily believe that the Jews in Britain were in a majority. And once Susanna came home from school to ask me, 'Dad, who is Leonardo de Vinsky?' I did not argue with Leo. It was not the occasion for one of our common fraternal disputations. Our quarrels about politics or aesthetics, however passionately grounded, nearly always deteriorated to mere logomachy. Leo walked me to the top of Whitehall. Then we said, 'Goodbye'. He turned back to the Palace of Westminster and I took the return journey to my semi-detached house in Golders Green.

25. For Love and Money

In her office near St Martin's Lane, Peggy Ramsay, the drama agent, sat on a table, her skirt characteristically creeping up to mid-thigh level. 'Mr Abse,' she said to me, 'you come into my office a duck. One day you will leave here a swan.' She seemed quite emphatic about my future metamorphosis. My play, *House of Cowards*, had been produced at the Questors Theatre in Ealing and had won the Charles Henry Foyle Award for 1960. When Donald Albery bought an option on my play I had daydreams of a West End production.

It would be nice if some money came our way. It would be useful to own a car, sensible to buy the freehold of our house in Golders Green from the Church of England. My medical job was a limited one: it had the advantage of giving me time to write but I could not save any cash as a result of it. Alas, Albery let the option on *House of Cowards* lapse after a year and it was not produced again until January 1963 – and then that was at, of all places, The Prince of Wales Theatre, Cardiff!

Standing in St Mary's Street, I looked up at the Father Christmas-red advertisement plastered on the billboards of the theatre:

THE WELSH THEATRE COMPANY PRESENTS

HOUSE OF COWARDS

BY DANNIE ABSE.

It was marvellous. They had even spelt my name correctly. There was but one snag. The winter of 1963 was the coldest for centuries and January was the coldest month of that winter. A rapier arctic wind howled down St Mary's Street without ceasing and few pedestrians threaded their way between the ruined igloos on the pavements. Any human being obliged to pass The Prince of Wales Theatre kept his head down as the refrigerated wind howled around the corner towards Westgate Street. So nobody gazed up at those beautiful posters which bore my name so conspicuously. 'Hey,' I wanted to shout. 'Hey, look up there, fellers. That's me, folks.'

It was a pity that the old heating system inside the theatre had broken down, that both actors and audience had to risk frost-bite. For by some arcane reason of thermodynamics it was actually colder inside the theatre than outside in St Mary's Street. My father, quite rightly, because of his chronic, wheezing bronchitis and increasingly troublesome emphysema, never ventured out of the house at all that January. Each night he would ask me in his best ex-cinema proprietor voice, 'Good house tonight, son?' Warren Jenkins, the director, tried to cheer me up about the sparse audiences. 'It was even worse for our last production, *The Glass Menagerie*,' he said. It was true I had more relations in Cardiff than Tennessee Williams – but given the weather Pontypridd Williams would have fared no better. More people sent me warm telegrams than actually braved the cold nights.

House of Cowards never had a further professional production following that Cardiff freeze-out. Plays I wrote later were mostly produced at non-commercial theatres in England or abroad. True, TV companies wanted to commission me to write plays but I was not keen. I would never even produce a bit of a synopsis. I preferred to earn any extra money by writing para-medical features for a national Sunday newspaper (using a pseudonym). No wonder Peggy Ramsay eventually became impatient with me and began all her conversations with 'Robert Bolt said . . .' All very sad; and as a result I cannot claim to be the second swan of the Avon or, come to that, the duck of the Taff.

Writing the occasional para-medical feature was altogether more lucrative. There were other rewards too. For instance, because of these journalistic features I have journeyed to places I would not otherwise have visited and interviewed people I would otherwise not have met: Professor Paul Niehans of Vevey and Dr Ana Aslan at Bucharest, for instance. Both these doctors had claimed that they had discovered a rejuvenating agent and thus could issue the aged with a passport to Shangri-la. So I went first to Vevey and later to Bucharest.

'Four million *Sunday Express* readers want to know what I think about the matter,' I said to Joan.

Both rejuvenating doctors had treated some very famous, pampered people. Professor Niehans had given injections of fresh embryo cells (taken from the newly killed foetus of a ewe) to such ageing celebrities as Pope Pius XII, Dr Adenauer, King Ibn Saud, Somerset Maugham, Georges Braque, Furtwangler, and Gloria Swanson. But

Noël Coward watching it all from his Swiss home had commented, 'Kings and Prime Ministers notwithstanding, the Professor's patients, judging from the look of those that enter his clinic, are decidedly non-ewe.'

Niehans claimed that fresh embryo animal heart cells could revitalise a failing human heart, fresh foetal liver cells could stimulate a worn-out human liver, fresh foetal brain cells could reactivate an ageing brain, and so on. His theories had no scientific rationale. Hence I left Heathrow airport for Geneva profoundly sceptical to say the least. I recalled, during my flight, that when the young, dazzling Abishag lay down on old King David's bosom because 'he gat no heat', though she cherished the King, and ministered to him, King David knew her not. Could Niehans' clinical cellular therapy succeed where the rejuvenating treatment of the fairest damsel of Israel had failed? I doubted it.

Arthur, the *Express* Geneva correspondent, met me at the airport. He was most tastefully dressed in a grey suit and tactful soft moss-coloured tie. I felt disadvantaged in my Harris tweed coat, tieless sweater shirt, old slacks. Of course in my Marks and Spencer grip I had packed a clean shirt *and* a tie – but I could hardly boast about that. In his much-polished or rather burnished car I tried not to breathe out dirty bacteria. Arthur asked me if I knew Wystan and Stephen who had been his contemporaries at Oxford. Soon we arrived at a new, luxurious hotel, higher up the hillside than the Palais des Nations, that is to say, splendidly aloft distant Lake Geneva.

'I've booked you in here,' Arthur said. 'Tomorrow, early, I'll drive you out to Vevey. We have an appointment at 10 a.m. at his mansion which is near his Clinique Générale La Prairie.'

I walked with stamping ataxia over the too-thick foyer carpet and overheard someone ask in ventriloquist English, 'Have you come here for the Esperanto conference?'

They would not admit me to the dining room without a tie. It did not matter: I did not feel at ease in that ambience. I felt like Prufrock. The house detectives surely were watching my every move. What a role! Here I was booked into a hotel that had so many stars it outshone the American flag. Also drinks were free, food was free. I merely had to sign my name; and the *Express*, generously, had also provided me with about £80 for petty cash expenses. True, I had to account for the spending of it. On the other hand they expected me to be inventive about such matters. 'Taxi!' I shouted. 'Cab!' I made many friends that night in a bar in the picturesque old section of Geneva; nor would my new friends allow me to pay for *every* drink.

Next morning, after a rushed breakfast, Arthur hustled me, aspirined, into his waiting limousine. We drove through the precision of clear-cut, Swiss March sunshine. Soon Arthur reminded me I was not on holiday. 'Niehans,' he said, 'is now eighty-one years of age. Sprightly, I'm told, having given himself his own treatment. Do you know he is the great nephew of Kaiser Wilhelm II?'

'Yes,' I said.

'Generally he doesn't give interviews. It's only because you're a doctor that he's said yes this time.'

'I've looked up the cuttings in the *Express* library,' I said. 'He's given several interviews before.'

'Not for some time,' insisted Arthur.

I gazed out of the car window at the calm lake, at the snow-capped mountains towering above and behind the lake, at the adagio clouds and blue sky above the mountains. It was too beautiful. It was so beautiful it seemed a fake.

At five minutes past ten we parked outside Professor Niehans' large house in Burier-Vevey. Arthur, evidently a punctual man, seemed agitated that we were late. 'You sit here,' he commanded me. He intended to knock on the door and announce my arrival to Niehans, thus upgrading my importance. He knocked on the door. No one replied. He rang the bell. Still no one responded. He thumped the door. Silence. He leaned on the bell. It was now ten past ten and the doors remained adamantly closed. All the windows in the house were shuttered. 'Maybe Professor Niehans has died,' I thought. Arthur disappeared round the side of the house. Several minutes later he came back into sight and shrugged his shoulders at me, almost a Yiddish shrug. Again he approached the main door and hammered on it. When he returned to the car he looked pensive, even worried. It was twenty past ten.

'Maybe he's at the clinic,' Arthur said flatly, without conviction.

The doors of the Clinique Générale La Prairie at least were not locked. We stood in the foyer. A nurse appeared and, simultaneously, upstairs, we heard the heartbreaking cry of a child.

At once I felt aggressive towards Niehans. Unorthodox doctors using his cell therapy had claimed that mongoloids under five years of age had responded astonishingly to injections of foetal brain cells. I did not believe these extravagant claims. I also knew how desperate mothers of such children could become and how their natural yearnings for a miracle prompted them to try any outlandish therapy however expensive.

The nurse, puzzled when Arthur told her we had received no reply at the house, telephoned Niehans. Subsequently she informed us in French, 'The Professor has been expecting you since ten o'clock. If you proceed immediately to his home he will receive you.'

As we drove back to Niehans' house Arthur said, 'After I've dropped you off I'll get myself a coffee and return at twelve. So any time after that you will find me waiting for you. You'll be through by one o'clock, do you think?'

But at Professor Niehans' home again we received no reply to our constant knockings and bellringings. Arthur became angry. 'This is bloody ridiculous,' he said, hammering at the front door.

'Perhaps you have the wrong place?' I said, inspired.

Just then we heard a movement from within, a distant door close, a faint suggestion of footsteps, a shadow against the glass, bolts were drawn back and the heavy door pulled inwards at last to present a gloomy, scrupulous-looking woman who said, staring into the distance beyond us, 'The Professor is now ready to receive you.' At exactly eleven o'clock (no grandfather Swiss clock chimed within) a tall, elderly but still athletic gentleman approached us, his hand outstretched towards Arthur. 'Dr Abse?' he said.

Once more I decided Arthur was too well dressed. I touched the knot in my tie while, embarrassed, Arthur said, '*This* is Dr Abse,' presenting me like a magician out of a top hat. I forced myself not to say, 'Ye-es, I am Dr Abse.' Niehans unsmilingly aimed his arm in slow motion towards me. We shook hands. 'Come in,' the Professor said. Arthur winked and the door closed, leaving him stranded outside in the drive. I followed the Professor through dark, spacious, shuttered rooms until we came to his study. The voluminous rooms, the study, all yielded a sense of elegance without laughter.

'Please sit down,' Professor Niehans said rather harshly.

I turned towards the window. Below, the lake should have posed for us but it was hardly visible because of a honey mist of wet sunlight. Looming upwards, further behind, breathlessly perfect, unreal as a stage backcloth, again I saw the snow-capped mountains merging now into the clouds. In that dream landscape it was impossible to tell where the snow peaks ended and where the brilliant, silver-edged clouds began.

'You have a splendid view,' I said to the Professor.

'Indeed,' he said. Then with a remarkable rhetorical flourish he embarked on what surely must have been a prepared speech. 'The Creator has placed a magnificent power in the fresh foetal cell – and if one thousand injections do not guarantee one thousand cures, we can nevertheless ameliorate certain conditions at present incurable in a number of patients.'

I realised the interview had begun and I reached for my pen to make notes. Almost at once Professor Niehans said, 'Excuse me. I won't be a moment.' He quit the study.

I sat with pen in hand staring at a signed portrait of Pope Pius XII on the wall and musing that Niehans, for a man in his ninth decade, appeared vigorous, agile, even military. Such a straight back. If I straightened my back like that I would be two inches taller, surely? I sneaked a glance at the scores of littered airmail letters on the desk. Obviously people wrote to him from all over the world. So many people wanted a package tour to Shangri-la. Near a small delicate table I espied a fancy scimitar, no doubt a gift from Ibn Saud or some other Arab potentate. Leo would like that on his wall, I thought. His wife, Marjorie, would have loved it, the bejewelled handle, the exotic elegance. That would be something to take into the House of Commons on Budget Day.

By the time I had finished a cigarette and squashed out the dibby in what I *hoped* was an ashtray I had become anxious about the Professor. *Where the devil was he?* I opened the study door and listened. The house listened to me listening.

At half past eleven he still had not returned and desperately I quit the study and walked over the hushed carpets of the shuttered rooms that led to the hall. There I gazed at the ascending staircase. Where was the woman whose aspect had been that of one listening to a perpetual sermon? Where was she? Where was the Professor? I did not dare practise a Swiss yodel in that great empty furnished silence. A cough was the pathetic best I could do. Then I decided to go out through the front door and knock on it, and ring the bell loud and clear. That would be best, I determined. Dismayed, I discovered the front door to be locked. Did I then hear something clatter faintly? I scampered back to the study thinking that the Professor might have arrived there from a different direction. The study was empty. 'Fuck it,' I said quietly to the Pope. Once again I trod my way to the hall. It was almost quarter to twelve. Fortunately, as I gazed blankly through the window, I saw Arthur's car progressing up the gravel driveway. He had returned early. Arthur waved to me. I urgently signalled to him. Some minutes later we had a lip-reading conversation through the glass pane and Arthur, baffled, rang the front door bell forcefully as I instructed him to do. Arthur's banging rose to an embarrassing pitch and the lady of the sermon aspect at last materialised.

I explained to her that the Professor had dropped through some invisible trapdoor and please could I see him? 'He's on his way to you. If you return to the study,' she said tersely, 'he will be with you in five minutes.' Arthur said he would wait in the car and I, pondering, returned to the study.

When Niehans entered some minutes later he murmured a minimal apology for keeping me waiting. He offered no explanation for his prolonged absence. Instead he talked to me about his fresh foetal cell therapy. I was not impressed by his soliloquy. He was an ex-surgeon but his remarks, medically speaking, were bizarre or did not make scientific sense. His knowledge of endocrinology seemed limited and vague. Had his memory holes in it? He talked all the while with religious fervour and, sometimes, disturbingly, referred to himself in the third person.

'Niehans is a revolutionary,' he said, 'and revolutionaries in medicine have much opposition. That is why I kept my discoveries secret for twenty years. I gave three thousand injections before I released information about what I was doing. Niehans had to be absolutely sure.'

He turned away from me and gazed through the window. 'I have been working lately on diabetes,' he said quietly. 'I hope to publish my results soon and then, heavens, there will be another terrible storm. They will cry out against me again.'

'The American Medical Association and other orthodox bodies have rejected your rejuvenating treatment,' I said as benignly as possible.

'There are many people against Niehans,' the Professor said severely. 'They tried to take my clinic away from me. They have succeeded now in barring me from the slaughterhouse in Clarens where I have procured the foetal cells from the embryos of ewes.'

'Who are *they*, Professor?' I asked.

'I do not know,' he said smiling conspiratorially – as if he knew perfectly well the identity of these mephitic, anonymous figures. He added, 'Do not forget, doctor, many drug houses would lose money if my fresh foetal cell therapy was universally adopted. Many drugs would be superseded by my therapy.'

It was time to go. Professor Paul Niehans presented me with a book of scientific papers by his disciples. He signed it for me grandiosely: *Niehans*. We were standing up and I must have been facing the photograph of Pope Pius XII. 'He was a beautiful patient,' Professor Niehans remarked. 'Of all the people I have treated none were so wise, none so learned, none so interested in science as Pope Pius. I had a great esteem for him. He was not only a man. He was a saint.'

I knew that those close to the Pope credited Niehans with the last vigorous five years of the old Pope's life. Even on his death-bed, in October 1958, the Pope had whispered to the German nun, Pasqualina, 'Send for Niehans.' But as I told Arthur on our journey back to Geneva, I had altogether less faith in the Professor.

'You're prejudiced,' Arthur said, 'because of your orthodox training.'

'We all have yearnings to find the god-like personage of our childhood,' I argued. 'Someone wise and omnipotent. These yearnings are activated when we are ill and dependent. If the official doctor, full of doubts in his white coat, has nothing to offer us from his materia medica, no wonder some turn to the self-confident medicaster with his wand and purple cloak.'

Arthur and I had a farewell drink at the posh hotel. Then we shook hands. I never met him again. That night I decided to return to the same bar in old Geneva. 'Cab,' I shouted. It was my last night in the role of roving correspondent. Next day the plane sped back to London where I became myself, comfortably myself again. 'This house is a hole,' I told Joan, 'compared with the standard of comfort I'm used to.'

A few months later I prepared to travel to Rumania, and felt half excited and half worried at the prospect. I have always suffered from a degree of anomic anxiety when I quit familiar surroundings. I persuade myself that I like being in strange, even exotic, places and that it is simply the travelling that I abhor. As a child, to be sure, I loathed moving even from one Cardiff house to another. From Albany Street to Sandringham Road seemed an excursion of fearful proportions such as the Israelites must have experienced when Moses led them across the wilderness. 'I'm happy in this place,' I would tell my parents hopefully. 'What do you want to move for?' My mother had told me wrongly that Wales ended at that bridge in Newport Road. To the east of that bridge I believed lay chaos, darkness, wolves, danger. And to the west, at least west of Ogmore, why, dragons roamed the country, dangerous dragons and Ammanford relatives. No, I did not want to go too far from my home patch.

There was not even a decent flight to Bucharest. I had to pick up a Rumanian plane at Prague. 'How am I going to understand them telling me in Czechoslovakian, or whatever they speak, that I am to board the plane at Gate Z,' I complained to Joan, 'when I can't even understand the English that is spoken over the tannoy at White Hart Lane?'

The Rumanian plane looked relatively airworthy; the nuts and bolts appeared to be firmly in place. 'This is the right aircraft for Bucharest?' I asked the air hostess twice whose French, unlike mine, was perfect. '*Pour Bucharest . . . oui?*' I also asked the passenger next to me (just in case) who turned out to be a bulky, crew-cut East German. He looked bugged. It was night – dark, anonymous night – next to the window, and I could have been flying from anywhere to anywhere. Later, on the left, as the plane descended, we could see the lights of Bucharest. The noise of the engines changed its tune and the usual signs illuminated: FASTEN YOUR SEAT BELTS and NO SMOKING – in English, I noted, surprised. Most of the passengers ignored these instructions. On the contrary, despite the Captain's announcement over the tannoy, presumably endorsing the illuminated commands, they stood up, speaking in excited Rumanian, pointing out Bucharest reeling below, or heaving their luggage from the racks as the plane banked alarmingly. The German next to me began muttering. Finally, he could stand it no longer, screaming at me in English, '*No deescipline. No deescipline,*' pointing at the Latin Rumanians in the gangway. I half cocked my head, a non-committal gesture, halfway between Yes and No.

At Bucharest airport, Dr Aslan's male secretary (who had been educated at Birmingham University) took charge of me and with magical Rumanian passwords transported me from the back of the queue to the front and through the barrier.

'Is that *all* your luggage?' he asked, and again I felt deficient. Soon after, we strode through the doors of the Lido Hotel and a porter with such large teeth that he looked as if he had just eaten Red Riding Hood relieved me of my grip. Hurriedly Dr Aslan's secretary said, 'I'll call for you tomorrow morning and take you directly to Dr Aslan at her clinic.' Upstairs in the hotel I unpacked in a pleasant ample room which featured a *triple* bed. I gazed at the three pillows lying next to each other and wondered whether one was for the photographer. Some friends in London, including a busy PEN figure, had given me the names of some official Rumanian writers. I also had the address of an 'underground' Jewish Rumanian novelist who had recently been released from jail.

Having nothing better to do I sought him out and soon we were walking through Bucharest streets together. In his stiff English he told me, 'Rumania has changed. Things are better now.' He also gave me inklings of his horrific jail experiences. When we spoke of the assassination of Kennedy the previous autumn, he was confident, as other Rumanians were to whom I spoke later, that President Johnson had been the direct instigator of that murder.

My new friend was very earnest, indeed humourless, and after an hour and a half I thought perhaps I would retire to the hotel. 'I should ring X,' I lied, naming one of the official writers' names that I had been given.

'What!' he said with disgust. 'Your choice is clear. Either you spend the evening and have dinner with me or you telephone X who will provide you with two or three beautiful young girls.' I had dinner with him, of course.

He led me to a 'student' restaurant. As we crossed the very wide boulevards of Bucharest he appeared to be surprised when I hung back to let a car go by. (The traffic was relatively sparse.) 'Don't worry,' he said seriously. 'If a car knocked you down the driver would go to jail.' He was not joking. He did not joke, it would appear, ever. At the restaurant I enjoyed the food until I asked him what I was eating. 'Pigs' testicles,' he told me. A fine Jewish boy, I thought. When we quit the restaurant I said, 'Hello' to the man who had been following me since I had left the Lido Hotel. He seemed surprised. It was not the done thing.

Next day I interviewed Dr Ana Aslan who had treated not only the usual seekers after lost youth – Adenauer, Ibn Saud, etc. – but also (or so it was reported) Mao Tse-Tung and Nikita Krushchev. In 1959 Professor Aslan had been officially invited to Britain by Lord Amulree, president of the Medical Society for the Care of the Elderly. The drug that Dr Aslan used was called H3 which she maintained could reverse hardening of the arteries, improve the impaired hearing of premature senility, loosen old arthritic joints, make wrinkled skin smooth again and even repigment white hair. She presented her clinical reports to the startled British doctors. With lantern slides she demonstrated how her patients had looked before and after she had given them H3.

The orthodox medical response was summed up by a leader in the *British Medical Journal* at the time: 'A study of the clinical reports makes sad reading for the clinician trained in scientific method. There is an almost complete absence of controls, and blind trials were never used. At the Apothecaries' Hall last week, Professor Aslan created a most favourable personal impression as a woman gifted with humour, charm, enthusiasm, and boundless therapeutic optimism . . .'

After Dr Aslan returned to Rumania some British doctors carried out trials with a form of H3 on geriatric patients. These trials were a total failure. But when I interviewed her at the Institute of Geriatrics in Bucharest of which she was head, she argued that the British doctors had not carried out real trials.

'First they selected desperate cases,' she insisted, 'whose life expectancy was no longer than one year. Second, they only gave two injections a week instead of three. Third, they did not treat the patients over a long enough period. Fourth, they did not give H3 – they gave procaine injections. So that is why they had poor results.'

'But isn't H3 nothing more than the local anaesthetic, procaine?' I asked her.

'We have potassium in our solution,' Professor Aslan replied. 'This potentiates the action of procaine. With procaine solution such as you used in England I would only expect to get a 25 per cent success. With H3 I obtain a 60 per cent success.'

In her clinic she introduced me to many of her old patients. A number of them, I was told, were over 100. One of these I shall never forget; after shaking hands with him my fingers were crushed white by his strong Samson grip. That he had a formidable handshake was indisputable. That he was vigorous could not be denied. That he had a peculiar sense of humour was evident. But whether this was all a result of H3 I do not know. Professor Aslan pointed to another old person with raven hair. 'You have heard of people going white,' she said, 'but have you ever known of a white-haired man go black?'

Before I left Bucharest I saw once more the 'underground' Rumanian-Jewish writer and we discussed Dr Aslan. I told him that I thought she was sincere but misguided. What I could not understand was why she received the backing of the official Rumanian Medical Association.

'Ah,' explained my friend. 'Don't you realise that foreigners come to Bucharest specifically to see Dr Aslan? They stay in her clinic, they pay money. Rumania needs foreign currency. So she has official sanction. The Medical Association is not free of politics. The ends justify the means. You will give her publicity. You are a most welcome guest.'

'Yes,' I said, nodding at the same fellow who was again clumsily following me, 'but I am under constant surveillance.'

'Of course,' said my friend.

'Aren't you worried? Isn't it dangerous just talking to me – a representative of the capitalist Press?'

'Things are better now,' he said vaguely.

I returned to London with a whole box of H3 that Dr Aslan had given me. I did not use them on anybody, not even myself. Now Abishag would have been another matter.

26. Poetry Readings and All That Jazz

The first real poetry reading I gave was at the Ethical Church, Bayswater, a venue, in the immediate post-war years, for regular evenings of Poetry and Music. The week before my reading the audience had been electrified by balding Roy Campbell who, drunk, staggered towards the rostrum where Stephen Spender was reciting, 'I think continually of those who were truly great.' He gently pushed Spender on the chest. After that clumsy violation Mr Campbell was led away by two earnest young men as he protested nonsensically, 'But I've been flirtin' with him in the bar.' Mr Spender, meanwhile, stood tall and goodlooking and tortured with an unlit cigarette in his mouth, stood there like Murder in the Cathedral before continuing his interrupted, but dignified reading.

My own reading fortunately did not provoke such overt aggression. True, one spreading lady in the front row kept on yawning throughout but I did my best to ignore her; and when she moaned censoriously to her startled neighbour, 'I could have been at the Pushkin Society tonight,' no usher led her away to the stocks.

Most poetry readings used to be deadly dull. Until the 1960s too many poets mumbled or read at 100 m.p.h. or chose poems entirely unsuitable for public recital. No wonder, so often, the audience suffered on those Windsor chairs, crossing and uncrossing their legs, occasionally coughing and glancing at the clock. In more recent years, poets have become more practised in presenting their poetry out loud and it is possible to enjoy a poetry reading.

After such readings are concluded, as a result of a keen chairman's prompting, the poet may well be asked scattered questions. Don't you think modern poetry is needlessly obscure? (This from someone devoted to the 'tis, 'twas, myriad, womb diction of yesteryear.) Shouldn't poets be more committed? How do you write a poem? When the questions are less predictable the poet is forced to make new clarifications for himself. Too frequently the questions have been posed a hundred times before and he merely restates his own, by now stale, definitions.

Certainly I find myself often replying, 'I do not know how to write a poem. If I did, I would be able to write one at will. But I can't. I can't be commissioned to write a poem. Poetry is written in the brain but the brain is bathed in blood. At best I can tell you how once I wrote that or this poem – the genesis always being different, and the procedure never quite the same.' Or, 'I do not think modern poetry is any more obscure than poetry written centuries ago. I know I try to write poems that *appear* clear, that are in fact deceptions, that a reader can enter and believe at first he can see through – until once inside these apparent translucencies he finds that something below is arcane and he cannot quite touch bottom.'

The chairman then winds up the evening with one or two announcements and perhaps utters a brief vote of thanks. 'I have heard,' the chairman might well say with the knowledge of an insider, 'that after a recent poetry reading given by Dr Abse in South Wales a vote of thanks was proffered by a certain Mr Jones who referred to our guest-poet here tonight as Dr Abs. Afterwards, Mr Jones asked if his vote of thanks was OK. Fine, came the answer, but in future, Mr Jones, do please call me Abse. Oh, that's very nice of you, boyo, said Mr Jones, and in future why don't you call me Jonesy . . .'

In February 1961, I became involved in the Poetry and Jazz

concerts that were to take place regularly in Britain during the rest of the decade. A young man called Jeremy Robson telephoned and kindly invited me to read at the Hampstead Town Hall with Jon Silkin and Boris Pasternak's sister, Lydia Slater, who would be reading translations of her brother's poems. He did not mention to me anything about Jazz. And I am sure he did not remark the name Spike Milligan.

I set out for Hampstead Town Hall not expecting a particularly large audience. So when I saw in the distance an extraordinary long queue stretching between the Odeon and the Town Hall I briefly wondered what popular film was being shown that night in the cinema. Then I observed the queue was facing the wrong way. When I struggled through the crowds on the steps of the Town Hall a man tried to close the doors as he barked irritably, 'Full up.' By the time I managed to enter the Town Hall that first Poetry and Jazz concert had commenced and I was startled to hear Spike Milligan saying, 'I thought I would begin by reading you some sonnets of Shakespeare – but then I thought, Why should I? He never reads any of mine.' Afterwards, the jazz, blaring, raucous, too near.

Jeremy Robson, who later became a valued friend, organised hundreds of concerts over the next six years, at Town Halls, at theatres, for Arnold Wesker's Centre 42, for city councils and Arts councils, inviting different poets to participate. I read at a number of these concerts though never with a jazz backing. I always arrived, it seems to me now, in one or another provincial city at lighting-up time when every town resembled each other. Later, I would hear from back stage, as I nervously awaited my turn to go on, the sudden explosion of the distant audience laughing or applauding. And, eventually, after all the beer, the winding-down, the backchat, the almost obligatory Indian meal, we would journey homeward, as often as not down the rainblown M1. In the early hours of the morning I would be dropped off in abandoned Golders Green Road where the orange belishas continued to blink, though no one else was in sight, and the wind blew damp pavements under the bridge. 'Goodbye, see you,' to Douglas Hill or Vernon Scannell or whoever it was, and a car, changing gear, would then progress further into London.

I recall many of the poems read and the jazz played. I also recall Stevie Smith throwing her book at a persistent photographer while she continued to sing (out of tune as usual) one of her dirge-like poems; John Heath-Stubbs, tall and blind, gradually turning around as he read each consecutive poem so that, finally, he had his back to a very quiet, tense audience; Thomas Blackburn breaking off in the middle of a poem suddenly to deliver a fierce anti-religious sermon to a startled clergyman who happened to be sitting in the front row.★

One Friday night we were to give a concert, sponsored by the Welsh Arts Council, at the King's Hall, Aberystwyth. Ten minutes before it was due to start I sat in the pub across the road from the King's Hall with Joe Hariott, that fine West Indian alto-saxophone player. The radio was on. 'I think I'll have another Scotch,' said Joe to an admirer. 'After all I may not pass this way again.' Not far away the waves were flinging themselves on to the Aberystwyth promenade with an autumn harshness and inland, near a gasometer, hundreds of white seagulls had settled on an empty, green football pitch. Joe's admirer was talking about other jazzmen and I heard Joe say, 'Parker? There's them over here that can play a few aces too.' Then we abruptly became aware that the volume of the radio had increased remarkably. A wild voice said, 'Kennedy, Kennedy, Kennedy. Shot. Assassinated. Dead. Kennedy.'

We quit the pub and crossed the road to the stage-door of the King's Hall. It was half past seven. The manager thought it too late to cancel the concert. He decided that before it began he would announce the death of the President and, following that, there would be a two-minute silence. 'Yes,' said John Smith, one of the poets that

---

★ Tom Blackburn's father had been an irascible, haunted Anglican priest who had savagely beaten his son. Tom, as his daughter, the novelist Julia Blackburn reveals, was also 'a tormented man'. Indeed, he could be, on occasions, difficult to be with. I recall how at a dinner party, accompanied by his chain-smoking second wife, Peggy Maguire (who had a ceaseless, repetitive, tomb-hollow cough), he addressed me after looking across the table at John Malcolm Brinnin and Brinnin's male companion. In an audible hoarse whisper Tom persisted in enquiring, 'Is this Brinnin fellow queer, Dannie? Mmm? Mmm? Is this his boyfriend? Mmm? Mmm? Did you hear me, Dannie? Is this guy a queen, is he? Mmm?'

Tom wrote some most affecting verse which should be better known. He was also one of the best readers of poetry in Britain. I shared a platform with him several times and the audience always responded to his dark-voiced recitations. Following performances his behaviour could be somewhat Dionysian. Once, after we had read together at Southampton University, we were whisked off to a student party. By 2 a.m. Tom had fortunately sobered up but we found ourselves in a room with one narrow bed and a mattress on the floor. 'Toss for the bed,' he said. I won. 'You're not going to take advantage of that are you? Mmm? Mmm?' he complained. 'I'm older than you.' Later, when I lay in the bed, too wide awake, and Tom appeared to be sleeping on the mattress on the other side of the room I happened to cough. In the darkness I heard Tom's commanding voice cry out, 'Quiet Peggy!'

night, 'that would be best.' But somebody stupidly inferred that Kennedy had probably been assassinated by someone in the Black Power movement. Joe Hariott and the trumpet player, Shake Keane, drew together, stood close together talking passionately about something beyond our hearing. We overheard the sense of it only. They suddenly were two black men and we, temporarily, had become white, devoid of the necessary milligrams of melanin.

'If you'll follow me,' the manager was saying to Laurie Lee.

After his announcement we stood on the stage, the jazzmen and the poets, now neither black nor white, facing the hushed audience who had been told 'to please rise as a mark of respect'. The silence stretched into a millimetre of the future, elongated further, and finally snapped with the audience unaccountably clapping and clapping. They were in a theatre. And how do people express emotion in a theatre? They clap.

They clapped all through the concert, they laughed louder than any audience I have ever heard.

'It was the right thing to do, to carry on with the concert, don't you think?' the manager asked us afterwards.

Laurie Lee took the pipe out of his mouth to reply but before he could do so Joe Hariott said, 'Man, the Windmill never closed.'

Unlike us, many Americans were all First Names and Superlatives. It was simply a difference of style. We said Thank you and they said You're welcome. Their generosity so outpaced our own that, occasionally, quite unjustly, we questioned their sincerity or suspiciously picked underneath for ulterior motives. So, much to my discredit, I wondered why John Malcolm Brinnin was putting himself out in a way no British poet would have done. I reminded Joan that Brinnin had been responsible for Dylan Thomas's American tours and that it was ten years – *ten* years since that famous death in New York. Also I was Welsh. Could those two facts, even unconsciously, I asked, have contributed to his kind busyness in arranging an East Coast reading tour for me? The original invitation from the YHMA Poetry Center, where *Under Milk Wood* was performed, had materialised because of Brinnin's active suggestion.

'I doubt it,' Joan said. 'John is being himself – typically decent – generous in a way some Americans are and their European counterparts are not.'

I accepted the invitation. In April 1964 I would go on a three-week poetry-reading tour the other side of the Atlantic where I had never been before. It would be interesting and I would see Huldah in New York, Wilfred at the University of Virginia; renew acquaintance, I hoped, with old friends such as Denise Levertov; meet up again with those American poets whom I had come to know and like from their repeated sojourns in London – Daniel Hoffman, M. L. Rosenthal, Jack Sweeney, and John Brinnin himself.

Alas, John Brinnin became very ill even before I arrived in the USA, and had to be admitted to a Boston hospital for a major operation. Generous as ever he first arranged for friends of his, and therefore often friends of Dylan Thomas also, to look after me.

In the event it seemed to me as if I were ghosting for the ghost of Dylan Thomas. The advertisements announcing events at the Poetry Center billed me as 'Dannie Abse – Welsh Poet'. Soon I was told, 'You look like Dylan Thomas,' which I do not; or 'You write like Dylan Thomas,' which I do not; or 'You read like Dylan Thomas,' which I do not. Once, in New York a stranger said, 'Do you know you resemble Dylan Thomas,' and I replied aggressively, 'You mean I look like an unmade bed?'

'No, no,' he stammered, 'I mean you look like the Dylan Thomas that Alec Guinness is playing currently – in a play called *Dylan*.'

'Really?'

'Alec Guinness wears a wig – a ginger wig.'

'I haven't ginger hair.'

'No,' said the stranger.

I mentioned my being taken for Dylan Thomas to Denise Levertov's husband, Mitch Goodman, who happened to resemble facially the actor, Anthony Quinn. We joked about doppelgangers and I added, 'My mother used to warn me when I was a boy – Don't look into the mirror too long or you will see the devil.' We were walking up Fifth Avenue and Mitch, as if he had been struck, swung me round, his eyes wild, and said with sincere passion, 'Once, once in a lifetime, just once, it is privileged to all to look in the mirror and see someone beautiful, pure, innocent – utterly beautiful.'

In New York, in Boston, in Philadelphia, at various East Coast universities where Dylan Thomas had read over ten years earlier and had become a legend I continued to be asked, 'Did you know *Dai-len*?' I smiled, my smile became fixed like an air hostess's, and with a steady fatigue (because of Greenwich Mean Time in my head), I said 'No, I did not know Dylan,' and refused half the drinks and other proper and improper offers of hospitality. Some people obviously wanted me to behave like Dylan Thomas and perversely I, at once, became nicer than myself, more polite, better behaved.

At the University of Connecticut, at Storrs, I stayed with the Deans who were friends of Brinnin's. I did not know Pete and Dorothy then, I did not admire them as I now do, and I listened neutrally to someone murmuring, 'Dylan Thomas stole shirts from Professor Dean when he stayed with him.' During the usual after-the-reading party, Pete Dean, embarrassed, drew me aside. 'You don't happen to have put one of the students' pens in your pocket by mistake?' he asked. When the reading had finished, some of the students had asked me to sign books and I had borrowed a pen. I thought that I had returned it. Now I searched through my pockets while Pete Dean smiled fretfully. 'No,' I said at last – and blushed because unreasonably I felt guilty, remembering the rumoured shirt-stealing episode. Worse, I added:

> Taffy is a Welshman
> Taffy is a thief
> Taffy came to my house
> And stole a piece of beef.

Blankly Pete Dean stared at the plate I had put down when I had gone through my pockets. Mrs Dean had kindly supplied everybody with a beef supper. Next day he drove me to Boston where I was to stay in John Brinnin's apartment. There Brinnin's mother looked after me and, between readings in the Boston area, I visited John in hospital. He was flat out, in post-operative distress, blood drips, tubes in his arms, was wan, spoke in a whisper. 'Sorry,' he said needlessly.

I told him how the readings had gone; how pleased I had been to meet William Meredith at Connecticut College and X. J. Kennedy at Tufts; how concerned Richard Eberhart and Howard Nemerov had been about his illness. Even as I dispensed this small talk I could not but help recalling John's own account of how he had visited the dying Dylan Thomas – Dylan in hospital, flat out, blood drips, tubes in his arms. In John's apartment, delicately, John's mother had knocked on my door to inquire if I wanted anything. I looked up from the airmail letter I was writing home and she said softly, 'Dylan used to write on that desk.' She turned her head briefly toward the wall where hung a signed photograph of Dylan Thomas. I wanted to say unfairly, harshly, 'No doubt Dylan slept on that bed too.' He had.

When I left the hospital I found myself, almost at once, near the Charles River. My gaze rested on a pigeon's shadow skimming across the water. It seemed as if it were a ghostly double of the pigeon that careered above the river. Then, at the bank, that shadow drowned, became no more, and the real pigeon, alive, wheeled higher and higher to fly over land, on and on.

27. In Llandough Hospital

Sadly, in autumn, the circumstances dire, the patient this time my father. After I returned to London my parents had stayed with us and, in June, had come to a play of mine (*In the Cage*) at The Questors Theatre. Climbing the steps to the foyer of the theatre my father had to rest and wait for his breath. He had become a pulmonary cripple.

His condition deteriorated in late October and he had to be admitted to Llandough Hospital in Cardiff. An X-ray revealed a shadow not present on a film taken six months earlier. With Dr Phillips I examined my father's X-rays on the blazing screens. Shocked I saw that the new shadow near the left hemidiaphragm looked solid and as big as an egg. It would grow bigger and bigger and hatch death.

'Maybe two months, maybe three,' Dr Phillips said quietly.

Nothing radical could be done. In a week's time my father would be seventy-seven. People would think, 'Ah well, he has had a good innings.' To those who love a dying man his age matters not. I went back to the ward, joined Leo, and exchanged banter as usual with my father. Soon after, I returned to London. For the time being Leo would visit him during the week and I would come to Cardiff weekends. But at the chest clinic where I worked, each time a stranger's X-ray was put on the screen, I would compulsively stare first at the left base, at that area just above the left hemidiaphragm.

Weekends I saw my father go down hill; that malignant shadow was growing, growing wild. My father never complained, never asked unanswerable questions. He seemed interested only in my news and in showing me off to a favourite nurse. 'Now this is the son which is the poet.'

'Not the well-dressed one, not the MP,' the nurse said. 'My brother Leo wears my cast-offs,' I told the nurse so that my father should laugh.

In December, my father was moved to a single, private room next to the public ward. Through its window which I was to stare through long and often enough I saw 'the inexhaustible adventure of a gravelled yard'.

'I've cabled Huldah and Wilfred,' Leo told me. 'I think they ought to come now.'

My father had turned a pale yellow, jaundiced, and each day he began to resemble more and more an inmate of some terrible concentration camp. He would be drowsy with drugs and say to me, 'You don't have to stay, son. I'm sure you have a lot to do.' He wanted to let me off the butcher's hook. He did not want *me* to suffer. He would drop off to sleep again and I would stare through the window or sit thinking.

In a confessional mood, the previous summer, my father had told me that he had once had a secret desire to become a watch-maker. It had been his secret lifetime ambition, he had told me. Now he opened his eyes and whispered, knowing no time at all, 'What day is it?' When he learnt that it was Saturday he urged me to go and watch Cardiff City play, if they were playing . . . 'You would like that, son, though why I dunno.' Again he slipped down into sleep and again, in the chair near the wash basin, I kept vigil. I remembered that time he had played a practical joke on me, frightening me. I must have been about eight years old. It had been a late summer evening.

I had turned into the back lane of Albany Road before it was dark – though the moon was visible. It was bedtime and there would be a row when I returned home. My mother's voice would scold, 'Where have you been? I've been worried stiff about you.' So I hurried between the shuttered walls of the lane. Windows in the backs of houses must have been open because I could hear distant dance music from radios. Jack Payne or Henry Hall and his orchestra, I don't know. I stopped alarmed. In the distance, I could make out an apparently headless figure zigzagging from one wall of the lane to the other and progressing toward me. As the creature drew nearer, I decided it was a man with a jacket pulled over his head, his face almost obliterated. He careered in a frenzy from right to left, from left to right, and my heart beat fast. I was about to fly from this oncoming monster when the coat came off revealing my father grinning hugely. 'Your mother sent me out to look for you,' he laughed.

Another time, other occasions, those Saturdays he took me to the cinema in Aberdare, on the new bit of road near Mountain Ash, he would let me sit on his lap and steer for a straight mile. The road was usually empty and as we hurled forward at 20 m.p.h. I experienced an inward squeal of pleasure. In the dark, going back home after the cinema closed, my father would say, 'I'll give you a shilling if you keep awake. See if you can this time. Bet you can't.' Always I determined to keep awake. Always when the car reached Cardiff I was asleep and, in my father's arms, had to be carried into the house.

His arms, now, were so famine thin.

Once my father appeared from the garage. We played cricket in the lane. He watched us. 'Bowl faster,' he commanded me. I bowled faster. 'Not fast enough,' he said. I tried to put more pace into it, to become Larwood. 'Duw, you're no fast bowler,' my father sighed.

My cousin, Derek, came into the room and sat down quietly. An hour later we left the hospital together. 'I'm very fond of Uncle Rudy,' Derek said. He spoke in a measured, unnatural voice. 'I know,' I said.

Next day Wilfred and Huldah arrived. It was an unhappy family reunion: my mother reticent, shrunken, passive, and the rest of us uncharacteristically quiet. We went to the hospital. Huldah, though it was now mid-December, had managed to procure some peaches. 'Here's your favourite fruit, Dad,' she said. She peeled one and put it gently in his dry mouth. When, later, my father recognised Wilfred his hand reached out to grasp his eldest son's wrist – like a drowning man reaching for something stable. My brother, no god descending from a whirring machine, could offer nothing but soft words, and my father closed his eyes resigned. Startled, then, we heard Wilfred minutely sob, and quickly Huldah brought a handkerchief to her mouth.

A few nights later, my father addressed me for the last time. 'I may tell you, Dannie,' he said, quite unaware that he was about to echo the ancient gods, the wisdom written in the temple of Delphi, 'it's important that each man should know himself.' He spoke hoarsely, urgently, as if he were passing on to me, like a legacy, the hard-won accumulated wisdom of a lifetime. He rested his hand gently on mine, and never uttered a conscious word to me again. I stayed there, hand in hand, in a room that seemed desolate with the breathing of that emaciated man who once had helped to make me. There was the wash basin, the radiator for the central heating, the vase of carnations that my sister's husband had brought. And beyond those curtains, night, dark night and, no doubt, 'the inexhaustible adventure of a gravel yard'.

That time soon after my father became unemployed, when he no longer managed the Aberdare cinema, my parents for a few months separated. They had quarrelled bitterly. My father used to wait for me outside Marlborough Road Elementary School after the four o'clock bell. When I appeared he would say, 'Come with me to Grandma's.' I did not want to go with him to Grandma's. I did not want to betray my mother who had said Dad was no good, that he was too trusting, too easily fooled by others, too willing to gamble on the horses – and other things, darker things, unmentionable things too, my mother hinted. My father had assumed the temporary disguise of a villain. 'If you don't mind, Dada,' I had said, 'I'd rather not come to Grandma's. I'm expected home.' My father appeared wounded. 'Come for an icecream,' he bribed me, 'at the Empire!' I succumbed, felt guilty. He watched me eat a fruit sundae, or a peach melba, or a banana split, or even, on some afternoons, a knickerbocker glory. Never had I been allowed such grand ices; still I felt deeply uneasy. When, after the icecream, Dad would plead, 'Come back to Grandma's just for a moment,' little swine that I was, I replied, 'I must go home, Dada.' He nodded sorrowfully. When he bent down to kiss me goodbye, the skin on his cheeks or chin seemed as rough as sandpaper and the lapels of his coat smelt faintly of tobacco.

Wilfred pushed open the door. Once again he had been urging the night-nurse not to be frugal with the dose of morphine. A week earlier he had persuaded them, with my concurrence, to stop the antibiotics. What was the point? Doctors, nurses, they are all trained to keep patients alive; like everybody else in this world they find it difficult to cope with death. 'I'm all in,' Wilfred said. 'There are some beds in the solarium. I'm going to take a nap.'

'I'll join you soon,' I said.

My father seemed peaceful though his head seemed too heavy for his neck. He never opened his eyes again. In the early hours of the morning of December 19th, I walked quietly through the large public ward towards the solarium. On each side, sick people in their beds snored or moaned. They could have been sleepers imagined by Henry Moore.

In the solarium I climbed on to a bed, lay back and gazed upward through the glass roof at the clear night sky with all its humbling lights until I experienced some brief, small refreshment. While my brother catnapped on the next bed it seemed to me that a huge inhuman right hand held up the spinning earth while the left hand reached up higher and higher to light the furthest stars. Nearer, conspicuous, the moon hung mercilessly white. I did not know then, that never again would I be able to see a moon anywhere in the world, moon distinct and round, or moon a mere sliver, or a swollen mist-crashing moon appearing low on the horizon, without remembering my father, my father dying.

Later that morning, my father irrevocably dead, Wilfred said to me, 'No man who has ever watched his father die can ever be quite the same man again.'

I became mortal the night my father died.

28. Confessions, Confessions

I started to write a poem about that recent experience in Llandough Hospital. Then I put my pen down listlessly. To convert that raw finale into a mere wordy resemblance of it seemed wrong. Why should I allow myself to pull back the curtain on a scene so intimate to me? Yet since poetry was my *raison d'être* – my ambition, I had said often enough, was to write the next poem – then surely not to try and make a poem about that urgent eye-brimming experience would be to admit that poetry-making was a trivial act, a silly useless fiddle with words, and that my own life, its direction and centre, was silly and useless also?

I began to feel I must write a poem called 'In Llandough Hospital'. I had written poems about a stunted tree, about a railway shunter, about a piece of chalk even, about the halls of houses, about odours, about a school-teacher who taught French, about a stage magician, about a hundred things, hundreds of things, so not to write about my father's death would almost be an insult to my father's memory. This, he had said, showing me off like a prize, is the Poet in the Family, to his friends, to strangers, to the nurse even. So the poet in the family wrote a poem called 'In Llandough Hospital', and published it, but could never read it out loud at poetry readings to strangers. He did not want to squander something as valuably private as that and feel the anaesthetic numbness that comes from the repetition of a story told over and over, or a poem read again and again.

After the candle in the glass tumbler had been lit, the prayer murmured, and the mirrors covered, after the funeral, my mother came back to London with us. She sat for hours in sunken silence, her face tilted towards the dust-flecked window that was grey with shining pencil December light. That year Christmas day came and went without jollity and we tasted the age in our own mouths. There was more than a hole in the air, more than a mere painting removed from a wall leaving a blank oblong.

On New Year's Eve, I fancied I heard from our black, wiped-out garden an owl's deep-throated, solitary cry. Even in surburban Golders Green a night bird's melancholy haunting could evoke the new dead who had resumed the silence of God and who 'lay under the stars . . . unable to rejoice'.

'I don't think I shall wait up for the New Year to come in, son,' my mother said, rising from her chair.

'I've put a hot water bottle in your bed,' said Joan.

An hour passed before the mathematical clock struck twelve times and it was 1965. Sirens and hooters. Elsewhere, no doubt, at parties they were singing, Should Auld Acquaintance Be Forgot. Before going to bed I counted up vacantly the number of Christmas cards on the mantelpiece. Confessions, confessions!

Four months later it was still 1965 and sometimes, for a week at a time, only a certain overcoat in the wardrobe or the sailing moon at night would remind me of my father's body disrobing in Glamorgan's sanitary earth. It was the springtime of the year. Springtime, and in the daylit, bird-singing gardens of Hodford Road the branches burst jubilant with apple blossom, with cherry blossom, with the blatant yellow of laburnum. My mother had returned to Cardiff and David, now aged six, accompanied me to see a one-act play of mine, *The Eccentric*.

'Yes, I think you'll like it,' I said. 'It's rather funny as a matter of fact.'

Off we went, to the other side of the River Thames, towards the wastes of South London, the males of the family, David munching Cadbury's milk chocolate and I appealing, as we swung wildly around the Elephant and Castle roundabout, 'Who's the best driver in the world?'

On the way back, I asked my small son, who seemed quite cheerful, what he had thought of *The Eccentric*. He nodded. He cleared his throat. He hesitated. He turned his head towards me, serious, big-eyed, and pronounced, 'Only one thing wrong with it, Dad.'

'What's that?'

'It's boring,' he said.

A few days later, though, he came into the living room with Josh, one of his friends, and, as I looked up from my newspaper, he pointed to one of the books I had written that, for some reason, happened to be lying on top of the bookcase.

'See that thick book there, Josh,' he said.

Pleased, I pretended to read the newspaper.

'What?'

'That book. That book on top of the bookcase.'

'Yes.'

Absent-mindedly, I turned to the sports page.

'Well,' continued David, proudly, 'my mother typed all of that.'

That was April, and then it was May when all things stayed the same and became, once more, beautifully different. The one hawthorn tree in bloom in our garden was splendidly stranded in the coarse grass that, as usual, badly needed shearing.

At the chest clinic a colleague, Neville Rogers, came into my consulting room and put some X-rays on the illuminated screens. He wanted my opinion. I gazed at the bilateral enlarged hilar glands and the infiltration of both lung fields. 'Looks like sarcoidosis to me,' I said. 'Where's the patient?'

'He's coming to see me this afternoon,' Neville replied.

'How long has it been there? Have we any old films?'

While they searched for earlier films in the X-ray Department Neville Rogers and I talked of this and that. Suddenly Neville asked, 'What sort of poems are you writing these days?' I was surprised by his question. My colleagues usually did not engage comfortably in literary conversation. I hesitated. I did not know how to answer him briefly.

'I would really like to know,' Neville said, as if he had accurately read my thoughts.

Just then the telephone rang and I picked up the receiver. A covert voice asked, 'Is Dr Rogers there, please?' I passed the telephone over to Neville.

What could I say about the poems that I was presently writing? They were the poems of a much-married man who was almost as happy as possible – yet felt threatened sometimes, and uneasy. For, as a doctor, he was clearly aware of other people's dissatisfactions and suffering. He was increasingly aware, too, of his own mortality – how the apple flesh was always turning brown after the bite. In addition, there were those man-made threats: he took his wife to the Academy Cinema in Oxford Street only to be assaulted by a film about Auschwitz; or he would observe his children switch on the TV set only to be exposed to the obscene, derelict war images of Vietnam. There was no running away. Writing poetry, too, was an immersion into common reality not an escape from it.

I turned to scrutinise the X-rays on the blazing screens again and thought of how Chekhov had once written in a letter, 'You advise me not to hunt after two hares . . . I feel more confident and more satisfied with myself when I reflect that I have two professions and not one. Medicine is my lawful wife and literature is my mistress. When I get tired of one I spend the night with the other. Though it's disorderly, it's not dull, and besides, neither of them loses anything from my infidelity.' Neville Rogers put down the telephone receiver and walked towards the screens. The sarcoid infiltration seemed severe. I suspected that his patient might well need some steroid therapy. 'They are going to be quite a time searching out those old X-rays,' Neville Rogers said. 'Sorry – you were about to tell me what kind of poems you are writing nowadays?'

I had not expected him to persist with his question and I sat down in the chair near my desk. 'They are the poems of a fortunate man,' I replied.

PART TWO

Goodbye, Twentieth Century

Consciousness walks on tiptoe through what happens. So much is felt, so little of it said.

ANNE STEVENSON

The memory of far-off things brings objects back to us renewed, no longer habitual, but broken into new facets by time and forgetfulness and so made into something that spurs our imagination, all the more so because things remembered are new, yet mysteriously our own.

CESARE PAVESE

Goodbye, Twentieth Century.
What should I mourn?
Hiroshima? Auschwitz?
Our friend, Carmi, said.
'Thank forgetfulness
else we could not live;
thank memory
else we'd have no life!

From 'A Letter from Ogmore-by-sea'

1. In Autumn Sunlight

Once more I was preparing to visit the USA. I had been invited to give readings mainly in the South, in Virginia and Georgia, before coming back to New York via Washington. Joan had small reservations about my taking three weeks' leave from the chest clinic to chase the green dollar: too often, as we lounged in the lotus comfort of our Golders Green home, we had been assaulted by the tawdry images of the Vietnapalm war on the television screen. But most of our American friends also opposed the war though none so vigorously as Denise Levertov and her husband, Mitch Goodman, whom I hoped to see in New York. They, along with Dr Spock, had organised unignorable anti-war demonstrations.

Television, with vile immediacy, had, for the first time, brought the mutilations and ignominy of modern warfare into the kitchen and drawing room. All over Europe, too, the buzz of anti-American demonstrations. Days before I began my journey from Heathrow, on an amber-lit October afternoon in 1968, Joan and I and our three youngsters boarded a Number 13 bus and soon joined the hundreds of thousands milling around and about Trafalgar Square. Nearing the erected forum under the soaring column of Nelson's omnipotent statue, crowds held banners aloft: WILSON CONDEMN BOMB-ING OF VIETNAM and HALT US AGGRESSION, while disembodied voices fuzzed tinnily through the loudspeakers: 'Awak-ened humanity . . . Might of the Pentagon . . . Napalm . . . Suffering . . . Torment . . .' Nearby, the fountains' silvering, sunlit fringes of water collapsed ceaselessly into the huge, greenish, copper-sulphate stained basins. Because of the general background of noise, the red London buses the other side of Trafalgar Square passed by in eerie silence, a cotton-wool dream, a slow carnival.

Suddenly the frugal autumn sunlight cleared the clouds, making gossamer of the fountains and spotlighting details of the crowd: men holding children on their shoulders, students in their informal gear, isolated groups of families, solitary men puffing pipes and, further away, more banners held high: LONG LIVE HO CHI MINH and

CHE LIVES. Doubtless, members of the Communist Party had joined the rally but most were not in any way fanatical ideologues. They felt simply as Joan did, as I did, that one had to make a gesture of protest however impotent.

As the pigeons wheeled overhead, no electrifying Sermon on the Mount was preached through the loudspeakers that Sunday afternoon but the crowd discerned through the clichés and the stale layers of hesitant political speech and jargon, another language, one more magisterial, one seldom spoken. After the routine vocabulary of protest against the ravages of napalm a message from Bertrand Russell was relayed. Then a thin scattered patter of clapping before the loudspeakers were switched off and suddenly we were no longer deaf to the quotidian sounds of Trafalgar Square: the traffic thrum, the thresh of the fountains, the occasional padded flapping of pigeons' wings when some invisible signal sent them soaring into the air.

We waited opposite the National Gallery as a long procession began its journey to the American Embassy in Grosvenor Square, shepherded by policemen who stopped the traffic, who restarted it, who halted the people marching, then restarted them. As we stood on the pavement, collecting boxes were shaken like castanets at us and one forlorn-looking, extremely tall and thin man, detached from everybody else, called without ardour to the onlookers beside us, 'Three shillings – *Thoughts of Mao* – three shillings.' Soon we heard a small shouting as a score of men and women approached nearer and nearer. They carried orange banners and cried, 'Yanks out, Yanks out out out.' The policemen held them up, let traffic through, before they were allowed to proceed, their hoarse 'Yanks out, Yanks out out out' rhythmically fading in the distance. Then a van appeared on which was written incongruously THE LORD JESUS CHRIST IS RETURNING.

The October sun slid down behind the buildings, a dazzle of licked orange on the highest office windows as if fires had been lit within. Still the procession filed past through the Square, group after group, interminably with their identifying banners: THE CAMBRIDGE LABOUR PARTY, THE UNION OF LIBERAL STUDENTS, THE IRISH WORKERS' GROUP – all waving slogans such as STOP YANKEE BUTCHERS NOW and VIETNAM FOR THE VIETNAMESE. An estimated quarter of a million people were marching to the US Embassy in Grosvenor Square.

A year earlier a riot had followed a large London rally protesting against the US military involvement in the Vietnam war. We would therefore not risk taking the children to Grosvenor Square. Already we knew that television crews had been sent to cover any outbreak of violence. As darkness inhabited London the ruthless arc lights would be focused on the crowds outside the Embassy and they would be singing, 'We shall not be moved . . . We shall overcome . . .' while riot policemen, squadrons of them, would be waiting for their hour.

We walked away from the crowds, our family, the five of us, in search of a café that would serve us a late reviving tea. It all seemed so ironic, so pathetic, our protest about barbarous war and then our taking civilised tea and cakes. I remember thinking about my brother's speech in Parliament, how he, Leo, had thundered that the Wilson government should not condone actions which allowed the war to continue, that we should not sycophantically curry favour with the Americans, with sickening hypocrisy approve their policy. Yet a speech in the House of Commons had no more impact than this protesting public rally.

Privately Leo had spoken to me about the psychodynamics of the American government's deeds. He suggested that the psyche can apprehend defeat in a way that is analogous to death and that the Americans had more difficulty than some nations in accepting defeat. I had objected to this generalisation but he continued, 'Look at their gardens of rest, their morticians, their embalmers, their massive funeral industry. They are bound to lose in Vietnam but, like the Pharoahs of old, they cannot accept the finality of death . . . defeat. They should learn how to turn defeat into triumph, as we did over Dunkirk, as De Gaulle achieved for France out of the total loss of Algeria.'

The No. 13 bus home took ages and the children, tired, especially Susanna, became fractious. It is said that the second-born child tends to be more rebellious than other siblings and, to be sure, Susanna could sometimes explode into an expressive verbal tantrum. We arrived home to witness one such. From the hallway I heard discordant voices from the kitchen and Joan saying forcefully, 'Now Susanna, behave yourself. When you're grown up you won't be able to carry on like this.'

Susanna's response to that admonition has become for us a comic family legend. My eleven-year-old daughter, always articulate, in anger rivalled the inflamed rhetoric of a soapbox politician. 'Yes, I will,' she shouted shrilly, her schoolgirl voice daring higher and higher decibels. 'When I grow up, I shall behave as I please. I shall lie and I shall steal. I shall burn and I shall kill. I shall be like Mussolini. I shall be like Hitler. I shall be worse than Hitler. I shall . . . I shall . . . I shall VOTE FOR THE CONSERVATIVE PARTY.'

While in New York I called on Denise and Mitch at their home in Greenwich Street. Denise had become a celebrated American poet. I had renewed our acquaintance when I first visited the USA in 1964. Then she had given me her New Directions book, *The Jacob's Ladder*. Why that title? Martin Buber in his *Tales of the Hasidim* had related how Rabbi Moshe taught: 'It is written: "And he dreamed, and behold a ladder set up on the earth." That "he" is every man. Every man must know: I am clay, I am one of the countless shards of clay, but "the top of it reached to heaven" – my soul reaches to heaven; "and behold the angels of God ascending and descending on it" – even the ascent and descent of the angels depend on my deeds.' Denise asserted, as long ago as 1964, that writing a poem was a deed, that a political poem could have detonating social consequences. On the flyleaf of *The Jacob's Ladder*, which I have before me now as I write, there is an inscription: 'To my almost twin – 18 years later, is it possible? And in America . . .'

Not long before I met Denise, when I, wide-eyed, first walked the wards at Westminster Hospital, Leo had confided in me that between his birth and mine my mother had suffered a stillbirth, a girl. This was news to me and because I shared with Denise a Welsh and Jewish background, because we both wrote poetry and published in the same magazines such as *Poetry Quarterly*, because she had been a nurse, I, a medical student, felt absurdly that Denise seemed like an embodiment of my dead-at-birth sister. I even wrote a poem about such imaginings which was published in the Spring 1947 issue of *Poetry Quarterly*. Denise must have divined I had such feelings for she had written, 'To my almost twin . . .'

My almost twin, though, now appeared to believe that the poetry was in the politics – she had recently published passionate elegies about the Vietnam war. I mentioned that I had recently written a poem about the demonstration in Trafalgar Square but felt uneasy about it because I realised one could unconsciously do things, experience things, not purely for their own sake but because one could write about them. After a hesitating silence, Mitch replied,

'Didn't your mother used to say, Dannie, if you look in the mirror too long, you see the devil?'

It so happened that after I left New York and halfway through my tour, on a flight from Atlanta, I sat next to a talkative farmer's son who had been conscripted into the army. Having just taken embarkation leave he was rejoining his unit. 'I've been posted to Vietnam,' he told me. 'I've been back home to get married.' He looked so young, hardly needed to shave.

'You'll miss everybody at home,' I said uselessly. He nodded, turned away from me, looked out of the window. I sensed his avalanche of emotion. Eventually he said, 'I'll certainly miss Robbie.'

'Your new wife?'

'What?'

'Robbie? Your new wife?'

'My dog,' he said. 'My dog's called Robbie. I'll miss him.' He spoke without irony and now it was my turn to gaze beyond him to glimpse through the window so much interminable blueness that I felt the plane was motionless.

'Where do you come from?' he asked me.

The fact that I was from Britain seemed to amaze him and he cross-examined me innocently – with a familiarity alien to Englishmen. Eventually, on an uncharacteristic impulse, I gave him a paperback of my poems.

'Gee, I've never met a poet before.'

The young conscript thanked me profusely and insisted that I gave him my home address so that his mother could write to me.

'Your mother?' I said, surprised.

Eight months later I heard from her, learned of his untimely death in Vietnam. His mother, a farmer's wife whom I did not know, had never met, mother of a son with whom I had shared an hour on an aeroplane flight, sent me for several years an annual Xmas card.

At the University of Georgia in Athens I witnessed a particularly acrimonious anti-war demonstration. At Hampden Sidney College, though, the possible consequences of local race riots preoccupied them more than the war in Vietnam. Arriving late at that all-male college in Southern Virginia, I was immediately propelled on to an immense stage before an audience waiting patiently in the great hall. Upstairs in the balcony, downstairs, row after row, hundreds of young men glowered at me, unsmiling.

Readings at Hampden Sidney were rare events and the students had been forced to attend. It was evident that most of my audience would have preferred to be at their dentist's. The chairman, a distinguished professor in the English Department, rose to introduce me. His prepared peroration was pleasant enough, unremarkable, until the surprise of its conclusion.

'When this poetry-reading is over,' he barked, 'will you please all hand in your guns.'

He sat down. Pause. I stood up. I ventured into the silence. 'Perhaps you would all like to give in your guns *before* my reading.' It was a mistake. Nobody sniggered, nobody smiled. I plodded on. I had almost as hard a time as the audience.

Afterwards the professor confirmed that the students carried guns. There had been local outbreaks of violence following the murder of Martin Luther King the previous April.

'Where do you give your next reading?' he said quickly, changing the subject.

'In Washington. Afterwards I go home.'

The day before my reading engagement at the Institute of Contemporary Arts in Washington, left to my own devices, I visited the National Gallery. I was missing my wife and kids, and I was impatient to return home so when I moved into the gallery of French paintings and saw a tall familiar figure I knew from London I was particularly pleased. He had his back to me, half absent from this world as he peered at a painting by Manet.

'Stephen?'

When Stephen Spender turned he, too, seemed glad to see someone from home. Besides, he evidently wanted to share his enthusiasm for the painting we both now faced – Manet's *Gare Saint-Lazare* which, if I remember correctly, depicted a young girl gazing through railings at smoke left trailing from a train.

In 1956, Elizabeth Jennings and I had co-edited a PEN anthology with Stephen Spender and so had come to half-know this senior, somewhat shy poet who was now the resident laureate at the Library of Congress. Even before I had met him he had accepted poems of mine for *Encounter* and had bothered to write to me about them. When Elizabeth Jennings and I consulted him at his St John's Wood home he had shown us intriguing snapshots taken in pre-war Germany, including some of the famous Sally Bowles who, surprisingly, looked very bourgeois and respectable.

He used to startle us when he spoke bitchily of his friends,

Isherwood, Auden, Herbert Read and Eliot; yet on later occasions, when anyone else levelled a snide remark about any of them, Stephen would righteously bridle, redden alarmingly, and loyally defend their writings, their reputation, their honour.

Not a few poets of my own generation would make sneering comments about Stephen Spender himself – as much about him as about his poetry. Were they irritated by the vulnerable, too truthful, vain nature of some of his public statements? 'When I read a newspaper,' he once confessed, 'I'm disappointed if I don't find in its pages some reference to myself.' Or was it his spoilt good looks, his tall bearing, his upper class, rather cissy voice, that aroused their enmity?

I found his statements, his prejudices and patent ambivalences about so many things, somewhat comical. For instance, among poems submitted to the 1956 PEN anthology was one by Louis Adeane that had, unaccountably, raised Stephen's hackles. Though it was excessively romantic and rhythmically Swinburnian, Elizabeth and I were inclined to accept it.

'No no no,' Stephen Spender had insisted. 'We can't take it.'

'Why not?'

'NO. We can't accept a poem by someone of that name.'

'How do you mean?'

'LOUIS! No genuine poet could have the name LOUIS.'

For a moment silence held dominion in that St John's Wood drawing room. When he was reminded of his contemporary, Louis MacNeice, Stephen Spender blushed deeply. No one in that room needed Freud to interpret the basis of Stephen's absurd prejudice.

We eventually left the National Gallery together. It transpired he had been invited to give an after-lunch literary speech to a minion of lawyers. He kindly invited me to be his guest at this lunch so together we walked in the aurulent sunlight of the Washington streets. The leaves were falling as they would be at home; but the colours of the American foliage were altogether more blatant, more varied – like the clothes some Americans wear when on holiday. In this political capital of the world, the leaves on the trees and the bushes varied from a shade of canary yellow to that of a colour resembling candid blood. The Pentagon was not far away.

2. The End of a Decade

Some of the jazz musicians I encountered at the Poetry and Jazz concerts seemed less interested in tobacco than in smoking reefers in order – as they used to say in the Sixties – to be 'sent' and, thus, uninhibitedly enhance their improvisatory compositions. Before the concert began at the Victoria Theatre, Stoke-on-Trent, in the 'green room' I listened to an argument about hashish. Suddenly I was elevated to the status of expert because of my presumed medical textbook knowledge!

'It may be an aphrodisiac,' Joe Harriot grumbled, 'but it don't do much for me, man.'

I knew that an initiate inhaling the smoke of burning cannabis could occasionally improve his sexual performance by its enabling him to achieve a formidable erection. That was the good news. The bad news was that the same initiate often did not experience an orgasm. Indeed, I think I sabotaged their usual zestful creativity that evening for I told them that monks in the East used to take hashish in order to reduce their sexual appetites and how the French poet, Theophile Gautier, had written in the 19th century that a hashish addict would not have lifted a single finger for the favours of the most beautiful maiden in Verona.

In June 1969 Jeremy Robson decided to stage a final concert at the Queen Elizabeth Hall in London. It was intended to be not only a valediction to the successful and exciting Poetry and Jazz concerts he had originally initiated in 1961 but a goodbye also to the spirit of the 1960s which was perceived not so much as a low, dishonest decade but as ten swinging years of Liberty Hall morality in which the young men in Carnaby Street gear and young women in mini-skirts slid down the long seductive banisters of happy irreverence – despite the crimes in blood-soaked Vietnam, the vicious life sentence imposed on Nelson Mandela, the gunning down of the Kennedys and Martin Luther King.

Remembering how on 11 June 1961 3000 people had attended the second triumphant concert at the Royal Festival Hall, for this valedictory occasion Jeremy Robson had lined up the old gang – Laurie Lee, Tom Blackburn, Vernon Scannell, John Smith, Douglas Hill, and myself, along with the Michael Garrick Quartet. The record company, Argo, intended to record the concert live. Spike Milligan, who had appeared at the very first concert at Hampstead Town Hall, had volunteered to conclude the evening's jubilations. Christopher Logue had also been invited but we were told that, late in the day, he had dropped out when the Argo producer, Harvey Usill, quite unsurprisingly had refused him top billing!★

Soon I was listening from the wings – for some reason Peter Sellers was skulking nearby in the shadows – to Laurie Lee's leisurely burring, cidery, Gloucestershire patter between poems: 'A small boy came up to me and said, "Are you Mr Lee?" "Yes." "Did you write a poem called Apples?" (Pause) "Yes." (Pause) "Our teacher made us learn it." (Longer pause) We spent a moment of scowling intimacy together.'

Lifting his spectacles slightly and then letting them settle again on his nose, he suddenly tore up the sheet of paper he was holding, scattered it on the stage and remarked, 'I don't think I'll read "Apples". I'll read instead a poem called "Day of These Days". I wrote it on top of an 88 bus. I was going down Great Smith Street to Lambeth. Ask the conductor! It cost me threepence to write. (Pause) If I wrote the same poem today it would cost me three bob.'

> . . . Such a day it is when time
> piles up the hills like pumpkins,
> and the streams run golden.
>
> When all men smell good,
> and the cheeks of girls
> are as baked bread to the mouth.
>
> As bread and beanflowers
> the touch of their lips,
> and their white teeth sweeter than cucumbers.

★ In April 1965 when I travelled with Logue by train from Paddington to Bristol for a Poetry and Jazz concert at the University he was annoyed that we were not met at Temple Meads Station. I suggested that we took a taxi to the University. He refused and, instead, immediately took a train to Paddington!

I think Laurie's patter charmed the packed audience as much as his poems, many of which were themselves intoxicated with lyrical affirmations. At the conclusion of his reading Laurie Lee held up his 48-page Vista paperback, *Selected Poems* (I happened to have a similar slim volume in the same series), and pronounced, 'Ladies and Gentlemen, this 48-page little book is my Life's work. (Pause) It costs two and six. (Pause) Don't mix it up with Dannie Abse's slim volume, the colour of which is a much paler yellow, a much more *unpleasant* yellow. (Pause) Mine is a really *strong* yellow. Like the yolk of a potent egg. (Pause) It's only two and six, Ladies and Gentlemen.'

During the Sixties I had often read with Laurie at Poetry and Jazz concerts. He was always a pleasure to be with, though on one occasion while on tour he somehow secretly deposited some black knickers in my case – almost causing me trouble when I returned home to my wife. He also, on our train journeys, taught me a word game he had learnt in his childhood. We would play for sixpences. At first Laurie always won. Later, when I became accustomed to the game, he would cheat transparently and grin like a chastened schoolboy when challenged. Finally he massaged his conscience by giving my daughter, Susanna, a large coin with the note, 'Ha ha ha, he he he, here's a half crown from Laurie Lee.'

I could have looked back on the decade with some satisfaction. I felt, rightly or wrongly, that my own poetry-writing continued to progress. In 1962, the judges of the Poetry Book Society, Ted Hughes and Anthony Thwaite, had selected my *Poems, Golders Green* as the Society's Choice. In retrospect, I had decided that that volume displayed my stylistic development in uncertain transition – that my new book of 1968, *A Small Desperation*, was more stylistically homogeneous and stable, more confident. Of course, I realised that I might have been deluded about its worth. After all, when my first book was published I thought that volume to be great until my second book appeared four years later; and only when my third book, *Tenants of the House*, was published in 1957 did I realise how defective my second volume proved to be also. Besides, I had met several of my contemporaries who believed they were the cat's ten whiskers yet I *knew* many of them produced dud poems. So could I, too, be wrong about my belief in the authenticity of the poems I was writing in the later Sixties?

I did not think I was wrong. I had, for the first time, been able, in poetry, to confront traumatic medical experience; and I was happy about this because, as I have said earlier, I believed, emphatically, that poetry writing should not be an escape from reality but an immersion into reality. And that reality had been for me one that included the discords of disease. I agreed with the German poet, Rainer Maria Rilke, who judged that verses usually amount to little when one writes them initially. Rilke advised: 'One ought to wait and gather sense and sweetness, a whole life long, and a long life if possible, and then, quite at the end, one might perhaps be able to write ten good lines. For verses are not, as people imagine, simply feelings (we have those soon enough); they are experiences.' And these experiences, Rilke suggested, should include listening to the screams of women in labour as well as having sat beside the dying.

There is something ageing about the end of the year and also the conclusion of a decade. That interval, that patient enjambment between Christmas and January 1st, in itself turns the hair grey: the Christmas cards still on the mantelpiece; the unseasonable flowers withering in the vase; the post post-mortem turkey in the kitchen; the whole family extra-calorie heavy. No post. The Old Year yawning in the Waiting Room of Eternity, the New Year somewhere else, limping in slowly each afternoon as the lampposts come on too early.

Still, on 1 January 1970 I would not have to resolve to give up smoking yet again. I had seen its deleterious effects day in, day out at the chest clinic. Besides, I could not forget my own father's X-ray, that oval shadow, Death's small egg, nestling above the left hemi-diaphragm – and how years of coughing out the smoke of Ardath cigarettes, Kensitas, Players, had led him to become, even before his terminal illness, a pulmonary cripple. Anyway, I had managed to give up smoking in 1969 and now could tell patients that they must kick the habit without feeling a hypocrite. Strange that tobacco had once been considered a cure-all. In the 16th century its leaves had been applied to wounds and it was thought that its smoke blown up the rectum had a therapeutic beneficence.

But giving up smoking did not stop my hair turning grey. Just there! On the sides, look! I know that I felt my age at the ash-end of 1969. For opposite 29 December in my old W.H. Smith pocket diary, which I have now in front of me, I had entered a name: *Fred Astaire*, and I remember why I did so.

On the evening of 29 December I had switched on the radio in our living room to discover some orchestra playing, 'Putting on my top hat, brushing up my coat-tails . . .' To amuse the children and myself I danced solo a little and when I observed I had captured their interest – they began to clap enthusiastically – I told my six-eyed audience that I was *the* Fred Astaire. I whirled an invisible Ginger Rogers this way and that with wonderful vitality until the music stopped and Susanna asked, 'Who's Fred Astaire, Dad?'

As the radio resumed playing some other tune, I, torpedoed, collapsed into a chair. 'You've heard of Fred Astaire?' I said, worried, to my elder daughter, Keren.

'No,' she said.

'Never 'eard of him,' added my son David, triumphantly.

At once I felt my age that these three kids now magnified. They had their own music, the music of the 1960s: 'I've got a ticket to ride', 'Blowin' in the Wind', 'Where Have all the Flowers Gone?' Why should they know the passé popular music of my youth? Gosh, in five years' time I would be the cemetery side of 50. It was the end of the year, the end of a decade and now, outside, snow was falling on snow with all its deletions.

3. Lunch Hours

At the chest clinic I continued to see patients who suffered one of the same score of pathologies over and over: tuberculosis, bronchiectases, Hodgkin's Disease, sarcoidosis, neoplasms, lung cysts, pneumothoraces, etc. Specialisation for the doctor can lead to some monotony; but as an old French medical proverb insists, 'There are no diseases, only sick people.' True, I saw patients too briefly to know them well. If they needed treatment they would be referred to hospital; when I saw them again, as was often the case, it was only for observational purposes. Still, keeping office hours as I did, involved only in diagnostic work, had the advantage of allowing me some leisure time to write.

Besides, to discover an abnormal, intriguing shadow on an X-ray, and then to rely on one's knowledge and experience to make a diagnosis could be a satisfying experience for the doctor if not for the patient! To reassure a passive or mutinous patient that all is well or will be well could be uplifting; to clarify the bewilderments of someone ill and, at the same time, to avoid the violence of articulated drastic truth could make the physician feel virtuous. And sometimes I felt virtuous.

Nevertheless there were occasions during these office hours when I felt captive within my 5th-floor consulting room. I would stand at the window and see, below, the chimney pots and patched rooftops of Fitzrovia. And beyond them the noisy pubs and convivial cafés of Charlotte Street. Down there awaited unpredictable colourful freedom. Here I had to keep to the known routines of the clinic with its row of lit X-rays, its dolorous Ministry of Works paint on the walls, the bored weighing machine near the bookcase, the sphygmomanometer and stethoscope on my desk and those hooks near the door on which I could discard my long white coat.

Frequently, too frequently perhaps, lunch hour would signal a welcome parole into a temporary liberty. I would walk towards the possible adventure of Soho close by or else progress westward to the nearby BBC pub, The George, in search of congenial, literary, more like-minded company.

I rarely had to stand at the bar in The George in regal solitude. Usually I would be able to join those BBC producers who happened to be there, some of whom I had worked for: John Gibson or Eric Ewans, George MacBeth or Bob Pocock. I was always conscious of sipping at a slow half-pint – often not finishing it – while others downed pints with speedy automation. The afternoon, for them, could elongate towards infinity whereas I, sober, had to return to patients or to scrutinise X-rays. That is why I was surprised when Peter Porter wrote in a book of critical essays and reminiscences, 'I had been recording a poem with George MacBeth at Broadcasting House and we went afterwards to the BBC's nearest pub, The George in Mortimer Street. Dannie was at the bar, and was not sober. I think it is the only time I have seen him the worse for drink.'

I don't remember. I do recall how once, once only, one afternoon, I did move on, past closing time, in a truant alcoholic happiness to a run-down afternoon club not far from The George with Louis MacNeice, leaving my patients to be seen by a surprised colleague at the clinic. Louis, then in his fifties, felt his reputation as a poet had, of late, steeply declined; but, in The George, gradually freed by the usual restraints of sobriety, I mentioned, with candour, my sincere admiration for his poetry. Louis was a shy man and that particular afternoon, as he responded to my earnest flattery, I got near him for the first and only time.

A decade earlier I had sent a poem, 'Sunsets', to J.R. Ackerley, the literary editor of *The Listener*. The poem was returned with an impersonal rejection slip. Shortly afterwards, astonished, I received a note from Ackerley (whom I had never met and never did meet) inviting me to resubmit 'Sunsets' as he wished to have a second look at it. It seemed he had had a conversation with Louis MacNeice who had made positive remarks about my work. This, of course, endeared MacNeice the man to me as well as his poetry. I also admired Ackerley for subsequently publishing a poem he had first rejected. Not many literary editors, proud creatures, would have dared that. At that afternoon drinking club, seedy enough to serve as a background to a Graham Greene scene, in tipsy companionability, I discovered how vulnerable to criticism Louis MacNeice was, how much – like all who obsessively write poetry – he needed, at certain punctured moments, reassurance and genuine appreciation of his work, a sincere 'Yes', a true 'thank you', the balm and manna of praise.

A few weeks before Louis MacNeice died of a viral pneumonia – most people recover from that condition – I happened, during the lunch hour to be loitering in The George. I had joined Eric Ewans and Bob Pocock who were being entertained by the bar stories of Dominic Behan. Soon Louis entered the pub and sidled towards us, hovering on the edge of the group. Behan continued to relate radiantly absurd Irish anecdotes that generated much laughter. Then, suddenly, as one paroxysm of cackling amusement subsided, Louis, who had hitherto not said one word, nor even smiled at Behan's exuberances, mournfully asked, 'Do you know of a young poet who'd be my literary executor?' The remark was so irrelevant and so opposed to the comic tenor of the group's mood that after a brief hyphen of stealthy silence, all of us began to laugh hugely again. But even as I echoed the general merriment I observed Louis MacNeice staring at me perplexed. Some three weeks later, perturbed, I read the outrageous news of Louis' unexpected death.

One magnet that drew me away from The George during the lunchtime break were the bookshops of Charing Cross Road. Apart from browsing, and occasionally buying a book, I would check how my own publications were faring. I would scan the top shelves where authors, unfortunate enough to own surnames beginning with A, are placed out of reach. If my volumes happened to be absent I'd think darkly that the publisher's rep. had not bothered to 'top up'. Should a number of my books be evident, up there with Amis and Auden, then I would assume my poems were not selling, so what's the use?!

Robert Lusty, the Managing Director of Hutchinson, once complained to me, 'Your poetry books don't sell as well as those by Mary Wilson' (the Prime Minister's wife). I was able to respond, 'Her name begins with W. Dwarfs read Mary Wilson. Giants read Dannie Abse.'

Then a certain Welsh bus would come to mind, one I had observed travelling along the coast from Llantwit Major to Bridgend. The vehicle had no passengers. Row after row of unoccupied seats. The driver had possibly not bothered to stop at St Brides or Ogmore-by-sea or wherever, for no passengers awaited. I had the feeling that the bus returning from Bridgend to Ogmore-by-sea, to St Brides, to Llantwit Major, would continue to remain bereft of passengers. The journey would be pointless, the driver, surely named Mr Sisyphus Jones, would feel purposeless – like an author without readers.

I'm sure most authors also look out for their books when they visit a Waterstone's or Dillons. I recall how Roy Jenkins confessed that soon after the publication of one of his biographies he had bookshop-crawled down Charing Cross Road and not finding one single copy on offer had become increasingly despondent. At last, a happy light lit his eyes for he suddenly saw in a window the notice RARE BOOKS FOR SALE.

One hazard of walking across Oxford Street through Soho Square (past the dejected stoned statue of King Charles II who faces the mocking erection of the Post Office Tower, spurning behind him the Nell Gwyn Club, the Nude Shows) into Greek, Dean or Frith Street was the chance of meeting Paul Potts who, on the scrounge, would divest me of, at least, a ten-shilling note. 'Dannie, Dannie, listen I'm a failure. I've only known two lovers in my life. One woman left me, the other killed herself. I've failed at poetry and I've failed with women. Yet I've had great friends who've been writers like you. Friends like Orwell and Ignazio Silone. Don't they say you can tell a man by his friends? Can you lend me ten bob, can you?'

It was rumoured that George Orwell had left Paul a small legacy. Perhaps Orwell had admired Paul's occasional aphoristic remarks: 'Poems are old before they are made and young after a hundred years' or 'Surely anything worth saying twice is worth listening to once'. The trouble was Paul recited his aphorisms over and over, especially, 'A slave is only a free man in chains'. In 1969 he had published *To Keep a Promise* and soon after I encountered him in New Compton Street. He button-holed me, saying, 'Did you see the review of my book in the *Observer*?' When, truthfully, I said, 'No,' he drew himself up to his full considerable height and shouted, 'You're not worth talking to,' and stalked away as if insulted.

Another occasion, one lunchtime in Soho, I had no sooner handed Paul a ten-shilling note – he had approached me saying, 'Dannie, I'm starving. I haven't eaten for days' – than a maroon-suited, peak-capped commissionaire, one who regularly stood outside a rather grand Indian restaurant nearby, raced up to us, demanding that Paul should pay for the banquet he had just consumed. Paul muttered something haughtily, looked down at the commissionaire as if he were ordure and strode away like an insulted General. The commissionaire, frustrated, grabbed *my* arm. 'Here's the bill for his lunch, sir,' he said, full of unjustified hope, as a small inquisitive crowd gathered.

There are some people one likes, feels half-affectionate towards, providing one does not have to be with them for longer than ten minutes. Paul was one such. He was cunning, unpredictable, amusing, quarrelsome, helpless, a self-accusing, naive, tremulous romantic who had volunteered to serve with the Israeli army in the War of Independence and who was destined to end his days Down and Out. Perhaps George Orwell had clairvoyantly perceived this and had realised that Paul was more of a poet than a number of those with considerable reputations. As Paul remarked himself, in one of his frequent confessional moods, 'I'm a poet who can't write poems.' Inevitably Paul did end up in a Camden Town doss house. There is an extraordinary, heart-breaking photograph of him during his last days, taken by Chris Barker and reproduced in *Portraits of Poets*, edited by Sebastian Barker (Carcanet). A four-line note by Paul accompanies the photograph:

> My dreams
> Watching me said
> One to the other
> This life has let me down.

4. The Most Alien of All

That February in 1971 at Heathrow, before boarding the El Al aircraft, D.J. Enright, Jeremy Robson, Ted Hughes, Peter Porter and I were being searched. We were armed only with books of poems for we had been invited, through the British Council, to join with Israeli poets in giving poetry recitals in Tel Aviv, Haifa and Jerusalem. Carol Hughes had joined our party for she and Ted had just married. For them this tour would be a honeymoon jaunt. Our minder, Charles Osborne, the literary director of the British Arts Council, for some reason was chuckling.

'What's this?' a plain-clothes security guard asked Ted Hughes, having discovered in Ted's pocket a long, sharp, ivory-coloured object.

'It's a tiger's tooth,' mumbled Ted Hughes.

'What?'

'A tiger's tooth.'

'A tiger's tooth?'

'Just a tiger's tooth.'

'This is a tiger's tooth?'

Charles Osborne continued to chuckle. In the coming weeks he would chuckle often for his coven of poets seemed adept in firing off puns and witty one-liners. We learned later that Ted Hughes intended the tooth to be a gift for his friend, the Israeli poet, Yehuda Amichai. Years earlier, Assia Gutmann, who had, as a refugee, spent her childhood in Palestine, helped Ted to translate Amichai's Hebrew poems into effective English.

Now, when introduced to Carol, I could not help recalling my meeting with Assia and Ted Hughes in Devon. Nor could I forget the clamour of salacious gossip. I remembered Assia as a glitteringly attractive young woman, tall and slender, sooty-haired with startling eyes. I glanced curiously at Carol Hughes, also tall and slender and attractive. They stood together, Ted and Carol Hughes, hand in hand as if posing for a happy wedding photograph, and one of Ted's pockets cradled the tooth of a once lethal tiger. (Strange that in a poem Ted would write decades later he referred to Assia Gutmann's 'tiger-painted' finger nails.) In the nearer future we would all be taken to, among many other haunted places, Mount Gilboa where King Saul was supposed to have committed suicide and where, ever since, it was said, the curse of God allowed no plant, no tree, no bush, no vegetation to grow.

I had visited Israel once before, in the summer of 1966, when I had attended an Anglo-Israeli Writers' Symposium at Tel Aviv. For the first time I had felt myself to be abroad. It was not only because of the strange fauna and flora, the orange groves and the giant banana monocotyledons of the North, the scrub and parched hills of the South, their scorpions and their snakes. Nor was it the ancient Hebrew language or the glimpses of the past made tantalisingly visible that made me feel I was visiting a foreign land. It was rather the people of Israel, those death-camp survivors, those children of survivors, their miraculous sabra-like transformations after unspeakable loss, crucial wounding and divestiture – their cocky phoenix energy and their arcane but abiding neuroses. Years before I had ever visited Israel, I had dared to write a flawed poem called 'Jew' in which I suggested that 'Stricken Ahaseurus no longer has to roam.' Then followed:

> One returns, another wanders still, will not cease.
> Israel or the Diaspora? Come, who's afraid?
> One upright in the sun, one sobbing in the shade,
> but which the robust fake, which the sick masterpiece?

Had that impudent quatrain, written out of partial ignorance, some truth in it? If the register of the Ashkenazi tribes of Israel could be called, there would be no homely, benign response such as I had known as a schoolboy in Wales – no Davies-Evans-Jones-Thomas-Williams would answer, 'Present, sir'. Instead, one would hear melancholy voices intoning, 'I am Auschwitz', 'I am Belsen', 'I am Buchenwald', 'I am Dachau'. 'Present sir, present sir, present.'

During that first esurine visit to Israel, before the Six Day War (Jordan still occupied Old Jerusalem), I had overlooked the city walls and espied dangerous enemy territory. And a week later, one night, I had stood on the high Lebanese frontier to gaze at the plains below, hyalescent under a gibbous moon. My Israeli companion had told me how, from east of that northern border, the Syrians, on night raids, would be liable to disembowel hideously their victims.

I had been discomforted by the Israelis' understandable but too vocal pride and by their assertive nationalism. Surrounded by enemies, under siege, they did not resemble the docile Jews of the diaspora. When challenged, they did not say softly, 'Leave me alone.' Rather they shouted imperiously, 'Go away.'

Across the gangway of the El Al plane, a long-bearded Hasid, who surely had stepped out of an oppressive, century-old ghetto to pose for a Chagall portrait, began to pray. His lips moved, he swayed back and forth, the stereotype (for anti-semites) of the eternal Jew of history. But as Max Diment wrote in *The Indestructible Jews* (the paperback I had brought with me to read on the plane) this figure across the gangway was but a caricature of the Jew.

The Jews in Hellenic times dressed like the Greeks; the Jews in the Islamic Empire were indistinguishable from their Arab contemporaries; the Jews in the Renaissance dressed in the silks and finery of that age. The ghetto Jew is the ill-begotten product of his three-century imprisonment, a travesty of the Jews and of Judaism. Yet the ghetto Jew, though he represents but a brief segment of Jewish history, even now is made to exemplify the Jew throughout the ages. But such a Jew would be unrecognisable by Moses, David or Isaiah, who never wore phylacteries or the garb of Hasids.

Something of this I remarked to Peter Porter. Yet when the pilot signalled there might be some air turbulence ahead and we should fasten our seatbelts, Peter, who seemed to fear air travel despite his trips to Australia, whispered to me with Protestant, humorous seriousness, 'I hope that rabbi's prayers will be answered.'

Days later, during our sojourn in liberated Jerusalem, we would see clones of that rhythmic fanatic facing the Wailing Wall – that supposed Western Wall of Herod's Temple thought by pilgrims to be holy with the divine presence. (Until 1948, when Jordanians captured the Old City, this wall had been the principal place for Jewish pilgrimage.) Standing enveloped in tasselled shawls, these devout but bigoted men hummed and swayed, thrusting their pelvises back and fore as if they were fornicating with invisible spirits. I thought of the exclusivity of prayer and how I, a secular Jew, could barely apprehend the intensity of their spiritual congress, their enthralled surrender of self.

> Take me to you, imprison me, for I,
> Except you enthrall me, never shall be free.
> Nor ever chaste, except you ravish me.

Nor could I feel anything but spiritual numbness when Yehuda Amichai led Ted Hughes and me to the gilded Dome of the Rock, one of Islam's holiest places which has been described as 'the utmost fulfilment of colour, rhythm and geometry'. Soon after this visit though, after we had quit the mosque and had donned our discarded shoes again to stroll across the paving adjacent to the Dome, I was shaken out of my feelings of dull neutrality by Ted Hughes's seemingly pagan supplication: suddenly he threw himself face down on to the stone, his arms outstretched. Surprised, Yehuda Amichai and I halted. Ted Hughes, all six feet of him, lay across a large iron grating interrupting the pavement and called to the darkness below.

'Dark,' he cooed softly, as one praying, 'dark, dark.' He appeared to be trying to summon up from the hidden depths below the Spirit of Darkness itself. But when he rose, he saw with delight how his hands bore the marks of the grating like stigmata. He held them towards us, smiling: 'Look, look.'

The audiences at the crowded theatres in Tel Aviv, Haifa and Jerusalem proved to be enthusiastic and our recitals which we shared with different Israeli poets were judged to be a triumph.★ We were working fairly hard but in between performances and after them Israeli hospitality was such that soon we all became red-eyed. Perhaps we were interviewed too often, shook too many hands, saw too many sights, attended too many parties, drank too many drinks. D.J. Enright descended to breakfast each morning a little more pale, a little more whacked. Soon he resembled, as he put it himself, 'the six-day whore'.

There were, at that time, few manifestations of war. True, there was news of night raids in the North and soldiers were in evidence on the streets. And once, when we were in a taxi, we heard the ear-shattering roar of an aircraft flying menacingly low above us. 'It was a

---

★ Ted Hughes read mainly from his then new book, *Crow*. One poem, 'How Water Began to Play' moved me each time I heard him read it. On returning to London Joan and I were visited by Robert Lowell and his wife Caroline Blackwood. When Lowell made derogatory remarks about current British poetry including *Crow*, I told him how much I had been touched by 'How Water Began to Play'. 'Read it to me,' Lowell urged. I did so. I read the poem slowly, feelingly. I waited for him to applaud the poem. The room was silent. I assumed Robert Lowell, too, had responded to the blackness, perhaps the autobiographical blackness, in the poem. At last Lowell shook his head. 'That poem's terrible,' he said. 'Slush.'

mirage,' said the driver proudly as the volts of thunderous noise faded. 'It seemed real enough to me,' countered Jeremy Robson.

At Nazareth, where messiah Osborne mounted a donkey, we visited the Basilica of the Annunciation, peered at the statue of the Virgin on the wall while the Christian Arab guide began his customary peroration. Suddenly, mid-sentence, he stopped. Silently he glared at Ted Hughes who had put his arm affectionately around Carol's waist. Then he boomed out, 'This is no place for love,' intending, of course, no irony. 'This is no place for love but I know a handy cowshed,' D.J. Enright was later to joke.

Our hosts took our party to other sites of particular Christian interest. We even swam in the February waters of the Sea of Galilee. It was very very cold. No wonder, I decided, Jesus *walked* on the water. After we left the Sea of Galilee where we saw no fishermen, no descendants of Simon called Peter, or of Andrew, casting their nets, we headed South and stopped at a kibbutz. There I encountered a married couple from Cardiff. Passionate Zionists, they had emigrated to Israel. I knew the husband's family name. Had I not seen it writ on those grave-tablets, those stone visiting cards of the Dead at Cardiff's Jewish cemetery, near Roath Park Lake, after the funeral of my own father? 'Home is where you start from,' argued T.S. Eliot ambiguously. Israel had become home for these two Welsh Jews. Yet I sensed their mood of hiraeth when they spoke of the Land of their Fathers.

'But I feel freer by here,' the wife said. 'No anti-semitism.'

'Freer? But there's hardly any anti-semitism in Wales.'

In her autobiography *Lost in Translation*, Eva Hoffman speaks of the country of her Jewish childhood. Despite what happened in Poland she affirms: 'No geometry of landscape, no haze in the air, will live in us as intensely as the landscape that we saw as the first, and to which we gave ourselves wholly and without reservation.' Such sentiments as these I repeated to the Cardiff couple but the husband merely replied, 'I feel more secure here and it's a happy place.'

Were they more safe? Happy? Like the sunset in the Judean hills the melancholy of Israel remained perceptible behind all the vocal and gesticulating vivacity of Israelis and days later, back in Jerusalem, Jeremy Robson and I happened to saunter away from the main group and found ourselves nowhere in particular. Small Arab boys began to follow us. Soon, their faces utterly hostile, they sent our way a useless rage of stones. 'This is no place for love,' the Arab guide had said. 'I feel more secure here,' that Cardiff Zionist had said. Those stone-throwing boys were sons of the Defeated and we were allies of the Victorious. Despite the prevailing euphoria that had followed the Six Day War Israel was still embattled, still threatened. Those small boys with stones in their right hands were an omen of things to come.

5. A Meeting with Robert Graves

Sam Wanamaker, the American-born actor who lived in Southwark, had a dream, a vision: of a Bankside once again thriving, bustling with denizens of London in search of serious entertainment – the Globe Playhouse, itself, reconstructed. To realise that vision Sam Wanamaker formed the Globe Theatre Centre and encouraged contemporary poets, each year, to honour on the page and on the platform the supreme dramatist of all time. For one of the Centre's commendable aims was 'to create a Shakespeare Birthday Fund which will commission new works of music, poetry, drama and art to be presented annually as the most appropriate tribute to Shakespeare's memory.'

In April 1972, Sam Wanamaker, accordingly, planned a concert in Southwark Cathedral. Nine contemporary composers were commissioned to contribute music, thirteen contemporary poets to write poems and speak them. I remember being somewhat pleased *and* worried when Christopher Hampton, on Mr Wanamaker's behalf, asked me to be one of the poets – pleased because Mr Hampton had invited, or intended to invite, a number of poets including W.H. Auden and Robert Graves whom I admired but had not met and now would meet; worried because I knew that poetry is something that cannot be willed, that I could not will a poem into existence, that I might not be able to keep a promise of providing a new poem for the occasion.

Nevertheless, persuaded by Christopher Hampton, I accepted the commission and eventually, armed with a new poem, I went along to Southwark Cathedral to read it.

I suppose many of us have wished sometimes, frail and silly wishes that we could turn back the clock, be transported, if only for an instant, to a certain place, at a certain time. Driving over towards Southwark, I wished uselessly that I could have attended a Shakespeare play at the original Globe Theatre – perhaps *Julius Caesar* – for I had read a description by a Thomas Platter of an evening at the Globe when he saw that play. 'After dinner, at about two o'clock, I went with my party across the water,' wrote Thomas Platter, 'in the straw-thatched house we saw the tragedy of the first Emperor Julius Caesar, very pleasantly performed, with approximately fifteen characters; at the end of the play they danced together admirably and exceedingly gracefully, according to their custom, two in each group dressed in men's and two in women's apparel.' Yes, it would have been interesting to have travelled across the water in that party; as a guest from another century it would be like being a stranger in a foreign land.

Instead I drove through twentieth-century London towards London Bridge in my Austin 1300. It was a lovely, fresh, April day; it was good to be alive. Soon, before me lay Southwark Cathedral where that afternoon I would discover, I hoped, one more sweet beginning and no unsavoury end. I parked the car, then walked into the Cathedral to meet, at once, Christopher Hampton who told me that Cecil Day Lewis was seriously ill, was, in fact, dying; also that W.H. Auden would not be with us for he was in New York.

'You'll be reading your poem in the second half, after an interval,' Christopher said. 'Is that all right? Let me show you where I want you to sit.'

As I followed Christopher I saw, near a door in the north aisle of the nave, Sam Wanamaker talking to Stephen Spender, Peter Porter, and an elderly man whom I did not know. Could it be Robert Graves, I wondered.

'Yes,' said Christopher, 'he looks pretty fit, doesn't he? He's 76 now, you know.'

I recalled Graves's own self-portrait:

> Crookedly broken nose – low tackling caused it;
> Cheeks, furrowed; coarse grey hair, flying frenetic;
> Forehead, wrinkled and high;
> Jowls, prominent; ears, large; jaw, pugilistic;
> Teeth, few; lips, full and ruddy; mouth, ascetic.

> I paused with razor poised, scowling derision
> At the mirrored man whose beard needs my attention
> And once more ask him why
> He still stands ready, with a boy's presumption,
> To court the queen in her high silk pavilion.

His face had softened with age evidently, but he still looked sprightly enough to chase that same queen and catch her. In the choir stalls Christopher pointed to the seat he wanted me to occupy, immediately after the interval. 'Between Graves and Adrian Mitchell, all right?'

I had liked Robert Graves's poetry for many years: it was always well-organised and lucid, always an internally directed soliloquy that the reader, as it were, was privileged to overhear. He composed poems in the central English lyric tradition and he used a conservative diction and a logical syntax without display, though not without the power to surprise. His was an essentially romantic sensibility with its belief in phantoms and miracle; in the terrifying and terrific supernatural; in his interest in myth as a living, operative power even in our so-called rational societies; and not least in his preoccupation with the creative and destructive element that waxes and wanes in a man-woman relationship. Yes, I looked forward to meeting Robert Graves; besides his reputation as a man was intriguing. I had heard how he could be iconoclastic, anti-academic; how he was quick to deflate lofty pretensions, how he could be wittily bitchy about his most celebrated contemporaries.

I was introduced to him in the Harvard Chapel which lay behind the north choir aisle as the buzzing audience were returning to their seats in the nave after the interval. 'John Harvard,' Robert Graves told me, 'was baptised here in 1607.' I assumed John Harvard was the gentleman who emigrated to Massachusetts to make a fortune and to found Harvard College. I was not sure, though, and not wishing to boob I said nothing. Soon Robert Graves was telling me, as we took our seats in the choir, all kinds of esoteric information about the Cathedral. He seemed anxious to instruct me. My knowledge of the Cathedral was small, my ignorance large – and even if I should have dared to pronounce on that which I did know, it would have been without confidence, like a blind man naming the colours in a rainbow. Instead, I told him the names of the poets who, one by one, faced the very large audience for he was most eager to identify them. 'Who's that?' he would spit out at me.

'Vernon Scannell,' I'd say and as soon as Vernon had finished his poem and the next piece of music commenced – by Richard Rodney Bennett or Lennox Berkeley or Peter Maxwell Davies or John Tavener – Robert Graves would generously impart to me his next small piece of scholarship: 'Edward Shakespeare, William's youngest brother, was buried in the churchyard here.' He pulled out a snuffbox, an antique, from his pocket and surreptitiously showed it to me. I learnt a few quick facts about that snuffbox, its provenance, before the music ended. 'Who's that?' asked Robert Graves a minute later. 'Peter Redgrove,' I said.

For the next twenty minutes we bartered information for information. His numerous facts for my one name. He mentioned Hollar's drawing of the Bankside three centuries past and, I believe, if the musical pieces had been more prolonged I would have learnt of 'the colouring of Titian, the grace of Raphael, the purity of Domenichino, the *corregiescity* of Correggio, the learning of Poussin, the airs of Guido, the taste of the Carracci, or the grand contours of Michael Angelo'. I began to feel that my contribution to the whispered dialogue was insufficient. I tried to think of some relevant piece of recondite information *I* could drop; but all I could think of was a conversation I had once with a man who worked at London Zoo who had told me that tortoises often died of diphtheria. Somehow, to state baldly there and then, 'Tortoises frequently die because of diphtheroid organisms in their throat,' did not seem right and proper.

In any event, suddenly, a whole group of strangers descended upon us and began to sing a song for Shakespeare's birthday, 1972. Robert Graves seemed pleased: he had written the words for it. We both listened intently as a maniacal conductor waved his arms and the choir *so near*, *so loud*, sang:

> When Will sat forging plays with busy friends
>   He wrote no worse than they;
> When he sat writing for his loves, and us,
>   Such play outshone all play.
>   And still it does today.

I had the sense *not* to say, 'That was pretty awful.' I smiled like a hypocrite when the audience applauded enthusiastically as the immoderate choir scurried away and Robert Graves stood to his feet. He raised two hands like a triumphant boxer who had knocked his opponent out. It was certainly hard to think of him as one aged 76.

Back in his corner, I mean his seat, he whispered to me, 'That was the best thing we've heard all afternoon.

'Who's that?' Robert Graves asked.

'George MacBeth,' I replied.

Eventually it was my turn to walk the twenty-two yards to the scaffold and face all those seated figures in the soaring, elongated nave (rebuilt, I think Robert Graves said, in 1897 to replace the er thirteenth-century nave destroyed er in 1838). It is not easy to read one poem only. As soon as you become used to the stressful situation, the hundreds of upturned faces, the different sources of light, the unfriendly microphone, the whole thing is over. You have been bowled out, the audience are clapping out of habit but you are walking back to the pavilion pulling off your batting gloves, knowing that you have made a duck. I sat down and took my own pulse.

Music began – by Harrison Birtwistle.

Robert Graves leaned over towards me. I thought he was going to say, 'Well done,' or 'That was a good poem' – something sensible like that. Instead he whispered most confidentially, 'He nodded at me, you know.'

'What?' I asked, wondering.

'He nodded at me.'

'Who?'

'The Prime Minister.'

I paused. When I was reading, I had spotted someone in the front row, in spitting distance, a man with a red, adipose, shining face who did, come to think of it, look very familiar.

'Edward Heath?' I asked.

'Of course,' Robert Graves said irritably, as if I were a dunce and did not know with certainty even the name of the present Prime Minister.

For my part, I felt irritated with Robert Graves. He was supposed to be a rebel, a non-conformist; and now here he was full of ridiculous pride, *hubris*, because the Prime Minister, a *Tory* Prime Minister (whom, of course, *I* did not vote for), had nodded at him.

'What did you do?' I whispered.

'I nodded back,' Robert Graves said.

At this point, Adrian Mitchell who had just arrived, late – at least he looked as if he had just parked his motorbike at the south transept door – took the empty seat on my left-hand side.

'Adrian,' I said quietly, 'Mr Graves is on nodding terms with our Prime Minister.'

I explained to Adrian that the Prime Minister was sitting in the front row. This information activated Adrian Mitchell – his skin, eyes, horns, altered. 'Is Heath here?' hissed Adrian between bared teeth, his face contorted, vivid with displeasure. Evidently Adrian regarded Heath as an amalgam of Caligula and Hitler. Just then Birtwistle's music ceased and the audience applauded again. 'Yes,' said Robert Graves benignly, cheerful, leaning over me towards Adrian Mitchell, 'Mr Heath's sitting in the front row.' But now it was Adrian's turn to read his poem. He almost ran towards the microphone.

'Who's that?' asked Robert Graves, startled.

There are those who hardly know what they think until they express it either vocally or on the page. That is not true of Adrian Mitchell. His political views are not shaded. They inform and energise his work, they translate him as a man, they draw him, as it were, as clearly as a pencil can draw a profile. I have a feeling that Adrian perceived no human being occupying that chair in the front row but a monstrous cartoon figure, one responsible for all the treachery in the world, all the injustice, coercion, easy manipulation, casual greed, inequality, unnecessary pain. Now, at last, here was a chance of a lifetime to confront bluntly that one who had previously stood in the shadow, that cartoon figure, that prime adversary. Adrian boiled with rage. He began to abuse Edward Heath, accused him of being partly responsible for the chemical warfare in Vietnam and those at the back of the nave, far away, clapped while those somewhat wealthier, in front, nearer to the presence of the Prime Minister, sat dumbly. Then Adrian Mitchell read his poem and afterwards, in reverse, curiously pale, rushed past us through the choir to disappear down the south transept whence he had come.

Some music started up – by Elizabeth Lutyens, I think – and Robert Graves said, 'You've seen the tomb of Lancelot Andrewes? He was buried originally in the Bishop's Chapel, you know.' The concert was almost over, this was the last musical composition and all the poets had read their commissioned poems. Sam Wanamaker had arranged for the concert to conclude with a reading by the actress Diane Cilento. She had been asked to recite the Epitaph by John Milton on the Admirable Dramatick Poet, W. Shakspeare. The attractive blonde actress moved to the microphone and I happened to glance at Robert Graves who seemed to be following her progress with exceptional interest – rather, I thought, as the elderly King David must have looked upon, for the first time, the beautiful Abishag. Before the microphone Miss Cilento recited without book:

> What needs my Shakespeare for his honour'd bones
> The labour of an age in piled stones?
> Or that his hallow'd reliques should be hid
> Under a starry pointing pyramid?
> What need'st thou such weak witness of thy name?
> Thou, in our wonder and astonishment
> Hast built thyself a live-long monument . . .

The Milton poem over, Diane Cilento bowed to the applauding audience with pleasing grace. 'Who's that?' asked Robert Graves once more.

'Diane Cilento,' I told him.

Robert Graves hesitated, furrowed his brows, nodded his head.

'Cilento,' he said.

'Yes.'

'Cilento. Quite a gifted poet,' he said.

'She's an actress,' I explained.

'An actress?' he asked.

'The poem was by Milton.'

'Quite. Ah yes, I thought that poem sounded familiar.'

I did not laugh. Robert Graves had made the sort of boob that I could have made. I looked at him with growing affection; he looked at me, puzzled.

Later, at the reception that followed the concert, near the entrance, I met Sam Wanamaker. 'Let me introduce you to Robert Graves,' he said. I looked across the crowded room and saw Mr Graves deep in dialogue with Mr Heath. 'It's OK,' I said. 'We've met. In fact, we've had quite an intermittent, instructive conversation. We both enjoyed the music so much.'

6. Return to Roots

At last we had saved enough money to put down a deposit for a mortgage on a house in South Wales, preferably, as far as I was concerned, at Ogmore-by-sea. My parents, when they had lived six miles away in Bridgend, had honeymooned at that lark-high, seaside village which overlooked the crinkling, silver-paper shine of the estuary below. After my mother and father had moved to Cardiff, every decent Sunday they would revisit Ogmore. I think my father's old Riley knew its own way along the A48, up Tumble-Down-Dick, past Cowbridge, on and on, to descend Crack Hill and take the sheep-obstructed, winding, narrow road to Ogmore-by-sea. There, my father would fish for obstinate salmon bass, dabs and ghosts, while the family swam or walked the cliffs above or played cricket on the coal-streaked sands and generally made a holiday of the hours.

It would make economic sense for us to invest in a second home. I had purchased no Life Insurance and now, in the middle reaches of middle age, I asked myself, 'Supposing something goes wrong? How would Joan cope with three children to support? An investment, useful and pleasure-giving, would surely be better than cash almost inert in a building society?'

My work at the chest clinic kept me in London but I needed, out of affection and duty, to return regularly to Cardiff to see my aged, widowed mother. Frankly, though, I was tired of sleeping in the front room of her ground-floor flat in Cathedral Road, missing my wife, missing my young family in London. How much better it would be if I could drive down with my family from London, pick up my mother in Cardiff, then westward, twenty-three miles later, stay in our own place in Ogmore, breathe out stale London air, breathe in the limitless Ogmore oxygen. And Saturday afternoons I would be able to sneak over to Ninian Park and sinfully watch Cardiff City play!

But my wish to return to South Wales in 1972 was not merely engendered by the pressures of convenience and rational economic assessment, nor even by my heart-felt love of the Ogmore locus itself. I sought also something less definable – perhaps it was those refreshments a writer can gain by returning to his birthplace.

One of my earliest published poems began, 'A man with no roots is lost/like the darkness in the forest.' And I agreed with James Hamilton Paterson when he opined, 'the creative urge does not march beneath a flag, although it may from time to time astutely invoke its shade.' When poems refused entrance I enjoyed portraying, in novels or plays, Welsh comic portentousness. I liked listening to the heirs of Iolo Morganwg, that renowned eighteenth-century Welsh poet, antiquary and forger of whom it was said that he could see seven sails where there was but one.

'Remember what Yeats advised Synge in Paris,' I said to Joan who, at that time, was not so enamoured of Ogmore. 'Go back home to Dublin and live in some inn. Then make a hole in the wooden planks so that you can eavesdrop on Irish voices. The dialogue you'll then write will be the richer for it.'

'He didn't say that.'

'Something like that.'

In South Wales literary activity was no longer dormant. Lively literary magazines, succoured by the Welsh Arts Council, had come into being and some writers had begun to vent militantly their sense of Welsh identity. I had congenial friends who had come to live in Cardiff – Aled Vaughan at the BBC and poets John Ormond and John Tripp among them.

John Ormond gradually became known and respected in Wales. I recall someone saying to me breathlessly, 'You're a friend of John Ormond, aren't you?' I nodded. Then the stranger, after a most magnificent pause, boasted, 'I stood next to him once in a cinema queue.'

As for John Tripp – well, he was a character who could have happily inhabited the cadging wastes of Soho rather than the respectable suburbs of north Cardiff. Even his closest friends never knew whether he, for no evident reason, would become angry or melt into an appeasing sweetness. In softer mood, he would confide, 'Dannie, there are only two real, remarkable poets in the whole of Wales. You and me, boy.' It was not long before I learnt he whispered those words to every Welsh poet he met. Hence the continued adoration by so many of the buttered poets of English-speaking Wales whom he had once, in alcoholic intimacy, sweetly flattered. One Saturday afternoon John Tripp accompanied me to Ninian Park to watch Cardiff City play. Throughout the ninety minutes John persisted in yelling at the referee who, according to him, was a monster of corruption who suffered from double cataracts and was a lecher without testicles.

When other Cardiffians began screaming abuse at one particular player on the opposing side because he had once played for Swansea John enthusiastically joined the chorus: *Cheat, Cheat, Cheat.* Then someone shouted, '*Clap 'ands if you 'ate Swansea*' and immediately John Tripp yelled with the others, clapped hands at the vile, depraved, noxious, wretched, detestable, execrable players who somewhere else in Britain that afternoon were wearing the impure, tainted, squalid, foul, crapulous white shirt of Swansea Town FC.

I am not, never have been, obsessed by nationality but when forced to do so I have of course proudly acknowledged my Welsh background as well as my Jewish origins. Once, during a BBC Wales TV interview, questioned about my identity, I remarked that I didn't wake up each morning screaming, 'I'm a 5ft 8½-inch Welsh Jew' – though even in Wales I'm sometimes made to feel I am the man from somewhere else.

I have two roots, that of Dafydd as well as David. My forebears, after all, have lived in South Wales since the 1870s. At my elementary school in Cardiff I was taught to sing Welsh songs and revere Welsh heroes. I see myself now, ten years old, sitting at a desk listening to our teacher, Mr Williams: 'The grave of our own Owain Glyndwr, princely Owain, who took up his sword in defence of justice and liberty, is not one visible, boys, but it's known. *Known.* Oh aye, you'll not find it in any old churchyard, no old tomb of his under the shadow of a yew. No stone tablet do bear his name. So where is it? I'll tell you where it is – in the heart and in the noble soul of every true Cymro. OK?'

While I attended Marlborough Road Elementary School where, among others apart from Mr Williams, I was taught by George Thomas. I was sent on a 2A tramcar one evening a week to the basement of the Windsor Place synagogue so that I could celebrate the dubiously moral deeds of the Old Testament heroes and learn the Hebrew alphabet. So, later in life, I found it natural to claim both traditions – Welsh and Jewish legends, Welsh and Jewish texts, Mabinogion and Midrach, Dafydd ap Gwilym and Yehuda Halevy.

Joan had reservations about owning a green patch in Ogmore. 'There are other places,' she said, irrefutably. Her memories of holidays at Ogmore were not of long sunny Augusts such as I had known as a boy when all the Abse family, winking uncles, nose-powdering aunts, nose-picking cousins, arrived from Cardiff, Swansea and Ammanford for their annual quarrels, for cards and beach games, for dips in the pencil-coloured sea, for the sing-songs – 'Stormy Weather', 'These Foolish Things', 'She Was a Good Girl until I Took Her to a Dance'. On the contrary, the very first August Joan and I and our clamorous toddlers joined my parents in the house they had rented, the rain became spiteful and the clouds suffered such lassitude they stayed motionless over Ogmore for weeks. And the next summer we visited Ogmore only to rendezvous with clammy sea mists so that we, indoors, listening to the foghorns moaning from nearby Nash Point, could do nothing more entertaining than write our names on the condensation shrouding the windowpanes. It was the kind of weather that could make the sheep, sheltering behind the old stone walls, know, for the first time, their fate.

In the future Joan would come to know and be captivated by the natural beauty of Ogmore: the gleaming estuary (overlooked by high sand-dunes), the cliffs and beaches that stretched past Southerndown's Trwyn-y-Witch (Witch's Nose). The nearby relics of history, too, would give her recurrent pleasure – Ewenny priory, Ogmore Castle and on the elevated cliffs the ruins of Dunraven Castle where, in the first century, tall, eagle-eyed Caradog (Caractus) perhaps looked down on the Roman soldiers bathing on the incoming tide. Now, though, she needed to be persuaded of the virtues of a second house in Ogmore.

She reluctantly agreed that the next time I visited South Wales I could, at least, reconnoitre for any FOR SALE signs at Ogmore. So, one warm afternoon, when Ogmore was at its winning best, as it can be, as it often is, I did exactly that. Alas, the only estate agents' boards I came across happened to be outside bungalows without invincible views. Somewhat defeated, I strolled away from the cluster of houses, over the springy turf, down the sheeptracks between the dark green ferns towards the cutlery-glinting sea. The larks twittered, hidden in the gorse, some gulls floated and mewed under the blue sky but such sounds as these only emphasised the encamped silence of Ogmore. Out at sea, a silhouetted ship edged noiselessly away from Cardiff or

Barry and further, on the horizon, the half-deleted blueish outline shores of Somerset and Devon held up the frankly bluer sky above.

Ernest Jones – Freud's disciple and biographer – had lived further along the coast, on the Gower peninsula, and when he was a small boy he misheard an adult conversation so that Master Jones believed that across the waters of the British Channel Heaven, not Devon, could be seen on a clear day. I, as a boy, thought Heaven, if it existed at all, would be very much like Ogmore-by-sea.

I walked away from the estuary towards the cliffs of Southern-down. Nobody seemed to be about, not one person on the sands. I felt I was the only person in the world alive that mid-week afternoon until, further on, I saw below a figure standing near the edge of the sea. Soon I could see it was a fisherman. He stood there with his oblique rod as my father used to do. Ahead of me, beyond the Witch's Nose of Southerndown, successive sunlit promontories, one after another, jutted out into the Bristol Channel as far as distant Nash Point. A small aeroplane, an old propellor Anson, presumably from RAF St Athans, buzzed the cloudless sky, then cut its engine off to admit a long hyphen of dramatic silence before resuming its safe drone. I turned back towards the estuary. I decided I would call on my Uncle Max who owned a bungalow close to Hardee's Bay.

Uncle Max, then some 80 years of age, a retired doctor who still saw an occasional patient and prescribed old-fashioned remedies such as the poisonous bromides, lived with his partner, middle-aged Stanley, and with their daft poodle, Peppy. Uncle, one of the younger brothers of my father, was the only homosexual in the family. My mother seemed to believe that Jews could not own such proclivities. 'Poor Max,' she used to say, 'he would have married and had a nice family if only he had met the right nice Jewish girl.' I liked my Uncle Max. I liked the way he uttered occasional, unintentional Sam Goldwynisms.

As I advanced towards his bungalow I could see that the front door gaped open invitingly. I walked down the path hearing the radio on within. No, not the radio, I suddenly realised. Max was playing the piano. From the hallway, at an open door, I watched Uncle's back swaying gently as he played. When he stopped abruptly I clapped and he swivelled round to face me, surprised. 'Do go on,' I said. He would not.

'I have some arthritis,' he said, looking at his hands. And then, not meaning to be humorous, he continued, 'Dannie, you should get your illnesses when you're young and healthy.'

I learnt that the front door remained open because Stanley had just taken Peppy out 'to do its stuff'. I also learnt from my Uncle Max that the house at the top of Craig-yr-eos Road, Green Hollows, was to be put up for auction. 'I know the house,' Max said. 'It belongs to the dentist. Splendid house. It would suit you and Joan. Nice garden, too.'

'Craig-yr-eos' in English means 'Rock-of-the-nightingale'. It was rumoured the 16th-century bard, Iorwerth Fynglwyd, settled for a time in Ogmore. Perhaps the nightingale was a bard not a bird?

'I read one of your books of poems,' Uncle Max said. 'Couldn't understand a word.'

Joan and I looked over several houses in South Wales before we finally decided to bid for Green Hollows. In November, 1972 it became ours. We did not realise then how much a second home would change the routines of our lives. It certainly meant that I, as a writer, was now reconnected to my roots. There were pebbles on the beach of Ogmore and perhaps sermons were hidden in some of them.

7. A Princeton Interlude

I've often thought that personal bad news arrives swiftly by telephone, good news at a slower, reluctant pace, by post. One of the letters that I picked up from the rough-haired brown doormat in our semi-dark hall that sunless winter morning would also change the direction of our lives – at least briefly.

The letter-heading announced Princeton University, Program in Creative Writing, 185 Nassau Street, New Jersey 06540, USA. Edmund Keeley, its Director, whose translations of such Greek poets as Seferis and Cavafy I had admired for some years, was inviting me to become Writer-in Residence, a Senior Fellow in Humanities, for an academic year at this Ivy League College. The salary offered beat that which I was receiving from my work at the chest clinic. More importantly, my duties would be light so that I could devote myself to my own writing. I would be expected, it seemed, to labour only one and a half days a week – on Tuesday mornings a workshop on poetry-writing; on Tuesday afternoons a workshop on prose; and on Wednesday afternoons I would be required to linger in my office so that any student who wished could converse with me.

Suddenly, amazingly, I had the opportunity to change my quotidian routines, to cease asking patients to breathe in, to breathe out; to turn away from the blazing screens subdued by X-rays. My work at the clinic had staled and I needed a break. Would the admin people allow me a sabbatical from September 1973 to early June 1974? Who would follow up my patients? What about the sarcoid survey I was engaged in? But after an interlude at Princeton perhaps I would return to my medical work refreshed?

'Joan,' I called out, taking the letter from the hall.

Our base at Ogmore-by-sea had already altered the grace-notes of our lives. Here was a more radical offering. Both Joan and I had obligations to ageing parents. Our eldest daughter, Keren, would continue her studies at Sussex University and, no doubt, she would visit my mother in her Cardiff flat. I did not know then that our worries should have been directed more towards Mary Mercer, Joan's mother. Susanna and David we would have to place in school in Princeton. Perhaps they would welcome that adventure?

The sabbatical from the chest clinic was reluctantly granted to me – leave without pay, but they generously offered to keep the post open for my return. So, at last, on September 11th, Joan and I and two of our three children boarded the Pan Am Jumbo plane at Heathrow. After our arrival at New York's Kennedy airport, we would have to travel the fifty miles or so down the New Jersey Turnpike, past the huge, monstrous outdoor chemistry sets, looming on and on, one after another, towards the oasis University town of Princeton where we had rented in advance, unseen, a house in Pine Street belonging to a music professor who, in turn, was already taking *his* sabbatical somewhere in Europe.

Pine Street was a quiet street of early-nineteenth-century, modest, clapboard houses, almost all white-painted. We had been instructed to collect the keys from the house next door. That done we climbed the shaky wooden steps to the creaking verandah and entered the tree-dark house. Heavy branches, a great show-jumping area for squirrels, overshadowed the roof of this house that would be our home for the next ten months.

Alas, the house was already occupied. As I examined the professor's records in his somewhat utilitarian living room – it was evident that the professor had a passionate attachment to Wagner – I heard shouts and cries from the kitchen.

'Fleas!'

The professor's dog and cat – presumably not the professor himself – had bequeathed the Abse family a live legacy. A bevy of black fleas sucked at Susanna's bare calf and David, too, was badly bitten. We would have to get the house fumigated. Meanwhile, carrying our luggage, forlorn, temporarily homeless, we abandoned the infested house, scratching and cursing all the professors of music in the world and their famished fleas. Bloody Wagner.

We took ourselves to Princeton's Nassau Inn, hoping for shelter, baths, showers, comfort, beds. We were exhausted, jet-lagged. The Nassau Inn was a quite posh, plush, air-conditioned hotel and, of course, wonderfully free of fleas. We entered it from its nearest back entrance so that in order to reach the Reception foyer we had to walk down a carpeted corridor so spongily thick that I felt I was suffering from the ataxia of inebriation. Near the open door of a Conference Room I rested the bags for a moment. Within, a man on a raised platform had evidently just finished some sales talk for he now addressed his audience who had their backs to the corridor. 'Any questions?' he asked. An awkward hush ensued. Suddenly the speaker raised his gaze and his eyes held mine. I felt impelled to shout, 'How do you get rid of fleas?' before moving quickly on to the Reception area. I stayed just long enough to witness the backs of the audience's heads becoming profiles.

The Creative Program building which contained artists' studios, classrooms, a cinema space, and several lofty, large offices, one of which had been assigned to me, lay close to the Princeton University Library and the Campus itself. Crossing the nearby, tree-lined side road into the Campus I was soon confronted by a conspicuous, outdoor, crude, gynaecological-looking sculpture by Lipchitz. Nor did I admire overmuch the Picasso sculpture which stood outside the magnificently endowed University Art Gallery.

The Campus itself, though, which faced Nassau Street's Hampstead-like row of shops and cafés, was most pleasing. Pathways led past ivy-clad, Victorian-Gothic colleges set strategically in a square mile or so of grassy parkland where students forever seemed to be throwing frisbees to one another. With the fall of darkness the heavy arches and buttresses, the towers and spires of the colleges, grew older by far, by centuries; and the night sky, unlike that familiar one regularly blotted out in London, grew infinite with all its hung stars.

I liked the large office that I inherited from the previous visiting writer, the American novelist, Robert Coover. In it, on my very first day, a student sat opposite me. 'I . . . er . . .' he began. He looked around the room, stared at the wall posters advertising a play by Robert Coover which had been staged in New York the previous year. 'I wonder if I might ask you . . .'

'What?'

'How did they come to invite you to Princeton?'

'How do you mean?'

'Um . . . Well, they asked Anthony Burgess, Kingsley Amis here. They're famous. But you? How come?'

'Maybe they've only got round to the As and Bs and Cs,' I said.

'It may be better for us,' the young man said, consoling me. 'I mean I'm not sure Anthony Burgess would give much of his time to students. I think if you're famous you haven't time to spend on students.'

Later, when he and the others presented me with their poems, I recalled my own apprentice work. Being untutored, reading Medicine not English, I owned no knowledge of theories about the craft of poetry and had made elementary mistakes. Some of these I might have avoided had someone pointed me towards, say, the 'Don'ts' of Ezra Pound. Politically evil Pound might have been, but he had climbed Parnassus and come down with a tablet of stone on which the Muse had written some vital commandments for the apprentice poet.

These and other critical strictures I passed on, pronouncing 'Don'ts' more often than 'Do's'. I doubted whether any of my students, though not a few were gifted, would become professional writers. But the workshops, I liked to think, were educative if only because, believing themselves to be budding authors, they read carefully the fine prose and poetry I introduced into the classes so that they could discover how others made the real thing strange.

I, myself, was being educated. As a medical student I had received only a technical education. Now, while the rich maple leaves began to haemorrhage on the Princeton trees, I attended illuminating lectures on Shakespeare and went to the Gauss seminars. I particularly looked forward to those that were to be conducted by Allen Tate who, years earlier, had visited us in London.

That summer evening Michael Hamburger had also joined us for dinner. Arriving late, flustered because half a mile away his car had broken down, Michael pronounced in a loud stricken voice that he must, at once, telephone the AA. Allen Tate assumed those initials stood for Alcoholics Anonymous (as they do in America) so when I suggested we should dine first he, alarmed, said, 'No, no, if Michael needs to, let him phone at once.'

'Where exactly is your car?' Joan said.

'In the Finchley Road.'

'Perhaps you shouldn't be driving,' said Allen solicitously, puzzling all of us.

We were shocked when we renewed our acquaintance with Allen Tate. He was thin, his head and face more skull-like. Because he was suffering from laryngitis, Tate's autobiographical talks at the Gauss seminars proved to be a distressing failure. Only those sitting in the front two rows could hear his weird, scratched whisper. From time to time, he would put out his tongue, as was his habit after making some wry joke. But since his humorous remarks could not be heard generally little laughter resulted. The silent audience, for the most part, merely witnessed that occasional grimace of his as he opened his mouth and grotesquely protruded his tongue.

We did not realise he was dying. Months later, along with Ted Weiss and Edmund 'Mike' Keeley, I sat at his hospital bedside as he whispered malicious anecdotes that illustrated the many frailties and vanities of John Berryman, Randall Jarrell and Robert Lowell. He had known these three poets well and now, as a critic of human behaviour, he was humorously merciless.

In October, while Allen Tate's Gauss seminars proceeded and the squirrel-haunted trees of Princeton had further ripened to become so much more spectacularly autumnal than those in Britain – more various, more colourful, blood-lit – we heard news of the Yom Kippur War, the attack on Israel by Egypt and Syria on two fronts. Syria had invaded the Golan Heights and advanced fifteen miles while President Sadat's troops had crossed the Suez Canal. Some 100,000 Egyptians had begun a massive offensive.

I listened to the news on the TV between repetitious advertisements for furniture stores (Hey Jerry, what's the story?); for washing powders (He's the bold one!); for spaghetti sauces (Dat's Italian!) and learnt that the Israelis had counterattacked and seemed about to crush the Egyptian army.

Each time Israel has been at war I have become involuntarily anxious and surprised by the charge of my own emotional involvement. What I have inherited of Judaism is a pious story that has faded on its scrolls and a voice out of earshot. For me the candles on the Menorah burn without heat or smoke and the glass of wine that waits for Elijah is set in somebody else's house; yet when Israel is threatened I become a conscious Jew. Only later, when the threat has dissipated, can I lower the flag, feel becalmed, listen sorrowfully to the dirge high on the walls and note the vultures sailing over.

I had felt that Israel's victory would not be the end of the blood-stained story and I tried to write a poem called 'Look out, someone's coming'. It did not work out; nor did I have the need those first few months in Princeton to fumble for other poems. I had leisure enough but somehow the Muse had not taken note of my change of address.

Joan and I enjoyed living in Princeton. We led a busy social life. Our sixteen-year-old daughter, Susanna, though, moped somewhat, missing her boyfriend in London. When I invited my male students to tea I could see they were attracted to her (she looked older than her years) but she took absolutely no notice of them. David, too, missed his friends and thought little of the school he attended. He must have felt bored for he asked if, on Tuesday afternoons, he could join my prose workshops as an auditor.

One of the things *I* missed was watching Cardiff City play. On leaving London I had made arrangements to subscribe not to the *TLS* or *The New Statesman* or *The London Magazine* but only to *The South Wales Football Echo*. But reading about games did not appease my addiction. One Saturday morning, David and I, desperate, watched the Princeton soccer team when they opposed Yale. The November sun shone without warmth and the air laden with gaseous ice made me feel the femurs in my thighs. Shivering, every quarter of an hour we shouted forlornly, without enthusiasm, 'PRINCE-TON, PRINCE-TON.' At half-time we were shocked to observe the other spectators produce from fur coats, briefcases, hampers, not flasks of hot coffee but cans of beer and Coca-Cola to which they added, teeth chattering, ICE CUBES.

In December the weather deteriorated further. This concerned us since we planned to hire a Toyota which, blizzards willing, would transport us for the Xmas break to Charlottesville where, at the

University of Virginia, Wilfred had practised as Clinical Professor of Psychiatry for several decades.

A sudden thaw promised an easier journey and made me think, during the end-of-term days, as I walked to my office across Nassau Street, how ice consisted not only of frozen water but of captive time. The half-anaesthetised winter sunlight released regular seconds of audible December Time, drip drip drip, from the small, glycerine-like, globular prisons on the twigs of the trees' branches. But by the end of the week the air razored again and, soon, serious snow drifted across the windscreen of our red Toyota as it made its way out of the precincts of Princeton, its windscreen wipers hysterically active.

Some weeks after we had arrived in Princeton we found ourselves attending occasional decorous dinner parties. The conversation frequently focused on Nixon and the Watergate scandal. In the New Year such intermittent party-going did not falter. The male American feet in English suede shoes continued to indent expensive carpets. It was all affluence and elegance but Joan and I no longer overheard worried discussions about the self-incriminating aberrations of Nixon and the illegitimacy of Watergate. It was as if, by 1974, our Princeton friends had become numb to further talk of tax evasion, lies, bugging, burglary.

I led a privileged life. I spent hours at the University Library, went with Joan to the University Art Gallery, to the cinema and to the McCarter Theater; and at the Weiss's attended a few chamber music recitals. In addition, English visitors came to give their one-off lectures, Donald Davie and Frank Kermode among them. And my own creative-writing sessions passed by pleasantly enough. I never felt enraged like one of my colleagues, the novelist Geoffrey Wolfe, whom one day I heard shouting from the adjacent classroom, 'How the hell can I teach you anything when not one of you has even read Hemingway!'

In Britain, so I read in the *New York Times*, industry was paralysed by disputes involving the coal mines, the railways and the power stations. It was the uncomfortable time of the three-day week. In Princeton, by contrast, all I had to worry about was my then temporary writer's block. Fortune changed soon enough. One night we heard a throat-gripping scream from the snowed-in darkness of Pine Street. We never did discover what or whom; but it was as if that thin, prolonged scream heralded the phone-call that awoke us from blank sleep some nights later. Joan's voice quivered, 'My mother has had a stroke.' For a little while the transatlantic call that summoned Joan to England, to Lancashire, left us each in our own head.

The morning after Joan had gone, I walked down freezing snow-locked Nassau Street and again it seemed like an omen when I heard the bell tolling from the nearby church. It was too apt, surely: the bell tolling, the hearse and the few cars lined up in the church drive. A small group, most facing in the same direction, stood between the church door and the long black car. They were motionless and the bell tolled. For me they were strangers mourning a stranger. And if one of them had looked up then, and smiled, how odd that would have been; but they stayed, solemn, uncertain in that interval, and I thought of my mother-in-law, Mary Mercer, as I raised my eyes towards the church's high tower where the great bell was swinging. When I next spoke on the phone to England, Joan's voice was small. Mary had died that night.

Six weeks or so later, soon after Joan and I were reunited in the Pine Street house, one of Theodore Weiss's postgraduate students, Mark Boada, arranged to meet me at my office. He wished to interview me for the Princeton student magazine, *The Nassau Literary Review*.

Sitting opposite me he stared at the posters about Robert Coover's play on the wall. 'I hear you're going to have a play of your own on in New York,' he said.

'Not until April.'

The Dogs of Pavlov had had its first production at The Questors Theatre, Ealing, in their New Plays Festival of 1969. Now, almost five years later, it was to have its American première at the small Cubiculo Theater at 414 West 51st Street.

'You'll be replacing Coover's posters with those advertising *The Dogs of Pavlov*,' Mark Boada said.

In the subsequent interview (I have the transcript on my desk as I write) I confessed, 'My predecessor in this office has left his marks, his books and pictures. I have not. I feel I'm a transient visitor, that I'm here and not here, that life in Princeton is real and pleasant enough yet it's also rather dreamlike. I can't even remember my own telephone number which worries me, but I suppose that's because I don't feel it's worth remembering. I do have a sense of being a visitor and that I will be moving on.'

Actually, Edmund Keeley had sounded me out about staying on as

Writer-in-Residence at Princeton for a further year; but I had the job at the chest clinic in London waiting for me. And now that Susanna had returned to London to live temporarily around the corner from our Golders Green home with our friends Lewis and Nan Greifer, we had two daughters the other side of the Atlantic. Besides, there was my ageing mother in Cardiff to consider and Joan's father, Jack, so recently a widower, in St Helens, Lancashire.

Apart from relatives, dreams and responsibilities, I missed many things back home – not the practice of medicine so much but friends; the sunsets of Ogmore-by-sea; watching Cardiff City play at Ninian Park; Welsh familiarity; my weekly chess games with John Watkins; British newspapers; our Health Service; the BBC; all manner of things.

In my conversation with Mark Boada he referred to my early (first) autobiographical novel, *Ash on a Young Man's Sleeve*, which, in turn, prompted me to remark how an autobiographer deletes the matter of his own past life and substitutes it with artifice, how the life that was real becomes extinct, or, at least for the most part, evaporates, goes into the mists . . .

I wonder, as I recall my agreeable months in Princeton, if that's what I am doing now: destroying my past by selecting and omitting certain memories. Is all autobiography a form of suicide?

Finally Mark Boada asked me, 'When do you go back to London?' and I replied, 'In May. But I don't want to jump ahead that far. I'm enjoying myself here.'

Before leaving London for Princeton I had agreed to choose, with Philip Larkin, the Poetry Book Society's quarterly selections for 1973–4. The Society was administered by the Arts Council and the Literary Director, Charles Osborne, had assured me that the books submitted would be forwarded to me promptly so that I would have time enough to confer, by post, with Philip Larkin in Hull.

Admirer though I was, and still am, of Larkin's memorable poetry – his poems are so sharp-eyed, appropriate with arresting detail and do not eschew sentiment – I had doubts whether our epistolary relationship would be entirely harmonious. We had been on opposing sides in the Maverick-Movement dispute of the 1950s which the Press had described as 'literary gang warfare'. Apart from linguistic disagreements, I had deplored the crassly nationalistic, right-wing Amis-Larkin views of the Movement and their consciously contrived philistinism.

I did not know, though, of Larkin's personal obsession about money, his almost comical stinginess which Andrew Motion was later to reveal in his biography. He had sent me a letter in which he opined about certain books which had not reached me in Princeton: they had gone astray. Because of a deadline a swift response from me was required. So I telephoned him.

'Could I speak to Philip Larkin?' I asked when, eventually, I got through to the University Library in Hull.

'Dr Larkin,' a woman's voice replied.

'Is Philip Larkin there?' I repeated.

'You want to speak to Dr Larkin?'

'Yes,' I said, 'Philip Larkin.'

'It's DOCTOR Larkin,' she insisted sternly.

'What?'

'DOCTOR Larkin. You desire to speak to DOCTOR Philip Larkin.'

'Oh,' I said. 'Yes, I do. So would you please tell him that DOCTOR Abse would like a word with him.'

It was not customary in 1974, nor as cheap, to make personal telephone calls to or from the USA as it is nowadays. So when Philip Larkin heard my voice he appeared understandably puzzled.

'Where . . . where are you speaking from?' he asked.

'From Princeton.'

'Princeton?'

'Yes, Princeton.'

'But that's where I've been writing to,' Larkin said.

'Well, I'm still here.'

'At the University?'

'Yes.'

'The University?'

'Yes, look those books . . .'

'You're phoning from the USA?'

'Yes.'

'The USA!'

'I want to talk to you about the books. Your letter . . .'

'Are you phoning from the University?'

'I'm phoning from home actually, but listen, the books never . . .'

'Are you paying for this call then?'

'Yes, I am. I haven't received the books from the Arts Council so I can't comment on . . .'

'Can you reclaim the money, do you think?'

'How do you mean?'

'From the Arts Council?'

'I don't think so. Look, in your letter . . .'

'I've never had a phone call from America before!'

'About the Choice and the Recommendation . . .'

'This must be costing you a packet.'

There is a story about the comedian, Jack Benny, who had the reputation of being miserly. A masked highwayman, gun in hand, says to Benny, 'Your money or your life.' Jack Benny pauses. 'Let me think.'

When *The Dogs of Pavlov* had originally been commissioned by the Questors Theatre in Ealing I had remembered a dubious experiment undertaken at a Psychology Laboratory in Yale. The Yale scientist had demonstrated how ordinary people would obey evil commands in deference to a respected authority and I had taken as theme for my drama the trust between two young lovers involved in such an experiment. After the first performance of *The Dogs of Pavlov*, thanks to generous notices and a BBC television focus on the play, the theatre had been packed. When I had read Gary O'Connor's review in the *Financial Times* – 'a work of exceptional merit, well worthy of a transfer' – I began to hope my play would have a West End production.

Eventually, recurring schemes for it to be re-staged broke down. As so often in the world of theatre, Hope was followed by its shadow, Disappointment.

But now it was receiving a production in New York, thanks to an enthusiastic recommendation by Joseph Frank, the biographer of Dostoevsky, who was then teaching at Princeton. That early April I frequently travelled from Princeton to the small Cubiculo Theater on West 51st Street to attend rehearsals and listen to American accents utter lines devised for British voices. Despite the best efforts of the director, Maurice Edwards, I did not think the production as good as the one at the Questors. Nevertheless, it received good notices and once more I thought it might transfer to a more commercial theatre. But a negative notice in *The Village Voice* by a Yale academic soon stopped a Broadway showing. Because of the high costs of a theatre production in a main theatre in New York, one bad review can deter any hesitating producer and leave the hopeful dramatist with a little infarct in his soul.

In early May, Wilfred and his wife Elizabeth, along with their friend Harriet Cooper, came to see my play. Afterwards, Wilfred, characteristically, enthused about *The Dogs of Pavlov*. Even when I was a fifth-form schoolboy and I had shown him my immature writings my 'big' brother was always unequivocally encouraging – unlike Leo who never shirked from unloosening a devastating arrow of a remark such as 'You should stick to poems, Dannie!'

After the final performance of *The Dogs of Pavlov* I realised that I had forgotten to pick up a poster from the Cubiculo Theater. No matter, we would be leaving Princeton in a matter of weeks. I decided I might as well leave Robert Coover's posters about *his* play triumphant on the office wall for the next incumbent, the next Visiting Writer-in-Residence.

8. Back to the Bright Prison

The excitements of renewals and return journeys. Home again! It was an Irishman who justly urged, 'Do not cry out against *la patrie*. Your native land, after all, will give you the two most exquisite pleasures of your life: that of leaving her and that of coming back.'

There is something smugly satisfying, a small primitive territorial victory, in reclaiming familiar possessions: this expansive second-hand desk I happen to be writing on now which my mother had once given me – 'Fit for an Emperor, son'; those well-thumbed books on the shelves; records bought years ago waiting to be replayed; paintings on the walls – this one by Jack Jones depicting a Welsh village which resembles a Lowry too much or that one by my father-in-law of two silhouetted children walking in dawn's strange light over the brow of a hill.

Everything seemed much the same. Our house told us we had hardly been away, and that it had preserved the same cracks in the ceilings. Outside, in Hodford Road, the winds of May had kept their annual appointment and brought down from the flowering cherry trees much of their spectacular pink blossom. The trees themselves appeared to be staring down at their own reflections on the pavement. Every year, each May, the sight of these rifled trees makes me think, for some odd reason, of a beautiful woman putting on lipstick before a mirror.

Having overcome, more or less, my jet-lag I decided to attend the Toynbee-Nicolson Wednesday lunch club. I rarely went to these Bertorelli lunches but having been away so long it would be good to see there my old friend Peter Vansittart and the other regulars. Besides, Bertorelli's was in Charlotte Street, a javelin throw from the Central Medical Establishment where, on the fifth floor, I supervised the chest clinic. My leave did not end until Monday, May 27th, but I thought that before lunch I would show my face at the clinic and discover what my work-load would be the following week.

In the foyer of the Central Medical Establishment the same porter presided as he had done for many years. It seemed he always had difficulty in pronouncing my surname. Occasionally, Joan, whom he recognised, would pick me up from the clinic when she had had a rendezvous somewhere else. As soon as she entered he would dial my number and say, 'Dr Asbe, your wife's here.' Having heard him mispronounce my name so many times one day Joan finally asked, 'Could you let Dr Asbe know I'm here.' He hesitated. 'You mean Dr Abse,' he said.

Now, though, he avoided uttering my name. His brow furrowed, his head sank into his shoulders deleting his neck as he stared hard at me. 'Are you feeling better, sir?' he asked. On the fifth floor, I discovered that my work-load the following week would be quite light. Importantly, among the letters piled into my in-tray was one which asserted that my salary had been raised to £5427 a year.

At Bertorelli's, in the usual upstairs room, over the usual veal and spaghetti lunch, I heard no one speak about the three-day week and other current economic problems. I found myself sitting between Freddie Ayer and William Coldstream. My conversation with the renowned philosopher focused on Tottenham Hotspur Football Club. For one winter I had traitorously not watched Cardiff City but, on Saturday afternoons, had joined my friend and neighbour, Lewis Greifer, in the Grandstand at White Hart Lane where I had peered over the tidy parting of Freddie Ayer and the non-existent one of music critic, Hans Keller. Behind me camped a more conventional soccer fan who, all through the match, sucked boiled sweets. Every time Spurs scored I had to extract a sticky lump of orange- or raspberry- or lemon-coloured carbohydrate from the back of my neck. If I had shut my eyes for ninety minutes I could still have known how many goals Tottenham had scored simply by counting the half-sucked acid drops that had unerringly landed above my collar.

In the following weeks I discovered that there were fewer patients to see at the clinic. Pulmonary tuberculosis had been, for some years, sharply on the wane. TB had been a scourge of man for thousands of years. Exhumed prehistoric skeletons of hunchbacks indicated that it had raged to wreck and twist and cripple its victims long before the era of recorded history. In the 14th century BC the priests of the Indo-Aryans treated the disease by chanting, 'Oh Fever, with thy Brother Consumption, with thy Sister Cough, go to the people below.' In ancient China, tuberculosis of the lungs was known as *lao-ting*. The Greeks suffered from the disease and they bore it with better gifts to the Romans who, in their turn, spread it throughout the conquered countries of Europe.

It was not until 1882 that the tubercle bacillus was discovered by the German bacteriologist, Robert Koch, who demonstrated that the various manifestations of TB – the bone malformations, scrofula, the lung disease and so on – were all due to the same crafty destructive germ. It was remarkable that in my time, in our time, after such a long and terrible and dramatic history, the disease, tuberculosis, could at last be defeated because of the discovery of streptomycin, PAS and INAH. Only a score of years or so earlier I overheard a distressed patient saying, 'TB, doctor? That stands for totally buggered, doesn't it?' It was wonderful that the phthisic casualty lists were now being so radically reduced, at least in Europe; but it meant that the nature of my work at the chest clinic was changing.*

In August, our whole family was reunited at Ogmore, including my mother and Joan's father. Once more we breathed in the sweet air; watched the seagulls, high up, freewheeling; sunbathed in the sand-dunes; and, on the beach, listened to the irregularities of breaking waves, the pitch and tone of them, the long hush of disturbed shingle

* In recent years there has been a recrudescence of tuberculosis in Britain affecting, in particular, those suffering from Aids and those exiled Down-and-Outs who made their reappearance in the selfish streets of Thatcher's Britain.

and then the sand sizzling – the noise in a frying pan – as the tide receded.

There are occasions and sights at Ogmore that I have never been able nor wished to forget. I remember, for instance, one early morning walk on the Ogmore sands when the tide was out. The sun bequeathed a mercury-backed dazzle to the sea. The beach, at that time of the morning, was empty. I looked towards the barely outlined coast of Somerset across the Bristol Channel and walked on, half aware of the erratic rhythm of the sea. Then, ahead of me, I saw a man, alone, sitting on the pebbles, his trousers tucked into his socks. Nearby lay a white stick. The man gazed outward, seemingly towards Somerset, but, of course, he was blind. And I, walking on sand, and hence silently, suddenly felt myself to be a voyeur, watching him watch nothing.

I noticed how he was feeling the pebbles around him, one by one. He picked them up, weighed them, felt perhaps the early sun's faint warmth in them before replacing each one deliberately. He looked my way, so that I wondered what parable is this? From behind a rock suddenly a woman appeared, obviously his companion, and I strolled on listening once more to the sea and to the sorrowing of the seagulls.

Not everything was dazzle and dapple and candy at Ogmore that summer of 1974. I discovered that opposite Green Hollows we had to endure a strangely aggressive neighbour, one we nicknamed the Butcher because of his hypertensive, beefy appearance. I did not know initially that his behaviour matched to a 'T' his looks. My son and one of his young friends had been throwing a frisbee to each other as they strolled up Craig-yr-eos Road from the beach. The disc had eventually swerved into our neighbour's front garden. The Butcher would not return the frisbee and shouted oaths at the boys. 'Don't worry,' I told David for I assumed that if I spoke to the neighbour, adult to adult, sweetly, he would not fail to return it.

Later, over his hedge, I observed him gardening. I approached and greeted him, I hope, pleasantly. But when I requested the boys' frisbee, for no evident reason he began to visibly boil. He screamed and suddenly threw the pitchfork he was holding towards me. I stood close to the hedge, amazed. 'You're mad,' I said. He lumbered into his house slamming the door forcefully. I retired not out, not hurt, but without the frisbee. I did not feel it was worth tangling further with my neighbour. I was no hero and the Butcher seemed afflicted with psychic, seething, unknown resentments that could surface too easily. A year or so later we were all delighted when we observed the FOR SALE placard outside his house.

By then, though, once again I began to feel even more than I used to that the clinic had become a bright prison. I had been asked to begin a survey of people who had been exposed to blue asbestos (crocidolite). All I had to do was to check their X-rays annually and urge them to cease smoking since there was a known powerful synergistic effect of tobacco smoke on any inhaled and trapped asbestos fibres. It was a monotonous surveillance task that did not extend me.

One advantage of only rarely being stretched at the clinic was that I continued to have time and space enough to write. When I was invited to become the full-time book editor of the *Sunday Express*, I had no hesitation in declining. It was not a paper I admired. I preferred in any case to be an occasionally bored doctor who could write what he wished rather than become a journalist subject to the caprices and prejudices of a Fleet Street editor. I like the story told by Graham Lord, a more recent employee of the *Sunday Express*. He relates how John Junor, the *Express*'s editor, in sacking one of his feature writers, had thundered, 'Sometimes you are very good, sometimes slipshod and awful. What I want is consistent mediocrity.'

Sometimes I felt pleased that I pursued two vocations; other times I wished I did not have to visit the clinic but could instead work on the poem in my head or the one in recent drafts on the page. Poetry, alas, could not help me to relieve my financial responsibilities – most of the family to support, house mortgages to pay off. On such occasions I felt trapped.

9. A Meeting with Elias Canetti

I was quite close to Hampstead Tube Station when, across the road, I spotted Elias Canetti sitting at one of the outdoor tables of The Coffee Cup. How typical, I thought, that he should still, in his now ripe maturity, still haunt cafés. Though decades older than when we had last met, he continued to resemble, with his squarish large head and lavish moustache, one of his heroes, Stendhal. 'I owe to Stendhal the conviction that all individuals if they could reveal themselves fully, would be extraordinary and exciting,' he had once rebuked me after I had remarked that a certain common acquaintance of ours frankly bored me. Canetti, to be sure, had a scalpel-sharp curiosity about people as, indeed, a novelist should.

Yet he was not given to satisfying inquisitiveness about himself. As if offering me a birthday present many years ago he, clandestinely, whispered to me his telephone number. When, rarely, I did happen to dial that number, a high-pitched voice, claiming to be Canetti's Chinese cook, responded. Only after he had discovered the caller's name would Canetti deign to unmask his true acoustic identity. It was surprising that such a costively secretive man as Canetti would, in future years, publish for public exposure autobiographical books about his early upbringing in Bulgaria, Vienna and Zurich. These vastly interesting books would contribute to win him the Nobel Prize for Literature in 1981.

It was a pleasant, warm, summer night. I decided to postpone my journey home and cross the road to The Coffee Cup. I could not help recalling those immediate post-war years when I had first met Canetti. I was then a medical student lodging in Swiss Cottage. Not long after I had arrived there, hung up my overcoat in the wardrobe's vertical coffin, eaten the Welsh cakes and the apple packed for me by my mother, I had ventured forth from 38 Aberdare Gardens to discover that I had settled in a cosmopolitan area with a remarkably vivid café life initiated by refugees from Austria and Germany. There, in The Cosmo, among the aspiring artists and the other youthful denizens, Elias Canetti stood out, not only because he was middle-aged, some twenty years older than most of us, but because of his unswerving courtesy, his evident spectacular erudition, his formidable aura and presence. Besides, he was a published author, the begetter of that strange, admired novel *Auto-da-Fe*, written, he told us, when he was only twenty-one. When questioned about what he was presently writing he made it clear that it would be a masterpiece, a book about crowds and power. '*Crowds and Power?* When will it be finished?' Canetti explained that he had been working on this monumental book for more than ten years. 'I don't want to contradict myself as Freud once did,' he asserted with a sonorous seriousness, amazing us. I was one who thought his immodesty wonderfully breathtaking. On winning the Nobel Prize, Canetti must have been unsurprised when the honour came his way . . .

He insisted we call him Canetti, not Elias, since he loathed his first name. Was that the true reason? His own heroes, Stendhal, Kafka, Musil among them, were hardly thought of by us as Henri, Franz and Bobby! Canetti was a lord spiritually and lords in England are not known by their first names. He was also, to my mind, because of his aphoristic remarks and wild imagination, a scholar poet – a poet, however, who wrote prose. He uttered remarks like 'The truly noble doctor invents a new disease for each patient' and 'The true Last Judgment will be when the resurrected accuse God in all languages'. Silly or poetic?

Canetti had such a sacred view of books by great authors that he even cared passionately where they were placed in the bookcase. In *The Play of the Eyes* he relates how he caught sight of a Buchner volume in a Vienna bookshop. He extracted the book and placed it in a holy position on the shelf – next to four volumes of Kleist! I remember what he told me about his visit to Graham Greene: how Greene had expressed his admiration for *Auto-da-Fé*; how he would be grateful if Canetti would sign his copy of the book for him. Canetti, it seemed, as he sat in his chair, had observed a wall of books opposite him and had noted how his own novel was placed right at the bottom – 'Right-hand side, in the servile position of Z,' Canetti exclaimed indignantly. Meanwhile, as Canetti took in the insignificant, inferior, and therefore to him, insulting position of his book, Greene had scrambled about in search of it, up down, right, left, centre, and though *on his knees* could not locate Canetti's novel. And Canetti had pretended he did not know where to look either.

The story depended, of course, so much on Canetti's animated engagement with it as he relived the incident and how, with startling skill, he mimicked Graham Greene's voice, mannerisms, posture, hesitations. In his telling of the story, Canetti had given me, his auditor, a comical glimpse of a trivial power struggle, human rivalry.

Canetti's anecdotes revealed something of himself, his interest – an obsessive interest perhaps – in the relationships of dominion: the power of one individual over another or others. No wonder conductors of orchestras fascinated him. Only Canetti would have noticed that the conductor, Hermann Scherchen (an acquaintance of Anna Mahler in Vienna), in extending his hand in greeting would raise it very high, so high that the other person reaching for it would feel, according to Canetti, inferior and experience a minim of temporary humiliation.

When *Crowds and Power* was published in England in 1962 I discovered a remarkable, peculiarly innovative piece about the omniscient role of the conductor – how the maestro's performance so aptly demonstrates the nature of power. Canetti pointed out how the conductor, unlike the audience and the orchestra, stands on a dais before the sitting and obedient orchestra, while the audience sits, still and quietly submissive behind him. 'Quite small movements are all he needs to wake this or that instrument to life or to silence it at will. He has the power of life and death over the voices of the instruments.' As for the audience they are 'as much part of the conductor's design as the obedience of the orchestra' – when the conductor appears everyone becomes still and remains still until he, the conductor, ceases. 'The applause he receives is the ancient salute to the victor, and the magnitude of his victory is measured by its volume.'

I suppose, being young, I was also impressed by the fact that Canetti had known so many celebrated authors such as Brecht, Babel, Musil. Some few he venerated, praised without stint; but when contemptuous of them he was contemptuous with enthusiasm. When I happened to mention that I had read and liked a poem by C. Day Lewis, he bridled. 'Day Lewis,' he said, 'no, no, worthless, he pot-boils detective stories under another name.' Even Brecht he damned as a person. 'A wretched man, only interested in writing for money.'

Once, in The Cosmo, I happened to share a table with Wolf Mankowitz who had graduated from being a 'pure' Leavisite contributor to the Cambridge magazine *Scrutiny* to become a 'commercial' novelist – and had recently contributed articles on dieting to the *Evening Standard*. I became aware of Canetti glowering at me from the other side of the restaurant. After Wolf quit I was beckoned to Canetti's table where he passionately declared, 'You shouldn't talk to that man. He's worthless. Have you seen his articles, how he uses words? You'll be polluted by people like that.'

It seemed to me then no less than now that the notion that journalism could corrupt a serious writer was a romantic cliché and, unlike many clichés, did not even encapsulate a truth. Yet I shared Canetti's righteous concern for words. Words do seem to own divine attributes: one can believe they are the source of revelation and that if one could discover some secret combination of them one might attain eternal beatitude. They are like gods in a way, immortal and dangerous. We summon them to help us – to curse and to praise; they allow us some measure of understanding within them and, beyond their definitions, there is only mystery and silence. To let them stray into a mere detective novel or, worse, into an inconsequential article for the *Evening Standard* was, for Canetti, surely to demean the gods themselves and to sell them into dark bondage as slaves.

When I arrived at The Coffee Cup, he rose from his seat as courteously as ever. 'May I join you?' I asked. When I spoke he paid attention as a great physician would. He had the habit of holding his head on one side in a listening posture. 'Are you still, in your poetry, approaching the quotidian with barbs?' he asked.

It was not long before our conversation was interrupted by two people at the next table who began to raise their voices. 'You're talking rubbish,' one shouted. 'You're marvellously stupid.' The other glared before saying imperiously, 'Calm down, angry lamb.' They seemed to be discussing the virtue of a woman known to them both.

'They're twins,' Canetti whispered to me.

I had not noticed until then how much the two men resembled each other. At least they had opposing views of a certain lady. When, eventually, the twins left the café, one could be seen to be much taller than the other. This imbalance of stature seemed to excite Canetti. 'The shorter one spoke louder than the tall one,' he said, agitated. He then launched into a story about twins and how one of them had died. 'As that dying twin lost flesh,' he said, 'and grew thinner and thinner, his brother got fatter and fatter. Finally, when the sick twin died, the survivor had become utterly gross, twice his original size.'

I could not help but smile at this typical Canetti anecdote. Once more I was reminded that this future Nobel Prizewinner, sitting across the table from me, was an extraordinary man, one relentlessly obsessed by the grotesque, by supremacy and control.

Soon a figure, one not grotesque but certainly odd, stood close to our table. It was Arthur Jacobs. He hovered nearby, mute, evidently waiting for me to ask him to join us. Arthur, a Glaswegian Jew, wrote modest poetry of particular Jewish interest, which revealed how aware he was of his alienation from the lost world of his grandparents and great grandparents – of a piety that was once commonplace, its Yiddish jokes, poetry and folksongs.*

When I introduced Arthur to Canetti, Arthur blushed as was his wont and, characteristically, remained silent. I was used to Arthur's aphasia. Occasionally he would ring our doorbell in Golders Green and soon I would find myself in our living room asking him questions in order to prompt him to speak. 'How are things, Arthur?' 'OK.' Silence. 'Have you seen Jon Silkin lately?' 'Yes.' 'You've been to Newcastle?' 'Yes.' 'You saw Jon there?' 'Yes.' Silence. 'Have you written any poems lately?' 'Not much.'

Now it was Canetti who found himself interrogating Arthur and the less Arthur spoke the more I sensed Canetti becoming interested in him. Perhaps Arthur's penetrating silences reminded Canetti of Hermann Broch, the Austrian novelist whom Canetti admired as a young man? Of Broch Canetti had said that his silences were something physical.

After I left The Coffee Cup, I kept remembering how kind Canetti had been to me when I was young: had shown me texts I would not otherwise have encountered; listened to my youthful, opinionated vapourings as if they were important; told me of writers I had not yet heard of, such as Cesare Pavese and a not yet published young novelist called Iris Murdoch; introduced me to Kathleen Raine, thinking she might be a useful person for me to know; even arranged a desperately flawed verse-play of mine to be presented at the Institute of Contemporary Arts. I was in debt to him for many long-ago things – remembered and unremembered, not least a 1905 book of Bushmen legends.

Kathleen Raine, in her autobiography, *The Lion's Mouth*, portrays Canetti as a kind of demi-god, a master, a prophet, endowed with a peculiar greatness and one who owned 'the magical power of evoking from us, ourselves'. She confesses that she had 'admired Canetti more unreservedly, taken more pleasure in the riches of his imagination, that robber's den of treasures that reveals itself to those who possess the open, sesame, than in the mind of any other person I have known well.' I had known Canetti only a little and merely for a few years in my youth – even so, I count that acquaintanceship a rare privilege and an enrichment.

---

* Arthur, alas, died in 1994, aged 57. His interesting *Collected Poems* was published in 1996 by the Menard Press and Hearing Eye.

10. Pythagoras (Smith)

A few weeks before we left Princeton Joan and I attended a party partly given in honour of Howard Nemerov who, since 1969, had been Professor of English at Washington University, St Louis. On my first trip to the USA I had shared a platform with him and Richard Eberhart for a poetry reading at Boston College. He had been, I remembered, very witty. Physically, he had resembled a lithe, professional tennis player.

A decade had passed since then and here he was, now somewhat more adipose. Hearing about *The Dogs of Pavlov* currently being performed in New York, Nemerov, himself the author of plays as well as poetry, introduced me to one of the guests who, as a theatre critic, wrote for the *Tulane Drama Review*.

'Theatre critics,' smiled Howard Nemerov. 'Father forgive them for they know not what I'm doing.'

Nemerov's acquaintance told me about Washington University's prestigious New Play Competition – the winning play would be staged at St Louis and the playwright would be rewarded with a VERY large cash prize.

'Of course, they receive hundreds and HUNDREDS of scripts,' this friendly drama critic mused. 'The plays submitted must never have had a production so you couldn't offer them *The Dogs of Pavlov*. You'll have to write another one.'

When I was a medical student, I too had become a sporadic critic for a theatre magazine. The magazine, published fortnightly, was not important enough to be offered first-night free tickets by theatre managements and I was not important enough to cover the main plays in the West End. This, the editor, Roy Walker, did himself. So, on second-night performances of plays, frequently new plays and frequently staged, it seemed to me, in the vicinity of Notting Hill Gate – I was forever taking a 31 bus – I claimed my seat in row G amongst a sparse audience. How sparse depended on how many friends the actors had, the size of the cast and whether or not the dramatist was alive and well and living in Notting Hill Gate. Before the house lights went down and the curtain went up, there I sat with my swanky chest stuck out, an invisible sceptre in my hand and my two eyes narrowed, ready to write my worst. I had every opportunity to be acidulous; almost all the new plays I saw were inept.

Some imagine writers to be encouraged by other writers' impoverished creations. They believe that an aspiring dramatist, for instance, might well think, 'I can do better than that.' This notion is wrong. Rather it is those rare plays that thrill one that prove to be seminal. Later, when I ceased to be a theatre critic and saw, as a paying customer, such twentieth-century plays as Pirandello's *As You Desire Me*, Eugene O'Neill's *The Iceman Cometh* and Tennessee Williams's *The Glass Menagerie* I felt the urge myself to write for the stage.

In an essay about the theatre, T.S. Eliot spoke of his abiding desire to write a play free of the faults of his last work and how that desire had acted as 'a very powerful and useful incentive' to write the next one. Such an incentive has also prompted me, every five years or so, to attempt working on another play. 'We are only undefeated because we go on trying,' Eliot had averred in another context.

I was proud of having written such a strong moral drama as *The Dogs of Pavlov* but when I returned home from Princeton I resolved that if ever I should write another play I would try for more inner gaiety than was present in *The Dogs* – 'gaiety transforming all that dread' or, at least, one that would allow more proliferating blossom to disguise the underlying nettle. If I wrote such a play, maybe I would enter it for the Washington University New Play Competition.

Before many months had passed I had begun to work on a script that eventually became a play, *Pythagoras (Smith)*. Oddly, as in my first play, *House of Cowards*, its source was one of my own poems. The poet and BBC producer, George MacBeth, had presented a long poem of mine called 'Funland' on Radio 3. George had asked me to introduce it. And when I spoke of its starting point I had referred to T.S. Eliot's lines from 'East Coker':

> The whole earth is our hospital
> Endowed by the ruined millionaire.

'My experience of human irrationality,' I continued, 'the discovery of it in my own behaviour and in others; as I encounter it in my personal life and in my medical practice; as I'm affected by it in the absurdity of public political action; as indeed I'm threatened by it in the clash of public powers; makes me feel sometimes, as I'm sure it does others, that the earth is no ordinary hospital but a lunatic asylum whose inmates live out suffering lives of black comedy. Technically in "Funland", I have attempted to use surrealistic images and effects with humour. For if a long poem is to be sad, then perhaps there must be points in it when the reader should laugh.'

Not long after the broadcast of 'Funland' I accepted an invitation to visit the New College of Speech and Drama at Pavlova House. Working from the BBC script of 'Funland' the students had, much to my surprise, made a dramatisation of the poem. That student production gave me the idea that 'Funland' could be dramatised in a more radical way than they had envisaged.

This – my own dramatisation of 'Funland' – was presented at the Questors Theatre New Plays Festival of 1975. It was far from being a success. I needed to start again, to forgo the actual lines of the poem and to concentrate instead on the people named in the poem, on developing especially the character of the asylum inmate called Pythagoras.

When I had finally completed the play, my agent forwarded it to the Royal Court Theatre. And I myself, as an afterthought, posted a spare copy off to the judges of the New Play Competition at Washington University, St Louis. I had never entered a competition before – nor have I since. I knew the chances of winning would be slim; but someone has to win a lottery.

Many months passed, almost time enough for a baby to be conceived and born, before I heard that someone at the Royal Court had passed my play on to Peter Farago who, happily, wished to direct it at the Birmingham Repertory Theatre. We met for lunch in a restaurant close to the chest clinic and discussed the play at length. 'Have you any ideas of who should play Pythagoras?' he asked me. 'I have in mind Roger Sloman.'

Peter Farago, fortunately, did not seem to be one of those self-infatuated directors who decide the script needs pepping up a bit: that *Lysistrata* requires an all-male cast; that dwarfs only are to appear in *Julius Caesar*; that *The Cherry Orchard* should be set in industrial Newark, New Jersey, in the 22nd century. On the contrary, he seemed sensitive to the text and open to suggestions about the direction.

The play was to go into rehearsal when a letter arrived from Washington University. They informed me that *Pythagoras* was one of three plays shortlisted for the generous cash prize. And would I please confirm that my play had not had a previous theatre production before final judgement. Oh dear. Too late.

Pythagoras opened at the Birmingham Repertory Theatre on my birthday, September 22nd 1976. It received good reviews and soon, outside the theatre, they had posters up promoting the play. '*Theatrically exuberant as well as touchingly funny, sincerely free of sentimentality and eminently actable.*' *Daily Telegraph*. And from Michael Billington in the *Guardian*: '*A play that blends intelligence with delight in theatrical effect.*'

I had great hopes of the play moving to London. Birmingham Rep had made arrangements for three of their productions to be staged at the National Theatre: *Measure for Measure* and Ben Jonson's *The Devil is an Ass* at the Olivier and Lyttleton and *Pythagoras* at the Cottesloe.

Once more, disappointment. The Birmingham Rep Theatre suddenly were encumbered with a very stiff bill for their central heating requirements! For economy's sake, something had to go. Shakespeare and Ben Jonson were transferred to the National. Dannie Abse . . . who?★

Peter Farago hoped I would write another play for the Birmingham Rep but my ambition had reverted to writing the next poem and then the one after. True, at the request of the Ensemble Theatre Company, I did extend an early one-act play of mine, *Gone*, for a fringe production at the Edinburgh Festival of 1977. Afterwards, under the title of *Gone in January*, it transferred to the Young Vic studio theatre. Alas, Denise Coffey's production of it, unlike that of Spencer Butler at Edinburgh, made me wince. I was reminded of Chekhov's assertion, 'The stage is a scaffold on which the playwright is executed.'†

★ In 1990 Seren Books published *Pythagoras (Smith)* along with *House of Cowards* and *The Dogs of Pavlov* under the title of *The View from Row G*. The editor was James A. Davies who wrote an introduction to the book. Once more I hoped that its publication would lead to a significant production of this or that play. Alas, *The View from Row G* was largely ignored by reviewers and remains one more book little known.

† The first play I ever wrote, a curtain-raiser called *The Eccentric*, led me to the precincts of that scaffold. It was at the Arts Theatre in London's West End. The main actor literally went 'mad' and subsequently had to receive radical psychiatric treatment. Not only did he forget his lines, but he improvised by uttering unfunny 'dirty' jokes which, of course, the audience thought had been devised by me!

Disenchanted, I did not feel compelled to write another play. I did not think I could do better than *Pythagoras (Smith)*. Besides, there were miles to go and poems to write – my primary interest and need – while the gaudy British theatre wagon moved on and out of sight into the 1980s.

11. Volume One

I was fifty-three years of age in 1977 when the first edition of my *Collected Poems* appeared. The very word 'Collected' had the bleak, black noise of a full-stop about it, something sounding terminal, even posthumous. But my previous volumes of poetry were now out of print and so a *Collected* allowed the work I had written since 1948 to have a further airing.

When my complimentary author's copies arrived I saw that the book contained 204 pages. Quite fat. I thought of how Laurie Lee, at poetry readings, used to hold up his skimpy, slim 48-page paperback and say, in that burring accent of his, lugubriously, 'Me Life's work!' I flicked over the pages and saw something of my own life unfold.

Most of us hardly question what influences us and do not observe our barely fathomable metamorphoses steadily. We merely mark how our life situation may have changed or our interests have developed; how our children have grown up, how others we loved have become much older or have died. All authors, though, have visible concrete evidence of their own changes: they can turn to their writings – in my case to my prose as well as my poems – and see how these give witness to altering attitudes, preoccupations, arguments with oneself. They recall debts to other writers, textual influences, transient or repetitive experiences and moods, successes and failures, occasions and relationships. Poems on the page lie there and do not lie: their own progenitor can scrutinise them as if they were spiritual X-rays.

I had written an introductory note to the *Collected Poems* and in it had confessed how, during the late 1950s, I'd begun to eschew allegorical or symbolical structures and how my poems thereafter had become more often rooted in actual experience rather than in fancy. I had concluded the note by adding, 'For some time now my ambition has been to write poems which appear translucent but are in fact deceptions. I would have a reader enter them, be deceived he could see through them like sea-water, and be puzzled when he cannot quite touch bottom. That ambition endures as does my wish to look upon the world with the eyes of a perpetual convalescent. Perhaps without repetition there would be no character, no style. So I hope this is only Volume One of a *Collected Poems* . . .'

If there had been disappointments about the material success of my plays, I could hardly complain that my poetry was being neglected by readers for Hutchinson had to publish three successive editions of the *Collected Poems*. Apart from reviews, a few intermittent radio and television appearances helped to promote the book.

After one TV appearance and feeling rather pleased with myself, I was soon deflated by a tactless colleague, Dr H., who seriously, most seriously, remarked, 'You know, Dannie, you look *so* much better on television than you do in real life.' I hoped Dr H. was more tactful with his patients though I doubted it. When I had first met him at the clinic he had said, 'Oh . . . I nearly read a book of yours once.'

I was delighted when I learnt that the International Poetry Forum of the Carnegie Library in Pittsburgh had chosen my *Collected Poems* as its 1977 International Poetry Selection. The University of Pittsburgh Press would publish the volume and I would receive all expenses plus a generous honorarium for launching the book at the Forum. There would be a small ceremony and I would be given a medal! It didn't sound too much of an ordeal.

Not long after I had opened the letter from the Forum's Director, Samuel Hazo, the telephone brought me the American voice of my friend, Paul Fussell, who was visiting London. 'Come round,' I said, 'and join us for dinner.' Paul hesitated. 'I'd like to,' he said, 'but I'm staying with Kingsley Amis. Could he come with me, perhaps?'

London was an attraction to a number of our American friends, among them William Meredith and Dan and Liz Hoffman. Seeing them, on average biennially, we could tell old tales and laugh at gilded butterflies: of who loses and who wins; who's in, who's out. And we had even enticed other friends – Mack (M.L.) and Vicki Rosenthal and, on another occasion, Ted and Renée Weiss – to stay with us at Ogmore so that they could witness the mobile events of

Welsh weather while we grumbled about poets, loiterers and other malcontents.

When Paul Fussell and Kingsley Amis joined us at Hodford Road, Amis's grumbles featured a certain academic. 'Too clever by half,' he announced. Kingsley Amis regarded me pop-eyed when I referred to the Volga Bulgars of the 10th century who felt that a man who excelled through quickwittedness and knowledge was more fit to serve God than man. 'So they seized him, roped his neck, and hung him from a tree until he rotted away,' I said, deliberately trying to be too clever by half.

Some months after my *Collected Poems* came out I visited a friend of a friend, terminally ill in University College Hospital. I was surprised to see, at his bedside, a copy of my *Collected Poems*. When the dying man, so thin and wan, whispered he had found consoling poems in my book I felt perplexed. I had come to comfort him. Was he being considerate, kind to me, letting me believe I was someone of use, not just a dreaming Thing? I didn't know what to say, did not do very well.

Every poet must hope that his work, apart from offering linguistic pleasures and possible perdurable insights, may, on occasion, be of utilitarian use. And yet, I remember how I felt reading the proofs of my *Collected Poems*. So few of them touched on public, politically active themes. When I began to write aspiring poems as a sixth-form schoolboy, keenly aware of the paradox of war cripples and slums in a world of colours, I imagined I knew the answer to Stephen Spender's cry, 'What can we do in a world at war that matters?' I thought W.H. Auden defeatist when he resignedly complained, '. . . poetry makes nothing happen: it survives/In the valley of its saying where executives/Would never want to tamper.' Did not poets once sit at the Prince's right hand and praise the Princes and their lies, if beautiful enough, contribute to the myth-making of history?

In the 20th century, poets living in authoritarian societies, the genuine ones, no longer sat at the Prince's right hand but, like others, suffered the decisions of that powerful figure and were almost obligated to bear witness as best they could. Writing out of their own personal predicament they affected those who shared that predicament or who were in sympathy with that predicament. Some, as a result, were murdered. In liberal societies, though, such as our own, even when the poetry in its own ideoplasm suggests socio-historical implications, it can make only the smallest of detonations and is not heard in the great world.

> What canst thou do, or all thy tribe
> To the great world? Thou art a dreaming thing.

So wrote Keats. And yet I know that some poems, inadvertently, act as moral, didactic instruments. When I was young, some poems of the German poet, Rainer Maria Rilke, became guru-lessons for me. I think I am someone who tends to talk too much, to display rather than to listen – not a useful characteristic for a medical student or a doctor at a hospital bedside or in a consulting room. The ideal is to listen solely to patients, never having to silence the clamour that one's own senses might make. That I had done so often enough was helped by reminding myself of those religious lines by Rilke which, in Babette Deutsch's translation, I learnt by heart when a student.

I know that, in minor ways, my own poems have sometimes been of practical use or have made something happen or have influenced someone. Alfred Brendel once told me that after reading a poem of mine in the *Collected Poems* about childbirth, 'The Smile Was', he felt impelled to observe a child of his being born. I can boast, too, that an Epithalamion I wrote has been recited many times at wedding ceremonies – most recently at the marriage of the editor of my *Collected Poems*!

These are, I know, small boasts. Poems, in our society, cannot be bombs; at best they are small sparks in the margin that leave 'the great world' untouched, uninfluenced. No matter, with luck they may give some people some pleasure and that is no small thing. I hoped my *Collected Poems* would do as much. And here's the curious thing: after decades of writing poems, every poet, I believe, if he takes his own work seriously as he should, comes under the influence of it. When a poet begins to write a poem there is no reader; but as he concludes his poem, he himself becomes the first reader. Sometimes the last! He receives his own words. Thereafter, in subtle ways, his poems, even as they may recede for others, remain for him strangely active. They begin to determine not only how he will write but how he will live. Some may argue that poetry is a useless thing, that it influences no one. But whatever else poems do, or do not do, they profoundly alter the man or woman who writes them.

12. The Smiles of a Woman

When I was a schoolboy in Cardiff I heard whisperings about a close relative of mine: 'She had an abortion.' Following the abortion, she, luckless, had suffered an infection of the Fallopian tubes that had left her barren. 'Poor girl, she's devastated,' aunts whispered. It was the springtime of the year when the birds whistled assertively above the multiparous earth as they built their nests, when small green pointillist buds appeared on the trees and the sheep licked their sticky new-born lambs as if posing for a pre-Raphaelite artist. At cheder I learnt of the sorrows of Sarah when childless and how Rachel, too, envious of the children Leah had borne, cried out to her husband, 'Give me children or I shall die.'

When I was a medical student at Westminster Hospital I heard similar, if more muted cries, at gynaecological Outpatients. So many infertile women felt guilty, needlessly blamed themselves, sensed wrongly that they had failed as women, failed their menfolk and the world. The road they had not taken was the favoured one they could not take.

Some patients, informed by their gynaecologist that no doctor could do anything for them, did not, I'm sure, become irrevocably resigned to being infertile but in their continued desperation resorted to quack remedies, herbal and otherwise. In another century they might have bought their way into Dr James Graham's Celestial Bed at the Temple of Health in Pall Mall. This magneto-electric bed, it was claimed, could 'infallibly produce a genial and happy issue' when fornicated upon. (It is uncertain whether Dr Graham ever qualified in medicine.) By all accounts he was an extraordinarily handsome man with a charismatic personality – perhaps the only qualifications he needed. At the height of his career, in the late 18th century, he was charging £50 for a night on the bed, though a contemporary recorded that 'many a nobleman paid Graham £500 to draw the curtains'.

Other women in Outpatients, their hopes dashed like my relative, probably prayed to God that they might conceive. Sometimes, of course, the childless couple discover that, possibly, their problem may be solved – but none so easily or more pleasurefully, according to Mr Bell, the consultant gynaecologist at Westminster, than in the case of a certain priest and his wife. 'It's incredible that now, in the middle of this century, people can be so ignorant of sex,' Mr Bell told us, his students. 'This priest regularly, twice a week I daresay, ejaculates between his wife's breasts and wonders why, after five years of such love-making, there has been no happy outcome.'

I did not know, reading a newspaper in July 1978, that a front-page item would be of consequence to me: 'Around midnight it was announced that the world's first test-tube baby, Louise Brown, weighing five pounds twelve ounces, has been delivered by a Caesarean operation at Oldham District General Hospital, Greater Manchester.' The newspaper report then described the joy of the mother when the baby was presented to her, how her expression was so moving, her look so eloquent. I knew that look so eloquent. I had written a poem about the secretive, gentle, ineffable smile that invariably comes to inhabit a new mother's face when she hears for the very first time her baby's cry – her struggling face so magically transformed into one strangely calm, momentarily beautiful. During a concert for patients and staff at a Manchester hospital I had read this poem that celebrated childbirth not so long previously, and not too far from where Louise Brown was soon to be born. I realised that, as I proceeded, I was making an ungovernable faux-pas.

Before I had finished reading the first section of the poem I became aware of gasps, whisperings and sighings to the left of me. As I turned my head to glance wonderingly at the audience, I read on:

> That agreeable radiant smile
> no man can smile it
> no man can paint it
> as it develops without fail
> after the gross, physical, knotted,
> granular, bloody endeavour.
> Such a pure spirituality from all that!
> It occupies the face
> and commands it.

The audience on the left I came to realise consisted of women only, dozens of them, and they were all glowering at me. I was halfway through the poem before the penny dropped: these restless women were all probably from the gynaecological wards, and all probably had had, or were about to have, their pregnancies terminated. And there I was, fool, describing the mother's unadulterated, unambiguous, pure, happy smile.

After the concert, two of the disturbed women, still in their dressing gowns, followed me out into the corridor, one of whom it seemed to me had a fixed smile similar to that of *rigor mortis*, with all her 44 facial muscles tense. The other woman, surprisingly, thanked me for reading the poem and asked if I had had a particular new mother in mind.

What could I say? That I was aware of the ambivalence inhering in so many smiles, not least those related to or engineered by violence. Had I not observed, years earlier, a stranger enter a Swiss Cottage coffee-house and smack Glyn Davies's face? Accusing him of stealing, the stranger had slapped Glyn's cheeks over and over. Glyn had merely kept on smiling, sickly smiling. 'No,' I said. 'I had no particular woman in mind.'

With the coming of winter in 1978 many people, unhappily, were unemployed. Hundreds of thousands had been laid off and widespread unofficial strikes had followed. One lunchtime, I left the chest clinic to meet the chief editor at Hutchinson, Harold Harris, for lunch at Bertorelli's. He had telephoned to say that he wished to speak to me about Louise Brown.

'Who?'

'Louise Brown, the test-tube baby.'

'I can't tell you anything about that,' I said, surprised.

'No, no, I have something to show you. Have lunch with me.'

I was curious to know what Harold Harris wanted. Generally, my dealings with Hutchinson were through Tony Whittome, the poetry editor there and a long-standing friend of mine. As I passed the restaurants of Charlotte Street, I could see everywhere visible health hazards – rubbish piled high, waste overflowing, feasts for rats. The newspapers reported that even some cemetery workers had refused to dig graves.

Pleasantries over, but not the lunch, Harold Harris produced two manuscripts. He explained that at the Book Fair in Frankfurt they had bought the rights of a book by the pioneers of the 'test-tube' baby research, Patrick Steptoe and Robert Edwards. Steptoe was a consultant gynaecologist at an Oldham hospital, Edwards a scientist at a Cambridge laboratory. Their collaboration was one of Medicine and Science.

'It's an interesting story they have to tell but it needs to be rewritten and made publishable. They want you to work with them,' said Harold Harris, filling my wine glass up again to the brim.

'Why me?'

'Because you're a doctor.'

'Sorry, no,' I said. 'I'm just not interested in – '

'Read this,' pleaded Harold Harris, 'before you come to any decision. We've paid a lot of money for the rights of this book.'

Reluctantly, I took the manuscripts away. I discovered that Patrick Steptoe's offering was only a chapter length and, in any case, scientifically meagre. He did describe the actual birth of Louise Brown graphically and also how he witnessed the pioneer work of the Director of Infertility at a Paris Hospital; but for the rest he reminisced how he, as a boy, had helped the resident pianist at the local Palace cinema by playing, during matinées, the incidental music for the silent films of Tom Mix and Harold Lloyd. Harold Harris, I felt sure, had not bought the future book that he intended to call *A Matter of Life* in order to focus on Dr Steptoe's musical ability.

Robert Edwards's much more substantial contribution, though written in a style more fitted for a scientific paper than for a book, engaged me. I could not help but respond to his account of how the beginnings of life never failed to fascinate him; how through the microscope he had observed embryonic cells move elegantly and precisely along their appointed pathway, forming a succession of shapes before they emerged into the pattern of the human form.

Soon, in ludic mood, at first just for the hell of it, as an exercise, leaning on Bob Edwards's text, I ghost-wrote, in his persona, a paragraph or two on the drama of a beautiful triumph: 'I knew that instant we had reached our goal, the early stages of human life were all there in our culture fluids, just as we had wanted . . . I was thrilled when through the microscope I observed the embryos we had incubated divide into two cells, four cells, eight cells and more, each cell with its own nucleus . . . I am still thrilled as an egg divides and develops for, in addition to the beauty of its growth, the embryo is passing through a critical period of life of great exploration – it becomes magnificently organised, switching on its own biochemistry, increasing in size, and preparing itself quickly for implantation in the womb. After that, its organs form; the cells gradually become capable of development into heart, lung, brain, eye. What a unique and wonderful process it is as the increasing number of cells diverge and specialise in a delicate, integrated and co-ordinated manner. One day all the secrets of this early development may be known and those same secrets may help us to repair the ravages and defects in the tissues of sick and ageing men and women.'

'It would be a challenge, a sort of game, if I did agree to work on the book,' I said to Joan, who herself was working on a life of John Ruskin.

I thought of the long-ago births of our own three children, how we had been blessed, of the anxious concern before their so welcome entrance into our bewildered, fissured, unfathomable, amazing world, their seagull-like lusty cries, their flailing, helpless débuts. I recalled my own breathless moments of half-relief, half-exhilaration when, on each occasion, thankfully (a prayer of no words to the enigma), I learnt that mother and child were healthy and whole; and I shall never forget the proprietory, contented look on Joan's face as she held the baby in the sanctuary of her arms and glanced up at me proudly.

Then the visiting hours of the next perplexing days. Once, waiting to go into the midwifery ward, I was approached by another fumbling father, one extremely young, talkative and far from astute, who, without hesitation, buttonholed me, 'You got summat for the kid? I've got a bar of chocolate for mine.' When I remarked that a baby could not digest chocolate, he explained, trumping me, 'Aw, it's milk chocolate, see.'

I met Patrick Steptoe in London and I travelled several times to Cambridge to interview Robert Edwards and to visit his laboratory. To his great credit, Patrick Steptoe had developed the technique of laparoscopy in Britain, not only as a diagnostic tool but also to carry our operative procedures. In Paris he had learnt how to insert the laparoscope, the viewing instrument, into the abdominal cavity at the navel. The instrument worked like a telescope permitting a magnified view of the body organs. After a period of four or five months, having practised on some thirty corpses, Steptoe felt confident enough to try out a laparoscopic examination on a live patient.

I had met consultants similar to Patrick Steptoe ever since I had become a medical student at Westminster Hospital, though few as innovative and bold as he. His civilised demeanour and formality, even his interest in music, were for a medical consultant as stereotypical on the surface as the elegant suit he wore. Robert Edwards seemed to me something else. I had never met a pure scientist before. As I grew to know him a little, it seemed to me characteristic that when he had been a post-graduate in Edinburgh, perhaps for the first time theologically exercised, he had decided to attend *experimentally* all the different churches of the city – the Presbyterian, the Episcopal, the Free Church of Scotland, the Methodist, the Baptist, the Congregational, the Lutheran, the Catholic, the Plymouth Brethren, the Quakers. 'I lingered in churches with stained-glass windows and those with plain glass,' he told me. 'I looked up at hammer-beam roofs, at those with medieval vaulting and those that were plain. I knelt near walls with murals and those devoid of decoration. I was on a church-crawl, but eventually I found the mysterious and the numinous not so much in any church but in the laboratory where each night I peered through a microscope at primitive sex cells.'

Robert Edwards seemed to me a born scientist, one without side, without a mask, teeming with ideas; one prepared to take risks that would make most doctors blink, hesitate.* He knew that his work would open new horizons in human reproduction, not least the possibility of embryonic or genetic engineering. He recognised, for instance, that future cloning could well take place – 'a needless and unattractive exercise in genetic engineering . . .' yet one that may

---

* For instance, during the 1960s, it was thought (wrongly) that spermatozoa had to be exposed to secretions of the uterus or Fallopian tubes before the ovarian eggs could be fertilised.

In 1966, Edwards, working with gynaecologists in Chapel Hill, North Carolina, believed he needed for his laboratory fertilisation experiments somehow to collect such sperms from a woman's reproductive tract. He devised a very small chamber which could be filled with sperms before inserting it into the womb. This chamber, lined with porous membrane, would allow uterine secretions to pass into it but hopefully would not let sperms escape. Women volunteering for Edwards's experiments, reassured they would not become impregnated, allowed a chamber with its busy live spermatozoa to be inserted at night and removed next morning. Edwards confessed, 'I had sleepless nights fearing the chamber might burst inside the uterus with disastrous results.'

eventually be utilised for the benefit of humanity in ways that, at present, cannot be apprehended.

The more I learnt about Robert Edwards and the nature of his scientific work so paramount in the treatment of infertility, the more surprised I became that he and Steptoe never received the Nobel Prize for medicine. And yet it was not entirely surprising. Throughout their research they had been opposed on ethical grounds by the medical establishment. When they applied to the Medical Research Council for long-term research support they were told that the Council had serious doubts 'about the ethical aspects of the proposed investigation in humans, especially those relating to the implantation of oocytes fertilised in vitro which were considered premature in view of the lack of preliminary studies on primates and the present deficiency of detailed knowledge of the possible hazards involved . . .'

Their application was declined. There was opposition, too, from the theological establishment. In *The Journal of the American Medical Association* a prominent theologian from Princeton University, Paul Ramsey, thundered that Edwards and Steptoe ignored the sanctity of life, that they carried out immoral experiments on the unborn. The work was 'unethical medical experimentation on possible future human beings and therefore it is subject to absolute moral prohibition.'

Edwards and Steptoe felt confident that they would be successful eventually despite all the obstacles and the strident opposition, that their research would open up the whole world of embryology. There would be new approaches in medicine. They would bring hope to thousands upon thousands of infertile women and there might well be also all kinds of other extraordinary benefits to humankind.

During the next months I helped them both to shape *A Matter of Life*. By then 'the Winter of Discontent' was over. On May 4th, 1979 Margaret Thatcher became Prime Minister.* Quoting St Francis of

---

* I had encountered the MP for Finchley when she was a mere backbencher. I had been invited to join the panel of a local charity Brains Trust, one that Mrs Thatcher was to dominate. Initially, the affluent audience had beamed at the young blonde Conservative politician. I sensed, though, that they became somewhat disenchanted when she spoke too stridently and too much. When the famous architect responded to a question about architecture Margaret Thatcher bullied in, interrupting his decorous expertise. Soon after, a question was posed about the poetry of W.H. Auden. The chairman turned towards me. Before I could utter a word Thatcher's invincible voice ascended to its full volume, 'When I was at Oxford with Auden . . .'

Later, at home, I remarked to my wife with blithe confidence that I had, that evening, encountered an ambitious MP who, however, was so impossible she would, politically, never get anywhere!

Assisi, this most confrontational of women inappropriately declared, 'Where there is discord may we bring harmony, where there is despair may we bring hope.' She said this earnestly, she did not smile, she did not show her teeth. Soon her government would privatise industries, encourage private medicine at the expense of the Health Service, emasculate British Rail, introduce savage cuts in public spending, make the rich richer, make the poor poorer and bring discord where there was harmony and despair where there was hope.

13. A Weekend in Toronto

'Brezhnev arrived in Washington on June 16th. Somewhat of a hypochondriac, he turned the necessity of getting used to the time change into an obsession. He wore two watches, one set at Moscow time, the other for Washington time. He kept forgetting whether Moscow was ahead or behind Washington. When he reached San Clemente and three more hours were added, he gave up keeping track of the time difference but never ceased his grumbling about it.'
Henry Kissinger

In the autumn of 1980 I accepted an invitation to visit Canada. Three Canadian poets were to tour Britain, three British poets to tour Canada. It did not seem a fair exchange.

'Who else will be going from Britain?' I asked Pamela, the director of the Poetry Secretariat.

'We were thinking of Adrian Henri and Fleur Adcock,' she declared.

I knew Fleur Adcock and liked her; Adrian Henri I hardly knew at all but I had been told he was easy-going – 'very difficult to quarrel with'.

'It's an arduous schedule,' Pamela admitted, 'from coast to coast.'

I learned that our first reading would be in Toronto on a Saturday night, that we would leave London on Thursday and depart from

Toronto for Vancouver on Monday morning. I thought, I'll have Thursday night, Friday night, Saturday night, Sunday night to catch up on sleep – a long weekend to become accustomed to Toronto time and recover the five hours lost before the next long haul to the Canadian West Coast where everybody once again would be programmed younger, shouting eagerly, 'Have a nice day,' and 'You're welcome,' as we staggered, dehydrated, our baggage growing heavier, our arms longer, into the foyer of some overheated hotel. After that it would be easy: each flight eastward, homeward, and the clock would be turning clockwise.

As we progressed across the Atlantic towards Toronto I considered the three Canadian poets – George Johnston, Susan Musgrave and Bill Bissett – who at this very hour would be flying over the Atlantic in the opposite direction. I looked out of the Jumbo Jet window.

As my knowledge of Canadian poetry was somewhat limited I had not heard of these three poets. In order to reduce, in some measure, my ignorance I leafed through an anthology of Canadian poetry I had brought with me. Later, trying to ignore a 'movie' flickering to the left of my eyes, I browsed through a small reference manual put out by the League of Canadian Poets – a selected bibliography, quotes from reviews, that sort of thing. I looked up Bill Bissett first.

I had got it wrong. It was bill bisset, a lower-case man. Under the heading, WHAT CRITICS SAY, I read, 'Like Blake, bill bisset is a visionary, mystical poet who makes his own rules of poetry as he goes along.' *Queens Quarterly*. I felt somewhat dwarfed by the knowledge that Canada was sending us this Blake-like, visionary figure. Nobody had called *me* Blake-like. I felt certain too that neither Fleur Adcock nor Adrian Henri had been described as such. A little depressed, I turned the pages to discover Susan Musgrave. There she was – her photograph I mean: attractive. Moreover, under WHAT CRITICS SAY I read, 'Musgrave explores sexuality at the primal level of bone-hurt.' I looked out of the window again.

The critical remarks about George Johnston seemed more enigmatic. Lawrence Jones in *Canadian Literature* had written of him, 'Surely an anomaly among the present generation of Canadian poets.' And then it came to me, after six weary hours in the plane, a revelation of sorts – the reason why we particular three had been invited to Canada: why I had been asked, why Fleur Adcock had been asked, why Adrian Henri had been chosen for this jaunt. It was to match these three Canadian poets, blow for blow. Had I not seen, a month or so ago, a lower-case advertisement for an Adrian Henri poetry reading? That was it: adrian henri for bill bissett; our best-looking poet, Fleur Adcock, for Canada's best-looking poet, Susan Musgrave; and therefore, I pondered gloomily, QED, me for George Johnston whom they bloody well called 'an anomaly'.

At Toronto airport we were met by Arlene Lampert, executive director of the League of Canadian Poets, who handed us envelopes containing expenses money, a more detailed itinerary for us to study, and forms to sign. It seemed the first reading would be at the Harbor Front where we were part of an International Festival Week organised by one Greg Gatenby. That very evening Arnold Wesker and other dramatists were featured at the Harbor Front and on Saturday night we would be reading with the Polish poet, Czeslaw Milosz. Soon we discovered that the early posters which advertised the event had recently been supplanted by new ones. 'THREE BRITISH POETS: DANNIE ABSE, FLEUR ADCOCK, ADRIAN HENRI with Czeslaw Milosz', the original posters had proclaimed. But Milosz had then been awarded the Nobel Prize for literature so quickly new posters were printed. The copy had been altered to 'CZESLAW MILOSZ with three British poets: Dannie Abse, Fleur Adcock, Adrian Henri'. At least we had not been downgraded to lower case.

At 9.30 p.m. I decided to go to bed for it was now 2.30 a.m. real time and I was tired. With luck I would sleep for five or six hours before the clock in my head foolishly woke me up. As I walked towards the lifts, or rather elevators, I heard the familiar pleasant voice of Arnold Wesker talking about a new play of his. 'It begins with an orgasm,' he was saying. 'And no doubt ends with a bang,' another writer interrupted him.

In my room on the twenty-eighth floor I lay in the dark. The TV set waited in the same dark lifelessly. So did the radio, the ironing board, the central heating radiators, the telephone, the shower, the lav, the armchairs, the writing desk, the wardrobe, the whole caboodle. What did they say the name of this hotel was? I thought of Big Ben faraway, striking the hour on the hour, the *right* hour, every hour. I decided this was Hotel Insomnia. However, eventually I must have fallen asleep because I woke up, startled by the clamour of an active telephone. I struggled to put the light on, to focus my eyes on my wristwatch which read 1 a.m., i.e. 6 a.m. real time. Puzzled, I fumbled for the receiver. A Canadian voice, a man's, asked twangily, 'Is that you, Ginger?'

'What?'

'Ginger?'

'Ginger?' I repeated, dazed.

'Yeh. That you, Ginger?'

'No,' I said, 'I'm not Ginger.'

Annoyed, the anonymous caller grunted, 'Jesus,' and slammed the phone down. I did not sleep much that night. So the next night, after meeting some old friends who had emigrated to Canada a decade earlier and after visiting the museum to see the enormous and multiple Henry Moores etc., once more I decided to have an 'early' night. I was too tired even to read. I would, before sleep, have welcomed some consoling music perhaps, but nothing too loud, orchestral. What is sometimes engaging is to hear a solo performance, not in a concert hall or on the radio, but unexpectedly, fortuitously – an accordion in a street, a flute in a night train, a mouth organ in a field, picnic-time. None of that was possible. I fiddled with the radio and lost. So, resigned, I went to bed, turned off the lamp.

I did not expect a replay of the previous night. But again the telephone woke me up. Furious, I picked up the phone to shout at that heavy breather who wanted to talk to Ginger in the middle of the night. 'Hello,' the voice said. It was Arnold Wesker. Besides I saw that it was only 11 p.m. (Toronto time.) 'Dusty and I are going to Niagara Falls tomorrow,' Arnold said generously. 'There's a car picking us up. Would you like to join us?' Afterwards, again I found it difficult to fall asleep.

The next day there was a cloudburst or rather clouds burst one after the other over Toronto. Niagara Falls, as if summoned, had come to us. The car did not arrive. I was disappointed. I wanted to see the Horseshoe Fall, which I gathered was 149 feet high, width 2100 feet. But I had to imagine it all, the river below the falls rushing with great velocity down the sloping bottom of a narrow chasm for a distance of seven miles. We would not, in that strenuous rain, have seen very much anyway – merely heard the smoke that thundered.

Dusty, Arnold's wife, was a fan of the actor Walter Matthau. That afternoon we went to the cinema. I could have been anywhere, in an Odeon in London or Llantwit Major, Jerusalem or Pontardawe, as I sat with friends staring at a big screen, at the shagged face of Walter Matthau.

The rain stopped before the evening concert. I was surprised by the numbers who had come to the Harbor Front, almost a thousand I should think: every seat was taken. No doubt people were curious to hear the new Nobel Prizewinner.

I knew Milosz's work a little. A line of his had stuck in my head: 'When you leave your native land don't look back, the Erinyes are behind you.' How desolate to be a perpetual exile as Milosz was, to be separated from your own language, the true nationality of a poet. Bolingbroke, in his *Reflections on Exile*, suggested that that which is most valuable cannot be taken away from us, is out of reach of any political power, any tyranny. 'There is no part of the world,' declared Bolingbroke, 'from whence we may not admire those planets which roll, like ours, in different orbits round the same central sun; from whence we may not discover an object still more stupendous, that army of fixed stars hung up in the immense space of the universe, innumerable suns whose beams enlighten and cherish the unknown worlds which roll around them; and while I am ravished by such contemplations as these, whilst my soul is thus raised up to heaven, imports me little what ground I tread upon.' Consolations these are, but we are not elevated to the stars most of the time, and so the ground we return to and stand upon generally matters more and long.

I did not get to the hotel till the early hours of the morning. After the successful reading at the Harbor Front there had been a successful party. And there was a party too the next evening, on the Sunday, given by Arlene Lampert so that Adrian, Fleur and I could meet such considerable Canadian poets as Earle Birney, Patrick Lane and Eli Mandel. By 9.30 p.m. I was exhausted and knowing that I had to be up early to catch the flight to Vancouver I planned to slip away. A young poet, Giorgio Di Cicco, offered to drive Fleur (who was also very tired) and me to the hotel. We left Adrian Henri behind as our energetic representative whose glands obviously secreted natural Benzedrine. Or perhaps, simply, he had no telephone in his room.

Returned to my room, I could not resist looking up Giorgio Di Cicco in my little reference manual of Canadian poets. Under WHAT CRITICS SAY I read, '. . . a visionary in his own right . . .' *Joe Rosenblatt*. Curious, I turned to Eli Mandel to see how he was described. The *Winnipeg Free Press* labelled him as '. . . a would-be visionary'. There was no point in looking up other Canadian poets I had happened to meet earlier that evening: they were all, doubtless, visionaries or would-be visionaries or *visionaries in their own right* –

Blake-like figures every goddam one of them. I went to bed. Absurdly my watch read only 10.20 p.m. but my brain knew the real time — that which is recorded perpetually by the cenotaph clocks in the suburbs of hell: 3.20 a.m. I decided to take a Mogadon, a sleeping tablet, something I rarely need to do.

It seemed to me that I had only been asleep some five minutes when I was awakened by a noise much louder and more frightening than a frenetic telephone. I sat up in bed astonished. *It was a fire alarm.* I closed my eyes, squeezing the eyelids tight, thinking, 'This can't be true, I'm dreaming this.' The fire alarm continued on and on. 'This is the twenty-eighth floor,' I thought. I jumped out of bed and shifted smartly to the door. In the corridor, outside their doors stood several people looking anxious. The alarm ceased and a voice on a Tannoy said sedatively, 'Please be calm. A fire has been reported on the twenty-sixth floor. We are trying to confirm whether this is really so.'

'Hey,' said one of the men along the corridor, 'you can smell smoke, can'tcha?'

I sniffed. I smelt nothing. Since all was silent now I decided to get dressed.

'Nobody can get to the elevators,' the man was saying. 'It's not possible.'

I managed to dress in forty seconds flat and I was about to reach for my shoes when the Tannoy suddenly blared again. 'The fire on the twenty-sixth floor is being investigated. Nobody need be alarmed. We will come back to you as soon as we have definite news.'

I put on my shoes and stood again at my open door. The man who earlier could smell smoke now said, 'Hey, look, you can *see* smoke down there near the elevator, right?'

I looked down there. We all looked down there. I could not see any smoke. Somewhere, further along beyond the elevators, was Fleur Adcock's room. Possibly she would be anxious. I decided to call on her but near the elevators a fire barrier had descended obstructing the way through. I had to turn back and as I did so a door was flung open in front of me. A lady in a nightdress faced me, wildly shouting, 'He's looking at a pornographic movie in there and he won't fuckin' well come out.' I nodded sympathetically and returned to my own room as the Tannoy once more announced that the fire was being investigated on the twenty-sixth floor.

'Investigated?' said the man with the wonderfully acute senses, who, visionary as any Canadian poet, could smell nonexistent smoke, see nonexistent smoke. 'Jesus Christ, who're they trying to fool? They're trying to put it out, that's what. An' they're having problems.'

Maybe he was right. Inside my room I imagined a fire below, growing tall, blue and black whirling smoke among bouquets of glowing geraniums, proliferating neon wreaths of red roses. Then the Tannoy's bland voice told us that the *minor* conflagration on the twenty-sixth floor had been dealt with, that now all was well and all manner of things were well. 'We are sorry,' the voice said, 'that you have been disturbed.'

I went back to bed. I closed my eyes. My weekend in Toronto was over.

14. Exit

Even before her stroke my mother's mental health had steadily deteriorated over the previous two or three years. 'How's the children?' she would ask me. I would regale her with their news but within minutes she would forget our conversation and repeat the question, 'How are the children?' It seemed touchingly symbolic to me that she wore on her wrist a watch unaccountably devoid of hour, minute and second hands. Its glass simply covered a round blank whiteness featuring black numerals only. It was a watch that could have been devised by the Swedish film director, Ingmar Bergman.

Now, at the hospital bedside, I observed her, unconscious, breathing in and out ruinously, her face aged in repose. When young, my mother had been, according to her, 'the most beautiful girl in the Swansea valley'. It may well have been so judging from photographs. Whenever, in latter years, I had complimented her on her appearance, she had invariably responded, 'No, no, go away with you, son. I'm half dead. I look like the Wreck of the Hesperus.' Throughout her life, though, she had behaved with the confidence of one who had long been admired for her beauty.

She was ninety years of age when she suffered the ultimate stroke. Not that she ever knew the precise date of her own birthday. 'At the time of the Ystalyfera fair,' she always asserted in her lilting Welsh-accented voice. 'They came to our village every year, every springtime – the time of the daffodils, my favourite flower.' Eventually she decided to celebrate her birthday on March 15th, the birthdate of her eldest son, Wilfred.

Not long after her 85th birthday I visited Cardiff to record verses for the Welsh Arts Council Dial-a-Poem enterprise. Afterwards I proceeded to her Cathedral Road ground-floor flat. Not for the first time she served me kippers for lunch. 'I know you like them so much,' she remarked.

'It's Leo who's most partial to kippers,' I said yet again.

She ignored this. 'He took me to a terrible restaurant on my birthday,' she complained. I knew about that. Leo had told me how he had taken her to dinner at one of Cardiff's poshest restaurants. She had sat down, frowning because of the discreet lighting, the flickering candles on tables. Then, in a loud voice, she had scolded Leo, 'Son, this is the sort of place where men take other men's wives.'

After the kipper lunch she asked me if I was still giving poetry readings. 'I haven't heard you for a long time,' she said.

'You can hear me now, if you wish, on the telephone,' I responded.

She looked at me suspiciously. 'Go on, son,' she said, smiling. I dialled the Dial-a-Poem number before passing the telephone receiver over to her. She listened intently as I stood next to her. Suddenly she shouted out commandingly, 'Speak up, son.'

Now, however loud I spoke, she would not be able to hear me, could not. I held her right hand and Death indomitably held the other when Joan and my sister-in-law, Elizabeth, once more joined me at her bedside. My mother did not relinquish this one life of ours easily. For hours yet she raged, raged against the dying of the light.★

★ Hardly surprising: my mother could be dramatically combative. Her brothers would confirm, 'Duw, Kate's a real fighter.' She would spontaneously boil over if crossed or on witnessing some small injustice. Like Katherina Minola she could 'scold and raise up such a storm that mortal ears might hardly endure the din'. Her sheer wild energy, when she was younger, made her impulsive and unpredictable. I can remember so many occasions when she embarrassed me or startled me. There was that time when she remarked about a visitor in his hearing, 'He's got terrible BO, hasn't he, son?' Once she suddenly gave Jon Silkin a five-pound note because, as she explained later, 'He looked like a tramp.'

Of course I wanted her to be released from that torturing concentration camp for one. I spoke to the consultant urgently, persuasively.

Afterwards, when it was over, I drove the twenty-three miles back to Ogmore and continued for a further mile to reach Southerndown beach. The late August moon was up, immaculate in an almost cloudless sky. Elizabeth, Joan and I silently stared for a long time at the silvery glitter of its sweep across the sea's dark, swampy, undisciplined surface. The waves made their small thrashing sound but I heard my mother's voice, her favourite sayings: 'Every age has its compensations'; 'I look like the Wreck of the Hesperus'; 'That girl with her sheep's eyes – she needs a bucket of water over her to cool her ardour, son'; 'Duw there's plenty of land here for building'; 'There'd be no wars if women were in charge'.

The moon had been full when my father died in 1964. For years afterwards, whenever I've happened to look up at a revealed night sky, the moon in its ignorance has made me think momentarily of my father. Since my mother's death in 1981, the moon observed, whether in ascension or declension, has become for me a memorial for both of my parents – and one more potent than the two adjoining gravestones, unvisited, in the small Jewish cemetery near Cardiff's Roath Park Lake.

15. The Closing of the Clinic

The newspapers reported that more than three million were now unemployed in Britain, the highest number since the 1930s. The On-your-bike Employment Minister, Norman Tebbitt, who always made me think of a rat with an ulcer whenever I saw him on television, blamed the increased numbers on the atrocious winter weather.

I was to be made redundant myself on 1 February 1982 when the chest clinic was to be shut down as 'part of the contraction and rationalisation plan'. What with the government's festering economic failure and so happily few patients now contracting tuberculosis, how could it be otherwise? Each successive year, since my return from Princeton, each morning I arrived at the clinic at a later hour and because of unbusy afternoons I left earlier. The mobile X-ray units which I had supervised had been taken off the road; the three clerks in the office adjacent to my consulting room had been reduced to one; and visiting officials from the Ministry, assessing medical establishments, had justly decided that I no longer required a doctor to assist me.

All through the last snow-stricken week of January I took home my personal belongings from the consulting room I had occupied for more than a quarter of a century – so many books, so many ageing periodicals, medical and literary, that had accumulated in the tall bookcase. The walls seemed brazenly bare when I took down the pictures: my print of the ruined Ogmore Castle; the drawing a patient had given me; the night-school painting of Green Hollows by my father-in-law, Jack Mercer.

My desk, too, had been emptied and the waste-paper basket filled with the debris of the years. Discovering a library book that a decade earlier had somehow slipped down, jammed, behind one of the drawers of my desk, I was reminded of a great uncle of Joan's who, before the First World War, had felt it necessary to emigrate to India because he had failed to return a long overdue library book! I decided on no such drastic action. I would take it back to the local library from whence it came during the lunch hour. One scrap of paper found in a bottom drawer puzzled me. On it I had written, 'A Swansea councillor said that a town with no buildings is a very sad place.' Obviously I had meant to quote that banal, daft remark. But where and why? Memory, mother of the Muses, so much forgotten! And Themistocles could call by name more than twenty thousand citizens of Athens and Ben Jonson could repeat all that he had ever written and recite all the contents of the books that he had ever read.

I looked around the room. It had the appearance of one that had been burgled. It didn't matter. I had hardly any patients that last day. I felt uneasy, a sense of fleeting dread, and I think I know why. There are many people – I am one such – who are basically rooted, who experience a degree of anomie when their life situation changes. Part of me is me because of the introsumption of familiar landscape, seascape, objects, possessions, even those Ministry curtains, carpet, desk, bookcase, weighing machine, all the accoutrements of the office I was to abandon. When things are removed or I am removed from them there is a small assault on whomsoever I am.

The Powers-that-be wished to employ me later in the year on an occasional sessional basis for a few hours a couple of days a week to read an accumulation of chest X-rays and to see the odd patient. (In the future these sessions would become confined to Monday mornings only.) So on Friday 29 January, 1982 I felt my medical career had essentially come to an end, that the sessional work would only be a brief postscript.

Lunchtime, before I returned the library book to its rightful home, I examined, as I always did on a Friday, the current *Lancet*. Too many of the articles, as usual, I could not understand. Specialisation had brought with it an expertise and a jargon-language of its own so that it was no longer a question of two cultures – scientist could not speak to scientist, doctors could not understand doctors.

When Freud met Einstein they got on famously. Freud reported, 'Einstein understands as much about psychology as I do about physics so we had a very pleasant talk.' So many hospital doctors are lost when confronted by patients sick with ailments beyond their specialisation. I like the story of how some time ago in London, a semi-conscious man had been discovered sprawled on the pavement outside the Heart Hospital in Queens Square. The cardiac specialists, not feeling competent enough to deal with the patient who had obviously suffered an accident, suggested he should be taken across the Square to the Casualty Department of the General Hospital. A quarter of an hour later the Registrar in Casualty telephoned the Registrar at the Heart Hospital to ask, 'What do you want us to do with the patient who fell out of one of your third-floor windows?'

I sometimes wonder how I would have fared had I not specialised in chest work, had been more involved in therapy rather than in diagnosis. My relationship with patients referred to me for intermittent observation had, perforce, been glancing and temperate; that distancing had suited me. E.M. Forster once remarked that writers should be sensitive but tough. Doctors, though, I think, need to be tougher. My early experiences at Westminster Hospital and later, working as a locum for a General Practitioner, and later still, taking evening surgeries for an indisposed doctor friend, had taught me that

I was too inclined to empathise with distressed patients, much to my cost if not theirs.

Many doctor-writers, it would seem, have been endowed with an exaggerated ability to identify with their patients. Maybe this temperament has militated against their being truly successful doctors. Tobias Smollett was a surgeon who did not prosper. Oliver Goldsmith was advised 'to give up medicine for if he were resolved to kill, he should concentrate on his enemies'. And John Keats was another doctor defeated by having the extreme capacity to coalesce his whole life temporarily with a suffering patient or, indeed, with any living creature. 'If a sparrow comes before my window,' he wrote, 'I take part in its existence and pick about the gravel.' He even claimed he could feel himself unified with a billiard ball, and could apprehend 'its roundness, smoothness and the very volubility of its motion'. No wonder Dr Keats, at Guy's Hospital, confronted by a haemorrhaging Mr Smith or a Mr Robinson who had to have a gangrenous leg sawn off (without, of course, an anaesthetic) happily gave up medicine. Keats, concluding his medical career, confessed, 'My last operation was the opening of a man's temporal artery. I did it with the utmost nicety, but reflecting what had passed through my mind at the time, my dexterity seemed a miracle and I never took up the lancet again.'

On my return to the chest clinic from the Charing Cross Road Branch Library I walked through the soiled slush of Greek Street. Soho Square was uncharacteristically unpopulated. The secretaries and other office workers that picnicked on the grass during the lunch hours of the summer months remained hidden indoors munching their sandwiches. The ever increasing number of down and outs of Thatcher's England, who so listlessly sprawled on the wooden benches of the Square's south side during most of the year, had retreated to the comparative warmth of the nearby Tube stations. The snow had obliterated the small park's paths and like a genius craftsman had cleverly fitted a huge white carpet over the grass. The pigeons that roosted around and about wheeled on a carousel of air as if a fairground rifle had cracked. The statue of King Charles II, almost clear of snow except for his feet, neither shivered nor coughed. He simply stared sadly ahead at the potent phallic Post Office Tower – the Nell Gwyn Club, all of naughty Soho forever at his back.

By the time I reached the clinic it had begun to snow again. The large flakes drifted down in slow motion so that when I looked up some settled for a moment on my face. Above, I could see only dampness, the colour of meths, and was glad to enter the sheltered foyer of the Central Medical Establishment. As I waited for the lift to the fifth floor where the chest clinic was located I had a few inconsequential words with the porter who was a West Ham supporter, the one who sometimes called me Dr Asbe.

I thought the final afternoon at the clinic would end on a cheerful note for the last patient who had an appointment proved to be completely healthy and he left my office content. After writing up his notes, I was about to gather up my things and leave myself; but the radiographer in the X-ray department on the second floor phoned to ask me if I would read one more chest X-ray, a routine one.

It belonged to an officer in the RAF who had reached the age of fifty and who, therefore, was required to have a medical check-up including a chest X-ray. Because I could see a small opacity in the left mid-zone I had the film repeated together with a lateral view of his chest. It was no artifact. The opacity was clearly there; nor was it present on his earlier X-ray, taken in January 1977. Was it a tumour? If so, one malignant or benign?

'I don't think it's TB,' I told the radiographer. 'Could you ask the officer to come up from the X-ray department to see me?'

He would need further investigations. Following tomograms, he might well have to undergo a thoracotomy – have his chest opened – before the diagnosis became certain. I did not tell him this. It was better to state facts not guesses: that there was a shadow in his left lung that could be old or new, could be almost five years old and thus a scar of little significance; or else it could be something of more recent origin. 'That we must find out.'

'Can you tell me what it isn't?'

'No, I can't even do that,' I said truthfully, and then I leaned on a cliché: 'It's like looking at a black cat in a dark room. A light needs to be shone on it before it can be properly identified. That's why I want you to be investigated further.'

We talked some more. I learnt several other facts which could be relevant – that he did not smoke and, then, something that made me pause. It seemed, a few years ago, he had suffered an epididymo-orchitis. After a slow, cautious, clinical examination I telephoned the doctor at the RAF hospital chest unit at Wroughton and arranged for him to be admitted after the weekend was over. I tried to reassure my patient within limits, leaning once more on a medical adage: 'Everything in medicine is considered guilty until proved innocent. We have to make sure.' The flight lieutenant did not seem unduly perturbed and left for his RAF station.

I wrote my report and gathered a few personal papers from my desk before putting on my overcoat. Since, later in the year, I would now and then revisit CME I had no great farewells to make to colleagues. Soon I was standing in the darkness and snow opposite the peaceful, oblong, lit windows of the Middlesex Hospital.

16. My New Friend, John Betjeman

That Wednesday afternoon, I did not feel like working so I persuaded my philosopher friend, John Watkins, to have a game of chess with me. We usually played on languorous Sundays when we both happened to be in London. Somehow it seemed sinful to play mid-week, like going to the cinema during daylight. I was about to leave the house to walk to John Watkins's house in Hampstead Garden Suburb when the telephone clamoured in the hall.

'We're thinking of doing a series of programmes called *Friends of John Betjeman*,' the researcher working for London Weekend Television told me. 'We wondered if you'd like to take part in the pilot programme.'

I stood looking at the front door; a speckled shower of light tried to come through the glass.

'But I'm not a friend of John Betjeman,' I said, surprised. 'I've never even met him.'

'You like his poetry?'

'Well yes, the best of it.'

'What we have in mind,' the researcher continued, 'is that you have a discussion with Sir John about Edward Thomas's poetry and then read your own poem "Not Adlestrop".'

'I see.'

'We're not certain yet. At present, we just need to know if you're interested.'

I left the house soon after that telephone conversation with thoughts about Betjeman's poems persisting in my mind. His verses could make me smile though his humour was often a disguise, the blossom of the underlying nettle. And his serious poems owned a certain oddness if only because they were underpinned by rhythms best suited to comedy. For example, 'Death in Leamington' which had the jaunty cadences of 'Eskimo Nell':

> She died in the upstairs bedroom
> By the light of the ev'ning star
> That shone through the plate glass window
> From over Leamington Spa.

In his brief narratives I admired how he surprised the reader not only with the rhythm contrast but also that of mood. In 'Devonshire Street W.1.' he relates how a couple, having seen a specialist, have learnt that the husband is a dying man. Then his wife –

> . . . puts her fingers in his as, loving and silly,
> At long-past Kensington dances she used to do.
> 'It's cheaper to take a tube to Piccadilly
> And then we can catch a nineteen or a twenty-two.'

In life, I would stampede away from those awful upper–middle–class women Betjeman seemed to be ambivalently attracted to, but I was glad to meet them on the page: Miss J. Hunter Dunn, horsey Diana, and 'Pam, I adore you, Pam, you great big mountainous sports girl.' And I liked his evocation of place, his confessed hypochondria, his extreme fear of death. And who could resist a poem such as 'In a Bath Teashop':

> 'Let us not speak, for the love we bear one another –
> Let us hold hands and look.'
> She, such a very ordinary little woman;
> He, such a thumping crook;
> But both, for a moment, little lower than the angels
> In the teashop's ingle-nook.

Yes, I was for John Betjeman. Besides, had he not reviewed my first novel *Ash on a Young Man's Sleeve* hundreds of years ago, rather well? Remembering this I walked down Finchley Road, turning at Hoop Lane towards Hampstead Garden Suburb. It was a lovely sunlit day and I felt curiously cheerful. Then, as I approached the railings of the cemetery, I observed in front of me a black hearse with its flower-covered coffin, parked opposite the crematorium gate. Behind the hearse, another stationary black limousine waited by the kerb. Three people sat bolt upright in the back, unsmiling, motionless, not talking to each other. They had the melancholy faces of sleepers, except their eyes were open, their mouths firmly shut.

I walked up the incline towards the roundabout. Then came, silent as a conspiracy, a second funeral cortège. First the long car with the new coffin, followed by another shining black automobile, chauffeur-driven. And, again in the back seat, three mourners sat upright, looking neither to the left nor the right. They had similar despondent faces. I looked over my shoulder and saw behind me the parked, mourning car with its first three occupants and suddenly a possible line for a poem came into my head: 'Some talk in their sleep, very few sing.' I thought of a few more matching lines and I was struggling to get the sound of their meaning right when they became derailed as if I had been button-holed by a man from Porlock. For now, on the other side of the roundabout, a third hearse with a coffin approached. From poetic trance I was jolted into the ordinary, beautiful, common air of a Wednesday afternoon and was astonished. For it was as if, from diverse corners of London, funeral cars were converging on this focal point in Golders Green and each hearse, in its turn, with its chauffeur of Death, had to wait, had to idle the minutes away, rather like an aeroplane circling and circling, not given clearance to land at some crowded airport.

However, behind the third, so-controlled cortège there came, at last, another car – one not so sleek, one, as a matter of fact, battered, shabby, driven neither by a ceremonial chauffeur, nor carrying three exhausted occupants in the back. The driver was young and the window beside him had been wound down so that the raucous noise of Radio One assaulted the surrounding silence. The young driver had evidently turned the knob of his radio to half-past six because the volume of the pop-music was atrociously loud. The blaring noise that gradually diminished as the battered car progressed to the Finchley Road seemed, there and then, to celebrate informality, youth, vivid life, and for a moment I was glad of it.

On my way home I passed the red-brick crematorium again. No sleek black funeral cars lay in wait in the shadows. No battered car progressed, trailing its loud decibels. All was still, quiet, so that I could hear my own footsteps. Outside the gate of the crematorium I observed a board on which was written IN – like a command. No nascent words for a poem of my own came into my head. Instead, I recalled a few lines by John Betjeman:

> How straight the crematorium driveway lies!
> And little puffs of smoke without a sound
> Show what we loved dissolving in the skies.

When I reached Finchley Road, the lampposts suddenly became luminous.

Over a lively lunch at the London Weekend building John Betjeman told me that he intended to begin the pilot programme with Thomas Hood's poem, 'I remember, I remember, the house where I was born'. He continued, 'Some may think it sentimental but it isn't, it isn't, and I don't care if it is.' After Hood's poem the Poet Laureate then intended to air his enthusiasm for other poets, including Edward Thomas. He would request Prunella Scales to read Thomas's 'Adlestrop'. 'At this point you come into it,' he advised me. 'We'll talk about Edward Thomas before I ask you to read your poem, "Not Adlestrop", all right?'

It so happened that I had recently read a strange long poem by Thomas Hood called 'Miss Kilmansegg and Her Precious Leg'. I asked Betjeman whether he knew it. His response surprised me. He clapped his hands and with vulnerable passion turned to me as if I had given him something he had wanted all his life. He cried out, 'How *very* good of you to know that poem. Oh thank you, thank you so much!' I smiled suspiciously; but John Betjeman was patently sincere. He was grateful, in a most innocent way, that another individual had read and liked a poem he knew and cared for. He continued to thank me rhapsodically and his eyes glittered with pleasure as we discussed the merits of Thomas Hood's poetry.

Before we went into the studio I asked if he, Sir John, had been influenced by Thomas Hood, by, for instance, the rhythms of 'The Bridge of Sighs'. Sir John gave me a dazzling smile before opening his eyes wide and reciting by heart the whole of 'The Bridge of Sighs'. Hearing that poem mediated through his voice I discovered Hood sounded utterly Betjemanesque:

> . . . In she plunged boldly,
> No matter how coldly
> The rough river ran, —
> Over the brink of it,

Picture it — think of it
Dissolute man! . . .

Take her up tenderly,
Lift her with care;
Fashioned so slenderly,
Young and so fair! . . .

Thomas Hood, during his lifetime, had always been short of money
and harassed by ill-health. He had to live in Grub Street, contribute
verse for *Punch* in order to provide for his wife and children. I kept
thinking of his supposed dying words to his wife. Punning to the end
he had sighed, 'My dear, I fear you are losing your lively Hood.' On
Thomas Hood's gravestone, at his own request, the words engraved
were, *He sang the Song of the Shirt.*

As John Betjeman spoke to me about Charles Dickens's friendship
with Hood I could not but observe how frail Betjeman himself
appeared to be. He had a neurological condition and he would
probably have to be taken to the TV studio in a wheelchair.

Indeed, when he, Prunella Scales and I sat under the harsh TV
lights for a rehearsal Sir John's staccato performance agitated the
producer. His neurological illness had left him in decline and though
he could recite 'I remember, I remember, the house where I was
born' accurately, he displayed, subsequently, repeated memory lapses
which made the producer wonder whether Betjeman was now
capable of performing as 'anchor man' for the seven programmes
planned. Prunella Scales whispered to me, 'I'm accustomed to
working with Sir John. He's always like this at rehearsal. When we
actually do it, he'll be brilliant, you'll see.'

Alas, during the actual performance before the studio audience
John Betjeman did lose his place and did bumble rather. He forgot,
for instance, to mention Edward Thomas at all so I had to interject,
'Do you like Edward Thomas, his poem "Adlestrop"?'

'Oh yes. Yes, yes. Edward Thomas. I do so like his poetry.
"Adlestrop"? I'll read it for you. No no, Prunella Scales will read it.
Then you must read your "Not Adlestrop".' I did not think these
promptings, his unpredictability, mattered too much. His hesitations,
his transparent recoveries, his obvious vulnerability, surely made him
all the more likeable to a viewing audience? Certainly the studio
audience warmed to him. As soon as the programme was over many
of them approached Sir John with books to be signed. The books

piled up in front of him. It so happened that on the table lay my own *Collected Poems* from which I had read 'Not Adlestrop'. John Betjeman, signing book after book, accidentally wrote his shaky signature in mine. I can proudly boast that in my bookcase I have my own *Collected Poems* signed by John Betjeman.

The programme, though, was never relayed and the series was cancelled. The producer felt (wrongly in my view) that Betjeman could no longer function professionally enough.

At a presentation party a handsomely produced book, *A Garland for the Laureate*, was presented to Sir John Betjeman on his seventy-fifth birthday. Twenty-two poets, including Philip Larkin, Ted Hughes, R.S. Thomas, Elizabeth Jennings and Stephen Spender, contributed a poem to the volume, as indeed I had. How typical was his response to that Garland. He wrote, I presume, to all of us: 'Thursday, November 19th, was the happiest day of my life. I can hardly believe it has happened. I often feel myself an interloper who has got in under false pretences; now, with your wonderful generosity, you have established me in my own estimation as quite a good poet, for here you are, the most eminent poets in England, giving me a present of your original poems. What more can a man want? Thank you . . .'

Over the top? John Betjeman, that very English poet, could act in most unEnglish ways, to become a most typical atypical English eccentric!

I was thinking of his eccentricities, rapturous enthusiasms, at Westminster Abbey when I attended the Service of Thanksgiving for the Life and Work of Sir John Betjeman CBE, 1906–1984, on Friday 29 June 1984.

During the war Betjeman had written a satirical poem called 'In Westminster Abbey'. Would those who organised the Service dare to have it read? Two of its verses came to mind as I waited for the Service to begin:

> Gracious Lord, oh bomb the Germans.
>   Spare their women for Thy Sake,
> And if that is not too easy
>   We will pardon Thy Mistake.
> But gracious Lord, what e'er shall be,
> Don't let anyone bomb me.

and

> Although dear Lord I am a sinner,
>   I have done no major crime;
> Now I'll come to Evening Service
>   Whensoever I have the time.
> So, Lord, reserve for me a crown
> And do not let my shares go down.

Thomas Hood would have liked that. But now the Dean of Westminster had begun to speak: 'We meet to thank God for Sir John Betjeman, a national figure, whose death has eclipsed the gaiety of nations and whose kindly and eccentric personality, wit and humour, laughter and sense of fun, charmed his contemporaries and will be long remembered . . .'

17. Doctor as Patient

In Istanbul, after my lecture on British Poetry 1945–1984, we walked down a narrow dimly lit alleyway, a group of us, on our way to a recommended restaurant. 'How did it go in Ankara?' Mike Winter, one of the British Council representatives, asked me. I told him how the Dean at one University there had boasted, with evident satisfaction, 'We've had Elizabeth Jane Howard, Arnold Wesker and Margaret Drabble here before you. If Shakespeare were alive we'd have him too.'

As we emerged from the alleyway, a man strenuously beckoned our group to one side for he was guarding two cats who were copulating under the one lamppost. I was surprised by this public, outrageous sensuality. I had always thought cats to be secretive creatures. I have heard in the night their oriental cries but never seen them fastened to each other. Are well-bred English cats more reticent than their Turkish counterparts?

Once in the restaurant I referred to the gesticulating cat-guard, a lover of cats surely, sympathetic to their sensual needs. 'Are Turks, as a nation, allies of cats?' I asked. One of our party known as Ginger, an American lady married to a Turk, related how only weeks earlier she had encountered another pair of cats copulating publicly and a man watching them had been throwing stones at the feline lovers. She had suggested that this stone-thrower should desist, leave the cats alone, and nature be allowed healthily to take its course. 'But it's unhealthy, it's two male cats,' the man had protested.

I enjoyed Istanbul, the astonishing sights: the serene hush of the Blue Mosque and of St Sophia; the Topkapi Palace – the oldest of the remaining palaces of the world. But Turkey made me ill – weeks later after my return to London. One grey morning I looked out of our front bedroom window and the leprous snow on the pavements, on the hedges, front gardens, stark trees, on the slanting rooftops of Hodford Road, hurt my eyes intolerably. I drew the noise of closing curtains and went back to bed.

I had never suffered such a profound headache. I fumbled for a thermometer. Fever, headache, photophobia. Surely not meningitis? I examined my skin, thermometer in mouth. No neck rigidity, so perhaps I was merely experiencing the symptoms of a severe influenza with meningism – an irritation of the meninges, the coverings of the brain, rather than a frank inflammation there. But was I mistaken? Suddenly I recalled a party I had attended in Ankara. One of the guests had left early, apologising to the host because he felt unwell. A coincidence? What was the incubation period of a viral meningitis?

I wished my uncle, Joe Shepherd, was still alive. He had practised in Hampstead Garden Suburb and had looked after my family scrupulously for decades. Even a doctor wants above all, when ill, authoritative reassurance from another doctor. And Joe had been a kind, experienced general practitioner who kept up to date with advances in medicine. The mistakes Joe made tended to be non-medical ones, outside his practice.

There was that occasion, for instance, when we had been in a theatre foyer and James Mason had hovered nearby. Mason looked familiar to my uncle and he had assumed the film star to be one of his patients. 'Feeling better?' he asked James Mason who glanced back at him, astonished.* Aspirined, lying in bed with my back to the

---

* One other blunder of Joe's occurred when he took a holiday in Italy. In the hotel bar he struck up a conversation with a friendly Italian. Soon he told his new acquaintance that he was a doctor practising in Hampstead Garden Suburb in London. 'And what, sir, may I ask, do you do for a living?' The Italian replied, 'I'm Tito Gobbi.' My uncle responded by saying, 'Yes. My name is Joe Shepherd. But, as I said, what do you do for a living?' 'I'm Tito Gobbi,' repeated the Italian. My uncle decided that the stranger's English was somewhat deficient.

curtains drawn across the daylight windows, I dismissed the remembrance of that incident and stayed behind my eyelids. I wanted to fall asleep, deeply, refreshingly, and wake up free of the unrelenting headache.

The next morning I felt no better. I sat up in bed groggily while Joan took my temperature: 101. It would probably climb higher by the evening. I turned my head again towards the far wall for even the thin light, breaking through the curtains, bruised my eyes. 'I'd better call Dr Ross,' Joan said. (Dr Ross had become our National Health GP after my Uncle Joe died.) I attempted to dissuade her. I told her the diagnosis: not meningism merely but a viral meningitis or, as the textbook called it, Benign Lymphocytic Meningitis. 'Let's see what Dr Ross says,' she advised.

What was the point? There was no specific treatment for viral meningitis. Ross would come, take my temperature, perhaps test my reflexes, then admit me to hospital. There, they would extract a cubic inch or so of my cerebro-spinal fluid (a lumbar puncture) and send the fluid which would be as clear as gin to the laboratory; and after some weeks the diagnosis of benign lymphocytic meningitis would be confirmed. They called the condition benign because patients almost always survive it. It didn't *feel* benign. Headache, photophobia, dreaming blanks, time passing, analgesics, darkness, light, darkness, fever, analgesics. Plato believed that the best doctors would have experienced disease themselves. He reckoned that doctors should not be in robust health and 'should have had all manner of disease in their own persons'. If I came out of this illness alive and presumably it was not the more serious *bacterial* meningitis, I would, according to Plato, be a more skilful doctor, certainly one more sympathetic to those suffering from headache, photophobia and fever.

A couple of days passed before Joan called in Dr Ross. If anything I was worse. After he had examined me, listened to my short story of symptoms, he said, 'You'll have to go to hospital. What about the Royal Free in Hampstead? That's the nearest.'

'I don't fancy a lumbar puncture,' I grumbled.

Nor did I wish to lose Joan's sympathetic and tactful care – to exchange that for the more impersonal concern of hospital routine.

'There's only one place for you,' insisted Dr Ross. 'Hospital. I know the neurologist at the Royal Free. He's first class. I'll telephone him now.'

Soon enough I lay in bed in a darkened emergency room at the

Royal Free – the punishing headache, the photophobia unchanged, the temperature high. One of the nurses came and said, 'Could you manage to walk down to the X-ray Department by yourself for a brain scan and chest X-ray? I could get a porter to wheel you there but that may take a long time. We're so short-staffed.'

It was a long, long staggering walk to the X-ray Department and I cursed Margaret Thatcher's government that had so vandalised the National Health Service. Eventually I arrived, handed in the slip of a form and waited and waited with the other haggard-looking patients who sat on the long benches. Here I was a doctor – forget the poetry bit – here I was a doctor but on the wrong side of the counter. Selfishly, I wanted to say, 'Hurry up, let me go first, I'm a doctor. I want preferential treatment.' I said nothing, of course, but waited with my eyes closed, as a patient, patiently.

Afterwards, wheeled back to a darkened room (they had found a porter), I heard through my headache, beyond the open door, a patient in the ward shouting out penetrating cries in a language that hardly sounded human. His tortured screeches continued on and on and on unceasingly. This is how it must have been in Bedlam.

At last I was examined by the neurologist who suggested the provisional diagnosis of Benign Lymphocytic Meningitis. 'I'm not keen to have a lumbar puncture,' I said. 'Apart from confirming the diagnosis,' the neurologist persuaded me, 'it will relieve the pressure, relieve your headache a bit.'

The next couple of days after the two lumbar punctures – they mucked up the first one – passed by in a haze. Joan visited me each day, bringing me more tempting food. Everything at the hospital seemed in short supply. Despite my fever they did not have enough sheets available to change my bed.

Gradually I began to feel somewhat better and Joan told me that family and friends wished to visit me. I declined. I agreed with Ogden Nash when he wrote:

> Take the sight of a visitor trying to entertain a
>   patient or a patient trying to entertain a visitor.
> It would bring joy to the heart of the Grand
>   Inquisitor.

Another eight days passed before my fever seemed to truly abate. Then I asked to be allowed to go home, to go back to the care of my wife who would make for me 'some very special Welsh tomato soup which was absolutely necessary for my full recovery'.

When I returned home my fever also returned. I had hoped to sit quietly in the armchair in the bedroom, listening to the radio, perhaps feeling better every day – to claim, in convalescence, the regal right of the sick-bed, to be served and pampered. 'How sickness,' wrote Charles Lamb, 'enlarges the dimensions of a man's self to himself! he is his own exclusive object. Supreme selfishness is inculcated upon him as his only duty.'

Before I was released from the Royal Free the consultant neurologist had said, 'It'll take some time for you to be fully recovered. You'll probably get depressed. Don't worry, that's a normal sequel to meningitis. And don't go and see a psychiatrist. Just come to my Outpatients. OK? Mind you don't get a relapse when you leave here.'

That's what happened: a relapse – but I would not go back to hospital. I lay in bed again – headache, photophobia, fever, dreaming blanks, time passing, occasional visitors. Leo, Dr Ross, Keren, Susanna, David, darkness, light, day, night, and always Joan on call, near and reassuring.

Half dreaming, I knew with banal certainty, that the heart of reason was the reasoning of the heart and that when I listened to silence, absolute silence, I would hear the language of the spirits. Then, more awake, I thought how silence unheard could be the language of the spirits asleep. I opened my eyelids noiselessly. I was not walking down a branch-dark path, midge-haunted. I was here, home.

Recovered more or less I did not experience any depression such as the neurologist at the Royal Free Hospital had prophesied. But worryingly for a couple of weeks my cerebral nerves were affected. First I experienced a toothache and jawache, then an earache and finally I had some difficulty in focusing my eyes properly, seeing double. These symptoms all passed, fortunately, and before long I was able to resume, after months, my old routines of working in London at the chest clinic on Monday and Tuesday mornings; visiting Ogmore; watching Cardiff City play at Ninian Park; playing chess. And suddenly I had a particularly productive period of poetry-writing. I was looking at the world afresh with the grateful eyes of a convalescent.

18. My Brother Leo

The *Sunday Telegraph* decided to publish a weekly series in their colour supplement called, 'A Day Out'. They invited different people to go to any city they pleased and to describe their adventures during that one day.

'You'll pay for me and my wife to go anywhere for a day?' I asked the features editor on the *Telegraph* when he telephoned me.

'A day out, anywhere. Within reason.'

'How about Paris?'

'Sorry, Judi Dench has chosen Paris.'

'How about Amsterdam?'

'Sorry, it's already taken.'

'Copenhagen, then? I've never been to Copenhagen.'

'It's rather expensive there.'

'Oh – then what about Venice?'

I listened to fat silence before the features editor said, 'Look, wouldn't you like to do London?'

'What about Little Venice?' I asked sardonically.

Evidently the *Sunday Telegraph*'s expense account had been bombed; but then, hesitating, I thought why not? I had always wanted to take one of those boats from Camden Lock along the canal to Little Venice; and we had intended anyway to visit the Oskar Kokoschka exhibition at the Tate. We could take a taxi from Little Venice and besides we could lunch decently and dine expensively. A Day Out, yes. 'I could manage next Wednesday,' I said.

The next Wednesday proved to be a perfect English summer day. I remember opening the front door in the shadowed hall and how the bright light made me half close my eyes as I brought in the milk and picked up my mail from the doormat. Among the letters I recognised on one envelope the vertical clear handwriting of my brother Leo. Inside I discovered a piece he had written for a paperback book project on behalf of the Save the Children Fund. Evidently, various celebrities had been invited to pen a vivid memory from their childhood. 'I think the enclosed will interest you,' Leo wrote in his letter to me. The enclosed did. I read:

I remember well the details of that fateful day although I was only six years five months old. With my eight-year-old brother Wilfred, I had, for reasons then obscure to me, been dispatched to another part of the city to stay with my maternal grandparents. This was more acceptable to me since I was the favourite of my grandfather, a Talmudist who, I claim, was the first man to speak Welsh with a Yiddish accent; it was less congenial to my brother but, since he was the favourite of my paternal grandmother, a German-born, belligerent atheist, a woman of the Enlightenment, who lived but a few hundred yards away from the Talmudist, Wilfred was not over-fretful . . .

Leo continued to relate how 'after a few days we were told we could return home and that we would find there a splendid present, a new baby brother . . .'

Then followed the story that I had heard many a time when I was an adolescent: how Wilfred had bought for me, new-born, a copy of *Comic Cuts* whereas Leo, superior, decided on *The Children's Newspaper*. 'When my turn came to enter my brother's bedroom and I saw the sleeping babe, I became afflicted with doubts about his capacity to appreciate my gift,' Leo confessed.

Why, I wondered, had Leo chosen to focus on my birth when he must have had so many vivid memories of boyhood to relate? My birth day, he had remarked, was a 'fateful' day for him. He must have looked at our mother with those serious, chocolate-brown eyes of his, unsmiling, as he witnessed the temporary crowning of his new kid brother. I was amused how his piece revealed also his competitive spirit with Wilfred. He spoke about 'favourites'. He buys for me a sensible *Children's Newspaper*; Wilfred blunders with a comic. Leo 1, Wilfred 0. But, of course, later, I also was not free of the family's competitive nature.

As I put down Leo's letter I thought how routinely my views about politics or whatever tend to be discounted by my elder brothers. I was only seven when my sister, the eldest in the family, left home, so because she hardly knew me as a young teenager, she is likely to respect my opinions. But Wilfred and Leo, Leo in particular, knew me when I was even more ignorant than I am now! And so, affectionate as they are, and allowing me one province of expertise – poetry – about almost everything else I sense they won't, they can't, really take me seriously.

After all, when they were aged eighteen and sixteen and arguing the toss about Karl Marx and Sigmund Freud – remarkable that they should have been able to do so given the few books in our house – I was reading the *Gem* and the *Magnet*. I was a ten-year-old idiot who could not even pronounce 'dialectical materialism'. I should, by rights, have an outsize inferiority complex. 'Who wrote this, and about whom?' Leo would ask me in his best inquisitor voice:

> Just for a handful of silver he left us,
> Just for a riband to stick in his coat.

Yards of silence stretched. 'By Browning,' Leo would thunder triumphantly, 'and it's about Wordsworth selling out, becoming Poet Laureate. Any fool knows that.'

It was always so, the youngest ignorant and chided by elder brothers. Evidence of it is there in the history books, in the Bible, too, and in those fairy stories that begin, 'Once upon a time there was a king who had three sons. The first two were intelligent, but the youngest was stupid and called Dummling.' The nice thing is – nice if you're the youngest, that is – Dummling, in those fairy tales, always scores in the end. He is helped by earthly magical forces – an animal, a toad, a white cat – and near the last page scoops the prize and the Fair Lady. Even when the youngest is a girl, downtrodden, enslaved, wronged and vulnerable, she is finally favoured – seen by all the world as being the virtuous one – and her situation is magically transformed. I close my eyes, the reel of years revolves backward and I see the headline of a pre-war *South Wales Echo*: CINDERELLA WINS; further back still and I hear Cordelia say, 'Wasn't I right, Daddy?'

Before we ventured forth from Golders Green for our *Sunday Telegraph* Day Out, I telephoned Leo to thank him for his letter and for the interesting enclosure. When I remarked that later, during the afternoon, Joan and I would be close to Parliament at the Tate Gallery he invited us to join him afterwards for a strawberry and cream tea on the terrace of the House of Commons.

Though he had been an MP for almost twenty years my visits to Parliament over the two decades, as his guest, had been infrequent. Nor would they gather pace in the future as Leo, aged 68, had announced his irrevocable intention to resign at the General Election of 1987. 'I don't intend to be one more aging politician maniacally denying the aging process and death itself,' he had trumpeted.

I had last visited the House of Commons when Leo was speaking during a Welsh affairs debate. Entering the great voluminous Hall I had encountered the philosopher Bryan Magee, then an MP, who, it seemed, was awaiting the arrival of Kingsley Amis. Magee, whom I knew from the Ben Nicolson-Philip Toynbee lunchtime gatherings at Bertorelli's in Charlotte Street (near to the clinic), asked why I was there. When I explained, Bryan Magee appeared perplexed, even incredulous. 'For the Welsh debate. Good Lord! The *Welsh* debate!' Evidently Magee had no intention of taking varnished Amis into the Chamber despite the novelist's Welsh connections. And to be truthful, though Leo spoke with his customary eloquence, I did not find that particular debating interlude, with all its undramatised minutiae of locality, too engrossing. Strawberries and cream on the terrace on a cloudless summer day, beside the slow, brown, travelling Thames, appeared to be a much more entertaining prospect.

After a leisurely alfresco lunch at Camden Lock, we joined the boat that hummed along the canal's greenish water, passing the walkers on the tow-path, towards Regent's Park and the Zoo where it stopped to pick up a few passengers. Afterwards it thrust forward peacefully beneath occasional low bridges over which the frantic, busy traffic of London grumbled and grated. We, in our holiday mood, waved to canoeists and boys fishing – no doubt playing truant as we felt we were. Near Lord's the canal widened suddenly to a little dock of moored boats with pretty names: *Blue Rose, Nightjar, Harebell.*

Then came the long three-minute tunnel which was broad enough for only one boat to pass. In the darkness we could see the oval light at the end of the tunnel and I thought how Orpheus, returning from the Underworld, near the end of his journey, would have beheld a similar view. As we began to make an exit the O became excitingly wider and wider until we were born and borne into the more expansive canal of Little Venice.

From Little Venice we hailed a taxi which took us to the Tate Gallery and soon enough I found myself standing before a formidable portrait of Alma Mahler. I had first heard of this painting by Oskar Kokoschka years earlier when Canetti had enthused about it. He had excitedly informed me that the portrait of Gustav Mahler's widow seemed to depict a murderess. Alma Mahler had disgusted Canetti when he had met her in pre-war Vienna. She had not shown enough veneration for her greatly gifted husband. Worse she had injuriously confessed how she admired Aryan physique in men, and had then complained how many little Jews such as Gustav had fallen in love with her. Since Canetti happened to be a 'little Jew' himself no wonder he had bristled blood and found in the portrait some resembling kinship with Lucretia Borgia!

Oskar Kokoschka, no little Jew, had been one of many who had been in love with the composer's wife. After she had ditched him, love-lorn Kokoschka had made an effigy of her, a winsome, life-size doll for which he bought Parisian clothes and underwear. When he rode through the streets in his carriage he took The Silent One, as he called her, with him. At the opera, he arranged for the life-size doll to sit next to him in his private box.

All this I recalled as I stared at the portrait of a woman who had the reputation of being a kind of female rhapsody. 'Not my type,' was all I could say to Joan when she joined me to picture-gaze.

After we quit the Tate and progressed towards the Palace of Westminster, I pondered how my intermittent conversations with Leo over the last year had been too much about Time passing, too much about our eventual, inevitable assignment with Thanatos. Perhaps the prospect of quitting the House of Commons discomforted him emotionally more than he could consciously acknowledge. In his book *Private Member* (a typically humorous, brazen title) Leo confessed that entering Parliament had been a painful experience. 'The nights after I left the Commons for my lonely hotel room were full of nightmares and terror; seemingly for hours I would, in a twilight world between dream and wakefulness, be gripped by vertigo . . . I was unbalanced and had lost my bearings.' Leaving the Commons might also, perhaps, disconcert him? After all, so much of his life had revolved around politics. He had been an MP since 1958. Before that he had been a Cardiff councillor. When he was twenty-one, before he'd had the opportunity to vote himself, Leo had been adopted as a Labour councillor for one of the Cardiff wards. I, then a fourteen-year-old schoolboy, had found myself chanting:

> Vote vote vote for Leo Abse
> Kick old Whitey in the pants.

I have met remarkable people in my life – Canetti, for instance – but Leo is as vital a person as I have ever known. What startles those who do not know him is his tactless proclivity to offer them ceaseless Freudian explanations for their argued beliefs or their particular actions. Leo has always respected and been influenced by my eldest brother, Wilfred, a psychoanalyst. From early days, when we both lived in our parents' house in Cardiff, Leo productively borrowed Wilf's psychoanalytical spectacles. On his bedroom wall he pinned up a reproduction of Giorgione's *La Tempesta*. 'It shouldn't have been called *The Tempest*,' he argued. 'It's post-coital. Look how calm and serene the scene is. The storm has passed. The man is dressed, the naked woman feeding her child. Look how between them flows the river which represents Time flowing on to eternity. And note, in the foreground, how the column is broken, a spent-penis symbol. Right?'

Unpredictable, original, irritating, confrontational, extremely efficient, quick to understand a problem and to suggest a sensible solution, it must have been vexing for him to have watched fellow MPs, less gifted, though perhaps more wisely tactful, some associated with Cardiff like James Callaghan and George Thomas, achieve honours and positions of power while he remained a backbencher. Yet, as Michael Foot once said to me, 'Leo did more to raise the quality of life for many in Britain, through his private bills, than did the government under Wilson's long tenancy at 10 Downing Street.'

When Leo entered Parliament Aneurin Bevan advised him to 'cultivate irreverence'. Leo had never needed such advice. On the contrary, a dose of Foreign Office caution might have made him hesitate to impugn overtly the motives of some of his fellow MPs by informing them, man to man, that their actions were an expression of auto-erotic narcissism or repressed homosexuality or, as he once told a bewildered Richard Crossman, 'The trouble with you, Dick, is you're an obsessional; it's all to do with your early potty training.'

Leo's judgement of people, or rather his sometimes bizarre reasons for prejudice in favour of or against them, must have made his auditors wonder or squirm. When Robert Maxwell was an MP, long before he'd been unmasked, I asked Leo what he thought of him. 'I don't know him too well,' Leo said. 'Don't care for him though. He opens doors for me. He rushes ahead, right? Opens the door, you know? By being so subservient he must experience a feeling of power. I don't care for him.'

I recalled that soon after Leo was elected in 1958 I had stood with him in the medieval Westminster Hall and I asked him if he, one day, would like to be a Minister. He had replied with utter seriousness, 'To be a backbencher. That's enough, right? That's all I want. With luck one can be of use as a bankbencher.'

He had not spoken further and seemed overcome. Humble. This

was not the Leo who usually sounded so confident and buoyant, not the Leo who would generally assent to Nietzsche's 'the secret of the greatest fruitfulness and the greatest enjoyment of existence is: *to live dangerously*. Build your cities under Vesuvius! Send your ships into uncharted seas!' Even so, I did not guess then at my brother's uncertainties, or know of his disorientation. Later Leo recognised the source of his own vertigo symptoms for he wrote in *Private Member*, 'All achievements bring guilt, and those most yearned for in childhood, on attainment, bring the heaviest neurotic burdens.'

On the open-air terrace, close to where the Thames, in its summer slow-motion, flowed on to eternity, Leo offered us the promised strawberries and cream and introduced Joan and me to several of his colleagues, some of whom happened to be Welsh. Not one of them resembled a scrum half. They towered over Leo who is even more short-statured than Canetti was. 'This is my kid brother,' Leo declared.

How often, over the years, strangers have asked me peremptorily, 'Abse? Your name's Abse? Any relation to Leo Abse?'★ When I happily claimed our fraternity some let me know how much they had benefited from his intercession to right small injustices and had personal reasons for being grateful to him – unrecorded acts of kindness on his part – and some let me know how much they admired his maverick stances and his speeches. Ever since I've been so high, in Wales people have said to me, 'Duw, your Leo, he's got a mouth on 'im.' And indeed Leo is a superb orator, one who believes 'rhetoric can inspire, persuade and finally move men into the cause of justice and prompt them into action that improves our lot and theirs.'

★ Others say 'Abse? That's a curious name. Is it Welsh?'
Not long before the clinic closed a Lebanese patient whose name was Abse entered my consulting room. I asked him about the origin of our name. 'I don't suppose you've heard of the great poet, Abse?' he countered. I swallowed and said, 'Well . . . er . . .' but he continued, 'He was a sixth century Bedouin robber-prince poet, Antara al-Abse.'
Later I read an article by Bernard Lewis in *Encounter* about early Arab poetry. Antara's mother apparently was black. Racial prejudice made him write, 'Half of me comes from the family of Abse, the other half I defend with my sword.'
Many stories refer to Antara al-Abse's strength and wit. One concerns a group of men fearful of a huge bull. 'Only you, Antara, can deal with that bull,' they cried. 'Mmm,' said Antara, 'but does the bull know I'm Antara?'
In September, 1993, an American woman, a stranger to me, related one of Antara's boasts: 'My sword, in battle, was a doctor dispensing medicine to those complaining of headaches.' The more I learn of Antara's swanking, the more I wish I could claim him as an ancestor.

Others, less generous, or disagreeing with his politics, have to my face mocked his sartorial performances on Budget Day. In response, poker-faced, I've always said, 'Yes, he wears my cast-offs;' but privately, much to his irritation, I used to try to persuade him to relinquish his ostentatious dressing up. 'You're so bourgeois,' Leo would respond. 'You're so worried about what-the-neighbours-will-say,' and he would suggest that his sartorial gestures were 'acts in defiance of the covert sumptuary laws maintained by the Tories who patronisingly believed that finery was for them and that socialists should wear cloth caps.' But maybe James Callaghan had a point when he told Leo, after his first Budget Day extravagance, that such theatre would damage his political career irretrievably.

'My constituents thought otherwise,' Leo has recorded, 'and so did a substantial section of the public who having focused upon my attire, were now much more ready to focus on my words, on my campaigns, for social reform.'

As I helped myself to strawberries and listened to the ping-pong banter of a group of MPs, I could sense how many of them respected Leo, indeed felt affectionate towards him.* They would have assented to a recent appraisal by the broadcaster, Patrick Hannan, who declared that, for his money, Leo was 'one of the most gifted backbenchers of his time as a manipulator of Parliament'. 'You love Parliament, I use it,' Leo had once told Michael Foot.

One of the Welsh MPs addressed me. 'You're from Cardiff too.' I nodded. Merlyn Rees, who had been Home Secretary in a Labour Government, then went on to describe how when he was a Minister, a petitioner with an apparent Cardiff accent had approached him. 'I said, from Cardiff are you?' Rees continued, 'whereupon this fellow, clearly annoyed, promptly produced a gun and stuck it in my stomach. Fortunately, he was quickly disarmed by the alert body-guards.' Merlyn Rees hesitated, then with studied timing added, 'The fellow, you see, was from Newport.'

Leo steered me towards another group of MPs which included Robin Cook. Again he introduced me as his 'kid brother'. One of the MPs related a story involving one of his constituents; but I kept

---

* Not that everyone warms to Leo. Indeed he never hesitates to make an enemy. If crossed he reacts with a notable Old Testament belligerence. When a hostile reviewer of one of his books made certain factual errors Leo, with legal alacrity, announced, *'I'll make him crawl.'* It was no idle threat. I often wish he would heed the advice of Gore Vidal's grandmother who told the novelist, 'Don't stir up more snakes than you can kill.'

on thinking of the time I had accompanied Leo when he travelled up the industrial, damaged valley from Pontypool to Blaina, all around his constituency, visiting an old people's home here, attending a miners' meeting there, and how much respect my brother had commanded. I recalled, too, how a less grateful constituent plucked at Leo's lapels and demanded, 'What are you going to do about the bloody sheep – they keep getting in my front garden and eating the flowers?'

Late that evening, over an absurdly expensive dinner at Keats's restaurant in Hampstead, surrounded by those eating their business expenses, not for the first time Joan and I discussed Leo, his sibling rivalry and my own. Leo was highly conscious of being a second son. He reckoned that 'second sons with able elder brothers, from Stafford Cripps to Harold Laski to Tony Benn, have frequently provided significant leadership.'

'As for me,' I told Joan, 'I'm reduced by Leo to being just a kid – that's to say one rendered competitively benign. Did you notice how he introduced me to all those MPs as his *kid* brother?'

'He was being affectionately protective,' Joan opined. 'He sees you as being forever the baby of the family.'

Joan was right. Leo was right: the youngest children in families never do grow old. We may become grey-haired or bald, we may be wizened, our hands may tremble, our voices become thin as reeds, but this is all just a master disguise.

19. White Coat, Purple Coat

As the decade progressed my clinical sessions at the Central Medical Establishment became even more rare, dwindling to one morning a week before ceasing altogether. I had become an ex-doctor, aged 58. Looking back at my medical career I realised that I had much to be grateful for; it had afforded me satisfactions, not merely material; and clinical experiences that had even provided me, intermittently, with dramatic subject matter for my poetry and prose.

No doubt, too, the practice of medicine and my early training had left a watermark on my poetry-writing style. Medical students must memorise facts – physiological, anatomical, pathological. They cannot, like Eng. Lit. students, race through their text-books. The scientific hypotheses, along with the established concepts proffered, are often couched in abstract terms with frequent use of scandalous jargon. Hence, medical students need to clarify for themselves what they read. Later in life, they discover that not only do they tend to read more slowly than others educated differently but they also retain the habit of trying to make things lucid which, on first appearance, seem obscure. Encountering vagueness, they thirst for definition.

Perhaps this is why doctor-poets of our century – William Carlos Williams in the USA, Gottfried Benn in Germany, Miroslav Holub in Czechoslovakia, Rutger Kopland in Holland and Edward Low-bury in England, to name but a few – are not difficult to read. Their work, generally, is accessible. Because of their medical experience, and perhaps because of their physician's sense of community, they are not among those who, as Nietzsche remarked of the poets of his own time, 'muddy their waters so as to appear more deep'.

True, not all doctor-poets have allowed their medical experiences to colour the subject-matter of their poems. Until the mid-Sixties I, myself, had not been able to call upon my confrontations with patients, their triumphs and defeats. After poetry readings some people would approach me saying that they were surprised to learn that I was a doctor. 'You couldn't tell from your poems,' they would say. And I thought, consoling myself, what about Keats's poetry or that of Robert Bridges: reading their work, who would guess they had substantial medical experience?

All the same, I had felt uneasy about not being able to call upon that area of my life. Louis Pasteur once commented, 'Chance favours the prepared mind.' Gradually, my mind, as it were, became prepared to write poems with medical themes and chance favoured me with a number over the years. Indeed, months after I had become an ex-doctor, I put together for future publication in 1989, a second extended *Collected Poems* which I was to call *White Coat, Purple Coat* and of the 180 poems it contained, 28 were (are) indisputably medically coloured. One of them took as its theme the difficulty of pursuing two vocations:

> White coat and purple coat
> a sleeve from both he sews.

That white is always stained with blood
    that purple by the rose.

And phantom rose and blood most real
    compose a hybrid style;
white coat and purple coat
    few men can reconcile.

White coat and purple coat
    can each be worn in turn,
but in the white a man will freeze
    and in the purple burn.

Free from the chest clinic's schedules we were able to stay in Ogmore for longer periods if we so wished. Often while we were away William and Patricia Oxley moved into our Golders Green house and took care of our ginger cat, Caitlin. Sometimes when we sojourned in Ogmore, London friends would stay with us. One such was Tony Whittome and he was there when we witnessed something I, for one, will never forget.

On a windy day of intermittent sun and shadow we happened to be gazing down idly at the estuary, at the river's bright, snail-trailing exit into the sea. Suddenly we became aware of a vertical wall of rain being blown towards us. In front of it, a rainbow advanced rapidly and became more and more distinctly coloured. Soon one end of the rainbow was touching our side of the river while the other end dipped into the far marram-green sand-dunes. Just then, as we dumbly watched this mobile scene, a seagull flew right through the high zenith of the curved arch.

'I expect that seagull is no longer white,' I said to Joan and Tony.

As ever, we were called back to London soon enough. I had commitments there; so had Joan, not least the happy duty to baby-sit. For now we had three dulcet grandchildren to boast about and to cherish. Our children had taken to heart the Yiddish proverb, 'A grown-up daughter should live near to her parents but not so near that she can walk over in slippers.' Besides Joan needed the comprehensive libraries of London to pursue her research for a new book, provisionally entitled *Journey into Art*.

Joan had written a biography of John Ruskin and a guide book to the Art Galleries of Britain and Ireland, and we had together compiled an anthology of poems about paintings and sculpture which the Tate had published in 1986. In the past, century after century, painters and sculptors had been inspired by biblical themes, by mythological stories related by Homer, Ovid and Virgil, by the fictions of Shakespeare. So many Bathshebas had posed naked in artists' studios; so many Ledas had been disgraced; so many painters had drowned Ophelia. But the converse influence of painters on poets had come into its own during the twentieth century, probably due to the greater accessibility of paintings in public galleries. Poets of our time had turned frequently to art for their subject matter so we had no difficulty in choosing eighty fine poems and placing them in conjugating adjacency to the corresponding colour plates. In compiling that Tate book, Joan had had to visit a number of London libraries, including that of the Courtauld Institute where she had been a student. Now she needed to do so again.

My increased leisure allowed me to accept more frequently invitations to give poetry readings in Britain and abroad. One such invitation, from Swansea decades earlier, had seemed less than welcoming. The letter inviting me had read: 'Our chairman, Mr Vernon Watkins, has arranged for you to visit us in Swansea. As Secretary of the Poetry Society, I need to tell you that we expect an audience of about eighty people. I trust you will not read too long as really the audience would much prefer to hear my poems about the Gower Coast. Yours truly, E. Howard Harris.'

I am far from certain about what pleasure audiences receive from some poetry readings. After all, one has to have the scrupulous ear of a Schoenberg to plumb the depths of a suggestive poem on hearing it for the first time. Nevertheless, audiences do often seem to respond to poets when they present their own work. As for the eager poets, apart from the welcome fee, the post-war fashion for subsidised readings has produced for them, as William Oxley has put it, 'happenings that are adjuncts to the imaginative life.' In addition, it is now common practice to sell the poets' books at such readings. Indeed, one important reason to perform poems is to tempt diligent auditors to examine what they have heard on the page and investigate missed nuances.

Organisers of poetry readings do not always order books but ask the poet to bring them along. They provide a table and announce at the end of a reading that the poet's books are for sale and that he/she would be glad to sign them. Ordering books directly from a publisher however can be tricky. Once, when I was about to embark on a three-day poetry tour in Lancashire, I telephoned Tiptree, Hutchinson's warehouse, and ordered sixty copies of my *Collected Poems*. Two weeks later a parcel arrived. On opening it I discovered sixty copies of the *Collected Poems* of Kingsley Amis. 'We only deliver, not take back,' I was told when I telephoned Tiptree to point out their mistake. And when, eventually, I re-ordered my *Collected Poems* not only did the parcel arrive too late for my Lancashire tour but it contained the *Collected Poems* of the Pope!

I have wondered sometimes whether the regular practice of reading poems aloud to audiences affects, consciously or unconsciously, the poet's strategy in constructing poems. When Dylan Thomas began to read to increasingly large audiences the idioplasm of his poetry gradually altered. His poems, while growing more complex in their rhythmic orchestration, also became somewhat less dense, less recondite. There are seductive dangers in being exposed to large audiences and I daresay some poets – reaching for laughs or for an instant reponse – succumb and not in the way Dylan Thomas did. I do not think I have been so seduced though towards the end of the decade I was giving some thirty readings a year.

Some I remember for their sheer comedy: a reading at Uxbridge, for instance, at a local library. They had not organised a poetry reading there before. I was taken aback by my 'welcome'. At the door a stout woman sat behind a wooden table.

'One pound fifty,' she demanded.

'I'm ... er ... Dannie Abse,' I explained, noting behind her my name printed large above a poster announcement of the meeting.

'I don't care who you are,' she said. 'One pound fifty if you want to come to this poetry reading.'

'But I'm giving the reading.'

'What?'

'I'm Dannie Abse.'

'You're not the poet,' she said authoritatively.

'Yes,' I said.

She peered at me. I was being very closely examined. Worse, an impatient queue was forming behind me, one of whom seemed a little tipsy.

'Go on,' the stout lady jeered. 'You look ordinary.'

'Look – ?'

'You look ordinary,' she announced. 'I could cuddle you.'

'Let the bugger in,' shouted the tipsy man behind me.

This was very different from the welcome I received at the Cambridge International Poetry Festival. Then, when I arrived, I heard people say excitedly, 'Dannie Abse's here, Dannie Abse's here,' and I was surprised and warmed by their apparent delight at my arrival. As I moved through the corridor to the reception centre, again the murmuring, 'He's here, he's here.' This is the best welcome I've ever had, I thought. When I finally reached Reception one of the organisers sprang to her feet as if I was the Messiah at last manifest. 'Oh Dannie Abse. I'm so pleased you're here,' she said. 'Thank God. We're desperate. Could you please write a prescription for one of the Greek poets who has a terribly painful gum infection and is due to read tomorrow.'

I had brought half a dozen copies of *White Coat, Purple Coat* to the Uxbridge Library and as I placed them decoratively on a nearby polished table the chairs in the library gradually became occupied. Soon, the far from urbane chairman introduced me and complimented the valiant audience for bothering to turn up for a poetry reading on such a pleasant June evening. I had not read and chatted for more than five minutes before there was an untamed disturbance at the back. I could not see quite what was happening but suddenly a door slammed and the unwelcome cacophony subsided. I then read to an attentive audience. Some time later, I became aware of a figure in the street outside, standing near one of the half-open library windows. He remained there, statuesque, listening to my reading. After a further five minutes or so I invited him to come inside and take a seat.

'Can't,' he shouted. 'They threw me out. I'm pissed.'

20. In Llandaff Cathedral

As Joan and I drove from Ogmore to Cardiff that May morning to attend the memorial service for the poet and BBC Wales producer, John Ormond, at Llandaff Cathedral I could not help wondering who else from the compact literary world of Wales would be in respectful attendance – his friend Glyn Jones maybe, the best younger poets, Tony Curtis and Robert Minhinnick, or perhaps R.S. Thomas about whom, not long previously, John Ormond had made an engaging TV feature film. Probably also his publishers at Seren, Cary Archard and Mick Felton.

His friend, John Tripp, would not be there. Alas, he had suffered a heart attack and had died four years earlier while watching a boxing match on television. John Tripp and John Ormond, both born in the 1920s, belonged to what Leslie Norris and others had called 'a lost generation of poets' because of the dazzling performance of the somewhat older Dylan Thomas. It had been John Ormond who had introduced me to the work of John Tripp. 'He's truly gifted,' John Ormond had said, and then had added with sincere sadness, 'But John's got no integrity.'

Certainly Tripp would write instant verse at the drop of a Welsh Arts Council shilling. And his professed Welsh nationalism seemed to both of us to be one of opportunistic convenience since so much literary endeavour in Wales was sponsored by an Arts Council sympathetic to the ideals of Plaid Cymru. As another Welsh poet of 'the lost generation', Harri Webb, had put it:

> White Jesus bach, let no ill
> Befall Big Heads Arts Council,
> Pounds they have, many thousand,
> Like full till shop draper grand
> Good is the work they are at
> Soaped they shall be in Seiat . . .
> Praised let them be for this thing,
> Money they are distributin
> Like Beibl Moses his manna
> Tongue we all, bards Welsh, Ta!

Despite John Tripp's linguistic carelessness which John Ormond justly deplored, his relatively spontaneous pieces evoked an urban seediness of location worthy of a Graham Greene. Indeed John Tripp, himself, could have stepped out of the pages of one of Greene's novels.

To many of the literary people in Wales John Ormond was a much more complex and barbed presence, impatient of mediocrity, capable of verbal, puritanical malignancy. And yet, as I drove down the A48 to Cardiff, I could not help recalling John Ormond's frequent spurts of unexpected, efflorescent generosity. For instance, when I visited my mother, in her mid-eighties, I would sometimes find a vase of splendid fresh flowers on the sideboard in her Cathedral Road flat.

'Those are very nice,' I'd say. 'Did someone give them to you, Mother?'

It was John Ormond, of course, who lived nearby and who, doubtless on a whim, had bought an abundance of flowers, knocked at the front door, and standing in the porch had offered them, probably with a gallant gesture, to the small-statured, grey-haired old lady who was my mother.

I remembered other characteristic Ormond acts of unpremeditated kindness: how he would call on friends to help his other friends. Once he bullied me into buying a painting by Jack Jones because of the latter's economic plight. On another occasion, after the death of the painter, Graham Sutherland, John bought a copy of my *Collected Poems*, asked me to sign it and to take it personally, as a present from him, to Sutherland's widow who was then staying in London's posh Connaught.

And then I recalled, ridiculously, the time he and his wife, Glenys, had come to dinner at our house. The other guests had been Huw and Jay Wheldon. We had placed John next to Jay and soon we observed, to our surprise, the change in their sitting posture. Though side by side at the table they somehow, comically, had swivelled round to face each other, like contortionists, even as they sipped their soup. I assumed that they were much attracted to each other. I did not know that John was secretly deaf in his left ear and Jay deaf in her right one!

It was hardly any time at all since we had attended a memorial service for Huw Wheldon at Westminster Abbey and had cause to conjure up *his* neon-lit presence, *his* large gestures, *his* open-mouthed astonishments – 'You've never had an avocado pear before, Dannie?' – our long association with him, those Sunday-before-Xmas parties at his handsome house in Richmond where each year we would see the same guests: David Attenborough, Melvyn Bragg, Kingsley Amis, Dan Jacobson. One way and another there were too many Welsh ghosts about; among others, John Tripp, Huw Wheldon and, now, John Ormond.

I had first met John Ormond some twenty years earlier when he had presented himself not as a poet but as a BBC Wales TV producer. He had come to our house with a television crew to make an 'Arts' programme. On his return to Cardiff he sent me his first book of poems, *Requiem and Celebration*, which had been published by a small

Welsh press, Christopher Davies, and had received no significant critical attention. Surprised, I discovered that his poems were the real thing strange. Like so many other Welsh poets he had not eschewed the backward look and his existential search for roots had led him to quest for a 'glimpse of holy law'. This questing search in his poetry had taken him beyond a merely personal past. His historical imagination had latched on to objects that sent signals forward over the chasm of centuries: ruined farmhouses, ancient monuments, fossils, artifacts of a distant Celtic culture – shadows barbarously anonymous and mysterious.

He was also a vivid portraitist of Welsh characters. And these portraits were offered with a warmth of feeling unlike those, for instance, composed by R.S. Thomas. To Englishmen, the characters Ormond painted may seem rather histrionic, even operatic. The fact is, in Wales, the stage Welshman walks less on the boards of the theatre than on the ground of the not-so-green valleys where he holds forth with sublime and comic portentousness and sings expressively in a real choir.

When John made the TV film that featured R.S. Thomas, he came to London to overlook the final editing of it in a small Wardour Street studio-cinema. Proud of his film, John invited me to join him there. Though he was an admirer of R.S. Thomas's poetry he was less enthusiastic about the man. Nor did I, myself, particularly take to R.S. Thomas in later years when I shared a platform with him. There was something displeasing about the way Thomas miserably casti- gated himself for writing in English rather than in Welsh, as if in doing so he had been a traitor to the Welsh nation.

I was always surprised that R.S. Thomas's bad-tempered earlier verse triumphantly survived his carping attitudes and unexciting language – the clichés which a tired politician might resort to: 'virtue's defeat', 'A new truth'; or adjectives that did not work for their keep: 'red blood', 'the green tree'. Yet, paradoxically, R.S. Thomas was an original poet whose poems were not devoid of emotion or devotion. Sometimes he displayed the other, averted side of his personality – poems that turned away from grumbling social pessimism to reveal perdurable affirmations: the country landscape of Wales, the clean skies, the speckled thrushes, the cobbled water, the trouts' shadows. These and such allowed R.S. Thomas to return to sources which he claimed 'are as near now as the morning I set out from them'. And this is what Ormond's film focused on.

What John Ormond revered in R.S. Thomas was his creative spirit – as he did in most men and women, irrespective of whether that spirit resided in poet, musician, cathedral builder, or the neighbour who visited John's local pub, The Conway. John relished odd behaviour too – Welsh eccentricities, Welsh exaggerations, providing they were not phoney. In telling, in his poems, about the old cathedral builders, about the religious fanatic, Johnny Randall, about the cemetery attendant who 'had the eyes of a dying seal in a bankrupt circus', or about John Owen, market gardener and organist (that Benthamite of music), and others who could have escaped from *Under Milk Wood*, he was giving us more than amusing portrayals: he was writing a kind of love poetry. He was saying in a very open manner to his dusty kinsfolk, 'I love you', or, at least, 'I loved you.'

> Early and lately dead, each one
> Of you haunts me. Continue
> To tenant the air when I walk in the sun.
> Beyond the shadow of the yew
> I speak these words to you, my kin
> And friends, in requiem and celebration.

And now here we were, kin and friends, in Llandaff Cathedral, few of us far from the shadow of the yew. I looked around and saw among the congregation John's Conway pub acquaintances and his old BBC colleagues. Immediately behind Joan and me sat John Heath Stubbs and Eddie Linden who had travelled from London to signal their esteem for our dead friend and for his living poetry. Present, of course, were his wife, Glenys, and the two beautiful Ormond daughters and their son, their lamenting near and dear.

The organ played. The service began. In the past, boy or man, I had visited Llandaff Cathedral only when the pews were unoccupied. Now the church was peopled and Epstein's aluminium *Christ in Majesty* appeared to be a little less dominant. The last occasion I had strayed into the Cathedral had been at the time of the Chernobyl disaster. Four years earlier, on May 4th, I had written in my journal:

This morning an East wind was blowing so vigorously in Ogmore that our wooden gate had been thrust open. From the bedroom I could see that a ewe with two lambs had trespassed into our garden. They were munching the daffodils and narcissi, a nice, forbidden, wicked breakfast. I rushed downstairs, still in my pyjamas, to shoo them out.

As I closed the gate behind them I thought more of the east wind than the sheep. Probably it was bearing invisible death-seeds from Chernobyl. Perhaps radioactive raindrops were sipped from the daffodil cups by the ewe and the lambs. Information, so far, is meagre. In any case, who can believe the complacent, stealthy, reassuring voices of experts and politicians? How much has been covered up before, how much will be told to us now? Will radioactive iodine be taken up by small, thirsty thyroid glands? What about my new granddaughter and all those like her from Ogmore-by-sea to the Ukraine and beyond where Prometheus is still chained to his rock while the vulture eats his liver?

Last Friday in Cardiff, I visited Llandaff Cathedral. I just happened to be nearby, so popped in as I used to as a boy, passing the yellow celandines beneath the yew tree. Inside soaring spaces of worship – Jewish, Moslem or Christian – I feel not just secular but utterly estranged like one without history or memory. Once more, numb, I observed Epstein's dominating Resurrected Christ. And it was springtime, springtime in the real world and all seemingly dead things were coming alive again though a cancer sailed in from Chernobyl.

Inside the Cathedral, I ambled towards the Lady Chapel reredos where, on either side of the sculpted Madonna, six niches are filled with gold-leafed wreaths of wild flowers. In Welsh, dozens of flowers are named after the Virgin, as is proper in a nation that reveres the Mam of the family. The marigold is called Gold Mair – Mary's Gold; the buttercup, Mary's sweat; the briar rose, Mary's briar; the foxglove, Mary's thimble; the monkshood, Mary's slipper; the cowslip, Mary's primrose; and the snowdrop, Mary's taper. Tapr Mair.

If a man believed in a deity, any deity, goddess, god or God, he would, in that Cathedral, have prayed in English or Welsh or no language at all, for the neutralisation of the death wind. And in Ogmore, this morning, as I stood in my pyjamas while the opera-dramatic clouds, grey, cream, or frowning darker, tracked so visibly westwards, my own lips moved.

But they were now praying for the soul of my friend, John Ormond, and hymns were being sung. The congregation stood up and then, almost in unison, they sat down again. Soon we were listening to a priest's discourse; but all through the service I kept recalling insignificant things: how John had told me his favourite composer was Schubert; how John, when he was in London, favoured a certain restaurant in Old Compton Street; how proudly John had shown me snapshots of himself when young with Dylan Thomas; how John had fooled me once, phoning me with a Scots accent and pretending to be the Cardiff City football manager, Jimmy Andrews; and there was that time when John had steered a drunken John Tripp away from Sam Wanamaker whom he was threatening to attack physically.

Such thoughts retreated when I heard Purcell's 'Dido's Lament' being throbbingly sung and later listened to touching, considered addresses from Alun Richards and Dai Smith. Finally and fittingly, John's son recited his father's poem, the one not about Llandaff Cathedral but about Cathedral builders:

> They climbed on sketchy ladders towards God,
> With winch and pulley hoisted hewn rock into heaven,
> Inhabited sky with hammers, defied gravity,
> Deified stone, took up God's house to meet Him,
>
> And came down to their suppers and small beer;
> Every night slept, lay with their smelly wives,
> Quarrelled and cuffed the children, lied,
> Spat, sang, were happy or unhappy,
>
> And every day took to the ladders again;
> Impeded the rights of way of another summer's
> Swallows, grew greyer, shakier, became less inclined
> To fix a neighbour's roof of a fine evening,
>
> Saw naves sprout arches, clerestories soar,
> Cursed the loud fancy glaziers for their luck,
> Somehow escaped the plague, got rheumatism,
> Decided it was time to give it up,
>
> To leave the spire to others; stood in the crowd
> Well back from the vestments at the consecration,
> Envied the fat bishop his warm boots,
> Cocked up a squint eye and said, 'I bloody did that.'

21. Blood on the Carpet at the Poetry Society

My father-in-law, Jack, was staying with us that winter of 1979. We had just sat down for dinner when the telephone clamoured in the hall. Reluctantly I rested my knife and fork and quit the table. I was surprised by the phone-call. 'This is Gavin Ewart,' Gavin said solemnly. 'Hello,' I responded. 'How are you?' He ignored that. Excessively formal – I had the feeling he was standing to attention – he continued, 'The Council of the Poetry Society have charged me, instructed me, to ask you if you would be willing to become our President.'

'President of what?' I asked, stupidly.

'If you are willing, the Council will send you an official letter inviting you to become President of the Poetry Society.'

'I'm not a member of the Society.'

'That doesn't matter. The President doesn't have to be one.'

'What would I have to do?'

'Nothing. Well, hardly anything. It's an honour. You'd be our figurehead.'

'Who are on the Council, Gavin?'

'I am,' he said. 'And Alan Brownjohn, Jenny Joseph, Jon Silkin, Blake Morrison, John – '

'Then I am honoured,' I interrupted him.

Gavin Ewart obviously felt that my response had been somewhat tardy. 'The previous President was Basil Bunting,' Gavin reminded me, 'and before that Hugh MacDiarmid and before that – ' Again I interrupted him. 'Please tell the Council I should be pleased to accept their kind invitation.'

I wanted to laugh. Instead I asked after Gavin's wife, Margo, and uttered the usual clichés before concluding our phone-call. I returned to the dinner table and told Joan and my father-in-law that I had been invited to become the President of the Poetry Society and had accepted. Both of them looked rather left-wing and puzzled. I felt Joan would suddenly declaim, 'Just for a handful of silver he left us. Just for a ribbon to stick on his coat,' as if somehow I had joined the Establishment. 'In latter years,' I said defensively, 'the Poetry Society has made it a tradition to appoint Outsider poets such as Basil Bunting and Hugh MacDiarmid.'

'What happened to them?' asked Jack.

'They both died in office,' I said.

When I thought about it at all – which was rarely – I had identified myself as a maverick. Indeed, very recently, in a public letter-poem addressed to Donald Davie I had remarked on my feelings of 'oddness':

> I too am a reluctant puritan, feel uneasy
> sometimes as if I travelled without ticket.
> Yet here I am in England way out in the centre.

'Let's look at the Liverpool game,' I said to Jack after dinner.

In our front room we lounged before the TV set and listened to the rousing BBC signature tune of *Match of the Day*. My mild father-in-law had earlier watched the Six o'Clock News and perhaps had shouted, as was his wont, at some pontificating politician, 'No bloody idea.' He probably also knew the football results. It would spoil things for me if he should, inadvertently, let me know. 'Don't tell me the score, Jack,' I pleaded. Quick as a hare he replied, '2–0. Liverpool won.'

When I was a young poet I would not have wanted to be associated with the Poetry Society. After attending one of its poetry readings in the impressive library of its HQ at 33 Portman Square, I had determined never to repeat the experience. The audience about me appeared to be largely fugitives from a geriatric ward; worse, the poems recited were amateur, dimpled, and of Georgian hue. It seemed the clock on the wall had stopped in 1909 when the Society had been founded.

Only when the slender, youthful, blonde Muriel Spark had surprisingly become the Society's secretary and editor of its official journal, *The Poetry Review*, did the Society begin to move towards the present tense. It was an uphill struggle because the fossilised Board continued to grumble about the obscurity of modern poets such as T.S. Eliot and Dylan Thomas. Eventually, Muriel Spark left after a frenetic Annual General Meeting where her stewardship was furiously attacked.

Derek Stanford has described the tempestuous scene at that AGM in his amusing memoir, *Inside the Forties*. It seems that the sexologist and amateur poet, Marie Stopes, a stalwart of the Society, had become incensed when Tambimuttu, the editor of *Poetry London*, defended Muriel Spark. Yes, the financial resources of the Society had diminished, agreed Tambimuttu, but that was because Mrs Spark had paid the contributors to *The Poetry Review* properly. He argued, 'A poetry society should be for poets not for stockbrokers. Poets need money. Stockbrokers do not. If you reward poets justly, funds sink. That's how it should be. That's proof the editor is doing his job. A good poetry editor endangers his publisher. I've endangered several publishers several times. The best poetry editor shows devotion to the Muse and so should make his publisher bankrupt.' Tambimuttu, doubtless, would have continued this original thesis but now he was being threatened by Dr Marie Stopes who was waving her umbrella wildly above his head.

Six weeks after Gavin Ewart's telephone call, I received an invitation to inspect the Society's Headquarters at Earls Court Square where it had been situated for many decades, following the sale of their premises in Portman Square. Brian Mitchell, the chief employee of the Society, that is to say their Director and General Secretary, invited me for lunch at a nearby restaurant where we would be joined by Clifford Simmons, the Chairman of the Society, Alan Brownjohn, the future Chairman, and Pamela Clunies-Ross, the Director of the Poetry Secretariat.

I set out, I remember, on a very windy January day. The little sunlight could not make up its mind whether to go or stay. Something was happening in that bedlam January sky. No Ruisdael, Constable or Tiepolo could have caught the drift of it. Any moment, I thought, a rainbow would appear for the dayshift and then fade like a ghost.

I arrived too early. There was very little traffic about. I parked the car and wondered whether I should hang about for a bit. Surely a President should arrive late! But it was windy and cold. I climbed the stony steps to the front door of the five-storey building. The door was open and I lingered in the draughty foyer reading the multiple notices until I was greeted with, 'You're Dannie Abse, aren't you?'

He had a pronounced Welsh lilt to his voice. It seemed he was from Neath, that he wrote great poetry which Roger Garfitt, the editor of *Poetry Review*, had rejected. And he was 'by 'ere' to tell Mr Garfitt that he had made a mistake. 'I've won competitions,' he boasted.

I thought yet again how, generally speaking, Welshmen – and I was one such – tend to boast much more than their English counterparts. Shakespeare evidently felt this to be so. Did he not make Owain Glyndwr say, in *Henry IV, Part One*, 'At my nativity/ the front of heaven, was full of fiery shapes . . . and at my birth/the frame and huge foundation of the earth shak'd like a coward . . . These signs have mark'd me extraordinary . . .'?

Presumably Shakespeare knew many Welshmen. Was he conversant with Welsh boast poetry too? Twelfth-century Welsh language poets such as Gwalchmai ap Meilyr and Hywel ab Owain Gwynedd were swanky as the devil. 'It is splendid I am,' Gwalchmai declared, 'fearless in battle. Before the enemy I'm a lion, like lightning my onset.' Gwalchmai and Hywel ab Owain Gwynedd also liked to boast of the women they had conquered. Hywel, in one poem, remarked,

'I had seven and still the toil persisted.' These boasting poets reminded me of my Uncle David who could tame unicorns, cage a flaming phoenix.

When Brian Mitchell appeared, my Neath countryman scuttled away through the door. He seemed to be afraid of the Poetry Society's General Secretary who merely said, 'We have some strange people coming in here sometimes.'

Brian Mitchell, who seemed very efficient and pleasant, showed me over 21 Earls Court Square and pointed out this and that as if I were a prospective buyer of the property. He showed me the basement where members could print out their own work; the bookshop; the library; the offices; the stairs leading to the attic flat where the caretaker lived; and, of course, the vast 60 feet by 30 feet handsome performance room with its marbled Adam fireplace and ceiling patterned with mid-Victorian arabesques. True, most of the other rooms of the rambling edifice were somewhat shabby, in need of renovation, but Brian Mitchell was justly proud of the building.

'We're short of money, that's the problem,' Mitchell remarked. 'Even to heat this place is difficult.'

During the next seven years I returned to Earls Court Square only for an occasional poetry event, a party, or when I was asked to be present when the Society was visited by an Arts Council representative or by some literary functionary from abroad. Being President was, for the most part, as Gavin Ewart had promised, a figurehead appointment.

Though the Arts Council underfunded the Society and its employees were paid poorly, all seemed reasonably well. *Poetry Review*, under its new editor, Andrew Motion, in 1982, thrived – the cobwebs of Georgianism having been long swept away. The Poetry Secretariat, administered by Pamela Clunies-Ross who was responsible for sponsoring readings all over Britain, was universally admired. And other activities of the Society such as the Education Department, which sent poets into schools (courtesy of W.H. Smith), were much appreciated generally. And Alan Brownjohn had become a much-esteemed Chairman.

Of course, there were some poets who felt they had been neglected by the Secretariat or had received a rejection slip from *Poetry Review*. Meeting me they would air their resentments. I was sometimes reminded of Sir Lewis Morris who, after Tennyson's death, had told Oscar Wilde that there was a conspiracy of silence about his own work. 'Join it,' Oscar Wilde had succinctly demanded.

Some people seemed to think that the President of the Poetry Society had curious obligations. For instance, in the summer of 1986, before the marriage of Prince Charles and Diana, I had a phone call from Tambimuttu. He intended to present a handwritten anthology of 'wedding poems' to the royal couple. 'As President of the Poetry Society,' Tambi asserted, 'you have to contribute to the anthology. I want to include your wedding song, your "Epithalamion". I want you to dedicate the poem to them.'

'Certainly not.'

'You must. You're President of the Poetry Society.'

'No. I wrote that epithalamion before Diana was born.'

On that evening of fireworks and crowds, Tambimuttu, ready to flex and low-bend, tried to breach the walls of Buckingham Palace carrying his anthology. My 'Epithalamion' bore no dedication.

I had an actual brush with Royalty when another anthology, *The Orange Dove of Fiji*, edited by Simon Rae, was published. It was in aid of the World Wide Fund for Nature. The Duke of Edinburgh, in a preface, wrote, 'The contributions to this book of poems will have made a significant contribution to the conservation of nature if the readers are inspired to join the struggle to save the life of our planet from human folly and indulgence'; and when the anthology was launched at Soho's Groucho Club the Duke sent his youngest son, Prince Edward, to officiate.

In the crowded room I happened to be chatting to Gavin Ewart and Carol Ann Duffy when I was approached by Bridget Sleddon, the young PR of Hutchinson, the publishers of the book.

'Dannie, as President of the Poetry Society, would you talk to Prince Edward. Simon Rae's having a hard time. Their conversation has come to a full stop.'

'Now's your chance to get the Poetry Society a Royal patron,' Gavin half-joked.

After Bridget Sleddon had introduced me to the Prince as the Society's President and remarked that the Society had no royal patron, I asked the Prince if he was interested in poetry.

'No,' he said.

Taken aback by his peremptory reply, I hastened to say how many people are put off poetry because of the way it is presented to them at school. The Prince looked despondent. He evidently wished he was somewhere else and I, having received such an initial, unsmiling rebuff, nattered on about how when I was at school I, too, did not care for poetry. 'I was much more interested in playing football and chasing girls.'

Simon Rae shifted uneasily. Bridget Sleddon looked anxious. Then I tried to save the day. 'But you're in the theatre,' I said. 'You're fond of the theatre.'

'Not particularly,' replied the Prince.

Soon after, Bridget Sleddon bore the glum Prince away to be bored by someone else. I hardly noticed a tall man close by who had overheard the threadbare conversation. But now he asked me, 'You are President of the Poetry Society, aren't you?' I nodded. He wrote down something in a notebook and vanished.

I did not read the *Evening Standard* edition of Friday 10 November, 1989 – at least not until the following week when an angry Bridget Sleddon remarked on how our encounter with Prince Edward had been misrepresented in the newspaper. The Londoner's Diary headline read: PRINCE TURNS DOWN POETRY SOCIETY. The first paragraph of the report continued, 'Prince Edward's reputation as an aesthete was in question last night. The President of the Poetry Society, Dannie Abse, sharply rebuked him for preferring "soccer and rugby and chasing girls" to poetry. The prince, who had turned up for the launch of Abse's [sic] charity volume of verse, *The Orange Dove of Fiji*, at the Groucho Club, was challenged by Abse to become the first royal patron of the Poetry Society.' More inaccuracies followed and it was obvious that I was doomed for the Tower.

In 1988 Sebastian Barker had succeeded Alan Brownjohn as Chairman of the Society. After Brian Mitchell left his post for a better-paid job elsewhere, it seemed that the financial status of the Poetry Society had deteriorated. A new, effective, paid Director was required and more sponsorship needed. Sebastian Barker asked me if I would, in future, attend the executive meetings (as was my right according to the Society's constitution) and 'help sort things out'. I, credulous, agreed. I did not know then that I had made a mistake that would lead to much personal anguish.

Chris Green, a competent arts administrator who had effectively enlisted sponsorship in the past for the annual City of London Festivals, was appointed Director. Soon, at Green's instigation, 21

Earls Court Square was somewhat refurbished, the salaries of the Society's employees raised, the staff reduced from sixteen to nine, and a bank loan secured. Chris Green did not appear, at first, in 1989 and 1990, to be worried by the increasing debts and he assured the executive that he would soon find sponsors for the Society's activities. And no doubt he would have succeeded if Britain over the next few years had not suffered a dire economic recession. The Arts Council which subsidised the Society – more than £100,000 a year – could not increase its commitment significantly. Indeed, they complained that not enough people attended the events the Society arranged and that there should be more 'ethnic input'.

The dinsome executive meetings that I attended focused more and more on economic concerns as our debts mounted. To make matters worse a personal animosity between Alan Brownjohn and Sebastian Barker became transparent. Each, in turn, hatched their own explosive supporters regarding policies, economic and aesthetic. I often found myself acting as a reluctant umpire. I frequently returned home fretful after an executive meeting and wishing that I had some financial expertise.

By 1991, our debts had increased to over £100,000. 'In 1989 our debt was £24,000,' said Alan Brownjohn accusingly.

'£70,000,' argued Chris Green. 'I was optimistic. I thought that with the contacts I'd built up over a period of time I'd attract sponsorship. I thought I had a reasonable chance. But I arrived here when everybody was cutting back. I tried banks, insurance houses, property companies, oil companies. It was dispiriting. After a while, you decide you've just got to sit out the recession.'

'Our debt was only £24,000 in 1989,' Alan Brownjohn insisted.

Yet not all was inundating gloom. *The Poetry Review*, under its present editor, Peter Forbes, had spectacularly increased its readership and continued to be an engaging read. What worried me, as it did Alan Brownjohn, was the Arts Council's policy of access rather than excellence – for more 'bums on seats'. Too many of the new members of the executive committee pulled in by Chris Green and Sebastian – perhaps to neutralise the Brownjohn faction – favoured popular performance poetry.

At the Annual General Meeting of the Poetry Society I argued (I have the text in front of me – it was published in *Acumen* No. 15):

... One of the preoccupations of an Arts Minister and, consequently, a matter of concern for the professional officers of the Arts Council, is the size of the audience, the percentage of the electorate interested in the arts. Orpheus may have a wonderful lyre, he may play beautifully, but it would appear that so many around him are deaf. This is a particularly pressing problem for the administration responsible for encouraging the practice of writing poetry and the reading of it. It needs to be said – and said loudly – that in these days of faint intermittent private sponsorship and insufficient public subsidy this just commitment to quality appears to be even less muscular than it was fifteen years ago.

The emphasis appears to be more on access than on excellence. It won't be different under a Labour Government, if there is one, as they declare in their policy document *Arts and the Media*, 'We will expect organisations in receipt of public funds to make widening of their audience a priority and both monitor and report annually on who composes that audience.'

At present [I continued] too many organisers of Poetry Events in the regions are exercised by how many bums will occupy seats rather than by the true credentials of the hired poet. Every silly or dull poetry event is an act of sabotage against Poetry itself. That epitaph on Robert Southey comes to mind:

> Beneath these poppies buried deep
> The bones of Bob the bard lie hid.
> Peace to his manes; and may he sleep
> As soundly as his readers did.

. . . I want to ask, are we at the Poetry Society, we who are so strapped for money, so in need of private sponsorship, so dependent on Arts Council patronage, are we, perforce, also too preoccupied by the numbers game – the circulation of the *Poetry Review*, the size of the audience for our Poetry events, while not being concerned enough about excellence?

. . . We need to remind ourselves that Performance Poetry or Cabaret Poetry, as I prefer to call it, is not the real thing. Poetry is not a cabaret turn and cabaret performers, though calling themselves poets, surely should attract the patronage, if patronage is deserved, of the Drama rather than the Literature Department of the Arts Council . . .

Chris Green and Sebastian Barker felt that the only way to solve the Society's financial plight was to sell our Earls Court building and move into less grand premises. Alan Brownjohn advocated that 21 Earls Court Square could be saved if an aggressive national campaign to raise money for the Society could be instigated.★

★ In one moment of desperation Chris Green and I went along to Kettner's in Soho to see the Big White Chief of the Pizza Express chain. We hoped to persuade him to put on the menu a Poetry Pizza which would result in the Society receiving a penny or so for every such pizza ordered. I took my *Collected Poems* to give to the Big White Chief. He accepted it graciously and we were treated to pizzas and red wine. It was an affable lunch but our persuasive efforts were futile. The only consequence was that I have become a Pizza Express addict.

'Our debt's increasing all the time,' Chris Green reminded the squabbling executive. 'This building was worth £850,000 in 1990. Now, because of the recession and its dilapidation – including some dry rot – it will only fetch £650,000. In another year if we keep procrastinating it'll be worth even less.'

These powerful arguments persuaded me and others, though reluctantly, that Chris Green should seek another home for the Society. I was mindful that in the previous year £400,000 had been spent to pay bank charges and staff and support all the activities including the programme of Poetry Readings, the Poetry Speaking competitions, the quarterly *Poetry Review*, the Poets in Schools scheme, the annual European Translation Prize and the National Poetry Competition. Only £210,000 had been recouped to add to the Arts Council grant of £133,000. Presumably there would be a further shortfall during the present year.

Meanwhile I was persuaded to be the reluctant sole judge of the European Translation Prize. As I read the pile of books submitted I could not help recalling the International Poetry Festival I had attended in Macedonia. On that occasion each of the many poets, whether from Korea, Denmark or wherever, had one of their poems translated into Macedonian. I doubt if the surprisingly large audiences for the recitals enjoyed them very much because, after all, as Robert Frost sardonically remarked, 'Poetry is that which is lost in translation.' The poem of mine chosen to be translated took the space of two pages. Whichever town or venue was visited, each poet would read out their poem and then an actor would recite the Macedonian version. But, at Skopje, my poem, in translation, ended somewhat abruptly. The second page had evidently gone missing. Seamus Heaney, who was there representing Ireland, whispered to me, 'Ach, Dannie, now I know that poetry is truly that which is lost in translation.' Much of the poetry offered in the books of translations that I read over the next month seemed to be missing too.

Late in 1991, Chris Green announced that he had received an offer for 21 Earls Court Square and that he had located a suitable property to buy in Covent Garden. 'It will allow us to pay our debts and to start again,' Chris Green promised. Alas, when the executive committee members inspected the cramped Betterton Street building in Covent Garden the majority believed it to be far from suitable, above all because it had no performance space. The Society would have to hire a hall if it wanted to host a significant poetry event. So the committee charged Chris Green to seek for another building. William Oxley, a member of the Society's Council, has written in his autobiography, *No Accounting for Paradise*: 'No one seemed to wish for us a move to a building that would not be suitable enough to carry on all its constitutionally required activities, though it has to be said that, as time went on, there seemed to grow a willingness – possibly backed by the Arts Council? – on the part of some members and staff to settle for a new building of office premises alone . . .'

About this time I received an anonymous letter. It was not the first one. Whomsoever sent it obviously disliked Chris Green and seemed to be a toxic religious fanatic. I tore the letter up and pondered how much I disliked religious fundamentalists who claim God for their own. I was a secular Welsh Jew, though one who could be temporarily persuaded about the truths of revelation, not in the moral realm, but in attempts to write poetry while sitting comfortably, of course, under a sinless apple tree in our own back garden, far from the deserts of religion and the thistle-eating donkey.

When a special General Meeting was called on 22 January 1992, I had no intention of resigning. I had thought about doing so. I was tired of the unabated squabblings of the committee meetings; the continual boring talk about money; the unsavoury machinations of the opposing factions among whom I had so often to mediate; the reprobative comments of the Arts Council. Even so, I felt I should hang in there. I counted Alan Brownjohn, Sebastian Barker and Chris Green as being friends of mine.

But at the General Meeting the Society was presented with a fait accompli. I was utterly astonished and angry when I learnt that Chris Green had, it seemed, mobilised one faction of the committee, including Sebastian Barker and the treasurer, Piers Pottinger, so that he, perhaps with the approval of the Arts Council, could announce that he had accepted £660,000 for 21 Earls Court Square and now intended to buy the Betterton Street property for some £400,000.

There was a devious stain on the virtue of the enterprise. I made my protesting speech, spoke intemperately about what I thought of some of them, and went home to pluck a quill from a raven's wing and write my resignation letter.

What can I say now? Chris Green was an honourable man and his supporters all were honourable men, though some were like those Shakespeare-Romans who whispered behind their hands and paltered.

22. The Big Assertive Clock

Judging from newspaper reports the churlish factions at the Poetry Society continued their feuds months after being installed at Covent Garden's Betterton Street. Alan Brownjohn continued to rage: 'The Society is doing about 50 per cent of what it did five years ago. There is no national scheme for poetry readings, hardly any London events, no bookshop, no bar, no excitement. What we have in Covent Garden is a set of offices which the Arts Council may be content with but the poets and their readers and our 2500 members will be unimpressed.'

It was not until mid-1993 that the President's hollow, scratchy crown was passed to John Heath-Stubbs, the esteemed blind poet. He was a good choice, not only because of his considerable gifts as a poet but also because of his tact, his humour and his breadth of knowledge about literature. During the 1980s, when I frequently presented the BBC Radio 4 *Poetry Please* programme, one of the actors reading the requested poems would ask me sometimes to elucidate an obscure reference in the text. I could not always do so. Nor were the reference books at hand invariably helpful. Desperate, I would telephone John Heath-Stubbs and I would not only receive an instant answer to the conundrum but quite often an orotund scholarly lecture to go with it.

I first encountered John Heath-Stubbs when, as a student, I had dared to explore the literary configurations of Soho. He was famously tall, thin, and even then more or less sightless. His frayed jacket sleeves seemed much too short for his long spindly arms and his trousers displayed much too much sock. His was a face that could have been drawn by Leonardo. His bony forehead projected over hermetic eye sockets and as one drew close to him the morning's shaving cuts would become visible on his cheeks. He spoke in a loud rich voice and when he laughed he would throw his head back joyously, displaying well-separated teeth. He did not so much sit down but, in a double-jointed manner, collapse into a chair. He has described himself wittily in his memorable poem, 'Epitaph', which begins:

> Mr Heath-Stubbs as you must understand
> Came of a gentleman's family out of Staffordshire
> Of as good blood as any in England
> But he was wall-eyed and his legs too spare.
>
> His elbows and finger-joints could bend more ways than one
> And in frosty weather would creak audibly
> As to delight his friends he would give demonstration
> Which he might have done in public for a small fee.

Over the years, much to my gain, our paths have crossed many times. There was that time we read our poems in tandem at the House of Commons. Eddie Linden, a close friend of Heath-Stubbs, had persuaded an MP to organise a poetry reading there. 'The first,' John told me, 'since the days of Chaucer, when John Gower held forth in Norman-French, Latin and Middle-English.'

All the 1950s denizens of Soho, uncharacteristically wearing suits, ties, possibly refused by Oxfam, and mostly sober, passed through the contra-IRA security system of the House of Commons to support their popular old friend John Heath-Stubbs – among them ex-poet Sir John Waller, a most unlikely knight who, foppishly, always seemed to be exhausted.

In the corridor, beforehand, as the Heath-Stubbs supporters milled this way and that, John Waller announced that he was going to make a speech for 'Poetry is being honoured this day. It is a unique occasion so I think I had better say a few words.' Before his friend, John Heath-Stubbs, could respond, Waller had wandered away so the sightless poet, unaware that Waller had vamooshed, chastised empty air. 'You must not,' declared John, who appeared to be sternly addressing a wall. 'Not one word.' He then launched into a scholarly dissertation on why Waller should keep his mouth shut while strangers, astonished or worried, passed by in the corridor. I moved to divert John but I was button-holed by the coquetry of an American who kept saying, 'Gee, this is sumpthin, Mr Abs. This *is* sumpthin. Can't imagine anythin' like this in the White House. Look at this bearded lot coming in. You've got sumpthin to sell here, boy.'

I reckoned that the odd mixture of MPs and Soho's lively, unpredictable characters were fortunate that evening to hear John

Heath-Stubbs's fine rendering of his work – as, indeed, the Poetry Society was in his acceptance of their presidency.

I learnt about John Heath-Stubbs becoming President just before I travelled once again to the USA to give poetry readings, some of which had been arranged for me by Daniel Hoffman, including a memorable one in New York for the Academy of American Poets – memorable for me because among those in the audience were several poet friends of mine: Theodore and Renée Weiss, M.L. Rosenthal, Stanley Moss, Louis Simpson and, of course, Dan Hoffman himself. Even my American publisher (Persea Books) turned up and remarked that he owed me some royalties. 'You seem to have some American readers,' he said with utter surprise.

At Swarthmore, Dan Hoffman, who is a Quaker, took me to a Friends' Meeting. Never having been to one before I was startled by the silence of the hour, by individuals occasionally rising from the wooden benches to interrupt the silence by personal testimonies. But mostly I listened to Silence, to inaudible sacred music. I did not feel the secular hair rise on my head; rather I felt myself to be, as I would in a synagogue, in a mosque, in a chapel, in a vast cathedral, the man from somewhere else.

I don't know whether I'm religious or not. I do know that I have no desire to go to synagogue or observe Jewish ritualistic customs though some I recognise as being beautiful – others seem to be merely pathological. I can accept and assent to the fact that Judaism teaches there is a direct way between man and God. Judaism is intended to be a religion without mediator, sacrament or priests. But for me, and I recognise that this lacks humility, for me between man and that experience that is labelled as God is the synagogue and its schedules, the dull prayers of dead religious maniacs, symbols that have often lost their potency and restrictive disciplines. For me, though of course not necessarily for others, they are barriers not bridges. I have said earlier that Auschwitz made me more of a Jew than Moses did but, like Ilya Ehrenberg, I consider myself a Jew as long as there is one anti-semite alive. If one reaches 'God' it is through the senses, through the amazement of looking and hearing, of tasting and touching and smelling; or through certain pleasureful activities like making love when one is in love, or like singing and congenial working. And the writing of poetry, by the way, is a kind of singing and a kind of lovely work that names things. And the naming of things, be it a country or a star, a flower or a baby, is itself a kind of worship.

Not long after my return to London the family took me out to my favourite Camden Town restaurant for my 70th-birthday treat. Keren, politically involved as ever, began talking about the new Clinton government in Washington and other world events: the unchained monster prowling through Bosnia, its children waiting to be born; statesmen such as Milosevic by murder fed, by murder clothed. But soon the conversation came nearer home as we discussed family matters and the different attractions of city and country, of London and Ogmore. Paul, Susanna's husband, chief travel correspondent of the *Daily Telegraph*, has visited many beauty spots in the course of his work and delighted me when he rhapsodised about Ogmore-by-sea!

Before our party broke up Susanna related how, when driving in the car with her daughter Larne, aged 7, and son Max, aged 4, they heard a song about the human race on the radio. Larne asked her the meaning of 'race' and Susanna had endeavoured to explain to my granddaughter that human beings categorised themselves as Aryans, Semites, Celts and so forth. Max, listening attentively to Susanna's list, suddenly piped up, 'Mum, Mum, don't forget the egg-and-spoon race, Mum!'

The next weekend we visited Ogmore. I was walking along the shore towards Southerndown, preoccupied so I did not hear how quiet, muffled, everything had become. Looking towards the sea I saw a sea-mist making for the shore. It progressed with a sullen, indeed sinister, deliberation, deleting all animate and inanimate things. Was some psychopomp in a small boat, not wishing to be observed, about to land on the coast of Glamorgan, here at Ogmore-by-sea, at Hardee's Bay where I was standing? Ridiculous thought.

I felt not exactly afraid but alert. It was dream-like. No one was about, no one at all. Already the hooting, doleful foghorns from Nash Point warned and wailed. I walked through the swirling mist over the rocks to the pebbles, to the sound of the almost obliterated sea, to its obsessional ministrations. I thought of those lines of Walt Whitman when he speaks of the sea whispering, 'Death, Death, Death, Death.' I picked up a large pebble and threw it as hard as I could through the sleep-walking densities of sea-fog, at nobody, at nothing.

For the rest of the decade we continued to enjoy our usual sojourns in South Wales walking on the turfy cliffs in the different weathers and seasons, watching the waves below repeating themselves with infinite variations as they tamely spent themselves on the coal-streaked sand or, seemingly frustrated, wildly crashed against the rocks, white spray leaping.

Here I pleasantly wasted time as Time wasted us. So many anodyne unremarkable slow days when, apart from Joan's solicitous gardening, nothing much happened, at least nothing dramatic, except for wonderfully gaudy sunsets and, at night, sometimes the astonishment of prosperous delinquent moonlight on the shifting surface of the carbon-dark sea. Often in my life, I have, during such slow passive days felt a vague sense of guilt: the guilt of simply waiting, of not working, days of amnesia, of postponements on rainy nights, of things not done and words not said. 'He's guilty, your honour, guilty of inertia.'

I think I felt such even when I was a twenty-year-old medical student. Then I kept a skull in my room to contemplate so that I should be forced to acknowledge my own transience and be spurred into some kind of action, however trivial. I also counted on those adolescent skull meditations to prompt me to see all things with the grateful eyes of a convalescent, to perceive everything as fresh and rinsed and clear as Adam did in those nascent days of Eden.

Sometimes Ogmore seemed next door to Eden! – especially during week days when the village was deserted and so open-aired. Many times I would walk to the village Post Office to buy bread and milk and I'd observe the beach below as empty as the road I walked upon. Occasionally a single anonymous figure would be walking a dog over the sea-wet sands – the tide receding – the human black shadow and the dog's black shadow following them upside down across the mirror beneath their feet.

To be sure there were times when we extended our stay at Ogmore and I was able to work there – to fiddle at a poem or to work on prose. Or I would quit Green Hollows to give a poetry reading not too far away. At the Hay-on-Wye Festival, for instance, where once I saw in the window of one of the second-hand bookshops an out-of-print book of mine, *Way Out in the Centre*. Since I only owned one battered copy I decided to buy it. As I took out the money to pay for it the cashier said, 'It's signed, you know.' Glumly I turned to its flyleaf to read my own signature. Then the cashier added solemnly, 'We don't charge much extra, sir. Abse signs easily.'

When I was in Ogmore I could not help remembering my dead parents who loved the place – my mother who, so long ago, taught me my name, my father who taught me the time. This was their honeymoon rendezvous. Now, soon enough, I would be older than my father ever was. In such pensive moments, especially when the rim of the sun slipped down below the sea and a high-moored star signalled sea-birds to fly towards sleep, I'd look up at the occult advancing blackboard of the void and ask the question old as man: Why?

During the late Nineties I read a great deal of Anglo-Welsh verse because Cary Archard and Mick Felton had commissioned me to edit an anthology of *Twentieth Century Anglo-Welsh Poetry* for Seren Books. I was glad to do this because so many good poets working in Wales had been neglected west of Chepstow – John Ormond, John Tripp, Tony Curtis, Sheenagh Pugh, Robert Minhinnick and Gwyneth Lewis among them. Too many readers knew only about the work of Dylan Thomas, his stuff and sense, his gifted gabble, his word gymnastics, his adjectives on stilts, his vagrant verbs, his nimble nouns, all so evident in that popular, amazing verbal radio cartoon *Under Milk Wood*. Besides, I had changed my mind about the nature of English-language Welsh poetry. Some thirty years earlier during a BBC broadcast I had asserted, 'a poem about a magpie seen in Wales is no different basically from a poem about a magpie seen in England and a love poem is unlikely generally to have a Welsh connotation if written in English by a Welshman. To put it another way: there is no such thing as a specific Anglo-Welsh style or tone, and the Welshness of an English poem simply depends on what the poem is about.'

I had come to believe that that remark had portrayed only part of the truth and that it shunned complexity. During the 20th century the Welsh language itself remained in retreat in much of Wales but spoken English itself continued to be Welsh pollinated. Many Welsh poets believed themselves to be members of a defeated nation and that awareness led them, in the signature of their poems, to side with the losers of history and of life's processes – the underdogs, the outsiders, the downtrodden. And the poems, themselves, whether or not touching on such themes, not infrequently owned a higher emotional specific gravity than was evident in the work of most English poets. They were, to borrow Browning's phrase, 'unafraid of soul'. These views I reiterated and expanded in the introduction to *Twentieth Century Anglo-Welsh Poetry* which was published in 1997.

From time to leisurely time I would take a batch of poetry books to Ogmore which I had promised to review for *The Hampstead and Highgate Express*. I am still baffled by what happened in late 1999. That October, Ruth Gorb, the literary editor of the *Ham and High* (as it is affectionately known), sent me half a dozen slim poetry volumes to review, none of which I cared for very much. So I asked her to send me, instead, a book by Carol Ann Duffy, *The World's Wife*, which had recently been published. 'Sure. I'll ask Picador to send you a copy direct,' she said. When the book arrived I turned over the pages thinking of the review I would write. However, when I next visited Ogmore I accidentally left the book behind.

A month later, when I had returned to London, Ruth Gorb telephoned and as soon as I heard her voice I felt guilty, expecting her to chide me for not having, as yet, sent in my review of *The World's Wife*. But she simply said, 'Would you let me have your year's choice of poetry?'

'*The World's Wife* by Carol Ann Duffy,' I suggested apologetically.

'Yes. Fine. You gave it a very enthusiastic review. I'm sorry I had to cut it.'

'What?'

'I asked for 600 words and you gave me twice that number.'

'I've not reviewed the book,' I said.

'Yes you have. Of course you have. Don't you remember?'

I hesitated. With age I'm becoming more absent-minded. But I'm not demented.

'I'm sorry, Ruth, but I haven't yet reviewed Carol Ann Duffy's book.'

Now it was Ruth Gorb's turn to hesitate. 'We've already published it.'

'How could you when I haven't written it?'

'On November 5th. You sent it to me and we published it on November 5th. You're not suggesting, are you, that someone forged your name?'

'The only review I composed about Carol Ann Duffy's pleasing, lively book,' I insisted, 'was an embryonic one in my head.'

For a moment I held the receiver and listened to silence. It was just possible that someone who knew I wrote regular poetry reviews for the weekly had thieved my name.

'It wasn't like you,' Ruth admitted thoughtfully, 'to have sent me a longer piece than I asked for.'

A week or two before Christmas when I happened to be in our local library, I climbed the stairs to the reference section curious to read the review of *The World's Wife* in the November 5th issue of the *Ham and High*. There, in the Book Review section, was my name displayed above an over-the-top, sticky, laudatory review of the book. It did not resemble my style at all, its 'voice' was that of a stranger's. Besides, a few biographical facts about Carol Ann Duffy in this somewhat sesquipedalian notice were news to me. I certainly had not even somnambulistically written this review.

Early in the New Year I discovered that the fee for the review had been sent to my bank account.

'Perhaps I ought to sit back and let some ghost notice poetry books in my name for the *Ham and High* while I collect the fees,' I said to Joan.

'You should return the money,' my wife said.

'Not bloody likely,' I said. 'They've underpaid me for years.'

I did speak to Ruth again though, letting her know that I had read the review and that I certainly was not the author of it. This time she promised to exhume the original copy from her files. A few days later she told me how, startled, she had found the typewritten review. 'It was unsigned,' she said.

Since it had been sent in anonymously Ruth Gorb had assumed it was by me. After all, I had asked to review it and she had asked Picador to send me the book. The strange thing is nobody had and nobody has written in to correct the error or, indeed, claim the fee. The author of that review continues to remain mysteriously unmasked.

London, however, would soon enough call us back, not least because of our grown-up children and young grandchildren. They often joined us for a loquacious Sunday lunch. An American editor of *Harper's* magazine once remarked that the British at their dinner tables 'decline to be interrupted by the frivolity of talk upon the appearance of their favourite dishes'. He had not been at our house in Golders Green when my wife and I are joined by family. Usually the decibel level above the knives and forks is only just tolerable. It is an eisteddfod of affectionate verbal dissonances. Not one of the family heeds Oliver Wendell Holmes who justly asserted that talking is like playing the harp: 'There is as much in laying the hands on the strings to stop their vibration as in twanging them to bring out the music.'

As Keren, Susanna and David grew older I could not help recognising my own katabolic processes. Age is an inherited disease and the year 2000 seemed to loom ever nearer with its big, assertive clock. There have been moments when I was tempted to record the physiological changes I began to experience as I lived, happily enough, through the last years of the century. I have been reminded of the scientist, Charles Brown-Sequart, who, at the last outpost of his life, gave a detailed account of his own symptoms, correctly diagnosing his illness and stating his bleak progress. Fortunately my rustings and aches so far have been benign enough. But there are now, as I write, too many ghosts of relatives and friends about. I find it difficult to accept the inevitability of certain things: how people we know and love grow senile; how certain diseases cannot be cured; how Antigone is condemned and there is no reprieve.

Most recently, my regular chess partner, the blue-eyed, pipe-smoking, LSE philosopher, John Watkins (once the blue-eyed boy of Karl Popper), suddenly, while sailing in Devon, suffered a mortal coronary. For nearly forty years every Sunday afternoon when we were both in London, we would play aggressive competitive chess. Other friends, too, have gone during the last decade of the century, gone, as they used to say in South Wales, 'where they don't play billiards'. The list is long. I name but a few: Huw Wheldon and Hans Keller; Edward Blishen and Leslie Hamilton (the Cardiff City Football Club doctor); poets such as John Ormond, David Wright, Gavin Ewart and the Israeli, Carmi; Americans to whom I am indebted, Mack Rosenthal and Pete Dean. Not one reaching the hurdle of the year 2000. I miss their chatter and company.

Happily pleasures other than chess engage me, among them the solace and excitements of watching Cardiff City win, draw or lose at Ninian Park. Well the Bluebirds may lose too often but I know rainbows exist all the time. They are everywhere. Simply, most of the time they are invisible. And, of course, I still wait patiently for the visitation of the next poem and then the one after. When not visited I turn to prose which is so much easier to write than poetry – I write poetry uphill, prose downhill. During the Nineties – boast boast – I have continued to publish: a novel, *There was a Young Man from Cardiff* (1991); and poetry, *On the Evening Road* (1994) and *Arcadia, One Mile* (1998). As I write the latter two books have just been published as one volume in New York under the title *Be Seated, Thou*. Its epigraph is from Wallace Stevens's 'Mozart 1935':

> We may return to Mozart.
> He was young, and we, we are old.
> The snow is falling
> And the streets are full of cries
> Be seated, thou.

I know that my poems in *Be Seated, Thou* and in my earlier books have related the hidden narrative of my biography in ways I have not been able to do here in prose. Of course they have not remarked bare facts but there is hardly an important occasion in my life that is not covertly profiled or overtly re-inhabited in my poetry. So when I open, say, my Penguin *Selected Poems* (1994) and turn to page 61 I almost suffer an abreaction as I hold again my father's hand when he was dying in Llandough Hospital near Cardiff; or when the book falls open on page 77 I can remember altogether less painfully how with Joan and our then young children I attended a demonstration against the Vietnam War in 1968; or page 173 leads me back to a patient of mine with abhorrent Nazi sympathies.

Other pages may summon to mind mysteries and the mere ruins of an experience or may simply prompt an eidetic image of something quite trivial – perhaps an unimportant location such as the small parking lot situated outside the window of the building where I worked at Princeton University in 1973 to 1974, or of a certain broken stone wall not too far away from Ogmore-by-sea.

Poems can remind me of such things because they are rooted in my mental life, in my experiences – some mundane, some dramatic. I recall the words of Rilke whom I read when young, 'In order to write a single verse one must be able to return in thought ... to unexpected encounters ... to days of childhood that are still indistinct ... to nights of love ... But one must also have been beside the dying, must have sat beside the dead in a room with open windows and with fitful noises.' I have experienced such things as so many others have; and I have done my best to tell of these things in my poetry with what gifts I have. And it is the year 2001 and I have not finished yet. Meanwhile:

> In this exile people call old age
> I live between nostalgia and rage.
> This is the land of fools and fear.
> Thanks be. I'm lucky to be here.

Index